"This is simply an outstanding analysis of crucial and often difficult questions about heaven and hell. Although many today avoid discussing these topics, what we believe about heaven and hell has a massive influence on how we live our present lives, and Alan Gomes has produced a discussion that is exceptionally clear, thoughtful, carefully reasoned, fair to opposing views, and relentlessly faithful to Scripture. I expect to turn to it again and again for a detailed analysis of some of these challenging questions."

—Wayne Grudem,
Research Professor of Theology and Biblical Studies,
Phoenix Seminary

"A lot of us, even Christians, have non-Christian views of heaven and hell. Drawing on many years of teaching theology, Alan Gomes grounds his answers in Scripture. This is a superb resource!"

—Michael Horton,
J. Gresham Machen Professor of Systematic Theology and Apologetics,
Westminster Seminary California

"*40 Questions About Heaven and Hell* is a masterpiece. It exhibits fairness, rigor, deep theological acumen, and biblical fidelity. Gomes has given us a treasure trove of information about the biblical view of the afterlife and a hard-hitting critique of alternatives. Thoroughly researched, Gomes leaves no stone unturned, and he takes on virtually all of the hard questions people raise about heaven and hell. With the publication of this book, no one can write on these topics with intellectual integrity who does not interact with Gomes's book. It is a must-read for all who are interested in these issues, and would be an excellent text for courses that include the subject of the afterlife."

—J. P. Moreland,
Distinguished Professor of Philosophy,
Talbot School of Theology, Biola University

T0326822

40 QUESTIONS ABOUT
Heaven and Hell

Alan W. Gomes

Benjamin L. Merkle, Series Editor

KREGEL
A C A D E M I C

40 Questions About Heaven and Hell
© 2018 Alan W. Gomes

Published by Kregel Academic, an imprint of Kregel Publications, 2450 Oak Industrial Dr. NE, Grand Rapids, MI 49505-6020.

This book is a title in the 40 Questions Series, edited by Benjamin L. Merkle.

All rights reserved. No part of this book may be reproduced, stored in a retrieval system, or transmitted in any form or by any means—electronic, mechanical, photocopy, recording, or otherwise—without written permission of the publisher, except for brief quotations in printed reviews.

All Scripture quotations, unless otherwise indicated, are from The Holy Bible, English Standard Version, copyright © 2001 by Crossway Bibles, a division of Good News Publishers. Used by permission. All rights reserved.

Scripture quotations marked KJV are from the King James Version.

Scripture quotations marked NASB are from the New American Standard Bible®. Copyright © 1960, 1962, 1963, 1968, 1971, 1972, 1973, 1975, 1977 by The Lockman Foundation. Used by permission. www.Lockman.org

Scripture quotations marked NET are from the NET Bible® copyright ©1996–2006 by Biblical Studies Press, L.L.C. http://netbible.com All rights reserved

Scripture quotations marked NIV are from the Holy Bible, New International Version®, NIV®. Copyright © 1973, 1978, 1984, 2011 by Biblica, Inc.™ Used by permission of Zondervan. All rights reserved worldwide. www.zondervan.com

Scripture quotations marked NRSV are from the New Revised Standard Version Bible, copyright © 1989 by the Division of Christian Education of the National Council of the Churches of Christ in the U.S.A., and are used by permission. All rights reserved.

Scripture quotations marked RSV are from the Revised Standard Version of the Bible, copyright © 1946, 1952, and 1971 the Division of Christian Education of the National Council of the Churches of Christ in the United States of America. Used by permission. All rights reserved.

Cover artwork is a tapestry from the fourteenth century: The New Jerusalem, number 80 from "The Apocalypse of Angers" by Nicolas Bataille.

The Hebrew font, NewJerusalemU, and the Greek font, GraecaU, are available from www.linguistsoftware.com/lgku.htm, +1-425-775-1130.

ISBN 978-0-8254-4276-6, print
ISBN 978-0-8254-6838-4, Kindle
ISBN 978-0-8254-7649-5, epub

Printed in the United States of America

22 23 24 25 26 27 28 / 8 7 6 5 4 3 2

To Dr. Robert L. Saucy (1930–2015),
my dearest friend and brother in Christ,
who now knows beyond any doubt whether
I have answered these questions well
(1 Cor. 13:12).

Contents

Part 4: The Eternal State

Acknowledgements

I wish to offer my sincere appreciation to my colleagues Tom Finley, Henry Holloman, Kevin Lewis, Robert L. Saucy, and Ken Daughters, from whose helpful suggestions and insights I have benefited greatly. Thanks also go to research assistants Philip Powers, Shaun Deegan, and Mike Burbidge. I am especially grateful for the work of my colleague Joy Mosbarger, who labored very hard to help me prepare the manuscript for publication.

Abbreviations

AB	Anchor Bible
BBC	Broadman Bible Commentary
BDAG	Walter Bauer, Frederick W. Danker, William F. Arndt, and F. Wilbur Gingrich. *A Greek–English Lexicon of the New Testament and Other Early Christian Literature*. 3rd ed. Chicago: University of Chicago Press, 2000.
BDB	Francis Brown, S. R. Driver, and Charles A. Briggs. *A Hebrew and English Lexicon of the Old Testament*. Oxford: Oxford University Press, 1978.
BEB	Walter A. Elwell, ed. *Baker Encyclopedia of the Bible*. 4 vols. Grand Rapids: Baker, 1988.
BECNT	Baker Exegetical Commentary on the New Testament
BibSac	*Bibliotheca Sacra*
CBQ	*Catholic Biblical Quarterly*
CTR	*Criswell Theological Review*
DJG	Joel B. Green and Scot McKnight, eds. *Dictionary of Jesus and the Gospels*. Downers Grove, IL: InterVarsity Press, 1992.
DPL	Gerald F. Hawthorne and Ralph P. Martin, eds. *Dictionary of Paul and His Letters*. Downers Grove, IL: InterVarsity Press, 1993.
DT	Karl Rahner and Herbert Vorgrimler, eds. *Dictionary of Theology*. 2nd ed. New York: Crossroad, 1981.
EAR	J. Gordon Melton, ed. *Encyclopedia of American Religions*. 7th ed. Detroit: Gale, 2003.
EBC	*Expositor's Bible Commentary*, rev. ed.

EC	Erwin Fahlbusch, Jan Lochman, John Mbiti, Jaroslav Pelikan, and Lukas Vischer, eds. *Encyclopedia of Christianity.* 5 vols. Grand Rapids: Eerdmans, 2001.
ECT	Jean-Yves Lacoste, ed. *Encyclopedia of Christian Theology.* 3 vols. New York: Routledge, 2005.
EDB	David Noel Freeman, ed. *Eerdmans Dictionary of the Bible.* Grand Rapids: Eerdmans, 2000.
EDBT	Walter E. Elwell, ed. *Evangelical Dictionary of Biblical Theology.* Grand Rapids: Baker, 1996.
EDT	Walter E. Elwell, ed. *Evangelical Dictionary of Theology.* 2nd ed. Grand Rapids: Baker, 2001.
EOP	J. Gordon Melton, ed. *Encyclopedia of Occultism and Parapsychology.* 5th ed. 2 vols. Detroit: Gale, 2001. Gale Virtual Reference Library.
ICC	International Critical Commentary
JETS	*Journal of the Evangelical Theological Society*
NAC	New American Commentary
NCE	Thomas Carson and Joann Cerrito, eds. *New Catholic Encyclopedia.* 2nd ed. 15 vols. Detroit: Gale, 2003.
NDT	Sinclair B. Ferguson and David F. Wright, eds. *New Dictionary of Theology.* Downers Grove, IL: InterVarsity Press, 1988.
NIBC	New International Biblical Commentary
NICNT	New International Commentary on the New Testament
NICOT	New International Commentary on the Old Testament
NIDB	J. D. Douglas and Merrill C. Tenney, eds. *The New International Dictionary of the Bible.* Grand Rapids: Zondervan, 1987.
NIGTC	New International Greek Testament Commentary
NIVAC	New International Version Application Commentary
NTC	New Testament Commentary
PNTC	Pillar New Testament Commentary
TDNT	Gerhard Kittel, ed. *Theological Dictionary of the New Testament.* Translated by Geoffrey W. Bromiley. 10 vols. Grand Rapids: Eerdmans, 1964–1976.

TDNTW	Verlyn Verbrugge, ed. *The NIV Theological Dictionary of New Testament Words*. Grand Rapids: Zondervan, 2000.
TDOT	G. Johannes Botterweck, Helmer Rinngren, and Heinz-Josef Fabry, eds. *Theological Dictionary of the Old Testament*. Translated by John T. Willis, David E. Green, and Douglas W. Stott. 15 vols. Grand Rapids: Eerdmans, 1974–2006.
TNTC	Tyndale New Testament Commentaries
TOTC	Tyndale Old Testament Commentaries
TWOT	R. Laird Harris, Gleason J. Archer Jr., and Bruce K. Waltke. *Theological Wordbook of the Old Testament*. 2 vols. Chicago: Moody Press, 1980.
WBC	Word Biblical Commentary
WTJ	*Westminster Theological Journal*
ZECNT	Zondervan Exegetical Commentary on the New Testament

PART 1

An Overview of the Afterlife

Why Is It Important to Think about the Afterlife?

I know that many consider it a waste of time to think about the afterlife. After all, this present life has more than enough trouble. This book will not help you to pay off your mortgage, snag that promotion at work, or find the perfect mate. So why bother with it?

I am firmly convinced that thinking about death and what comes after it is the single most practical activity we can do. And yes, it affects *everything else* we do! Popular author Tim Keller put it like this: "The way you live now is completely controlled by what you believe about the future."[1] What you truly believe about the life beyond—or do not believe about it—determines your loves, your motivations, your goals, and how you direct all of your energies in this one. It cannot help but do so.

Why should this be so? It all comes down to a matter of "worldview." Worldview! That sounds like a word that escaped from an undergrad philosophy class. But our worldview drives everything we do, whether we realize it or not. Our beliefs about the afterlife, and all that is connected with those beliefs, form the center from which we may evaluate everything in life. *This life.*

When Worldviews Collide

In his popular song *Imagine*, John Lennon asks us to imagine a universe in which "there's no heaven" nor any "hell below us." In Lennon's ideal world, people would forget about living for some fictitious pie-in-the-sky afterlife but instead focus only on the real world, "living for today."

So let us accept Lennon's challenge and see how this cashes out practically. Imagine that all we have is the physical world as we know and see it.

---

1. Tim Keller, "The New Heaven and New Earth" (podcast of sermon, Redeemer Presbyterian Church, April 12, 2009), http://podbay.fm/show/352660924/e/1317415673.

There is no heaven above nor hell beneath. No spiritual realm populated by demons or angels—or even God, for that matter. The entire universe arose out of clumps of stardust banging together eons ago through random, impersonal, unguided processes. These same processes somehow brought forth human beings, evolving us into the highly complex biological machines, so to speak, that we are today. Eventually, though, the universe will wind down and burn itself out, passing away with a bang—or maybe only a whimper. But long before that happens, you and I will live for a time, die, and slip into quiet oblivion without leaving a trace, once the worms have had their fill. Sure, our loved ones may place flowers on our graves—maybe for a generation or two if we are especially beloved—but soon enough no one will remember and it will be as if we never were.

Now, if this describes our ultimate destiny, does such a view have any bearing on our *present* hopes, aspirations, and behavior? And, conversely, might the idea that we are more than corruptible biological machines—that we are eternal creatures, made in the likeness of a personal, loving, and just God—result in a different way of living our lives right now?

Where Afterlife Meets Practical Life

Let us consider just a few of the ways in which our vision of the future affects us now.

Our Hunger for Justice

We know that there is gross evil in this world, some of it so unspeakably horrible that we scarcely can contemplate it. Adolescent girls sold into sexual slavery for the financial gain of despicable human traffickers. Innocent lives cut short by gang members battling over drug turf. Entire populations decimated by genocide to advance selfish political and religious domination. Countries ravaged by despotic warlords and megalomaniacal dictators, who live a life of ease on the backs of their enslaved, starving subjects.

Picture the human trafficker, who has devastated the bodies and souls of innocent young girls. He lives a prosperous life of ease and then dies peacefully in his sleep. Or the oppressive dictator, enjoying fine imported cigars, exotic food, and his smuggled collection of classic cars, indifferent to the unimaginable suffering he has heaped upon his impoverished countrymen living in squalor. Does not everything within us rise up in revulsion and outrage? Is there no payback? Where is justice for the poor and oppressed?

If we imagine that there is no heaven or hell, and that all we have is "living for today," then we have also imagined a moral universe that remains seriously out of kilter, one in which the scales never balance. Sure, sometimes that warlord or dictator takes a bullet to his head—usually from an even worse warlord or dictator who just picks up where the previous one left off. No, we cannot deny that there is much unfinished business in this world. And so we have imagined a universe in which that business remains *forever* unfinished, and justice unsatisfied.

As bad as all this sounds, it is actually a good deal worse. A universe that came about through unguided collisions of inanimate matter strips us of any reason for our outrage. Why should we be incensed that the particular clumps of stardust that randomly fashioned the human trafficker also happened to dominate and subjugate the clumps that formed his victims? Because he has violated their "dignity"? What dignity? We humans have no more dignity than a rock or a tree; we are simply a different arrangement of clumps, after all—neither better nor worse. And from where do all these notions of *ought* and *should*, which trouble us so much, even arise in such a coldly impersonal universe? We are outraged, but for no good reason at all!

Yet, outraged we are. We know that such things ought not to be; and we cannot escape the certain feeling that something is deeply, profoundly, and desperately wrong, despite the fact that these feelings make no sense in a purely material and mechanical world.

Let us imagine instead that we are eternal creatures made in the image of an eternal God, endowed with a clear sense of right and wrong—the same sense that he himself has. Let us imagine that this God hates injustice even more than we do, and that he can and will do something about it—perhaps even at great personal cost to himself. Consider a universe in which this God holds his creatures morally accountable, who one day will "render to each one according to his works" (Rom. 2:6). This is a God who will set things right. He will compensate fully those who have suffered unjustly and will punish the guilty with perfect justice.

Imagine *that!*

Natural Evils in the World

Not all of the evils we encounter in this world are "moral evils" of the sort we have just considered. We also experience what we might call "natural evils," such as earthquakes, floods, and the ravages of old age. How do we make sense of these?

The famous actor and self-proclaimed agnostic Richard Dreyfuss said, "When I die I hope I'll have a chance to hit God in the face."[2] And just what did this God—who may or may not exist, according to Dreyfuss's agnostic philosophy—do to earn such scorn? "He deserves it," Dreyfuss tells us, "because of everything that happens to you in the third act of life: it's humiliating and debasing."

---

2. Richard Dreyfuss, "Richard Dreyfuss: 'When I Die I Want the Chance to Hit God in the Face,'" *The Guardian*, July 24, 2016, http://www.theguardian.com/lifeandstyle/2016/jul/24/richard-dreyfuss-reckless-when-i-die-i-want-the-chance-to-hit-god-in-the-face.

Again, we must inquire: If we are but the result of impersonal, mechanical, physical processes, why ought old age to be other than this? (There is that pesky word "ought" again!) Who is to say that death, disease, dying, and decay are "bad"? They just *are*. One may just as well rage against the wind or tides or any other impersonal force of nature as against the reality that our bodies disintegrate with age. Yet, here again, we know deep down that death and destruction and sickness and decay ought not to be. Something is seriously wrong. We know it and cannot shake this sense. We recoil against our own mortality and see it for the great and terrible evil that it is. And we long for something better: something that this world cannot provide.

Dreyfuss seems to acknowledge all this, whether he realizes it or not. Notice that he directs his rage against a presumably personal God, whom he wants to hold personally accountable with a punch in the face. His rage likewise points to a God who must have the power to do something about it—at least if his complaint is to make any sense at all. Fair enough. At least his anger is intelligible. But it is intelligible only in so far as he has set aside his agnosticism, and speaks from what his heart tells him is true.

Now, what if this personal creator God has revealed to us why natural evils, such as death, befall us in this life? Maybe there is a good reason for it that Dreyfuss has not considered. Perhaps also, this God is working a plan for dealing with death, the ultimate enemy of us all. Would it change anything to know that this same God will someday eliminate all the natural evils in this world by replacing our present universe with a new, glorious, and resplendent one? And that he offers to redeem these frail, weak, and mortal bodies by transforming them into immortal, imperishable, and vibrant ones—brimming with life, subject to none of the degrading effects of time and decay, full of energy and immortal youth?

Our Belief in the Afterlife Motivates Us to Live Sacrificially for Others
While most people "care deeply about justice for the poor, alleviating hunger and disease, and caring for the environment," Keller points out that the materialist worldview, which denies an afterlife, seriously diminishes our "motivation to make the world a better place." Indeed, Keller asks, "Why sacrifice for the needs of others if in the end nothing we do will make any difference?"[3] But a worldview that regards others as made in the image of a good and loving God, and therefore as beings of eternal value, spurs us to practical action in eliminating the misery of our fellow man and woman. What we do to help others now has no expiration date; it counts for eternity as well.

---

3. Tim Keller, *A Reason for God* (New York: Riverhead Books, 2008), 220.

Obviously, there are people who do not believe in an afterlife who make sacrifices for others. That is not the point. The issue is that their world-view undercuts any coherent reason to do so. The atheist and agnostic bear God's image as much as anyone else, and so we are not surprised that they sometimes live like the eternal beings they really are, despite what they may claim to believe. Nevertheless, how much greater motivation is there to do the right thing for the right reason! It is no wonder that Christians, who live today in light of eternity, have done more to alleviate the plight of the downtrodden and suffering than any other religion or philosophy ever have done.[4]

Consider the early Christians, who well understood the connection between time and eternity and lived it out to dramatic effect. What was it about the fledgling Christian movement—reviled, persecuted, outcast, and despised—that triumphed against all odds over mighty pagan Rome, one of the greatest empires in human history? Historians tell us that it was the Christians' selfless love, pouring themselves out in sacrifice to others. At the root of it all was the specifically Christian vision of the afterlife, which propelled these early believers to put their own lives on the line to minister to their countrymen at great personal cost. They did not fear their own deaths, for they knew something better lay in store for them.[5] To cite but one poignant example, these early followers of Christ risked their own lives to care for their pagan enemies who had contracted infection in a time of plague, when even their own family members cast them into the street to avoid contracting their disease.[6] The self-sacrifice of the early Christians, more than anything, commended Christianity to a culture that found such a lifestyle astonishing and inexplicable apart from a vibrant, living, and eternal hope.

---

4. For a book that addresses this theme well, see Rodney Stark, *The Triumph of Christianity* (New York: HarperCollins, 2011). See also David Bentley Hart, *Atheist Delusions* (New Haven, CT: Yale University Press, 2009). An interesting book that details the enormously positive effect that the introduction of Christianity has had on India is Vishal Mangalwadi, *The Book That Made Your World: How the Bible Created the Soul of Western Civilization* (Nashville: Thomas Nelson, 2011).

5. Even some of the most bitter, strident critics of Christianity had to admit as much. For instance, historian Howard Clark Kee cites Lucian as illustrative: "Lucian remarks, 'The activity of these people [Christians] in dealing with any matter that affects their community is something extraordinary: they spare neither trouble nor expense.' It is because 'these misguided creatures' believe that they are forever immortal that they scorn death and manifest the voluntary devotion that is so common among them" (Howard Clark Kee, et al., *Christianity: A Social and Cultural History* [New York: Macmillan, 1991], 82). Kee's citation of Lucian comes from his *Death of Peregrinus*, sec. 11–16. See also Kenneth Scott Latourette, *A History of Christianity* (New York: Harper & Row, 1953), 105–6.

6. Stark, *The Triumph of Christianity*, 114–18.

Our Belief in the Afterlife Gives Us Hope
Since I began writing this book, I have come to appreciate more and more just how much the truth of what God has in store for his children in the next life gives us hope for navigating the trials and disappointments of this one. If I might, I would like to speak to this point very personally and from my heart.

As I write this, it has been less than a week since we have concluded what may be the most contentious, polarizing, and dispiriting presidential election in United States history. Never have I been more discouraged about the prospects for this country. We are in a serious moral eclipse, and though I am hardly a prophet, I predict that we are in for some very dark days ahead. Those who seek their "salvation" in a political party or candidate would do well to heed the ancient admonition that we ought not to "Put [our] trust in princes" (Ps. 146:3). It is hard to have much hope in the current direction of things, both here and around the globe. The world is on fire, and there is little reason to think it will improve.

It is not just the world scene but also life closer to home that often disappoints and takes its toll. Since I began writing this book, I have lost two of my dearest friends in a space of only four months. First, there was Dennis, who died of brain cancer; and then Bob, who succumbed to his injuries from an auto collision three blocks from Talbot School of Theology, where I had taught with him since 1987. Dennis was my classmate at seminary; our kids grew up together, and he and I, with his wife Susan and my wife Diane, did life together for more than thirty years. As for Bob, he was not only my best friend but also a close professional colleague with a brilliant theological mind. Bob was my sounding board for all things theological, including many of the thoughts I had to work through in writing this book. It seems unreal that my intimate advisor, confidant, and friend—more like a father, really—has been ripped out of my life. I cannot call him for advice, encouragement, and help. The pain of this is still raw, and I feel it acutely as I type these words.

Now, it might be easy to conclude that if people would just stop dying and our politicians would shape up, then life would be perfect. But what of the self-inflicted misery of my own heart, welling up as a polluted spring and chargeable to myself alone? What about my miserable pride and arrogance, insecurity and envy, anger and impatience, raging doubts and fears, that surge from within, unbidden? I cannot blame this on the Democrats or the Republicans or bad Supreme Court appointees or anyone else who just lacks the good sense to see things my way. No, I alone am to blame for "the sin that dwells within me" and "which clings so closely" (Rom. 7:17; Heb. 12:1). Nor will I eliminate my misery by just "trying harder." "For I have the desire to do what is right, but not the ability to carry it out" (Rom. 7:18). And I am tired of it: tired of hurting others, weary of failing myself and especially my God. I know that I should do and think and speak and feel only what is right and pure, every moment of every day. I also know that I can no more do that than I can raise myself from the dead.[7]

Though I grieve over the state of our world and of the pain of personal loss, though I mourn over the depravity that lies within the secret places of my own heart, I do so as one who looks to an ultimate victory—to a day when every tear will be wiped away from my eyes and from the eyes of those I deeply love (Rev. 21:4). Someday the world will be ruled in righteousness by the man whom God has appointed heir of all things, the Lord Jesus Christ, "the root and the descendant of David, the bright morning star" (Heb. 1:2; Rev. 22:16). God will banish all wickedness and corruption from his universe, and we shall never again be enslaved. He shall remove all evils, moral and natural, from his world forever, including those lodged so firmly in my own sinful heart. There will be a new heavens and a new earth, in which there shall be no mourning, nor crying, nor pain, for the former things shall have passed away (Rev. 21:4). Knowing this gives us the strength not merely to endure but to thrive, confident in that glorious future that now awaits our unveiling as the sons of God (Rom. 8:19).

REFLECTION QUESTIONS

1. After reading this chapter, how would you reply to the well-known saying, "He is too heavenly minded for his own earthly good"?

2. Reflect on how one's worldview "cashes out" in such practical ways as our desire for justice, and our motivation to alleviate the pain and suffering of our fellow human beings.

3. Consider Richard Dreyfuss's statement about wanting to punch God in the face when he dies. Have you ever been angry with God for your own pain in this world? Has anything you have read in this chapter given you a new perspective on that?

4. Have any of the ideas presented in this chapter helped you to deal with some of your own hurts and disappointments?

5. Of everything discussed in this chapter, what aspect of the age to come do you most look forward to experiencing?

---

7. To paraphrase the great theologian Charles Hodge.

What Are the Most Common Views of Life after Death?

Recent Surveys of American Religious Belief, Including the Afterlife

The last ten years have seen several significant projects seeking to quantify and clarify American religious beliefs. Some of the results may be surprising, granting the conventional wisdom that our postmodern culture has become increasingly "secular," materialistic, and non- (or even anti-) religious. While some data do bear out certain secularist trends, the picture is not nearly as straightforward as one might expect. Other findings of these surveys, though, should not surprise us, such as the diversity of opinion that they highlight. This diversity is entirely consistent with the pluralistic ethos of American culture.

The General Social Survey (GSS), 1972–2014
Let us begin with one of the most current and large-scale surveys that provide a window into American religious opinion: The General Social Survey (GSS), conducted between 1972 and 2014. Researchers Twenge, Sherman, Exline, and Grubbs recently have analyzed this data, placing special emphasis on the most current trends between 2006 and 2014 in comparison to earlier decades.[1] On the one hand, the data from this survey show that a solid majority of American adults retain at least some commitment to such core issues as belief in God (78 percent) and prayer (85 percent). At the same time, the movement away from these is noteworthy, especially in the last eight years or so.

It is true that earlier studies have documented a growing decline in outward forms of religiosity and affiliation, such as identifying with a particular

---

1. See Jean M. Twenge, et al., "Declines in American Adults' Religious Participation and Beliefs, 1972–2014," *SAGE Open* 6, no. 1 (January–March 2016): 1–13.

church denomination, even as they showed that personal spirituality remained more or less resistant to such defections. The most recent data, however, reveal Americans' personal and private convictions and behaviors decreasing in a way commensurate with their diminished public practice, particularly among younger adults. For example, "eight times more 18- to 29-year-olds never prayed in 2014 versus the early 1980s."[2] Although this age group shows the most pronounced change, one finds this decrease in religious conviction among all adult Americans.[3]

The authors of this analysis summarize these trends as follows:

> American adults in the 2010s were less religious than those in previous decades, based on religious service attendance and more private religious expressions such as belief in God, praying, identifying as a religious person, and believing the Bible is the word of God. . . .
>
> While religious affiliation and service attendance have been declining since the 1990s, the decrease in more private religious expressions began fairly recently, becoming pronounced only after 2006. . . .
>
> Americans in 2014 were less likely to say they believed in God. In the late 1980s, only 13% of U.S. adults expressed serious doubts about the existence of God. . . . By 2014, however, 22% expressed doubts, a 69% increase. Among 18- to 29-year-olds, 30% had serious doubts by 2014, more than twice as many as in the late 1980s (12%).[4]

Again, we must note that a solid majority of Americans still profess belief in God and pray. What we are talking about here are trends, and it is clear that the tendency is away from traditional religious conviction and practice.

These developments may not surprise us, given the increasing secularization that we see in American culture generally. One trend, however, is surprising, and the authors of the study identify it as such: Despite a decreasing belief in God, prayer, and religious doctrine overall, Americans now register a slight *increase* in affirming the existence of an afterlife! "Thus, more Americans believe in life after death even as fewer belong to a religion, fewer attend religious services, and fewer pray."[5] Specifically, belief in the afterlife

---

2. Ibid., 1.
3. Ibid., 5 (Table 1), 7 (Table 2).
4. Ibid., 4, 6.
5. Ibid., 8.

continues to hover around 80 percent overall, and this number includes an increasing share of individuals who are otherwise nonreligious. This unusual phenomenon holds just as true for the eighteen- to twenty-nine-year-old demographic as it does for adult Americans generally. Moreover, compared to the 1970s, belief in the afterlife is greater in absolute terms.

The writers of this study admit that this finding about Americans' readiness to embrace a belief in the afterlife "might seem paradoxical" in light of their general defection from conventional religious belief and practice. Though they cannot offer a definitive reason for this anomaly, they speculate that the increasingly friendly posture toward the afterlife may correlate with the growing "entitlement mentality" of many Americans, who expect "special privileges without effort." Such entitlement "appears in religious and spiritual domains when people see themselves as deserving spiritual rewards or blessings due to their special status."[6] However, the study's authors caution that this hypothesis, though suggested by other research on contemporary American attitudes, is only speculative and cannot be answered by the data the GSS itself furnishes.

The Pew and Baylor Studies

Other recent investigations present a picture in many respects consistent with the above. Consider a study conducted by the Pew Forum on Religion and Public Life.[7] Updated in 2014, this survey attempted to outline the varieties of religious belief and affiliation in the United States by polling more than 35,000 Americans, age eighteen and older. It found that a strong majority of Americans (72 percent) believe in an afterlife, specifically heaven. A lesser number, but still a solid majority (58 percent), likewise affirm belief in hell, understood as a place "where people who have led bad lives and die without repenting are eternally punished."[8]

The findings of the second "wave" or phase of the Baylor Religion Survey (2006–2007) turned in numbers consistent with this. According to this study, 82 percent of Americans believe in heaven, while 73 percent believe that hell either "absolutely" or "probably" exists.[9] Observe that in both studies, belief in heaven is slightly more common than a belief in hell, though the strong belief in hell is still "much higher than most commentators on American religion seem to have assumed."[10]

---

6. Ibid., 11.
7. Pew Research Center, "Religious Landscape Study: Belief in Heaven," Pew Forum, http://www.pewforum.org/religious-landscape-study/belief-in-heaven/.
8. Pew Research Center, "Religious Landscape Study: Belief in Hell," Pew Forum, http://www.pewforum.org/religious-landscape-study/belief-in-hell/.
9. Rodney Stark, *What Americans Really Believe: New Findings from the Baylor Surveys of Religion* (Waco, TX: Baylor University Press, 2008), 73.
10. Ibid.

What do people think about their own postmortem fate? Rodney Stark, summarizing "wave two" of the aforementioned 2006–2007 Baylor study, concluded, "Americans overwhelmingly believe in an afterlife, in heaven, and equally in hell," but "most of them expect to go to heaven."[11] Specifically, fully 66 percent of Americans are either "somewhat certain" or "quite certain" that they will go to heaven when they die. Though this particular survey did not explicitly broach the question of whether anyone thought he or she was going to hell, the Barna Group conducted one three years earlier that did just that and concluded, "Most Americans do not expect to experience Hell first-hand: just one-half of 1 percent expect to go to Hell upon their death."[12]

The widespread affirmation of heaven and hell in our culture might seem at first glance to be an endorsement of traditional Christian belief, at least when it comes to the afterlife. However, one significant departure is a widespread denial of a future bodily resurrection, a key component of orthodox Christian theology.[13] In other words, while there is general belief in an afterlife, people tend to conceive of it in spiritualized terms—namely, as the ongoing existence of the soul in a disembodied state. A 2006 study performed by Scripps Howard News Service and Ohio University bears this out. As reported by Thomas Hargrove and Guido H. Stempel III, "Most Americans don't believe they will experience a resurrection of their bodies when they die, putting them at odds with a core teaching of Christianity."[14] The researchers found that "only 36 percent of the 1,007 adults interviewed . . . said 'yes' to the question: 'Do you believe that, after you die, your physical body will be resurrected someday'? Fifty-four percent said they do not believe and 10 percent were undecided." Consistent with a denial of one's own bodily resurrection is a declining belief in Christ's own literal resurrection from the grave. A 2012 Rasmussen poll showed that 64 percent of Americans believe in Christ's literal resurrection as a historical fact. Though still a majority opinion, it reflects a marked drop from a poll asking the identical question only one year earlier, which then registered 77 percent agreement.[15]

11. Ibid., 74.
12. Barna Research Group, "Americans Describe Their Views about Life after Death," October 21, 2003, https://www.barna.com/research/americans-describe-their-views-about-life-after-death/. Just like the later 2006–2007 Baylor study, the Barna study gives an almost identical percentage of people who believe that they will go to heaven upon death (i.e., 64 percent).
13. We shall discuss the bodily resurrection in considerable detail in Question 19, "What Will the Resurrection Body Be Like?"
14. Thomas Hargrove and Guido H. Stempel III, "People Doubt Physical Resurrection," *Casper Star Tribune*, April 6, 2006, http://trib.com/news/national/article_0c4bbda9-194a-5abd-a3ca-01c31c89269e.html.
15. Dan Joseph, "Percent of Americans Believing in the Resurrection Drops to 64% from 77% Last Easter," *CNSnews.com*, April 1, 2013, http://trib.com/news/national/article_0c4bbda9-194a-5abd-a3ca-01c31c89269e.html.

What Is Heaven Like?

Granting the large number of Americans who embrace the existence of heaven and see it as their own ultimate destiny, what do they think heaven will be like?

We find a confusing picture at best. As we have just observed, most conceive of it as a disembodied state. At the same time, people often describe it using a variety of concrete, physical terms. Lisa Miller, citing a *Newsweek* poll, tells us: "Nineteen percent think heaven looks like a garden, 13 percent say it looks like a city—and 17 percent don't know."[16] Miller continues:

> In the peaceful, prosperous West, visions of heaven are increasingly individualistic; a best-selling novel, *The Lovely Bones*, is narrated by a 14-year-old girl who has gone to heaven, and her paradise contains puppies, big fields and Victorian cupolas.[17]

Maria Shriver, former wife of former California Governor Arnold Schwarzenegger, paints a similarly fanciful portrait of heaven in her children's book, *What's Heaven?* British New Testament scholar N. T. Wright, commenting on this book, provides this description:

> The book . . . is aimed at children, with lots of large pictures of fluffy clouds in blue skies. . . . Heaven, says Shriver, is . . . "a beautiful place where you can sit on soft clouds and talk to other people who are there. At night you can sit next to the stars, which are the brightest of anywhere in the universe. . . . If you're good throughout your life, then you get to go to heaven. . . . When your life is finished here on earth, God sends angels down to take you up to Heaven to be with him."[18]

American Views of the Afterlife in Non-Christian-based Traditions

Until now, I have framed our discussion of American views of the hereafter in the broadly Christian categories of heaven and hell. This is appropriate, granting that the United States is in a very generic sense a "Christian" nation, given its Christian roots and heritage. At the same time, one finds other views of the afterlife among the non-Christian, minority religious traditions in this country. For example, based on a 2008 study, about six in ten American

---

16. Lisa Miller, "Why We Need Heaven," *Newsweek*, August 11, 2002, http://www.newsweek.com/why-we-need-heaven-143873.
17. Ibid.
18. Wright, *Surprised by Hope*, 17; citing Maria Shriver, *What's Heaven?* (New York: St. Martin's Press, 1999).

Hindus believe in reincarnation.[19] The so-called New Age Movement also popularly embraces this tenet.[20] What is especially surprising, however, is that close to 20 percent of all adult Americans claim to believe in reincarnation, with 10 percent of self-described "born-again Christians" holding this view.[21]

Among Americans who identify with the Buddhist faith, about six in ten profess belief in the attainment of "nirvana" at death, understood as "the ultimate state transcending pain and desire in which individual consciousness ends."[22]

Islam is another minority religion in the US that has garnered increasing attention, particularly since the events of 9/11. The Pew study shows that American Muslims believe in heaven and hell in greater numbers than the population as a whole, registering 85 percent and 80 percent belief respectively.[23] Indeed, one of the commonly identified motivations of so-called Islamic fundamentalism around the globe is the belief "that if killed fighting in the name of Islam, [the jihadist] will go straight to the seventh level of heaven and delight in the company of beautiful virgins." Lisa Miller quotes Hamas leader Ismail Abu Shanab as touting the power of this belief, which, he claims, "gives Palestinians the advantage over the Israelis."[24]

Contacting the Dead

Many think it possible to contact those who have passed "to the other side." As the Barna study notes, one third of Americans "believe that it is possible to communicate with others after their death." In proof that this idea is "gaining traction," Barna shows that, demographically, the idea is more prevalent among 48 percent of the so-called Busters (i.e., those born from 1965 to 1983) vs. just 35 percent of "Boomers" (born 1946 through 1964), with only 15 percent of "Elders" (born 1927–1945) registering agreement.[25] Especially surprising is that this same study shows nearly one third of those who identify as born-again Christians believe it is possible to contact the dead.

Modern-day movements and groups that practice communication with the dead include members of the National Spiritualist Association of the

---

19. The Pew Forum on Religion and Public Life, "U.S. Religious Landscape Survey," June 2008, 10, http://www.pewforum.org/files/2008/06/report2-religious-landscape-study-full.pdf. What I find a bit surprising about this is that the percentage is so low, given that reincarnation is a core belief in the Hindu tradition. But then, as noted in this section, some serious discrepancies exist between orthodox Christian doctrine and what self-professed Christians claim to hold.
20. Ron Rhodes, *New Age Movement,* Zondervan Guide to Cults and Religious Movements, ed. Alan W. Gomes (Grand Rapids: Zondervan, 1995), 16–17, 64, 66.
21. Barna, "Americans Describe Their Views about Life after Death."
22. Pew Forum, "U.S. Religious Landscape Survey," 10.
23. Ibid., 11.
24. Miller, "Why We Need Heaven."
25. Barna, "Americans Describe Their Views about Life after Death."

United States, the National Spiritualist Association of Churches (NSAC), and New Age trance "channelers."[26]

Concluding Thoughts

American opinion on the afterlife is not especially friendly to a biblical view. If we are to believe the surveys—and I see no reason to doubt them—the main threat may not arise from militant secularism, anti-supernaturalism, nor atheism. While there are trends in that direction that we cannot ignore, such views do not yet reflect the thinking of the culture at large. Rather, the biggest departures seem to be an overly spiritualized depiction of the eternal state, the conviction that nearly everybody will make it into heaven, and a corresponding belief in hell as merely theoretical, practically speaking. Underlying these ideas and attitudes, in turn, is either an ignorance or a rejection of the Bible's teaching on heaven, hell, salvation, and the bodily resurrection.

This raises for us the critical issue of authority. On what source or sources *should* we rely for accurate information about the afterlife?

REFLECTION QUESTIONS

1. Did you find surprising any of the survey results discussed in this chapter? Which ones?

2. Why do you suppose people continue to retain a belief in the afterlife even as they abandon other traditional religious beliefs?

3. Consider the surveys that show that Americans tend to see the afterlife purely in spiritualized terms, over and against a future bodily resurrection. What has your own thinking been on this?

4. Reflect on memorial or funeral services that you may have attended recently. What sort of picture of this afterlife did these services present?

5. Consider the picture of "heaven" that one finds in popular presentations of it. How does this compare to your own thoughts about the matter?

---

26. See Question 12, "Is It Possible for Us to Communicate with the Dead?"

Can We Really Know Anything about the Afterlife?

Given the diversity of opinion about the afterlife that we observed in the previous question, some may be tempted to throw up their hands and side with those who say that we really cannot know anything about life after death. As Thomas Wintle, a self-professed Unitarian Universalist "Christian" declares, "I don't know what happens to us after we die, whether there is nothing or there is light. No one does, neither the orthodox believer nor the secular atheist."[1] George N. Marshall, also a member of Wintle's Unitarian Universalist tradition, conveys the same skepticism when he states, "We simply do not know . . . it is common to hear said, 'No one has ever returned to tell us about the afterlife.' We simply do not know, and we question scriptural passages that seem to say otherwise."[2] Similarly, Lisa Miller, in the *Newsweek* article cited in the previous chapter, declares dogmatically,

> For more than 2,000 years, theologians and children have been asking the same, *unanswerable* questions: Do we keep our bodies in heaven? Are we reunited with loved ones? Can

---

1. Jane Rzepka, ed., *Death and Immortality: Unitarian Universalist Views* (Boston: Unitarian Universalist Association, 1994), 5, citing Thomas Wintle. The reason I put the word "Christian" in quotes is because I do not regard Unitarian Universalist "Christians" actually to be such. (Note that most Unitarian Universalists do not even make this claim about themselves, though some, such as Wintle, do.) See Alan W. Gomes, *Unitarian Universalism*, Zondervan Guide to Cults and Religious Movements, ed. Alan W. Gomes (Grand Rapids: Zondervan, 1998).
2. George N. Marshall, "Unitarian Universalism," in *Encounters with Eternity: Religious Views of Death and Life after Death*, ed. Christopher Jay Johnson and Marsha G. McGee (New York: The Philosophical Library, 1986), 300.

we eat, drink, make love? Can you go to my heaven? Can I go
to yours? How do you get there?[3]

If the Unitarian Universalists are correct, if Lisa Miller is correct, and if
a host of other secularists and agnostics and atheists are correct, then no answers are forthcoming and there is no need for a book like this. However, this
extreme skepticism is altogether unwarranted.

Jesus Christ: His Resurrection, Authority, and the Afterlife

When Marshall states, "No one has ever returned to tell us about the afterlife," he is simply wrong. This is precisely what Jesus Christ himself did,
presenting himself alive to his disciples for a period of forty days, offering
many convincing proofs (Acts 1:3; 1 Cor. 15:4–8; cf. Luke 24). Marshall's (and
others') rejection of Christ's bodily resurrection ignores that his resurrection
was a well-attested historical event. The gospel accounts have all of the hall-
marks of authenticity and plausibility from an historical perspective and are
worthy of credence.[4]

Jesus did not merely teach about life after death—he experienced life after
death and came back to demonstrate the truth of it. However, he did teach
about it a great deal as well. Jesus taught that he himself would rise bodily
from the dead.[5] He taught that others would rise from the dead.[6] He taught
that those who believe in him would experience eternal life.[7] And he also
taught that those who reject him would exist forever but in hell, banished
from his presence.[8]

---

3. Lisa Miller, "Why We Need Heaven," *Newsweek*, August 11, 2002, http://www.newsweek.
   com/why-we-need-heaven-143873; emphasis added. If Miller is correct in assuming that
   (apparently) only "theologians and children" ask such questions, then I am certain to be
   disappointed in the sales of this book!
4. William Lane Craig, *Assessing the New Testament Evidence for the Historicity of the
   Resurrection of Jesus* (Lewiston, NY: Edwin Mellen Press, 1989); and William Lane Craig,
   Knowing the Truth about the Resurrection: Our Response to the Empty Tomb, rev. ed. (Ann
   Arbor, MI: Servant Books, 1988). For a condensed treatment by Craig, see his chapter "Did
   Jesus Rise from the Dead?," in *Jesus Under Fire*, eds. Michael J. Wilkins and J. P. Moreland
   (Grand Rapids: Zondervan, 1995), 141–76. See also Gary R. Habermas, *The Historical
   Jesus: Ancient Evidence for the Life of Christ* (Joplin, MO: College Press, 1996); and N. T.
   Wright, *The Resurrection of the Son of God* (Minneapolis: Fortress, 2003). Wright's work is
   the most magisterial and commanding in scope in recent years.
5. Matthew 16:21; 17:23; 20:19; Mark 10:34; Luke 9:22; John 2:19; 10:17.
6. Matthew 22:30; John 5:21, 25, 26, 29; 6:40, 54; 11:24.
7. Matthew 5:12; 6:20; 8:11; 18:8–9; 19:21, 23, 29; 25:46; Mark 10:21, 30; Luke 6:23; 16:9;
   18:30; 20:35–36, 38; John 3:15–16, 36; 4:14, 36; 5:24; 6:40, 51, 54, 58; 10:28; 12:25; 17:2–3.
8. Matthew 5:22, 30; 10:28; 23:33; 25:41, 46; Mark 9:43, 45, 47; Luke 12:5; 16:23; John 3:18, 36.
   We shall elaborate more on each of these points in a variety of the questions that follow.

What Approach Shall I Take in Answering the Remaining Questions in This Book?

For the purposes of this present book, I now stipulate my key working assumptions. These are (1) that Jesus Christ rose bodily from the dead; (2) that everything he told us and demonstrated personally about the afterlife (and anything else) is true; and (3) that whatever the Scriptures convey about the afterlife or anything else (whether taught by his apostles, prophets, or other spokespersons) is absolutely true and reliable. I am not going to prove these statements but just take them for granted, for the purposes of this book. I do so because I have written this book primarily for Christians, who (presumably) already accept the premise that the Bible is a God-inspired book and is therefore authoritative. I am writing for those whose main interest is to know what the Bible teaches specifically on the afterlife.

The Bible Is the Only *Authoritative Source for Truth on the Afterlife*

In my view, the only things we can know about the afterlife with any degree of confidence are what Scripture presents. The Bible is not merely *a* reliable source of information about the afterlife but is the *only* source of trustworthy information about the afterlife.

Now, I am fully aware, for example, that numerous individuals allege to have had visions of heaven and hell, or claim to have gone there and returned to tell us about it—sometimes in lurid, full Technicolor detail.[9] Regardless, such claims are not the material out of which we should construct our opinions on the afterlife, especially when they contradict anything found in Scripture. Only the words of Christ, his apostles, or the writers of Scripture generally must be our guide. So if someone like the famous Swedish mystic, philosopher, and scientist Emmanuel Swedenborg (1688–1772) would have us assent to his fanciful visions of heaven and hell, let him first raise himself bodily from the dead after three days in the grave, and perhaps then we shall give him a hearing.

As shall become evident throughout the rest of this volume, this view of Scripture's central and complete authority will work itself out in how I answer each of the questions contained in this book. Practically speaking, this means that I shall draw all of my conclusions either from direct biblical statements— which I shall do my best to interpret correctly in their own proper context— or from what must follow necessarily from such direct biblical statements.[10]

We Cannot Know Everything about the Afterlife

We must surely reject the skeptical position about the afterlife that I cited at the beginning of this chapter. However, we must be careful not to go to

---

9. We address some of these claims in Question 9.
10. See the *Westminster Confession of Faith* 1.6., http://www.pcaac.org/wp-content/uploads/2012/11/WCFScriptureProofs.pdf.

the opposite extreme and conclude that we can know more about it than we really can. I find that many of the books on this subject, some written by well-intentioned Christians, often attempt to be too smart by half, "helpfully" furnishing us with all manner of fanciful details about the life beyond. The truth is, there is a great deal that we do not and cannot know.

Some matters about the afterlife that the Bible does address involve interpretive challenges. For example, the book of Revelation contains a great deal of information about the age to come. However, in places it is beastly difficult to interpret.[11] It is a book chock-full of symbolism. Sometimes the meaning of the symbols is not obvious. Furthermore, it is not always clear what one ought to take symbolically and what one should understand as literal. Sometimes the meaning in a particular passage is clear, but in other passages not so much. For example, should we understand the dimensions and description of the New Jerusalem (Rev. 21) literally or symbolically?[12] And if symbolically, how do we decode the symbols?

The fact that certain passages in Scripture pose special challenges ought not to lead us to despair nor cast us into a defeated agnosticism about the afterlife or about any other teaching of the faith. The venerable Westminster Confession of Faith gets the balance just right when it states, "All things in Scripture are not alike plain in themselves, nor alike clear unto all." It then adds this important qualification: In matters "which are necessary to be known, believed, and observed for salvation," these "are so clearly propounded, and opened in some place of Scripture or other, that not only the learned, but the unlearned . . . may attain unto a sufficient understanding of them."[13] In other words, on the essentials, one does not have to be a Bible scholar or a theologian to get it right. Where the issue is important enough, the Bible addresses it with sufficient clarity.

On some of the questions we shall explore, I believe we can be certain and I shall present my conclusions as such. There is a heaven. There is a hell. There will be a bodily resurrection. God will create a new heavens and a new earth. Not only that, but we can even know for sure some of the details about these matters. Hell is of eternal duration. It is a place of conscious punishment. God resurrects the same body that died. On other issues, though, we may not be quite so sure because Scripture may have little to say, or because what it does say may not be totally clear to us. Sometimes we may need to reason from what Scripture does tell us to what might be the most probable conclusion on a matter about which the Bible is not directly forthcoming. And on yet other matters, we must frankly admit that we do not have a clue.

---

11. Pun intended.
12. See the discussion of the New Jerusalem in Question 23.
13. Westminster Confession of Faith 1.7.

Extra biblical Arguments Are of Some, though Limited, Value

I do think that arguments drawn from sources other than Scripture may be of some (though limited) value, but only after we have decided the case by the Bible. For instance, as creatures created in God's image, I believe we can leverage our moral intuitions and feelings in order to understand why justice demands that sin be punished, both in this life and in the next. However, I would look to these intuitions only after first examining what God has to say about the matter. To cite another example, I think that there is merit to the argument that C. S. Lewis and others have offered, reasoning that the inability of this present world to satisfy us shows that we were made for another one.[14] I find arguments like these interesting and suggestive, but not determinative.

Conclusion

To sum up the matter, I can do no better than to quote the great nineteenth-century linguist and biblical scholar Moses Stuart, when he said, "The Bible, then, is the only *sure* source of knowledge, in regard to the future destiny of our race. This alone is to be relied on, in the ultimate settlement of the great question, whether we are to be forever happy or miserable."[15]

REFLECTION QUESTIONS

1. Evaluate this statement: "People have so many different opinions on the afterlife that there is no way to know who is right!"

2. In what way is the resurrection of Jesus important for our knowledge of the afterlife?

3. On what sources have you drawn upon in forming your views about life after death? Has anything in this chapter either changed your thinking, or perhaps reinforced your preexisting views?

4. Do you find it unsettling that we cannot know everything we might want to know about the afterlife? How about the fact that some biblical passages may be difficult to interpret?

---

14. C. S. Lewis, *The Weight of Glory: And Other Addresses,* rev. ed. (New York: HarperCollins, 1980), 32–34.
15. Moses Stuart, *Exegetical Essays on Several Words Relating to Future Punishment* (Andover, MA: Perkins & Marvin, 1830), 9.

5. What value do you place on the experiences of those who claim to have died and come back with information about life beyond the grave? (Note: You may wish to revisit this question after you have read Question 9, "What Should We Conclude about Those Who Claim to Have Seen Heaven or Hell?")

Why Do People Die?

The question of what may await us after we die requires us to explore why it is that we die in the first place. If we can get a handle on why death is the common experience of humankind, this will help us better understand what we might expect to occur after it.

When we deal with "why" questions such as this, we can approach them from several different angles. One obvious answer would be that people die because their bodies—the "biological machine," as it were—wears out or otherwise stops functioning. A "natural" process of decay and corruption besets all biological organisms and human beings are not exempt. Sometimes, though, we might not live long enough to perish from these so-called "natural causes" and meet our demise instead through accidents, natural disasters, homicide, etc. Regardless, people die when and because their bodies sustain damage to the point where they can no longer maintain life.

So much for death's most immediate cause. But what if we push the "why" question back even further? We could certainly imagine a world in which human beings do not wear out and decay. Why is that not the kind of world in which we find ourselves? In fact, if a loving and all-powerful God, such as Christians profess, really created this world, would we not expect him to have created a deathless world? Is this really the best that God could do? How are we to explain the presence of death and destruction in our universe?

The Scriptures give us some insight into the more remote or ultimate reasons behind why we die. We start first with the biblical understanding of what death is, in its most basic sense, and then move on to what the Bible tells us about its cause.

Defining Death, according to the Bible

As many biblical scholars and theologians have observed, the Bible teaches that the essence of death is *separation*. This is so whether it uses the word "death" literally or figuratively. Laidlaw states that for human beings, "death means separation, cutting off: primarily, of his spiritual life from God; secondarily, of his soul from his body."[1]

Speaking of physical death, the seventeenth-century Lutheran theologian J. A. Quenstedt defined it succinctly: "[Physical] death, properly speaking, signifies the separation of the soul from the body, and its deprivation of animal life."[2] A number of biblical passages bear out this understanding. Consider James 2:26, which reads, "For as the body apart from (*chōris*)[3] the spirit (*pneumatos*) is dead, so also faith apart from works is dead." Here, the "spirit" (Gk. *pneuma*) is seen in its capacity of giving life to or "vivifying" the body on the physical level.[4] Along the same lines is Genesis 35:18, which speaks of Rachel's "soul" (Heb. *nefesh*) "departing" when she died. The word *nefesh* has a range of meaning, variously defined as "life," "soul," or "person."[5] The Old Testament conveys the same idea by the Hebrew word *ruakh*, or "spirit," as in Psalm 31:5: "Into your hand I commit my spirit." Likewise, some New Testament passages speak of "yielding up" one's spirit (*pneuma*), resulting in physical death (Matt. 27:50; John 19:30; Acts 7:59).

The Bible also uses the word "death" in various metaphorical ways. As with the literal use of death, the metaphorical or figurative uses also feature the idea of separation—specifically, the separation or estrangement of the person from God and from the benefits of his divine life. So, for instance, we have Ephesians 2:1, which declares that before conversion to Christ a person is "dead" in trespasses and sins, described several verses later as being "separated from Christ" (v. 12). Yet another metaphorical use of "death" in the Bible is the expression "second death," used to describe the final fate of those who die in ultimate rejection of God's provision for salvation. The second death is "a metaphorical term for eternal separation from the presence and glory of God (2 Thess. 1:7–10; Rev. 2:11; 20:6, 14–15)."[6] The Bible equates this "second death" with the "lake of fire"—also spoken of as "hell."[7]

---

1. John Laidlaw, *The Bible Doctrine of Man* (Edinburgh: T. & T. Clark, 1895), 245.
2. J. A. Quenstedt, *Theologica didactico-polemica* (1685), 4.535, cited in Heinrich Schmid, *Doctrinal Theology of the Evangelical Lutheran Church*, trans. Charles A. Hay and Henry E. Jacobs (Minneapolis: Augsburg, 1961), 443.
3. The Greek preposition *chōris* in this passage means "without the presence of," and so well conveys the idea of separation. J. B. Bauer, "χωρις," *Exegetical Dictionary of the New Testament*, 3 vols., ed. Horst Balz and Gerhard Schneider (Grand Rapids: Eerdmans, 1993), 3:493.
4. See Question 5, "What Does the Bible Mean When It Speaks of Our 'Soul' and 'Spirit'?" for more detail.
5. Robert Culver, *Systematic Theology: Biblical and Historical* (Fearn, Ross-shire, UK: Mentor, 2005), 1021. For a detailed and careful discussion on the meaning of the word *nephesh*, see Question 5.
6. Paul Ferguson, "Death, Mortality," *EDBT*, 156.
7. See Revelation 20:6, 14–15; 21:8. We shall address the "second death" and the lake of fire more in Question 8 (concerning the biblical words for hell) and also under Section B of

Determining the "Cause of Death," according to Scripture

Having defined death from a biblical perspective, let us see what the Bible tells us about its cause. We shall consider the ultimate reason people die and not more immediate explanations, such as heart attacks or car accidents.

Biblically speaking, we may answer this question simply enough, though the implications of this simple answer are many. "The answer to this question is summed up by Paul: 'The wages of sin is death' (Rom. 6:23)."[8] In other words, death is the punishment for sin.

In saying that death is the punishment for sin, I am not suggesting that everyone dies for committing some particular misdeed or other, such as when a police officer shoots and fatally wounds a bank robber. Indeed, infants die all the time and yet they do not rob banks, use profanity, or exceed the speed limit. Rather, we are talking about something much more fundamental here: the fall of the entire human race into sin, resulting from Adam and Eve's original transgression in the garden. This "fall" is what we commonly consider under what theologians call the doctrine of "original sin." (We shall consider this doctrine in more detail in Question 11.)

One of the earliest verses in the Bible presents the truth of the fall and its consequences in all of its stark reality. In Genesis 2:17, God commanded Adam and Eve not to eat from the tree of the knowledge of good and evil, warning them, "in the day that you eat of it you shall surely die." Whether this verse is referring to a literal tree or to something symbolic is irrelevant to the point.[9] If the verse means anything, it surely means this: Adam and Eve were to obey God's direct command, and failure to do so—which is sin—would result in punishment, namely death. Of course, the biblical record shows clearly what happened: Adam and Eve disobeyed and thereby set in motion the wheels of death.[10]

In the New Testament, the apostle Paul gives what is perhaps the most extended discussion of death as the punishment for sin in Romans 5.[11] In the relevant portions of this passage, Paul states:

Part 4: "The Eternal State for Unbelievers (Hell)." For a good discussion of the second death, see René Pache, *The Future Life* (Chicago: Moody, 1962), 286.

8. "θάνατος," *TDNTW*, 534.
9. Personally, I think it refers to a literal tree.
10. In saying that Adam and Eve would die "in the day" that they ate the forbidden fruit, the text does not mean that they were to keel over dead on the spot. Indeed, according to Genesis 5:5, Adam did not die until he reached the age of 930. Rather, it means that the death sentence would be pronounced in that day, judicially speaking, even though the execution of that sentence would work itself out over time through an ongoing process of decay.
11. Speaking of Paul generally, *TDNTW* notes, "It is Paul who, among the NT writers, reflects most on the connection between guilt and one's mortal destiny" ("θάνατος," 535).

Therefore, just as sin came into the world through one man, and death through sin, and so death spread to all men because all sinned. . . . For if many died through one man's trespass, much more have the grace of God and the free gift by the grace of that one man Jesus Christ abounded for many. And the free gift is not like the result of that one man's sin. For the judgment following one trespass brought condemnation, but the free gift following many trespasses brought justification. For if, because of one man's trespass, death reigned through that one man, much more will those who receive the abundance of grace and the free gift of righteousness reign in life through the one man Jesus Christ. Therefore, as one trespass led to condemnation for all men, so one act of righteousness leads to justification and life for all men . . . so that, as sin reigned in death, grace also might reign through righteousness leading to eternal life through Jesus Christ our Lord. (Rom. 5:12, 15–18, 21)

Observe the following conclusions that we can draw from this text.

Death, in All Its Parts, Entered the World through Sin
First, Paul tells us explicitly that death entered the world through sin. The death here is both spiritual and physical.[12] The relationship between this death and condemnation (v. 16) shows that it is certainly spiritual in nature. However, Adam's sin brought in physical death as well. This is entirely consistent with what Paul states elsewhere, when he declares that all die in Adam physically (1 Cor. 15:21–22). Note, too, that when God punished Adam and Eve for their disobedience, as recorded in Genesis, he very clearly included physical death in this. Genesis 3:19 makes this plain, when God states, "to dust you shall return." Thus, death—both physical and spiritual—is the punishment for sin.

Had Adam and Eve Not Sinned, They Would Not Have Died
The second conclusion that we can draw is that had Adam and Eve not sinned, they would not have died. In other words, death is in one very important sense unnatural; it was not part of God's original or ultimate plan.[13]

---

12. See Augustine, *City of God* 13.15, as proof that the divine threatening includes both physical and spiritual death.
13. This includes not only human death but animal death as well: "If death is the consequence of human sin, then why are nonhuman living creatures likewise subject to mortality? To this Paul replies that the 'creation' has been subjected, not by its own will but as a result of human sin, to futility and impermanence. It now waits to be set free from death, together with the 'children of God' (Rom. 8:19–22). Thus, Paul does not regard even death in nature

This is obvious on its face. If Adam and Eve would have died anyway (i.e., apart from their disobedience), then it makes absolutely no sense for God to have threatened them with death as a consequence for their disobedience. It was only "in the day that they ate of it" that they would "surely die" and not before. In any case, Genesis 3:22 removes all doubt: Had God allowed them ongoing access to the tree of life, they would have lived forever.

Does this mean that God created Adam and Eve immortal, but that they lost their immortality through sin? Well, that depends upon what we mean by "immortal."

Let us consider their physical immortality first. As Augustine described it, in their innocent state as originally created (i.e., before they sinned), Adam and Eve were "able not to die." That is, God provided them with the means of living free from death and disease. Now, we should not confuse being "able not to die" with being "unable to die," or being absolutely indestructible. Even apart from sin, Adam *could* have died in principle (e.g., if someone had dropped an anvil on his head or if he had been run over by a freight train). But God, in his providence, kept all external dangers from harming them in the garden and would have continued to do so for as long as they had remained in that garden without sin. As for death through internal causes, such as disease and old age, God provided them with the tree of life, through which they would maintain their youthful vitality and be free of all such maladies.[14] In that sense, then, we could say that Adam and Eve were "immortal" in their unfallen state: not inherently, but in the sense that they *would not* have died. Nevertheless, as we shall see when we consider the nature of the resurrection body, a higher form of bodily immortality awaits us—a grade or quality of immortality that Adam and Eve never had. Believers will someday possess bodies that are, more properly speaking, immortal in the sense of being absolutely impervious to death (1 Cor. 15:53–54). Such bodies are not merely "able not to die" but are "unable to die."[15]

As for whether God created Adam and Eve with immortal souls, for now it is enough to note that Adam and Eve's soul/spirit survived the death of their bodies. This will be true for us as well. (I shall treat that in more detail in Question 6, "Does Our Soul or Spirit Survive the Death of Our Body?")

---

as a 'natural' phenomenon. From all that we have said, it is evident that in the NT death is regarded not as a natural process, but as a historical event resulting from the sinful human condition" ("θάνατος," *TDNTW*, 535).

14. "They were, then, nourished by other fruit, which they took, that their animal bodies might not suffer the discomfort of hunger of thirst; but they tasted the tree of life, that death might not steal upon them from any quarter, and that they might not, spent with age, decay" (Augustine, *City of God* 13.20). See also *City of God* 13.23; 14.26; *On the Merits of Forgiveness of Sins, and on the Baptism of Infants* 2.35.

15. For an excellent discussion of Adam and Eve's pre- and post-fall condition, see Laidlaw, *The Bible Doctrine of Man*, 233–46.

Adam and Eve's Sin Brought Death to All
The third conclusion that we must draw from that text in Romans is that Adam and Eve's sin brought physical and spiritual death on you and me, as well as on themselves. I have alluded to this earlier when I mentioned the doctrine of original sin. Since I examine this doctrine in more detail in Question 11, I shall not elaborate upon it here.

God Has Provided a Solution to the Scourge of Death
The final point is that God has provided a solution to death: the free gift of salvation through Jesus Christ. He alone has conquered death and provided deliverance from its power. Through Christ's work, God has addressed the problem of death, both in its spiritual and in its physical aspects. Spiritually, he has brought us into a right relationship with God, so that we are no longer alienated from him but are declared "not guilty" of our sins (i.e., we are "justified"). Even more than that, we become his children by adoption (Rom. 8:15, 23; Gal. 4:5; Eph. 1:5). In addition, those who put their faith in Christ will have bodies one day that are better than the bodies of Adam and Eve ever were, even before they fell into sin. God will animate these new glorified bodies with a dynamic, vital, spiritual principle of life that will make them impervious to death, disease, and decay. We shall save our consideration of the astonishing characteristics of our resurrection bodies for Question 19, "What Will the Resurrection Body Be Like?" For now, it is enough to say that Jesus Christ is the answer to death in any and every sense of the word.

REFLECTION QUESTIONS

1. Many—including even Yoda from *Star Wars*(!)—declare that "death is a natural part of life." In light of what you read in this chapter, how would you evaluate such a statement?

2. Read Genesis 2:17. What do we learn from this passage about the relationship between death and sin?

3. When Paul teaches that "death entered the world through sin," is he speaking of physical death, spiritual death, or both? How do we know?

4. Did God create Adam and Eve "immortal"? If so, what did that mean in their case?

5. Is there any difference between the "immortality" that God's adopted children will experience someday and the "immortality" that Adam and Eve experienced at their creation? How would you describe this difference?

What Does the Bible Mean When It Speaks of Our "Soul" and "Spirit"?

In discussions about life after death, people ask whether some "part" of us continues to exist consciously after our bodies die. People commonly speak of our "souls" or "spirits" living on, even as our bodies molder in the grave.

Does the Bible support the idea that there is some "immortal" part of us—i.e., our "soul" or "spirit"—that survives bodily death?

Because of the many interconnected issues involved, I have decided to break our treatment into two questions. In this question, I shall first clarify what the Bible means when it talks about our "soul" and/or our "spirit." Then, having established what the Bible says about how we are put together, so to speak, we shall examine in Question 6 whether the soul or spirit survives bodily death.[1]

General Observations about the Biblical View of Human Persons

Before we explore the specific biblical vocabulary that translates into English as "soul" and/or "spirit," a few overarching observations about how the Bible views the human person or self may prove helpful.

Both Testaments of Scripture tend to look at human beings holistically. Typically, the Bible depicts us as beings in which the body, the mind, the emotions, our physical biological life, etc., all cohere to make a unified, integrated whole—i.e., a living human being. Such a position stands in contrast to religions or philosophical systems, such as Platonism and gnosticism, that see humans as essentially "spirit-selves," who find themselves somehow trapped in material bodies. In those systems, the goal is for people to shed their bodily

---

1. At a few points in this present chapter, I shall assume that the "soul" or "spirit" survives the death of the body, even though I shall not formally demonstrate that until the next question.

prison house, enabling their souls or spirits to live unencumbered in disembodied bliss. Such a perspective is altogether alien from Scripture, as will become clear when we study the various uses of "soul" and "spirit" throughout the Bible.

Scripture's Use of "Soul" and "Spirit" to Describe the Human Constitution

When describing the human constitution, the Bible, in both the Old and New Testaments, uses several different terms that Bible translators render as "soul" and "spirit" in our English translations.

Soul and Spirit in the Old Testament

The word most commonly translated "soul" in the Hebrew Old Testament is *nefesh*, which refers to a vital, energetic, living being—whether man or beast.

Its use in Genesis 2:7 is significant and provides the key passage that unlocks its meaning. This text recounts man's creation, in which God forms his body from the dust of the earth and breathes life into his nostrils. The result is that man "became a *nefesh khayah*," which some translations render as "living soul" or "living creature."[2] Note here that the word "soul" (*nefesh*) does not denote something that man possesses or some "part" of him, but rather what he *is* (i.e., as seen in his totality as "the comprehensive and unified manifestation of sentient life").[3] As Seebass puts it, "According to Gen. 2:7 a person does not *have* a vital self but *is* a vital self."[4]

Nefesh, then, refers to a living being in totality. It is not restricted to human beings, however. *Nefesh* also describes animals in passages such as Genesis 1:20, 21, 24; 9:10; Leviticus 11:10; Job 12:10; and Proverbs 12:10.[5] Of course, our focus in this question is on a particular kind of living being, namely human beings. Since *nefesh* refers to the living being in his/her/its totality, in the case of humans—but not animals—it is roughly equivalent in meaning to the word "person." This is because humans, unlike animals, are *persons*, and we use the word "person" to describe a human being in his or her totality.

We see *nefesh* as equivalent to "person" in Genesis 46:26, which speaks of sixty-six *nefesh* that came with Jacob into Egypt. Also, Leviticus 21:11 and Numbers 6:6 refer to a "dead *nefesh*" (*nafshoth meth*), which some translators render as "dead body" (e.g., ESV, KJV), while others, perhaps more correctly,

---

2. *Khayah* is from the Hebrew adjective *khay*, which means "alive, living."
3. Aubrey R. Johnson, *The Vitality of the Individual in the Thought of Ancient Israel* (Cardiff: University of Wales Press, 1964), 10.
4. H. Seebass, "נֶפֶשׁ," *TDOT* 9:511–12.
5. See Robert L. Saucy, *Minding the Heart: The Way of Spiritual Transformation* (Grand Rapids: Kregel, 2013), 32.

translate as "dead person" (e.g., NASB, NAB). Regardless, these latter two instances surely demonstrate that one cannot take *nefesh*, in these passages at least, as referring to some disembodied part of the person.

Because *nefesh* so represents the totality of the individual's expressive life, the Bible sometimes uses *nefesh* as equivalent to the pronoun "I," "me," "my," etc., as in expressions such as "my soul." Here, "my soul" is equivalent to "me," but perhaps with the added nuance of stressing the individual as an energetic or "vital self."[6] So, a passage such as Psalm 103:1, which reads, "Bless the Lord, O my soul (*nefesh*)," means, in effect, "*I* bless the Lord with every fiber of my being"—or, as the words of the second half of the verse make clear, with "all that is within me."

If the "soul," then, stands for a complete living individual, how does the "spirit" relate to this?[7]

Our English translations commonly render the Hebrew word *ruakh* as "spirit." Its basic definition is "wind" or "breath," and the Bible uses it as such in a number of passages (e.g., Gen. 3:8; Exod. 10:13; Job 15:30). *Ruakh* also stands for the life force, both in men and in animals (Gen. 6:17; Ezek. 37:5), which departs the body at death (Eccl. 3:21; 8:8; Ps. 31:5).[8]

Note that in human beings, the *ruakh* does more than merely enliven the being on a strictly biological level. While it certainly does that, the human spirit also includes personal capacities as essential to it. It is the ground of self-conscious emotions, volitions (i.e., choices), and desires (e.g., Isa. 26:9), as well as "the seat or organ of mental acts" (Job 20:3; Ps. 77:6; Isa. 29:24; Ezek. 20:32).[9] In contrast, the *ruakh* of animals does not possess the higher mental capacities of the human *ruakh*.

Ruakh relates to *nefesh* in the following way. If the *nefesh* (i.e., soul) refers to a living being, then the *ruakh* is the life principle; it is that which makes the living being alive. A soul is a living soul by virtue of the presence of *ruakh* in it.

Again, the creation account in Genesis 2 serves as our guide. Notice that man became a "living soul" (*nefesh khayah*) once God "breathed into his nostrils the breath of life" (i.e., his spirit into him).[10]

---

6. Seebass, "נֶפֶשׁ," *TDOT* 9:510; Johnson, *The Vitality of the Individual in the Thought of Ancient Israel*, 15–16.

7. For the understanding of the relationship between spirit and soul (*ruakh* and *nefesh*) that follows, I am indebted primarily to the work of, and my discussions with, my good friend and colleague Robert Saucy. See his book *Minding the Heart*, 31–34, for a compact treatment of these issues.

8. For the meanings of *ruakh* that follow, see BDB, "רוּחַ," 924–25.

9. BDB, "רוּחַ," 925.

10. Though this passage does not specifically use the word *ruakh,* the meaning is nonetheless the same. Here Moses employs the verb *nafakh,* "to breathe; blow," followed by a form of the word *neshama*, which means "breath." Though used much less frequently than *ruakh,* its meaning is often synonymous with it. For clarification, see Genesis 6:17 and 7:15, which

Based on passages such as these, Saucy provides a helpful sketch of how we are to understand our makeup as human beings:

> As human beings we are a union of material substance, "dust from the ground," and immaterial substance, "the breath of life," or spirit. This union of material (body) and immaterial (spirit) results in "a living soul." Soul is thus the term for man's total human nature—the total person, what he is, not just what he has. Soul represents the human as alive with life that consists of emotions, passions, drives, and appetite. . . . *Spirit* is life as effective power; *soul* is the subject or bearer of that life, or life actively realized in the creature. *Soul* emphasizes the living individual, *spirit* the vitalizing power by which the individual or *soul* lives.[11]

Soul and Spirit in the New Testament

The New Testament presents a structure of the human person consistent with the Old.

Psychē is the Greek word most commonly translated "soul" in the New Testament. In many ways, *psychē* is virtually equivalent to the Hebrew *nefesh*; in fact, in the Septuagint, which is a Greek translation of the Hebrew Old Testament, the translators picked this word to render the various instances of *nefesh*.

As with *nefesh*, the Bible uses the term *psychē* in its most comprehensive sense; the *psychē* "embraces the whole natural being and life of a human being for which one concerns oneself and of which one takes constant care."[12] Like *nefesh*, the word *psychē* can also stand for "that which possesses life," which is to say the person as a whole.[13]

The word for "spirit" in the New Testament is *pneuma*. As with *ruakh*, the basic meaning of *pneuma* is wind and, related to it, breath. The Bible uses it in this sense in such passages as John 3:8 and (most likely) Hebrews 1:7. It also

---

uses *ruakh khayim* for the life principle of living beings. Note especially Genesis 7:22, which has *nishmat ruakh khayim*, "the breath of the spirit of life." Here *ruakh* is in an appositional construct to *nishmat*, which therefore could be translated "the breath (*nishmat*) that is the spirit (*ruakh*) of life." We find the same construction in 2 Samuel 22:16, with the same meaning. Job 4:9 is yet another verse that shows the synonymous sense of *nishmat* and *ruakh*. See the discussion in Saucy, *Minding the Heart*, 32.

11. Ibid., 32–33.
12. "ψυχή," *TDNTW*, 1374.
13. BDAG, "ψυχή," 1099. See Acts 2:41, 43; 3:23; 7:14; 27:37; Romans 2:9; 1 Corinthians 15:45; 1 Peter 3:20.

uses *pneuma* to designate the vital life force that animates the body. This is clear from James 2:26, which declares, "The body without the spirit is dead."[14]

Pneuma can also specify that which furnishes the thinking and feeling capacities of a person, including the emotions and the will. Thus, one's *pneuma* can be "troubled" (John 11:33; 13:21), provoked (Acts 17:16), and can rejoice (Luke 1:46–47).

How Do We Explain Passages Where Soul and Spirit Seem to Mean the Same Thing?

In the treatment above, I have stressed that the spirit refers to the immaterial part of a human being, while the word "soul" refers to the person in his or her totality. That is, a person *has* a spirit and *is* a soul. Yet, discussions on this topic commonly speak of the "soul" as the immaterial part of a person, thus making it equivalent in meaning to spirit. Furthermore, in the New Testament in particular, we encounter some passages that might seem to make the same equation. For instance, in Matthew 10:28 Jesus states, "And do not fear those who kill the body but cannot kill the soul. Rather fear him who can destroy both soul and body in hell." Here, it seems that "soul" refers to the immaterial part of the person, in contrast to the body, which is the material part. Likewise, Hebrews 12:23 refers to deceased saints existing in heaven as the "spirits of the righteous made perfect," whereas Revelation 6:9 describes deceased (here, martyred) saints as the souls "under the altar." Granting that the deceased saints in these two texts are disembodied, should we conclude that these passages use "soul" and "spirit" interchangeably, and that both texts refer to the immaterial part of the person, which is the part that survives bodily death?

Not quite. It is important to realize that what is true of one of the parts of a person is also true of the person him/herself. Take the eye as an example. It would just as correct to say, "*I* see 20–20," as it would be to say, "*My eyes* see 20–20." This does not mean that there is no distinction between our bodily parts, such as the eyes, and the person composed of those parts. Yet, what is true of the body is true of the person because the body in question belongs to that person.

Now, let us consider how this works specifically in relationship to the immaterial part of the person, which is properly called the person's spirit. While the person (or soul) is alive on this earth, he or she is a two-part person (or soul), consisting of a body (material part) and a spirit (immaterial part). However, as I shall demonstrate in the answer to Question 6, at death the spirit separates from the body and consciously survives bodily death, even as the body decomposes in the earth. So when the person was alive on earth, he/she was a two-part soul or person (body and spirit), whereas after

---

14. See also, for example, Matthew 27:50; Luke 8:55; John 19:30; and Acts 7:59.

he/she dies, we now have a one-part soul or person, consisting only of the person's spirit. Remember that the spirit includes not only the biological life that animates the body (e.g., so that the lungs breathe air and the heart beats and circulates blood), but the spirit also is the seat of the intellect, emotions, will, reason, self-consciousness, and all of the other mental functions of the person. It is the root of the personal life in which all of these capacities are grounded. Although the spirit no longer can keep the body alive once it has separated from it, it still continues its other mental kinds of functions. And it is these higher intellectual functions (such as reason, self-consciousness, and the like) that are essential to personhood; they are what humans have that animals do not. Simply stated, the essential elements of personhood survive bodily death because it is the spirit that "carries" the personhood, so to speak, and not the body.

Therefore, when we have a "disembodied soul," what we have is an incomplete human person, whom we may rightly call a "soul" (person) in an incomplete state, possessing only his or her spirit and no longer a body. Thus, when we have examples of Scripture referring to people who have died as "souls" (Rev. 6:9) or "spirits" (Heb. 12:23), both words refer to incomplete people awaiting resurrection. In the first case, the stress is on the *person* (i.e., soul) who no longer has a body. In the latter case, the passage refers to the incomplete person by naming the *part* of him or her that has survived bodily death (i.e., the spirit).

The Special Use of the Adjectives "Soulish" and "Spiritual" in the New Testament

Thus far, we have looked at the biblical words translated "soul" and "spirit" and examined their use in describing the makeup of the human person. However, certain New Testament writers, particularly Paul, employ the corresponding adjectives "soulish" (*psychikos*) and "spiritual" (*pneumatikos*) in related though somewhat different senses from what we have seen above.

Paul speaks of the "soulish" man (*psychikos anthrōpos*), who "does not accept the things of the Spirit of God . . . because they are spiritually discerned (*pneumatikōs anakrinetai*)" (1 Cor. 2:14). He also characterizes our present, weak, and frail body as *psychikos*, in contrast to our future resurrection body, which he terms a "spiritual body" (*sōma pneumatikon*) (1 Cor. 15:44).

Most modern translations render *psychikos* as "natural." This refers to human beings in their natural state and condition, apart from any special empowerment by God's Spirit. This term applies not only to humans as originally created and endowed with a natural or animal principle of life (as Adam was in the garden), but also to humankind as we find ourselves now, which is to say ravaged by the degrading effects of sin. In contrast, the adjective *pneumatikos*, or "spiritual," refers to the energy by which God specially empowers human beings. Here, the reference is not to our own human spirit or *pneuma* (as we considered earlier) but rather to God's own Spirit as an energizing principle of life, whether operating on our physical bodies or on own personal spirits. As Laidlaw summarizes:

> The contrast or antithesis . . . is plainly one between human nature in its own native elements and human nature under the higher power which has entered it in the New Birth. The former is *psychic*, the latter is *pneumatic*. The psychical or "soulish" man is man as nature now constitutes him, and as sin has infected him. . . . The pneumatic or spiritual man . . . is man as grace has re-constituted him, and as God's Spirit dwells in him and bestows gifts upon him (1 Cor. 2:15).[15]

This Pauline use of *psychikos* and *pneumatikos* in 1 Corinthians 15 will be most important for our examination of the nature of the resurrection body in Question 19. When I unpack this text later, we shall see that Paul contrasts the purely "animal" principle of life that enlivens the "natural" or "soulish" body over and against the coming "spiritual" body that we will receive in the resurrection. This latter body, every bit as physical as the former, nevertheless is one specially empowered by God's own Spirit, with all the glory that this will entail.

REFLECTION QUESTIONS

1. This chapter began by making the general observation that the Bible takes a "holistic" view of the human person. What does this mean, and why is it significant?

2. What is the Hebrew word most commonly translated "soul" in the Old Testament? How does this relate to the previous point, i.e., that the Bible takes a holistic view?

3. What is the Hebrew word most commonly translated "spirit"? Compare the meaning of "soul" and "spirit" in the Old Testament passages discussed in this chapter.

4. What are the New Testament words translated "soul" and "spirit"? What is the sense of each of these words and how do they relate to one another, as well as to their Old Testament counterparts?

---

15. John Laidlaw, *The Bible Doctrine of Man* (Edinburgh: T. & T. Clark, 1895), 94.

5. When a person's spirit departs his or her body at death, is he or she still a "human person"? If so, what *kind* of person? What is the significance of this for the doctrine of the future resurrection?

Does Our Soul or Spirit Survive the Death of Our Body?

Having examined the biblical uses of the words "soul" and "spirit," we are now prepared to address the question of whether the human soul or spirit survives bodily death.

The Holistic View of Humans in Relation to the Afterlife

In treating the previous question, I stressed that the biblical view of human beings is holistic. This holistic emphasis carries over into the Bible's treatment of the afterlife. We see this in the biblical emphasis on the eventual bodily resurrection of the person; it is as complete human beings, body and spirit, that believers will "glorify God and enjoy him forever."[1] In other words, complete, biblical salvation is most definitely not about shucking our bodies so we can spend eternity on clouds as bodiless ghosts. Rather, biblical salvation entails a glorious existence as whole human persons, including immortal, transformed, resurrected bodies, which will be well suited for life on an equally spectacular and transformed new earth.[2]

Some take the holistic view of human nature too far, however. Wrongly reducing human beings to highly complex biological machines, these scholars incorrectly conclude that the disintegration of the body marks the disintegration of the entire person, thereby precluding the survival of bodily death. John Hick points to thinkers who reject continuing consciousness after death because, they say, "we have to accept the general assumption among scientifically minded contemporaries that mental life is absolutely dependent

---

1. As we shall see later in Question 20, unbelievers likewise will spend eternity in an unglorified but nonetheless embodied state in the lake of fire.
2. See Question 19, "What Will the Resurrection Body Be Like?" and Question 21, "What Are the New Heavens and the New Earth?"

upon—if not identical with—the functioning of the cerebral system."[3] Those of this opinion, who also deny the future resurrection of the body, would therefore deny any possibility of life after death.

Others with similar reasoning take a less extreme, though still incorrect, position. They, too, hold that bodily disintegration marks the end of the person's existence. However, these argue that after a period of nonexistence, God will reconstitute the person in a future bodily resurrection. Adherents of this more moderate position, then, *do* believe in an afterlife, but only one that takes place after an intervening period of nonexistence. Theologians commonly refer to this doctrine as "soul sleep," though this label is actually rather misleading. According to this theory, the "soul" (or person) does not exist—sleeping or otherwise—while it has no body. At any rate, these individuals say that on the last day, God creates the person anew from his memory, endowing the newly recreated person with a body that makes conscious life possible.[4]

Now if, contrary to the above theories, the Bible teaches that the person experiences conscious existence after death, including also the period in which the individual's body remains in the grave, then we may conclude (1) that the person can and does continue in a mode of existence that retains the personality; and (2) that this personal existence is unrelated to and distinguishable from the person's earthly body or "tent" (2 Cor. 5:1). This would mean, then, that there must be something about persons that transcends their bodily life—including their physical brains—which somehow survives the body's death and "carries," so to speak, the personality of the individual. This "something" is what we identified in the previous question as the person's *spirit*. This spirit endures without interruption throughout the various conditions and states of the person's life: whether during the soul's this-earthly, embodied existence; during the soul's disembodied existence awaiting resurrection (known as the "intermediate state");[5] or throughout the soul's "eternal state" after reembodiment in a new, glorified, physical form.[6]

---

3. John Hick, "Life after Death," *Westminster Dictionary of Christian Theology*, eds. Alan Richardson and John Bowden (Philadelphia: Westminster Press, 1983), 332.
4. See Robert Culver, *Systematic Theology: Biblical and Historical* (Fearn, Ross-shire, UK: Mentor, 2005), 1034; E. F. Harrison, "Soul Sleep," *EDT*, 1130–31; and J. J. Scott Jr., "Immortality," *DPL*, eds. Gerald F. Hawthorne and Ralph P. Martin (Downers Grove, IL: InterVarsity Press, 1993), 432–33.
5. See Question 10, "What Fate Awaits Those Who Die in This Present Age, Immediately upon Death?"
6. In reference to the distinction between "spirit" and "soul" that I argued in Question 5, I should note that theological discussions often will use the terms "soul" and "spirit" interchangeably, using either one to refer to the immaterial part of the person. This does not in itself indicate disagreement with the view that I am presenting in this question, even though it may highlight a disagreement on the most scriptural way to express the view.

Biblical Evidence That the Person Survives the Death of the Body

Both testaments furnish sufficient evidence that the person survives bodily death, and that there is a continuity of one's conscious existence before and after death.

As we examine the following texts, note that we are only interested in whether they teach that people experience conscious existence after bodily death. We are not here interested in the quality of that existence (i.e., whether it is happy or miserable or ambivalent). For now, we are interested only in the *fact* of conscious life as such, after the death of the body.

Psalms 16:11; 17:15; 49:15; 73:23–26; 119:43–44; Isaiah 26:4

These psalms convey, in the words of Geerhardus Vos, "the confidence of uninterrupted fellowship with Jehovah." This, in turn, is "based on the belief in a future blessed life after death."[7] Consider, as representative, Psalm 73:23–26:

> Nevertheless, I am continually with you; you hold my right hand. You guide me with your counsel, and afterward you will receive me to glory. Whom have I in heaven but you? And there is nothing on earth that I desire besides you. My flesh and my heart may fail, but God is the strength of my heart and my portion forever.

The continual, unbroken enjoyment of God "forever" in "glory" would be impossible to understand if the psalmist thought that death marked the end of his existence. This is likewise true for the passages that speak of "trusting in the Lord forever" (Isa. 26:4), enjoying "pleasures at his right hand forevermore" (Ps. 16:11), and so forth.

Isaiah 8:19

This is one of many verses condemning necromancy,[8] or communicating with the dead. The fact that the Old Testament condemns this practice shows that the ancient Israelites believed that the dead survive their physical deaths. Though some might wish to attribute such a belief to primitive, ancient superstition, it is significant that God himself condemns the practice in this verse, and nowhere corrects their assumption that people live on after their deaths.

---

7. Geerhardus Vos, *The Pauline Eschatology* (Grand Rapids: Eerdmans, 1961), 349.
8. "Necromancy" refers to the practice of communicating with the dead, typically for divining hidden or future information.

Verses Teaching the Resurrection of Jesus

In Question 3, "Can We Really Know Anything about the Afterlife?" I cited a large number of texts claiming that Jesus Christ rose from the dead; I shall not repeat them here. Suffice it to say, if Christ's resurrection was a literal, historical event, then this is the most cogent proof possible that life after death is not merely a possibility but a fact. Not only does his resurrection show that the person survives the death of the body, but it also shows that the body itself survives the death of the body (i.e., through resurrection).

Note that during the three days in which Jesus's body lay buried in the tomb, he was in a state of conscious existence. We know this because he expressly told the thief on the cross, "*today* you will be *with me* in paradise" (Luke 23:43, emphasis added). This utterly refutes the doctrine of soul sleep mentioned earlier. God did not recreate Jesus anew when he resurrected him, but rather joined his still-conscious, glorified human spirit to his resurrected body, made new and immortal.[9]

Matthew 17:1–9

These verses recount the so-called Mount of Transfiguration incident. In this passage, Jesus took three of his disciples to a high mountain, where he was gloriously transfigured before them (v. 2). At this time, Moses and Elijah appeared to them and conversed with Jesus. This shows that Moses and Elijah, though long dead, were fully conscious and capable of carrying on this discourse with Jesus.

Matthew 10:28

This text reads, "And do not fear those who kill the body but cannot kill the soul. Rather fear him who can destroy both soul and body in hell." Leaving aside for a moment any consideration of "hell" as such,[10] Jesus's words make it clear that the person survives the death of the body. If this were not so, then anyone who killed the body would thereby annihilate the entire person, thus making Jesus's statement false. Observe that the "destruction" that God is capable of inflicting is not just of the body but also of the *soul*, i.e., of the entire person. (As we shall see in Question 34, "What Do Annihilationists Teach about Hell?," this destruction [Gk.: *apolesai*] does not refer to the annihilation of the person but rather to his or her ruin and misery.)

Matthew 22:32

In this passage, Jesus refutes the Sadducees' denial of the resurrection by pointing to the statement that God is "the God of Abraham, and the God of Isaac, and the God of Jacob." Granting that God is called their God, and that

---

9. We shall discuss this in more detail, particularly in Question 20.
10. See Question 8, "What Does the Bible Mean When It Speaks of 'Hell'?"

"He is not the God of the dead but of the living," it inevitably follows that these patriarchs are yet alive—contrary to the Sadducees' rejection of an afterlife.

Luke 16:19–31

These verses comprise the story of the rich man and Lazarus.[11] I shall say more about this passage when I discuss Question 10 (on the intermediate state), Question 30 (on the nature of hell), and Question 31 (which deals with whether we should understand the fires of hell literally or figuratively).

The situation Jesus recounts occurs during the intermediate state between death and the future resurrection on judgment day, given that he declares the rich man to be in hades (v. 23).[12] In addition, reference to the rich man's kinsmen who were yet alive (vv. 27–31) further confirms that this was antecedent to the final judgment.[13]

The following features of this account are relevant here: (1) both of the main players in this story are dead (v. 22); (2) they have perception and recognition (v. 23); (3) they have memory of their past life (v. 25); (4) they continue to experience emotions, such as comfort and anguish (v. 25).

2 Corinthians 5:1–10

In this fascinating passage, Paul contrasts three states of existence: (1) our present earthly life in the mortal, corruptible bodies that we currently possess; (2) a life without our bodies but nevertheless "with the Lord," which

---

11. Some question whether one should take this passage as a parable or as narrating an actual, literal event. Among modern evangelical interpreters, Bock, Blomberg, Green, and Stein all take it as a parable. However, there are some features of this account that do not correspond to the normal format of Jesus's other parables, such as the fact that the participants in it are given specific names and not spoken of generically. Bock, who himself takes it as a parable, gives a good summary of the arguments for and against (Darrell Bock, *Luke 9:51–24:53*, BECNT [Grand Rapids: Baker, 1996], 1362–63; see also Robert H. Stein, *Luke*, NAC 24 [Nashville: Broadman, 1992], 422). Either way, "the fundamental theological affirmations about the afterlife . . . are true regardless of the genre classification. . . . It depicts a tragic and serious reality" (Darrell Bock, *Luke*, NIVAC [Grand Rapids: Zondervan, 1996], 432, 434–435). I believe this includes the truths that are relevant to answering the question before us. That is, even parables must be based on certain literal truths from which the parabolic meaning is derived.

12. As we shall see in Question 8, hades refers to the intermediate and not to the final state of the wicked dead. See also, e.g., Joachim Jeremias, "παράδεισος," *TDNT* 5:769 n37.

13. See Question 7, "What Does the Bible Mean When It Speaks of 'Heaven'?" Cooper also points to the fact that "the rich man's brothers are still alive on earth," showing that the final judgment had not yet taken place (John W. Cooper, *Body, Soul, and Life Everlasting: Biblical Anthropology and the Monism-Dualism Debate* [Grand Rapids: Eerdmans, 2000], 124). Note that Cooper himself takes this passage as a parable and is not convinced we can derive factual information about the intermediate state from it. At the same time, in light of other teachings in Luke, he avers, "Luke 16 cannot be dismissed as wholly irrelevant to the New Testament ideas about the afterlife" (p. 129).

happens when we die and our "earthly home" or "tent" is destroyed; and (3) the eternal phase of our existence, during which an immortal, glorified body or "heavenly dwelling" will clothe every believer.

I shall treat this passage in considerable detail under Question 10, "What Fate Awaits Those Who Die in This Present Age, Immediately upon Death?" For now it is sufficient to note that in Paul's estimation, so long as we dwell in our present bodies, we are "away from the Lord" (v. 6). Conversely, once we are "away from the body" we shall then be "home with the Lord" (v. 8). This shows the continuing, "personal communion with Christ immediately upon death."[14]

Philippians 1:21–25

Philippians 1:21–25, coupled with 2 Corinthians 5:1–10 (above), provide "the clearest and strongest passages . . . in Paul's writings" of "continuing consciousness after death."[15] In this text, Paul wrestles with his desire to remain on in the flesh so as to continue his fruitful ministry among the disciples, which stands in tension with his longing to "depart" his body in death in order to "be with Christ," which is "far better." One cannot reconcile such a sentiment with a doctrine of soul sleep, much less with a permanent extinction of being. It is difficult to see how passing into nonexistence, even for a time, is the same as being "with Christ" and therefore "much better."[16] As Paul Helm correctly notes concerning this passage:

> Physical death is not the total cessation of the life of the individual but the person lives on, not merely in the memories of those who survive, but as a distinct personality, and in the case of believers with awareness of the loving presence of God.[17]

Revelation 6:9–11

This scene depicts individuals who had been martyred during a period known as "the great tribulation" and who are now in heaven, imploring God to avenge their deaths. Now, it is certainly true that the book of Revelation

---

14. John W. Cooper, "Immortality," *EC*, 668. See also Murray Harris, "Intermediate State," *New Dictionary of Theology*, eds. Sinclair B. Ferguson and David F. Wright (Downers Grove, IL: InterVarsity Press, 1988), 339.
15. Harrison, "Soul Sleep," *EDT*, 1130–31.
16. Harris states, "[Paul] would hardly have viewed unconscious rest with Christ in heaven as 'far better' than conscious communion with Christ on earth." Harris, "Intermediate State," 339–40. However, as we noted earlier, those who hold to "soul sleep" typically, at least, do not believe that the person exists at all upon their deaths; they are not "resting unconsciously," as might be the case with someone in a coma or a dreamless state of sleep.
17. Paul Helm, "Intermediate State," *BEB*, 4:1043.

contains much symbolism, and so one has to tread carefully in determining what to take literally, what to understand figuratively, and how to interpret the meaning of those parts that are figurative. However, I believe that certain facts, relevant to the question before us, are clear from this passage.

First, the "souls" in these verses are believers who had experienced martyrdom. The passage explicitly declares them dead: they had been "slain" (v. 9) and had poured out their blood in sacrifice for their steadfast profession (vv. 9–10). It describes them as "under the altar"—symbolic imagery that further emphasizes their sacrificial deaths.[18] The point here, then, is that since they are dead, and since the resurrection has not yet happened, they are therefore disembodied. As such, they now reside in God's presence in heaven, in contrast to those "who dwell on the earth" (v. 10).

Second, these martyred saints remain fully conscious of their situation. They retain full recognition and memory of their slaughter at the hands of their persecutors and also know that God has not yet avenged their deaths. They strongly desire for God to mete out justice, and they cry out for him to effect this. The Lord himself communicates with them, for he comforts them and instructs them to "rest a little longer" before he grants their request. All of this makes no sense if death marks the extinction of one's consciousness.

REFLECTION QUESTIONS

1. In the previous question, we observed that the Bible teaches a holistic view of human nature. In what ways have some taken the holistic view of human nature too far?

2. Describe the position commonly known as "soul sleep." What do advocates of this position teach about the "soul" and the possibility of its existence after bodily death? In what way is the label "soul sleep" a misnomer?

3. Some have argued that the Old Testament has no teaching about an afterlife. In light of the Old Testament texts presented in this chapter, evaluate that claim.

4. How do we know that Christ, after his death but before his bodily resurrection, remained in a state of conscious existence?

---

18. Osborne remarks, "The imagery of these souls 'under the altar' has occasioned much discussion. No one doubts that it refers to the sacrificial system, where the blood of the sacrificial victim is poured 'under the altar.' . . . Here the martyred saints are clearly pictured as those sacrificed for Christ" (Grant R. Osborne, *Revelation*, BECNT [Grand Rapids: Baker, 2002], 284–85).

5. Which of the biblical passages presented in this chapter provide the strongest and clearest teaching about continuing, conscious existence after death? Can you think of any other such passages besides the ones we looked at?

What Does the Bible Mean When It Speaks of "Heaven"?

The Bible speaks a great deal about heaven. Sometimes it does so using words in the original biblical languages that we translate explicitly with our English word "heaven." In other instances, the biblical writers use synonyms for heaven, which we render with words or expressions such as "paradise" or "Abraham's bosom."

If we are to understand the Bible's teaching on heaven, it is important for us to attend to the language very carefully, to discern the reality to which these words point.

"Heaven"

The Old Testament word rendered "heaven" in our English translations is the Hebrew word *shamayim*. In the Greek New Testament, as well as in the Septuagint (i.e., the Greek translation of the Hebrew Old Testament), the word translated "heaven" is *ouranos*. Both words carry the same three primary meanings (with other nuances possible).[1]

The first meaning of "heaven" is what we might call the sky or atmosphere. This is the air around us, in which we find clouds, birds, the wind, and so forth. For example, the Bible refers to "the birds of the heavens" (1 Kings 21:24), "the rain from heaven" (Deut. 11:11; Acts 14:17), and also snow (Isa. 55:10), dew (Dan. 4:23), frost (Job 38:29), wind (1 Kings 18:45; Ps. 78:26),

---

1. See Robert Culver, *Systematic Theology: Biblical and Historical* (Fearn, Ross-shire, UK: Mentor, 2005), 1097; J. K. Grider, "Heaven," *EDT*, 541; Bradford A. Mullen, "Heaven, Heavens, Heavenlies," *EDBT*, 333; and René Pache, *The Future Life* (Chicago: Moody, 1962), 342.

clouds (Ps. 147:8), thunder (1 Sam. 2:10), and hail (Rev. 16:21; cf. Job 38:22) "from heaven."[2]

The second meaning is the expanse in which the celestial bodies are located, including the sun, moon, planets, and stars. Passages such as Genesis 1:14–16; Jeremiah 33:25; Nahum 3:16; Acts 7:42; and Hebrews 11:12 illustrate this use.

The third meaning of "heaven" is God's abode, "the place where God reigns, from which He governs the universe."[3] The apostle Paul speaks of this third sense of heaven as, appropriately enough, "the third heaven" (2 Cor. 12:2–4). The writer to the Hebrews calls it "heaven itself," the place of God's presence (Heb. 9:24). Paul refers to the same thing, using the plural form *ta ouriania,* which is translated "the heavenly places" (Eph. 1:3, 20; 2:6).

Note that God does not reside in heaven by himself. Angels also inhabit "heaven" in this sense of the word (e.g., Gen. 28:12; 1 Kings 22:19–22; Matt. 18:10; 22:30; 24:36; Gal. 1:8; etc.).[4] Furthermore, it is the current abode of Jesus the resurrected God-man (Eph. 6:9; Col. 4:1; cf. Rom. 8:34), and of the departed saints (Heb. 12:22–24; Rev. 19:1–6), who await their own resurrections.

Since our interest here is neither in meteorology nor in astronomy, we shall focus on the third use of the word "heaven," i.e., as the dwelling place of God, angels, Jesus, and the saints.

Heaven as God's Abode

Concerning heaven as God's abode, Ecclesiastes 5:2 states the matter succinctly: "God is in heaven and you are on earth." Jesus likewise expressed this same truth in the Lord's prayer, teaching his disciples to pray, "Our Father in heaven, hallowed be your name" (Matt. 6:9). Many other verses express the same thought, such as Deuteronomy 26:15; 1 Kings 8:30; 22:19; Psalms 14:2; 103:19; Isaiah 63:15; 66:1; and Matthew 5:16; 6:1; 7:21; 10:32.

First Kings 8 is a particularly noteworthy chapter that gives us some helpful insights on the nature of heaven as the place where God abides. On the one hand, verses 30 and 49 declare that heaven is God's "dwelling place." Repeatedly throughout this chapter, Solomon implores God to "hear in heaven" the petitions of his people (vv. 30, 32, 34, 36, 39, 43, 45, and 49). And yet, Solomon—speaking of the "exalted house" he built for God "to dwell in forever" (v. 13)—acknowledges in verse 27 that God actually transcends heaven itself:

---

2. See "Heaven," *BEB,* 2:940; J. Lunde, "Heaven and Hell," *Dictionary of Jesus and the Gospels,* eds. Joel B. Green and Scot McNight (Downers Grove, IL: InterVarsity Press), 308; and Mullen, "Heaven, Heavens, Heavenlies," 332.

3. Pache, *The Future Life,* 342. See also Culver, *Systematic Theology,* 1098.

4. "οὐρανός," *TDNTW,* 939.

But will God indeed dwell on the earth? Behold, heaven and the highest heaven cannot contain you; how much less this house that I have built!

The point is, we should not conceive of heaven as some location in the sky or a partitioned-off area of space that contains or houses God, for this would contradict the biblical truth of divine omnipresence and transcendence. God, being omnipresent, is everywhere present: all the time, all at once, and in a way that completely outstrips our understanding. God exists above and beyond all things whatsoever, including even the third heaven. Thus, although God in his omnipresence fills (so to speak) not only the earth but even heaven itself (Jer. 23:24), they in no way limit or circumscribe him.

So, when we speak of God dwelling *in* heaven, we should understand heaven as that location in which God directly manifests his presence and in which he reigns to a preeminent degree—the place, in other words, where God's will is now done completely (Matt. 6:10). At the same time, heaven is, as we shall see below, the place that includes his angels, the resurrected Jesus, and the saints who have died and abide in his presence awaiting the resurrection of their bodies.

Heaven as the Abode of Angels

Many verses demonstrate that God's good angels inhabit heaven. For example, we find numerous passages that use the expression "angel(s) of heaven" or "angel(s) in heaven" (e.g., Matt. 18:10; 22:30; 24:36; Mark 12:25; 13:32). The Bible describes them as coming from and ascending into heaven (e.g., Gen. 28:12; Matt. 28:2; Luke 2:15; John 1:51). We also see that the angels enjoy God's very presence in heaven (1 Kings 22:19; Isa. 6:2–3; Matt. 18:10).

Interestingly, Paul also uses the plural form "the heavenly places" to designate the realm in which evil spirits or fallen angels operate (Eph. 6:12).[5] Here "Paul likely is referring to Satan and his demonic hosts, calling them 'rulers,' 'authorities,' and 'spiritual forces' (Eph. 3:10; 6:12)."[6] At first glance this seems a bit strange, granting that "the heavenly realms" are also where Christ presently dwells and where Christians are said, figuratively speaking, to be "seated" with him (Eph. 1:20; 2:6 cf. 1:3). Surely, demons cannot be roommates with Christ and his saints!

Perhaps we can solve this seeming discrepancy by regarding the term "heavenlies" or "heavenly realms" as a broader and more comprehensive expression that includes the world of spiritual beings transcending our earthly sphere. However, within that broader realm we can distinguish between "heaven itself," where God and his good angels abide, and Satan's "more

---

5. See Culver, *Systematic Theology,* 1097.
6. Mullen, "Heaven, Heavens, Heavenlies," 334.

limited sphere" of operations.[7] Thus, the sphere of influence of Satan and his legions "is entirely on this side of God's realm of light."[8] In any event, the popular notion that Satan is currently in hell is assuredly false.[9]

Heaven as the Realm to Which Jesus Ascended and from Which He Shall Descend[10]

Christ, being eternally God, preexisted in heaven with the Father "before the world existed" (John 17:5). He came to earth "from heaven" when he took on flesh in the incarnation;[11] returned to heaven, "where he was before," after his resurrection;[12] is presently seated at the Father's right hand;[13] and will return from heaven at the end of the age.[14]

The fact that the resurrected Christ presently abides in heaven raises an interesting point for consideration. Some question whether we should consider heaven to be merely "a condition" rather than a "place."[15] Theologian Robert Culver believes that the nature of Christ's resurrection body as a tangible body of flesh and bones provides some helpful insights. As Culver states, "Since Jesus arose in a physical body now in heaven, then heaven has dimensions of a sort commensurable with physical existence. . . . The presence of the glorified, complete manhood of Christ (body and soul and spirit) in heaven renders certain that it is a place friendly to the flesh of holy human beings."[16]

New Testament scholar N. T. Wright fundamentally concurs, noting, "The idea of the human Jesus now being in heaven, in his thoroughly embodied risen state, comes as a shock to many people, including many Christians."[17] However "shocking" it may be, it is nevertheless true. However, Wright also cautions that it is one thing to affirm this fact and "quite another to be able to envisage or imagine it, to know what it is we're really talking about when we speak of Jesus being still human, still in fact an embodied human—actually,

---

7. Ibid., 335.
8. "οὐρανός," *TDNTW*, 941.
9. Kirk-Duggan is certainly incorrect when she states, "Matt. 25 portrays hell as the domain of Satan and his angels, and the damned" (Cheryl A. Kirk-Duggan, "Hell," *EDB*, 573). Satan and his demonic hosts will be cast into the lake or gehenna of fire (Rev. 20:10) one day, but that awaits the future judgment.
10. See Culver, *Systematic Theology*, 1097–99; and D. A. deSilva, "Heaven, New Heavens," *Dictionary of the Later New Testament and Its Developments*, eds. Ralph P. Martin and Peter H. Davids (Downers Grove, IL: InterVarsity Press, 1997), 440.
11. John 3:13; 6:33–51 (esp. vv. 38, 62); 1 Corinthians 15:47–49.
12. John 6:62; Acts 1:11; Hebrews 4:14.
13. Acts 3:21; Philippians 3:20; Hebrews 9:24; 1 Peter 3:22.
14. Matthew 26:64; Acts 1:11; Hebrews 8:1; 10:12; 1 Thessalonians 1:10; 4:16; 2 Thessalonians 1:7.
15. See the discussion in Culver, *Systematic Theology*, 1099–1100.
16. Ibid.
17. N. T. Wright, *Surprised by Hope: Rethinking Heaven, the Resurrection, and the Mission of the Church* (New York: HarperOne, 2008), 111.

a more solidly embodied human than we are—but absent from this present world."[18] I believe Wright is entirely correct when he speaks of this as a mystery, requiring us to recognize that we are dealing with a different dimension and category of reality than what our present experience can illuminate.[19]

Heaven as the Place Where Departed Saints Await Their Resurrections
In Question 10, I shall demonstrate in detail that believers who die experience disembodied, conscious existence in God's presence as they await the resurrection of their bodies at the end of the age. We may correctly describe such individuals as "being in heaven."

Yet, this raises a point about which there is profound and pervasive confusion among Christians and non-Christians alike. It is common to speak of heaven as the believer's "eternal home." But is this really so?

Despite how ingrained this notion may be, *the Bible does not teach that Christians will spend eternity in heaven.* Heaven is most assuredly not the eternal home of believers, even though believers who die in this present age reside there *temporarily.* The Christian's hope as taught in Scripture is to dwell in a physical body on a new, renovated, physical *earth* for all eternity.[20] Christians simply will not occupy heaven for all eternity, whether with or without a body.[21]

One finds this confusion firmly entrenched not only in popular preaching and in Christian music/hymns, but also even in scholarly sources. For instance, the *Eerdmans Dictionary of the Bible* states that heaven is "the ultimate home of Christ's disciples."[22] The *Baker Encyclopedia of the Bible* similarly declares, "All believers will ultimately dwell in heaven in their resurrection bodies, which they will receive when the Lord comes for them from heaven (1 Thes 4:16, 17; Rv 19:1–4)."[23] And among the definitions of "heaven" given in the *Dictionary of Paul and His Letters,* the fourth entry reads, "The eternal home of the believer."[24]

We shall defer to Question 21 our consideration of the new earth on which Christians will dwell forever. For now, I shall simply register my hearty agreement with N. T. Wright's observations, in which he states:

> It is simply assumed that the word heaven is the appropriate term for the ultimate destination, the final home, and that

---

18. Ibid., 114.
19. Ibid., 115.
20. Middleton makes this point forcefully throughout his book, *A New Heaven and a New Earth* (Grand Rapids: Baker, 2014). See, for example, 58, 72–73.
21. We shall discuss the new earth in detail in Question 21 below.
22. Cheryl A. Kirk-Duggan, "Heaven," 564.
23. "Heaven," *BEB*, 2:941.
24. J. F. Maile, "Heaven, Heavenlies, Paradise," *DPL*, 391.

the language of resurrection, and of the new earth as well as the new heavens, must somehow be fitted into that. . . .[25]

As we read Revelation, we must not allow the wonderful heavenly vision in chapters 4 and 5 to lull us into imagining that this is the final scene in the story, as though the narrative were simply to conclude (as in Charles Wesley's hymn) with the redeemed casting their crowns before the throne. . . . We must read on to the end, to the final vision of Revelation 21 and 22, the chapters that give final meaning to all that has gone before and indeed to the entire canon.[26]

Some Common Synonyms for "Heaven"

The Heavenly Jerusalem
    In certain passages, Scripture refers to a place called "the heavenly Jerusalem" (Heb. 12:22; cf. 11:10, 14–16; 13:14). Paul speaks of this heavenly Jerusalem as "the Jerusalem above" (Gal. 4:25–26). Ultimately, this heavenly Jerusalem is going to descend from heaven as a city designated "the New Jerusalem" and abide on a new earth (Rev. 21:2, 10).
    I shall discuss the New Jerusalem at greater length in Question 23.[27] At this point, it is sufficient to observe that the heavenly Jerusalem is the present abode of departed saints awaiting their resurrections. However, in the eternal state this entity, in the form of a literal city and its heavenly inhabitants, will relocate from its current position in heaven and reside instead on a new earth, populated by resurrected, embodied saints. Thus, the heavenly Jerusalem is not, strictly speaking, a synonym for heaven but points rather to a "city" or heavenly entity that will descend from heaven and exist on the new earth in physical form.

Paradise
    Another synonym for heaven is "paradise." This word derives from the Persian root *Pairi- daēza*, which means "a park surrounded by a wall," "a walled enclosure," or "wooded park-like garden."[28] Coming into the Greek language as *paradeisos*, it carries the general sense of a "garden, park, or paradise."[29]

25. Wright, *Surprised by Hope*, 19.
26. Ibid., 281.
27. Though not all commentators agree (e.g., Robert L. Thomas, *Revelation 1–7: An Exegetical Commentary* [Chicago: Moody, 1992], 441), I take the New Jerusalem to be the same entity as the heavenly Jerusalem.
28. Joachim Jeremias, "παράδεισος," *TDNT* 5:766; William R. Goodwin Jr., "Paradise," *EDB*, 1008.
29. "παράδεισος," *TDNTW*, 965.

The Septuagint translation of the Hebrew Old Testament uses it forty-seven times, "notably as a term for the garden of Eden."[30] In the New Testament, one finds only three references to paradise: Luke 23:43; 2 Corinthians 12:3; and Revelation 2:7.

Jesus mentions paradise in his promise to the thief on the cross, when he states, "Truly I say to you, today you will be with me in Paradise" (Luke 23:43). Granting that this promise would be fulfilled before the thief's—or even Jesus's own—resurrection, it is clear that in this verse "paradise" refers to the intermediate state between death and resurrection. As Jeremias observes, "In its present concealment Paradise is according to Luke 23:43 the abode of the souls of the redeemed in the intermediate state between death and resurrection."[31] As such, paradise and heaven are simply different words for the same reality.

Paul equates paradise with heaven even more explicitly in 2 Corinthians 12:2–3. In verse 2, he states that he was "caught up to the third heaven," which in verse 3 he calls "paradise."

Besides its use to designate "the place which receives the souls of the righteous departed after death,"[32] the word can also refer to the eternal or "eschatological" paradise at the end of the age, which will be on the new earth. Its use in Revelation 2:7 points to this, as seen "from the fact that the gift of enjoyment of the fruit of the tree of life is an established attribute of the paradise of the last time."[33] Even a cursory comparison of the tree of life in the original Edenic Paradise of Genesis 2:9 with the description of the ultimate paradise in Revelation 22:2, 14, and 19 makes this plain.

Abraham's Bosom

The final synonym for heaven that we shall consider briefly is "Abraham's bosom." This expression occurs in only one passage in the New Testament, which is Luke 16:22, the story of the rich man and Lazarus. As we noted in the previous question, the events narrated in this account occur during the intermediate state between death and resurrection.

Pache asserts that the Jews equated paradise with Abraham's bosom, which, as we saw above, refers to the place where the believing dead reside awaiting their resurrections.[34] If this is so, then Jesus simply followed rabbinic usage in his own selection of the term.[35]

---

30. Maile, "Heaven, Heavenlies, Paradise," 381.
31. Jeremias, *TDNT* 5:769.
32. Ibid., 771.
33. Ibid., 769–70.
34. Pache, *The Future Life*, 334. See also Luke L. Keefer Jr., "Paradise," *EDBT*, 590.
35. H. A. Kent Jr., "Paradise," *EDT*, 891.

REFLECTION QUESTIONS

1. What was your view of heaven before reading this chapter? Has it changed at all because of anything you have considered here?

2. In what sense is God "in" heaven? Explain your answer according to a proper view of God's omnipresence.

3. In what sense is Satan in "heaven" (or, rather, "in the heavenly places")? Does this mean that Satan enjoys God's direct presence? If not, what does it mean?

4. Is heaven an actual "place" or simply a "condition"? Give reasons for your view.

5. People commonly speak of heaven as "the Christian's eternal home." Was this your opinion before reading this chapter? How about now?

What Does the Bible Mean When It Speaks of "Hell"?

Our English Word "Hell"

According to the *Encyclopaedia Britannica*, "The Old English *hel* belongs to a family of Germanic words meaning 'to cover' or 'to conceal.'"[1] This notion of concealment ties in with its common definition, which the *Oxford English Dictionary* gives as "the dwelling place of the dead; the abode of departed spirits; the infernal regions regarded as a place of existence after death; the underworld; the grave; Hades."[2] This general definition, while expressing certain aspects of biblical teaching, is fundamentally inadequate, as we shall soon see.

Most English Bible translations rely on the single English word "hell" to translate several different words in the original Hebrew and Greek languages. This has created confusion, as these words sometimes point to rather different entities. For instance, certain words refer to a disembodied place of punishment during the intermediate state, i.e., between the death of the sinner and his or her resurrection on the day of judgment. In other cases, the eternal, embodied state is in view. In yet other contexts, some of the words in question refer simply to "the grave" in the sense of the state of physical death. Designating all of these places and concepts with the same word "hell" results in a tendency to mush together realities that one ought to distinguish carefully.

---

1. *Encyclopaedia Britannica*, s.v. "Hell," https://www.britannica.com/topic/hell. See also the *Oxford English Dictionary*.
2. "hell, n. and int.," *OED Online*, March 2017, Oxford University Press, http://www.oed.com/view/Entry/85636?result=1&rskey=HGcfjX&.

We shall look at five words or expressions that either are translated by the word "hell" in English translations of the Bible, or are referred to as "hell" in popular preaching or other discussions of the topic. The words or expressions are sheol, hades, gehenna, the lake of fire, and Tartarus.

Sheol

"Sheol" is a Hebrew word used in a variety of passages to describe the fate of the dead, or at least the fate of some of the dead. However, commentators, linguists, and theologians often strenuously disagree as to what exactly sheol designates.

One possible meaning of sheol is "the grave." This is the grave in the abstract sense, i.e., referring to the condition of physical death and not to a particular cemetery plot or physical tomb. (We use the word "grave" in this sense when we say something like, "This job is driving me to an early grave.") Another possible meaning is "the spirit world" or "realm of the dead." This refers to a place of disembodied existence, where the spirit resides after bodily death. Assuming that sheol can refer to such a postmortem disembodied state, we must then ask whether it describes the abode of the wicked and the righteous alike, or whether it applies to the wicked only.

One finds scholars holding every combination of the above. Some argue that sheol refers only to the grave and never to the spirit world.[3] Others assert that sheol refers only to the spirit world and never to the grave.[4] Yet others say that sheol can refer to either one, as determined by context.[5] Among those who say that sheol can refer or always refers to the spirit world, scholars further disagree over whether it comprehends the wicked and righteous dead alike,[6] or only the wicked, i.e., as a place of punishment.[7]

3. R. Laird Harris, "שְׁאוֹל," *TWOT* 2:892–93.
4. Buswell states that he is "inclined to that conclusion," though he admits he is uncertain (J. Oliver Buswell, *A Systematic Theology of the Christian Religion*, 2 vols. [Grand Rapids: Zondervan, 1962–63], 2:316). See also Archibald Alexander Hodge, *Popular Lectures on Theological Themes* (Philadelphia: Presbyterian Board of Publication, 1887), 427–28.
5. So W. G. T. Shedd, *The Doctrine of Endless Punishment* (1886; repr., Minneapolis: Klock & Klock, 1980); and numerous other scholars.
6. E.g., Buswell, *Systematic Theology*, 2:308–9; P. H. Davids, "Dead, Abode of," *EDT*, 321; Maurice Gilbert, "Sheol," *ECT*, 3:1473; R. P. Lightner, "Hell," *EDT*, 548; William B. Nelson Jr., "Sheol," *EDBT*, 735. Timothy R. Phillips, "Hades," *EDBT*, 321; Clarence B. Bass and J. A. Motyer, "Hell," *NIDB*, 431. According to Levenson, this would be "the consensus among scholars" (Jon D. Levenson, *Resurrection and the Restoration of Israel* [New Haven, CT: Yale University Press, 2006], 71).
7. As Shedd states, "Sheol, in the Old Testament, is gloom, and only gloom, and gloom continually" (*Doctrine of Endless Punishment*, 31). See also Alexander Heidel, *The Gilgamesh Epic and Old Testament Parallels* (Chicago: University of Chicago Press, 1949), 184, 186; and W. A. Van Gemeren, "Sheol," *EDT*, 1099.

I believe that the correct understanding of sheol is as follows: (1) in some contexts, sheol means "the grave"; (2) in other contexts, sheol refers to the spirit world; (3) when sheol refers to the spirit world, it always and only applies to the wicked, not to the righteous. As such, sheol, when used to refer to postmortem, disembodied existence, is a place of punishment. The righteous who die do not go to sheol but to heaven.

Sheol as the Grave

The King James Version uses the word "grave" thirty-one times to translate sheol. Other translations, such as the ESV and NASB, simply retain the Hebrew word "sheol," but the meaning of "grave" is clear from the context.

Consider, for instance, passages in which "sheol" appears in parallel with references to physical death.[8] First Samuel 2:6 reads, "The LORD kills and brings to life; he brings down to Sheol and raises up." Here it is evident that "to kill" is the same as "to bring down to sheol"—that is, to inflict physical death. Likewise, Psalm 89:48 presents a clear parallel between sheol and physical death. Reflecting on the shortness of his time on earth, David asks, "What man can live and never see death? Who can deliver his soul from the power of Sheol?" Similarly, in Psalm 88:3–5, the psalmist equates drawing near to sheol (v. 3) with "going down to the pit" (v. 4), which he further describes as lying in the "grave" (Heb. qeber).[9]

Other passages where sheol clearly means the grave include Job 24:19–20 and Psalm 141:7.

Sheol as the Place of Disembodied Punishment for the Wicked

Some passages point to the idea of sheol as a place of disembodied existence, specifically as a place of punishment for the wicked and the wicked alone. Though many scholars agree that sheol can refer to a place of disembodied existence, they often see it as including both the righteous and wicked dead. I believe the weight of evidence is against this latter conclusion.

First, the Old Testament indicates that the wicked and the righteous do not go to the same place after death.[10] Psalms 49 and 73 make this truth evident. In these texts, the psalmist wrestles with the question of divine justice and why the wicked often seem to fare better than the upright. In 49:8–13, the psalmist observes that all men without exception, the fool and the wise alike, go to the grave and that there is no deliverance from that certain fate. But then, in verse 15, the writer expresses confidence in God's ultimate deliverance *after*

---

8. Parallelism is a poetic device in Hebrew, in which a previously stated idea is restated using slightly different words.

9. *Qeber* means "grave, sepulcher." BDB, "קֶבֶר," 868. *Qeber* "is mostly used just for the literal tomb," as, for example, in "the cave of Macpelah, the graves of Egypt and the sepulchers of the kings as mentioned in Chronicles" (R. Laird Harris, "קבר," *TWOT* 2:784).

10. See Heidel, *The Gilgamesh Epic*, 183–87.

death, saying, "But God will ransom my soul from the power of Sheol, for he will receive me." As Heidel observes, to redeem or ransom from sheol does not imply that the righteous go there for a time and are subsequently removed out of it. Rather, they are redeemed from the necessity of going there at all.[11] Psalm 73 makes the same point, though this psalm does not use the word "sheol." Though the wicked may prosper for a time, and even have a superior lot to the righteous in this present life, their ultimate end will not be the same. The righteous will eventually be "receive[d] . . . into glory" (v. 24), which is "heaven" (v. 25), where they will have God as their "portion forever" (v. 26). Not so for the wicked, who will be "destroyed in a moment, swept away utterly by terrors!" (v. 19).

Second, consider certain passages where "sheol" can mean neither "the grave" nor the abode of the righteous in the afterlife, leaving the postmortem abode of the wicked as the only remaining possibility. Take Proverbs 23:13–14 as an example. This text speaks of disciplining a child in order to deliver him from sheol. Obviously, this cannot refer to delivering the child from the grave, since disciplined and undisciplined children alike all die eventually. But neither can it refer to an indiscriminate, postmortem state of existence for the righteous and the wicked alike. If the righteous and unrighteous both go to sheol when they die, in what sense would discipline hold out the prospect of delivering one from that fate? Then we have Proverbs 5:5 and 9:18, which speak of immoral sexual relationships as leading one to sheol. There is nothing about such relationships that would lead to a premature physical death, given that the modern diseases arising from illicit sexual relationship did not exist in those days. As Stuart observed long ago, "Neither sudden death, nor violent death, appears to have been specially attendant upon the practice of illicit intercourse, in ancient times. What then is the significancy of the texts before us, if they do not refer to *future retribution*?"[12]

A third and closely related line of argument is that Scripture threatens sheol against the wicked, never against the righteous. In order for the prospect of sheol to make sense as a threat against the wicked, it cannot apply equally to the righteous. As Shedd remarks in light of Psalm 9:17:

> To say that "the wicked shall be turned into Sheol," implies that the righteous shall *not* be; just as to say that "they who obey not the gospel of our Lord Jesus Christ shall be punished with everlasting destruction" (II Thess. 1:8, 9), implies that those who do obey it shall *not* be. . . . Sheol, when

11. Ibid., 185. He argues this based on its sense in verses 8–10, concluding that there is no reason to take it in a different sense in verse 15.
12. Moses Stuart, *Exegetical Essays on Several Words Relating to Future Punishment* (Andover, MA: Perkins and Marvin, 1830), 110.

denounced to the wicked, must be as peculiar to them, and as much confined to them, as when "the lake of fire and brimstone" is denounced to them.[13]

Consequently, sheol cannot refer merely to "the afterlife" or to "the underworld" generally, but must be a place of punishment reserved for the wicked alone.

Hades

We find the Greek word hades both in the New Testament and in the Septuagint (LXX). Though the word itself "is taken over from Greek mythology, in which *Hades* was the god of the lower regions," the New Testament connects its use with the meaning of the Old Testament sheol.[14] Specifically, the LXX uses it to translate the Hebrew word "sheol," which in turn carries over when the New Testament writers cite an Old Testament passage that employs the word. One also finds hades used in New Testament passages that are not specifically quotations from the Old.

Hades carries the same two meanings in the New Testament that sheol does in the Old: the grave, or a place of postmortem, disembodied punishment for the wicked only.

Hades as the Grave

Two New Testament passages use "hades" as a reference to the grave: 1 Corinthians 15:55 and Acts 2:27–31. Since there is a dispute about whether the word "hades" actually occurs in the original text of 1 Corinthians 15:55, I shall ignore that passage and consider only Acts 2:27–31.

Verses 27 and 31 are of particular interest here:

> For you will not abandon my soul (*psychē*) to Hades, or let your Holy One see corruption. . . . [David] foresaw and spoke about the resurrection of the Christ, that he was not abandoned to Hades, nor did his flesh see corruption.

The references here to Christ's bodily resurrection and to the fact that his flesh would not see corruption make Peter's meaning clear: God did not abandon Christ to the ravages of the grave, here designated "hades."[15]

As for Christ's *soul* not being abandoned to hades (v. 27), we have already observed that the word soul (*psychē*) refers to the entire person and not

---

13. Shedd, *Doctrine of Endless Punishment*, 25–26; see also 22–23.
14. Arthur B. Fowler, "Hades," *NIDB*, 409.
15. Van Gemeren, "Sheol," 1099.

merely to the immaterial part of a person that survives bodily death.[16] One could therefore render verse 27 as, "You will not abandon *me* to Hades (i.e., the grave), or let your Holy One see corruption." Besides, we already know from Luke 23:43 that Christ's immaterial spirit did not descend into hades but instead went directly to paradise.[17]

Hades as a Place of Disembodied Punishment

As with sheol, some scholars (incorrectly) contend that hades can refer to the disembodied realm of the dead generally and not just to a place of punishment for the wicked.[18] As advocates of this theory often present it, hades/sheol is divided into two compartments, with paradise or Abraham's bosom being "a separate section of Hades" for the righteous.[19] Some further add that upon Christ's resurrection and ascension, "Paradise has been removed from Hades to the third heaven, and that the 'host of captives' who ascended with Christ were the OT saints (Eph. 4:8, RSV)."[20] However, as I concluded in the previous discussion of sheol, when used in reference to the afterlife, hades only designates a temporary place of punishment for the wicked.

One of the main New Testament passages employing the word "hades" is Luke 16:19–31, which is the story of the rich man and Lazarus. This text presents hades as a place of punishment for the wicked, occurring during the intermediate state. Contrary to Green,[21] the rich man and Lazarus are not both in hades, albeit in different compartments of it. Rather, the text identifies only the rich man as suffering there.[22] Woudstra correctly states, "Hades is associated with being in torment; the latter appears to be the consequence of being in Hades. If Hades were a neutral concept here, then the contrast with the rich man's former sumptuous state would not have been expressed."[23]

Granting that hades describes the condition of sinners in the disembodied, intermediate state between death and resurrection, it follows that hades is only a temporary condition. Revelation 20:13–14 makes this fact explicit when it states, "Death and Hades gave up the dead who were in them . . . then Death and Hades were thrown into the lake of fire." The "lake of fire," which

---

16. See Question 5, "What Does the Bible Mean When It Speaks of Our 'Soul' and 'Spirit'?"
17. Note that Jesus said he would be in paradise that very day and not through some detour via hades. See the discussion of this verse in Question 6 and Question 10. See especially Question 39 and Question 40, which deal with the issue of whether Christ "descended into hell."
18. E.g., Peter Davids, "Hades," *BEB*, 2:912; Timothy R. Phillips, "Hades," *EDBT*, 322; Cheryl A. Kirk-Duggan, "Hell," *EDB*, 573.
19. H. A. Kent Jr., "Paradise," *EDT*, 891. See also Joel B. Green, *The Gospel of Luke*, NICNT (Grand Rapids: Eerdmans, 1997), 607; Stuart, *Exegetical Essays*, 128, 131–32, 136.
20. Kent, "Paradise," 891.
21. Green, *The Gospel of Luke*, 607.
22. Ralph E. Powell, "Hell," *BEB*, 2:954.
23. M. H. Woudstra, "Abraham's Bosom," *EDT*, 20.

is equivalent to "gehenna" (see below), is the final state of punishment for the wicked, occurring after the resurrection of their bodies.

Gehenna and the Lake of Fire

The word "gehenna" appears twelve times in the New Testament: eleven times in the Synoptic Gospels and once in James. In the Gospels, Jesus is always the one who speaks of it.[24] The word comes into Greek from the Aramaic *gehinnam*, which in turn derives from the Hebrew *gehinnom* (Josh. 15:8; 18:16), meaning "the Valley of Hinnom." This valley served as a place of child sacrifices to Molech in the reigns of Ahaz and Manasseh (2 Chron. 28:3; 33:6; cf. 2 Kings 16:3). Lunde observes, "This elicited prophetic condemnation on the valley, identifying it as the scene of future carnage and desolation resulting from God's judgment (Jer. 7:30–33; 19:1–13; 32:34–35; cf. also Isa. 31:9; 66:24; 2 Kings 23:10; Lev. 18:21)."[25] This despicable place, which the Jews also called "Tophet," meaning "abomination, desolation," was desecrated later under Josiah (2 Kings 23:10), after which the Jews, according to many scholars, used it as a garbage dump. Fires burned there continually, consuming the refuse, thus furnishing a graphic symbol for eternal fire.[26]

Jesus makes plain that gehenna is a place of *embodied* punishment for wicked human beings (Matt. 5:29–30; 10:28; 18:8–9; Mark 9:43–47).[27] This shows that gehenna is the final place of punishment for the wicked, occurring after the resurrection that takes place at the last judgment.[28] Consequently, it is equivalent to "the lake of fire" mentioned in Revelation 19 and 20.[29] Note especially Revelation 20:12–14, in which the human inhabitants of hades, now resurrected and embodied, are cast into the lake of fire to receive their ultimate punishment. Satan and demons also find their eternal punishment there (Rev. 20:10)—without bodies, of course, given that they are angels and therefore incorporeal.[30]

---

24. Shedd, *Doctrine of Endless Punishment,* 42–43; Robert Culver, *Systematic Theology: Biblical and Historical* (Fearn, Ross-shire, UK: Mentor, 2005), 1083; V. Cruz, "Gehenna," *EDT*, 480.
25. John Lunde, "Heaven and Hell," *DJG*, 310.
26. Stuart, *Exegetical Essays,* 141. See also Culver, *Systematic Theology,* 1083–84; René Pache, *The Future Life* (Chicago: Moody, 1962), 281; Robert L. Reymond, "Dr. Stott on Hell," *Presbyterion* 16 no. 1 (Spring 1990): 47; N. T. Wright, *Surprised by Hope: Rethinking Heaven, the Resurrection, and the Mission of the Church* (New York: HarperOne, 2008), 175; Emmet Russel, "Gehenna," *NIDB*, 378; "Gehenna," *BEB*, 2:844; Ralph E. Powell, "Hell," *BEB*, 2:954.
27. Stephen Von Wyrick, "Gehenna," *EDB*, 489; "γέεννα," *TDNTW*, 1151.
28. V. Cruz, "Gehenna," *EDT*, 480; "γέεννα," *TDNTW*, 1151.
29. The expression "lake of fire" occurs six times, all in the book of Revelation.
30. Some scholars, incorrectly in my view, equate gehenna/the lake of fire with hades. For example, see P. H. Davids, "Dead, Abode of," *EDT*, 321. So also Philip S. Johnston, "Gehenna," *The New Interpreter's Dictionary of the Bible*, 5 vols. (Nashville: Abingdon Press, 2007), 5:531. Rather, I agree with *BEB* ("Gehenna," 1:844) that these terms "must be carefully

Tartarus

In 2 Peter 2:4 we find a form of the verb "*tartaroō*," which means, "to cast into Tartarus." English translations typically render this as "cast into Hell," so I shall treat it briefly here.

In nonbiblical classical literature, Tartarus designates a place of punishment after death. Specifically, it was "the subterranean abyss to which disobedient gods and rebellious human beings were consigned."[31] In classical, nonbiblical usage, it is sometimes equivalent to hades, or perhaps to a region below it.[32] In other cases, it is the compartment of hades where punishment occurs, as distinguished from Elysium, the other region where the righteous receive their reward.[33] Certain Jewish works written in the period between the Old and New Testaments draw upon this word and use it to designate a place of punishment and/or detention for a certain class of wicked angels.[34] However, in employing this term, Peter is not endorsing extrabiblical Greek or Jewish speculations about the afterlife generally. Nor is Peter granting whatever else such sources may say about the fate of these angels specifically. Rather, he simply "desired to communicate with his readers in terms of their own idiom," granting that this word generally suited his purpose for conveying the concept he elaborates upon in this context.[35]

Note that 2 Peter 2:4 in particular does not have all angels in mind but only certain ones. Peter cannot be describing all fallen angels, since it is clear that there are demonic forces who operate in the heavenlies, and that Satan himself is "the prince of the power of the air" (Eph. 2:2). The angels that Peter is considering, whoever they are, have been committed "to chains of gloomy darkness to be kept until judgment."[36] Thus, it appears that for these particular angels, Tartarus is their place of confinement, where they await their future punishment in gehenna, and "by being held there, God limits

---

differentiated," and likewise with Russell ("Gehenna," *NIDB*, 377), who states that the New Testament "distinguishes sharply" between them.

31. Douglas J. Moo, *2 Peter, Jude*, NIVAC (Grand Rapids: Zondervan, 1996), 103.
32. Lightner, "Hell," 547; "ταρταρόω," *TDNTW*, 1232.
33. Shedd, *Doctrine of Endless Punishment*, 42.
34. On the use of Tartarus both in ancient Greek mythology and in intertestamental Jewish apocalyptic writings, in view of Peter's use of the term, see Richard Bauckham, *Jude, 2 Peter*, WBC 50 (Nashville: Thomas Nelson, 2003), 248–49; Davids, "Hades," 2:912; Peter H. Davids, *The Letters of 2 Peter and Jude*, PNTC (Grand Rapids: Eerdmans, 2006), 225–27; Gene L. Green, *Jude and 2 Peter*, BECNT (Grand Rapids: Baker, 2008), 250–51; Michael Green, *2 Peter and Jude*, TNTC 18 (Downers Grove, IL: InterVarsity, 2007), 110; Moo, *2 Peter, Jude*, 103; G. S. Shogren, "Hell, Abyss, Eternal Punishment," *Dictionary of the Later New Testament and Its Developments*, eds. Ralph P. Martin and Peter H. Davids (Downers Grove, IL: InterVarsity Press, 1997), 459.
35. Thomas Schreiner, *1, 2 Peter, Jude*, NAC 37 (Nashville: B&H, 2003), 336. See also Michael Green, *2 Peter and Jude*, 110.
36. Not a few commentators connect this passage with Jude 6, which expresses a similar idea in comparable terms.

their ability to wreak havoc on earth."[37] At any rate, this text has nothing to do with the fate of human beings.

REFLECTION QUESTIONS

1. What is there about modern English translations of the Bible that has resulted in confusion about the doctrine of hell?

2. What are the different meanings of the Hebrew word "sheol"? In the various Old Testament passages considered in this chapter, how can we tell which meaning is intended?

3. How does the Greek word "hades" compare to the Hebrew word "sheol"? What are the key New Testament passages that point to "hades" as a place of disembodied punishment after death?

4. How does gehenna differ from either hades or sheol, i.e., when these latter terms are used to refer to a place of punishment after death?

5. To what does the term "Tartarus" refer? Who or what inhabits Tartarus?

---

37. "ταρταρόω," *TDNTW*, 1232. Likewise, Schreiner states, "The angels who sinned are now restrained in some way because of their sin, that God has now limited their sphere of operation" (*1, 2 Peter, Jude*, 227). See also Moo, *2 Peter, Jude*, 103. Just who these particular angels are, as well as their specific sin, are not clear, and scholars advance several different theories. (Refer to the sources in footnote 34.)

What Should We Conclude about Those Who Claim to Have Seen Heaven or Hell?

This story will "make you love God more and fear death less."

"It will make earth more meaningful and the future more hopeful."

"A beautifully written glimpse into heaven that will encourage those who doubt and thrill those who believe."

This account "could have been in the New Testament—but God has chosen to speak to us in this twenty-first century through the unblemished eyes of a child, revealing some of the mysteries of heaven. . . . The truth [is] astonishing, creating a hunger for more."

So read the breathless publicity blurbs for *The New York Times* #1 bestseller *Heaven Is for Real*, which recounts the story of three-year-old Colton Burpo's purported near-death transport to heaven. The book, recently released as a movie, regales us with full Technicolor details of heaven's amazing sights and sounds. It treats us to vivid descriptions of myriad winged children and adults flying about the heavenly expanse—though a wingless Jesus "just went up and down like an elevator." We encounter animals of every kind: dogs, birds, friendly lions, and especially Jesus's rainbow-colored horse. We find also swashbuckling angels brandishing swords, holding Satan and his minions at bay. And Jesus also revealed to little Colton heretofore unknown details about the coming battle of Armageddon, "which is going to destroy this world." To his father's astonishment, Colton says of this battle, "But the men, they had to fight. And Dad, I watched you. You have to fight too."[1]

Then we have real estate agent Bill Wiese and his unexpected journey to hell.[2] Wiese sets before us hell's lurid particulars, including hideous, reptile-like yet semi-human looking demons who claw his flesh; fetid fumes and a suffocating, overpowering stench; and the piteous wails of the damned as they roast helplessly in a massive fiery pit.

What should we make of these stories? Should they form a basis for our faith? Might they supplement or enhance the convictions that we already have? How do we evaluate such claims and what is their practical use even if true?

Different Types of Accounts

Sometimes purported experiences of heaven or hell occur in the context of a so-called "near death experience" or NDE.[3] In such accounts, individuals typically experience "death" in a "clinical" sense, whether through a car crash, heart attack, or some other physically traumatic event. Such individuals are "dead" in the sense that they experienced (or claimed to have experienced) a cessation of certain vital biological functions, such as cardiac or brain activity. The accounts of Don Piper (*90 Minutes in Heaven*) and Betty Eadie (author of *The New York Times* bestseller *Embraced by the Light*) are of this sort. These contrast with Colton Burpo (*Heaven Is for Real*) who, though seriously ill, never ceased breathing nor had his heart stop.

Others claim to have had visions of heaven or hell quite apart from any physical trauma. The famous scientist, philosopher, and mystic Emmanuel Swedenborg (1668–1772), who detailed his visions in his book *Heaven and Hell*, falls into this category. The same is true for Bill Weise, who said that he experienced an unexpected transport to hell one morning simply while lying in bed.

The goal of this chapter is to establish principles for evaluating *any* such experiences, regardless of what may have precipitated them. It does not matter

---

1. Todd Burpo with Lynn Vincent, *Heaven Is for Real* (Nashville: Thomas Nelson, 2010), 72, 136–39.
2. Bill Wiese, *23 Minutes in Hell: One Man's Story about What He Saw, Heard, and Felt in That Place of Torment* (Lake Mary, FL: Charisma House, 2006).
3. For an excellent investigation of NDEs, see Richard Abanes, *Journey into the Light* (Grand Rapids: Baker, 1996). Abanes takes the view that these experiences do not provide objective information about the afterlife. For a contrary view, see the work by Christian philosophers J. P. Moreland and Gary Habermas, *Immortality: The Other Side of Death* (Nashville: Thomas Nelson, 1992), chapters 5 and 6. Moreland and Habermas do believe that some NDEs furnish objective evidentiary value in demonstrating life after death and the reality of the soul. At the same time, they do not believe that NDEs can "be used to describe (or interpret) details concerning heaven or hell" (Moreland and Habermas, *Immortality*, 93).

whether the claimant was "clinically dead," "all dead," "mostly dead," or simply snoozing on the couch. Nor does it matter whether the person claimed a literal transport to heaven or hell or merely purported to have had a vision. The same principles of evaluation will apply.

Principles for Evaluating These Claims

Here are some of the principles that should guide us:

1. The Bible is the only reliable guide for truth about the afterlife.

2. We must reject any alleged experience of heaven or hell that contradicts the Bible.

3. Consistency with the Bible is a necessary, but not sufficient, condition for accepting such a story.

4. A look at the biblical authors who gave (or withheld) information about the afterlife suggests the default pattern that we should expect to see.

5. When presented with such stories we must give due consideration to alternative explanations.

The Bible Is the Only Reliable Guide
As set forth in Question 3, the Bible is the only reliable and trustworthy source for Christian doctrine generally, and for information about the afterlife specifically.

Recently, I was talking to a woman about this book, which I was halfway through writing at the time. She told me that she herself had received some kind of dream or vision of hell. She then asked me, "How can you possibly write anything about hell when you haven't actually seen it firsthand?"

Good question! I replied that I am able to write about heaven and hell because the Scriptures give us completely true information about these realities. I also shared my conviction that the Bible is the only unquestionably reliable guide in such matters.

We Must Reject Any Experience That Contradicts Scripture
Since God is a God of truth, and because truth cannot contradict itself, we must reject any claims about the afterlife that contradict the Bible.

We can immediately dismiss visions or purported journeys to heaven and hell offered by occultists such as Betty Eadie or Emmanuel Swedenborg, since their visions invariably present information that opposes the Bible. For example, in Eadie's incredibly popular *Embraced by the Light*, she dishes up New

Age as well as Latter-day Saint (Mormon) teachings that Jesus supposedly communicated to her during her heavenly sojourn.[4] Since such teachings directly deny the Bible, we can reject her claims without further consideration.

Consider also Colton Burpo's account in *Heaven Is for Real*. Most of the fanciful extrabiblical details do not contradict Scripture as such. For example, Colton claims that he saw Jesus riding a rainbow-colored horse—a statement that does not contradict the Bible, but one about which the Bible is silent. However, other statements in his account conflict with biblical teaching. For example, Colton declared the following concerning his deceased grandfather, whom he claimed to see in heaven: "He's in heaven. He's got a new body. Jesus told me if you don't go to heaven, you don't get a new body."[5] Well, Jesus did not tell him this because it is false. We do *not* receive our new bodies in heaven; heaven is a bodiless state for deceased Christians, not an embodied one (see Question 7). Rather, we will receive our new, glorified bodies at the *resurrection*, which we will enjoy for all eternity on a newly renovated *earth* (see Question 21). Furthermore, as noted above, Colton provided the interesting detail that he saw his father, Todd Burpo, fighting on God's side during the battle of Armageddon, which takes place at the end of the age.[6] This is improbable in the extreme and certainly will be falsified if (when!) Mr. Burpo dies before this great and terrible battle takes place.

Consistency with Scripture Is Necessary but Not Sufficient

How should we evaluate accounts that do not contradict the Bible but that either repeat information found in the Bible or, at minimum, present descriptions that are compatible with it?

Here we need to distinguish between a necessary condition for accepting a claim and a sufficient one. While agreement with the Bible is necessary, it does not follow that we should automatically accept a biblically compatible account.

I drive a battered 2003 Toyota Tacoma pickup truck. Let us say that I announced to my students during class, "Guess what! God just transformed my pickup truck and reassembled the parts into a brand-new Mercedes, and it's out there in the parking lot! Take a look." The students rush to the window and see a brand-new Mercedes-Benz GT coupé parked in one of the faculty parking spaces. Figuring that I must be playing a joke on them, they groan in disbelief. Now, what if I were to chide them by saying, "What's the matter, O ye of little faith! Don't you believe that God is omnipotent? Is anything too hard for God (Jer. 32:17)? What I'm telling you is entirely consistent with Scripture!"

---

4. See Richard Abanes, *Embraced by the Light and the Bible* (Camp Hill, PA: Horizon, 1994).
5. Burpo, *Heaven Is for Real*, 136.
6. Ibid., 136–39. "Colton was describing the battle of Armageddon and saying I was going to fight in it" (ibid., 139).

Have I given my students sufficient reason to accept my claim? Certainly not! While I hope that my students would grant that God *could* do such a thing—God is, after all, omnipotent—I would also hope that they would not accept my assertion uncritically but would consider any number of alternative and more likely explanations to account for that Mercedes. Perhaps I was playing a joke on them (something that I am known to do). Maybe I truly believed my story but was sincerely confused because I accidentally took too much cold medication. Regardless, the burden of proof would be on me to demonstrate my claim—assuming that I could even demonstrate such a thing—and not on them to disprove it.

The Biblical Authors Suggest the Default Pattern
Since we know beyond any doubt that the Bible is an absolutely reliable guide to the afterlife, it would be reasonable for us to maintain a healthy skepticism about alleged experiences that deviate from the biblical pattern, even when such experiences do not contradict the Bible outright.

Consider heaven. Biblical authors who report seeing certain of heaven's features include Isaiah, Ezekiel, Daniel, Paul, and John. What are some of the characteristics of these experiences and the way in which the authors report them?

First, very few biblical writers recount such experiences. That alone should give us pause. Hitchcock notes, "Those who claim to have visited heaven and then come back to report what they saw are placing themselves in very select company."[7] Now, it makes sense that someone like the apostle John would have a vision of heaven, granting his role as an apostle in conveying God's full revelation to his people. Moreover, in order to convince us to pay attention to such men, God confirmed their prophetic "bona fides" in powerful and indisputable ways (Heb. 2:3–4). Can we say this for any of the more recent claimants?

Second, the biblical writers received their information either as visions or perhaps—in the case of the apostle Paul—through a literal, bodily transport into heaven (2 Cor. 12:2–3). As far as we know, none of these biblical accounts involves a near-death experience. On the other hand, those in the Bible who did come back from the dead—such as those recorded in Matthew 27:52–53; Mark 5:35–43; John 11:1–46; and Revelation 11:3–12—never "wrote a book about their experience or hit the talk show circuit."[8]

Third, the biblical writers who truly did have a heavenly encounter show considerable reserve in recounting what they saw and experienced. Consider the apostle Paul, whom God did not even allow to divulge the details of his

---

7. Mark Hitchcock, *55 Answers to Questions about Life after Death* (Sisters, OR: Multnomah, 2005), 137.
8. Ibid., 54.

experience (2 Cor. 12:4). As Hitchcock rightly asks, "Why would God forbid Paul from telling us about what he saw when he was caught up to paradise and yet let dozens of others in the last twenty years do it?"[9] Even John, who presents relatively more detail, nevertheless appears to confine himself to those elements essential to communicating his prophetic vision. Absent are the superfluous and trivial details one finds in so many modern stories, such as a description of the Devil's poor oral hygiene.[10]

We Must Consider Alternative Explanations
What are some possible alternative explanations to account for such stories? Below, I shall suggest some of the more obvious possible ones. We can determine whether one of these applies in a particular case only be examining the evidence specific to that case.[11]

Fraud and Deception
One cannot automatically rule out fraud or deliberate deception. People do lie, and for a variety of reasons. Sometimes it is for financial gain, such as in order to sell books, movies, or to line up paid speaking engagements. In other cases, it may be to gain celebrity status, popularity, or notoriety.

The Christian community has certainly seen its share of "pious frauds." Consider Mike Warnke, the supposed ex-high priest in the Church of Satan turned Christian comedian. An entire generation of Christians formed its estimate of Satanism based on his "insider information." However, painstaking investigative journalism demonstrated conclusively that Warnke made up the whole thing.[12]

People have lied about their "heavenly experiences" as well. For example, we have the story of (then) six-year-old Alex Malarkey, who recounts his 2004 near-fatal car crash and ensuing journey to heaven in the book *The Boy Who Came Back from Heaven,* written by his father Kevin. In January of 2015, Alex recanted his story in an open letter, stating, "I did not die. I did not go to heaven. I said I went to heaven because I thought it would get me attention."[13]

---

9. Ibid., 137.
10. "The Devil's mouth is funny looking, with only a few mouldy teeth" (Kevin Malarkey and Alex Malarkey, *The Boy Who Came Back from Heaven* [Carol Stream, IL: Tyndale House, 2010], 171).
11. Abanes, *Journey into the Light,* provides evidence for some of the alternatives I am suggesting here.
12. See Mike Heternstein and Jon Trott, *Selling Satan: The Evangelical Media and the Mike Warnke Scandal* (Chicago: Cornerstone, 1993).
13. See Sarah Eekhoff Zylstra, "The 'Boy Who Came Back from Heaven' Retracts Story," *Christianity Today,* January 15, 2015, http://www.christianitytoday.com/gleanings/2015/january/boy-who-came-back-from-heaven-retraction.html; and Ron Charles, "'Boy Who Came Back from Heaven' Actually Didn't; Books Recalled," *Washington Post,* January 16,

I am not accusing everyone who claims to have experienced heaven or hell of lying, as these people did. But neither would I rule out deliberate lying automatically. It has happened before.

Suggestibility

Some individuals are highly suggestible and fabricate experiences that seem real to them even though they are not objectively true. As NDE researcher and author Richard Abanes argues, there is a certain psychological profile that correlates with a greater susceptibility to NDE experiences. Consider also that people already steeped in Christian ideas have visions of heaven and hell that take a biblical shape, whereas the NDEs of individuals from non-Christian cultures tend to populate their descriptions of the afterlife with features consistent with their own cultural expectations. This suggests the possibility that the experiences in question are subjective, expressing features of their preexisting beliefs and not of objective reality.

Demonic or Occultic Causes

Demons may induce some of the alleged experiences of heaven and hell. This is especially so in cases where the individual claiming the experience has a background in occultic (including New Age) practices. Some of the experiences of Elizabeth Kübler-Ross and that of Betty Eadie may fall into this category.

It may be difficult or impossible to say definitively whether demons may have caused a particular vision of heaven or hell. However, as a practical matter, it may not matter. As we observed above, individuals steeped in occultic or other false religious systems invariably present features that conflict with biblical teaching in relating their accounts. For example, they often claim they were told that all religions lead to the same God, that there is no hell, that all will be saved, etc. Now, we know from Scripture that those who contradict the word of God "have no light in them" (Isa. 8:20, KJV). Therefore, we reject such stories regardless of their ultimate source.

Physiological/Biological/Chemical Explanations

Chemical processes in the brain—whether through drugs such as hashish or by naturally occurring physical events—can precipitate vivid experiences along the lines of what one commonly finds in reports of heaven and hell. We might expect this especially in the case of "near-death" induced visions, given

---

2015, http://www.washingtonpost.com/blogs/style-blog/wp/2015/01/15/boy-who-came-back-from-heaven-going-back-to-publisher/?hpid=z5.

the disruption and irregularities to the person's normal biological functions that are taking place, particularly in the brain.[14]

Assessing the Practical Value of These Claims

Even granting the theoretical possibility that some of the claimed experiences of heaven and hell might be literally true, we must consider the question of their practical value.

Even if someone truly did go to heaven and then accurately report his or her findings, how could *we know* whether the experience (and the report of it) corresponds to reality? Assuming, of course, that the story does not contain features that contradict Scripture, how could we rule out other possible causes, including some of the ones discussed above? It took considerable time, money, and effort to discredit Mike Warnke, for example. Assessing claims about heaven or hell presents an even more formidable challenge. Absent direct contradictions to the Bible, just how would one invalidate or confirm such assertions, granting their inherently subjective nature? At best, we would have to remain agnostic about it.

In addition, what could we glean from such stories that we really need to know anyway? That "heaven is for real"? We already know that from the Bible. That hell is a place of unutterable anguish while heaven is a place of glorious bliss? We already know that from the Bible, too. That Jesus traipses about heaven on a rainbow-colored horse? Even if true, somehow the church has done just fine for two millennia without knowing this particular detail.

But what about the great encouragement to faith that these stories provide? Indeed, does it not show a lack of faith to be so skeptical of these claims?

The Bible commands us to have faith in God and his word, not in the purported and unverifiable experiences of others. And speaking of a "lack of faith," reread the publicity blurbs cited at the very beginning of this chapter, then ask why stories like these would "encourage those who doubt and thrill those who believe" if the Bible does not already do that. Could this be what Jesus had in mind when he spoke of "an evil and adulterous generation [that] seeks for a sign" (Matt. 12:39)?

Perhaps some feel that merely presenting what the Bible says about the afterlife is not compelling enough. According to Wiese, Jesus supposedly told him that he received his vision of hell so he could share it with others, "because many people do not believe that hell truly exists. Even some of my own people do not believe that hell is real."[15] Perhaps the "Jesus" who told this to Wiese was "a different Jesus"[16] from the one who recounted the following:

---

14. Abanes, *Journey into the Light,* 101–2, relying upon the work of professors Saavedra-Aguilar and Gómez-Jeria.
15. Wiese, *23 Minutes in Hell,* 33.
16. Second Corinthians 11:4.

And [the rich man] said, "Then I beg you, father, to send him to my father's house—for I have five brothers—so that he may warn them, lest they also come into this place of torment." But Abraham said, "They have Moses and the Prophets; let them hear them." And he said, "No, father Abraham, but if someone goes to them from the dead, they will repent." He said to him, "If they do not hear Moses and the Prophets, neither will they be convinced if someone should rise from the dead." (Luke 16:27–31)[17]

REFLECTION QUESTIONS

1. What was your opinion about stories of people who said they saw heaven and hell *before* reading this chapter? Have you changed your mind because of anything we have considered here?

2. What five principles does this chapter present for evaluating the truth of alleged experiences of heaven or hell? Do you agree or disagree with them, and why?

3. How would you respond to someone who says, "These stories *must* be true! Just look at how God has blessed people through them!"

4. Reply to this statement: "These accounts have got to be real! So many of the descriptions in them line up so well with what we see in the Bible."

5. What is the practical value, if any, of the stories we are discussing in this chapter?

---

17. Someone might raise the trivial and irrelevant objection that Wiese did not claim to have returned from the dead, and so these verses do not apply to his case. Actually, that fact makes the argument even more powerful. If people who reject the Bible will not accept the reality of hell from someone who actually returns from the grave, how much less would they believe it from someone who claims merely to have had a vision of it while asleep in bed?

PART 2

The Intermediate State between Death and the Resurrection of the Body

What Fate Awaits Those Who Die, Immediately upon Death?

In Question 6, I demonstrated that the person survives the death of his or her body. What we have not yet considered in any detail, however, is the *nature* of this intermediate state, both for the righteous and for the wicked. Here we shall shift our attention from the fact of a conscious intermediate state to the nature and quality of life in that state.

A Summary of What the Intermediate State Is Like

We may summarize the nature of the intermediate state as follows:

1. The intermediate state, both for Christians and for unbelievers, is disembodied.

2. Christians have a direct and glorious communion with Christ and an immediate apprehension of God's presence—far more so than anything enjoyed in this present life.

3. Believers become morally perfect upon their deaths. All sinful inclinations, attitudes, thoughts, etc., are purged; and these are replaced by perfectly holy desires, thoughts, and actions.[1]

4. While the intermediate state is one of blessing for believers, they do not yet possess their glorified, resurrected bodies. Therefore, while this is a blessed state, it is not the *best* state, which is yet to come.

---

1. This stands in contrast to the Catholic doctrine of purgatory. See Question 13, "Is There Such a Place as Purgatory?"

5. Unbelievers go to "hell" (i.e., hades) upon their deaths, which entails separation from God's presence.

6. The hell in which unbelievers reside is one of conscious torment.

7. Unbelievers will also experience a bodily resurrection on the day of judgment, and their punishment will continue in physical (though not glorified) bodies.[2]

Does the Bible support the above conclusions about the intermediate state?

Biblical Verses on the Intermediate State

Luke 16:19–31

As noted earlier,[3] it is clear that Jesus, in this passage, recounts a situation occurring during the intermediate state.

First, consider the rich man. The text describes him as being in hell—or "Hades," to be specific.[4] The passage characterizes him as in "torment" (*basanois*) (v. 23) and in a state of "anguish" or "agony" (*odynaomai*) (v. 25).[5] Jesus conveys this agony using the metaphor of fire (v. 24).[6] Note, too, the large gulf separating him from the abode of the righteous (v. 23), depicted as a "great chasm" (v. 26, *chasma mega*), indicating the impossibility of escape.[7]

Consider next the situation of Lazarus. Upon his death, angels escorted him to Abraham's side (v. 22), most naturally suggesting an immediate transport into glory. The text portrays him as "comforted" (v. 25).

We must be careful to acknowledge the obviously figurative language in this text. Granting that this occurs in the intermediate state, the individuals in this account are disembodied. Yet, the passage speaks of the rich man asking Lazarus to dip the end of his finger in water in order to cool his tongue, which of course cannot be literally true for individuals lacking physical bodies. Nevertheless, we should not let the figurative language that Jesus employs here obscure the truth of what he tells us about the intermediate state. As we shall see in Question 31, "Are the Fires of Hell Literal?" the Bible also applies

---

2. We shall treat this in Question 20.
3. See Question 6.
4. See the discussion hades as discussed in Question 8, "What Does the Bible Mean When It Speaks of 'Hell'?"
5. "*Odynaomai* refers to continual pain and grief, especially mental pain, which is why 'anguish' is a good way to render the term" (Darrell Bock, *Luke 9:51–24:53*, BECNT [Grand Rapids: Baker, 1996], 1372).
6. I shall discuss this metaphor more in Question 31, "Are the Fires of Hell Literal?"
7. See Question 14, "Does God Give People an Opportunity for Conversion after They Die?"

the metaphor of fiery torment to demons and to Satan himself who, being (fallen) angels, also have no physical bodies. Yet, the meaning of this metaphor is not in doubt.

Luke 23:39–43

These verses present the words of Jesus to the thief on the cross. When the thief implores, "Jesus, remember me when you come into your kingdom" (v. 42), Jesus replies, "Truly, I say to you, today you will be with me in Paradise" (v. 43).

Note from this the following: (1) The thief will be in "paradise," which, as we saw earlier, is one of the biblical designations for heaven.[8] (2) Paradise includes fellowship in Christ's presence; Jesus says that the thief would be *with* him. (3) This would happen immediately upon his death—i.e., "today" (*sēmeron*)—with no intervening period of "soul sleep," probation, unconsciousness, etc.

2 Corinthians 5:1–10

This text furnishes some very important facts about the intermediate state for Christians. Therefore, we shall consider this one in more detail.

As noted in our brief discussion of this passage earlier,[9] Paul contrasts three states of existence for the believer: (1) our present earthly life in the mortal, corruptible bodies that we currently possess; (2) a life without our bodies but nevertheless "with the Lord," which happens when we die and our "earthly home" or "tent" (i.e., our body) is destroyed; and (3) the eternal phase of our existence, during which God will clothe every believer in an immortal, glorified body or "heavenly dwelling."

According to Paul, as long as we are in our present earthly and corruptible bodies we are "away from the Lord" (v. 6), meaning that we do not experience his direct, immediate, full presence. When we die and put off this present earthly body or "tent" (v. 1), we then find ourselves "at home with the Lord" (v. 8). This refers to a "heightened form of interpersonal communion" with Christ,[10] superior to any fellowship the believer experiences in this present life.[11] Given the choice between these two states, Paul declares his clear preference: He would "rather be away from the body and at home with the Lord" (v. 8).

---

8. See Question 7.
9. See Question 6.
10. Murray J. Harris, *The Second Epistle to the Corinthians*, NIGTC (Grand Rapids: Eerdmans, 2005), 401.
11. As Garland correctly observes, "This does not imply that the believer is not 'with Christ' now (see Gal. 2:20) or is alienated from him in some way, only that the believer is not with Christ fully" (David E. Garland, *2 Corinthians*, NAC 29 [Nashville: Broadman & Holman, 1999], 264).

At the same time, Paul does not aspire to this disembodied state, despite being in Christ's direct presence. Rather, Paul's eager expectation is to be clothed with an imperishable, glorified body, which he describes as "a building from God, a house not made with hands, eternal in the heavens" (v. 1).[12] Indeed, Paul "groans in longing" to replace his present corruptible body with an immortal one (v. 2). Far from regarding a disembodied, spirit-existence in heaven as his ultimate goal, he likens it to being "naked" (v. 3), which, in and of itself, is something to be shunned. He longs for his resurrection body so that he would not be "unclothed" (i.e., without a body) but would be "further clothed" (i.e., reembodied) after he dies (v. 4). This further clothing will take place at the resurrection.[13]

Thus, Paul's view of the intermediate state is, as many commentators have observed, "ambivalent"[14] and represents something of a "paradox."[15] On the one hand, it is superior to his present earthly existence, since it represents an immediate fellowship with Christ not possible here. On the other hand, the lack of a body as such is not a desirable state, and one from which Paul shrinks; this presents Paul with "a tension of some magnitude."[16] So considering the plusses and minuses, Paul looks at the blessing of Christ's direct presence as outweighing the downside of disembodied existence. And yet, his most earnest longing is for his immortal, resurrection body, for which he shall have to wait until Christ's return.[17] Simply stated, then, the intermediate state is *better*, but it is not the *best* nor the ultimate condition to which Paul aspires.

---

12. The description of this body as "eternal in the heavens" has fueled much speculation among some commentators. Some have concluded that the resurrection body somehow eternally preexists. See the discussion in Harris, *The Second Epistle to the Corinthians*, 375. However, Harris renders the phrase *oikian . . . aiōnion en tois ouranois* as "a permanent heavenly house," which better captures the idea (367; see also 373, on the meaning of *aiōnion* as "permanent"). This, Harris says, refers to the resurrection body's "future durability" (376). Furthermore, Harris argues that the prepositional phrase "in the heavens" (*en tois ouranois*) is best understood in a qualitative sense—as "heavenly" rather than as locative, i.e., "in heaven" (373).

13. "The intervention of death must be recognized as a distinct possibility, and with it a period of nakedness, a not-yet-embodied state, prior to the advent of the general resurrection" (Paul Barnett, *The Second Epistle to the Corinthians*, NICNT [Grand Rapids: Eerdmans, 1997], 267). See also Barnett, 262–63, 268.

14. So Barnett, *The Second Epistle to the Corinthians*, 263, 272; Walter Elwell, "Intermediate State," *EDBT*, 375; Harris, *The Second Epistle to the Corinthians*, 403.

15. S. M. Smith, "Intermediate State," *EDT*, 609.

16. Barnett, *The Second Epistle to the Corinthians*, 272. See also Simon J. Kistemaker, *Exposition of the Second Epistle to the Corinthians*, NTC (Grand Rapids: Baker, 1997), 172.

17. Though acknowledging that Paul is referring in this passage to the intermediate state, some understand the "building from God, a house not made with hands, eternal in the heavens" (v. 1) as pointing to some kind of temporary body in which believers will be clothed—so as not to be found naked (vv. 3–4)—until they receive their final, permanent, resurrection bodies at the second coming. According to this interpretation, the intermediate state is *not* a disembodied state at all but an embodied one, albeit with a temporary body that

Philippians 1:21–23
We already considered this passage in order to demonstrate that the person survives bodily death in a conscious state.[18] Beyond the mere fact of consciousness, however, note that for Paul, to cease living in the flesh (v. 22) means that he would "depart and be with Christ," which is "far better." As we observed when we examined 2 Corinthians 5:1–10, Paul recognizes that death affords him the occasion of an intimate fellowship with Christ not possible in his present mode of existence. Thus, according to this passage, the intermediate state is one of conscious blessedness in Christ's presence and is thereby superior to our present condition.

Hebrews 12:18–23
This passage depicts a heavenly scene, which includes in its number not only the living God but "innumerable angels in festal gathering" (v. 22), as well as "the church of the firstborn, whose names are written in heaven"[19] and "the spirits of the righteous made perfect" (v. 23, NIV). The reference to

---

God will replace later. For instance, Walvoord argues that the martyrs receiving clothing in Revelation 6:11 "would almost demand that they have a body of some kind" (John F. Walvoord, *The Revelation of Jesus Christ* [Chicago: Moody Press, 1966], 134). Baker, on philosophical grounds, also suggests the plausibility of this view (see Lynne Rudder Baker, "Need a Christian Be a Mind/Body Dualist?," *Faith and Philosophy* 12, no. 4 [October 1995]: 498). This speculation, however, is unwarranted (see Barnett, *The Second Epistle to the Corinthians*, 257–58, 265n55; Garland, *2 Corinthians*, 250–51; and Harris, *The Second Epistle to the Corinthians*, 372–73).

Even less convincing is the claim that we actually receive our permanent resurrection bodies at death and not at the second coming of Christ. For the arguments of an adherent of this view, see Garland, *2 Corinthians*, 251–52, 260. For a discussion of the serious problems with this view, see Harris, *The Second Epistle to the Corinthians*, 377–78; and Kistemaker, *Exposition of the Second Epistle to the Corinthians*, 173. In my estimation, 2 Timothy 2:18 is reason enough to reject this position.

As for Paul's assertion that "we have" (*echomen*—present tense) this body, Harris takes the force of the present tense as indicating an "ideal" possession now, with a "real" possession to follow (*The Second Epistle to the Corinthians*, 380). This would be consistent, for example, with Paul's thoughts on "eternal life," which he sees "as an ideal possession in the present that would become a real possession in the future" (ibid., 379). Other commentators aver that Paul used the present tense to stress the certainty of attaining it, i.e., that it is "a future possession which is so real and assured in the apostle's perspective that it is appropriately spoken of in the present tense" (Philip Edgcumbe Hughes, *Paul's Second Epistle to the Corinthians*, NICNT [Grand Rapids: Eerdmans, 1962], 163n19). See also Barnett, *The Second Epistle to the Corinthians*, 259; and Kistemaker, *Exposition of the Second Epistle to the Corinthians*, 168.

18. See Question 6.
19. Or, "enrolled (*apogegrammenōn*) in heaven." Such an expression shows clearly that the reference has shifted from angels to human beings. See Harold W. Attridge, *Hebrews*, Hermeneia (Philadelphia: Fortress, 1989), 375.

"the church of the firstborn" has all of God's people in view,[20] "gathered in ultimate encounter with him." This would include also the audience to whom the author of Hebrews is writing, who "in their conversion, have come to this heavenly city."[21] However, the reference to the "spirits of just people made perfect" is more restricted and "speaks of all faithful men and women who have died."[22] That is, "since the coming of Christ the righteous dead are with God in the heavenly Jerusalem awaiting the soon-to-be described last Judgment (12:25–29)."[23] Observe that these saints has have been "made perfect" (*teteleiōmenōn*), showing that believers in the intermediate state receive entire moral perfection upon their deaths; there is "nothing lacking in their relationship with God."[24] Notice also the believer's direct and joyful access to God, in stark contrast with the fearful, divine inapproachability at Mt. Sinai.[25]

2 Peter 2:9

This verse reads, "then the Lord knows how to rescue godly men from trials and to hold the unrighteous for the day of judgment" (NIV 1984). The most straightforward way of interpreting this passage, particularly when translated in this way, is that God keeps the wicked in a state of punishment as they await their ultimate punishment at the final judgment.

There is definite warrant for this translation based on the grammar, and a number of other Bible versions render this verse so as to convey the same idea (e.g., ESV, NASB, RSV, NEB). As Bauckham notes, such a translation leads one to "understand it to refer to a preliminary punishment before the last judgment ('to keep the wicked under punishment until the last judgment')."[26] In other

---

20. So Attridge, who says that the reference is "to all men and women of faith in distinction to angels" (*ibid.*).
21. Peter T. O'Brien, *The Letter to the Hebrews*, PNTC (Grand Rapids: Eerdmans, 2010), 487.
22. Ibid., 488.
23. Gareth Lee Cockerill, *The Epistle to the Hebrews*, NICNT (Grand Rapids: Eerdmans, 2012), 657n71; cf. 656–57. See also Lane: "In v. 23*b* the expression *pneumasi dikaiōn*, 'the spirits of righteous persons,' refers to those who have died (BAGD 810) but who now inhabit the heavenly city that is the goal of the pilgrimage of godly men and women under both covenants (11:10, 13–16; 13:14)" (William L. Lane, *Hebrews 9–13*, WBC 47B [Dallas: Word, 1991], 470). O'Brien points out that the expression "spirits of the righteous" is an expression commonly found in Jewish apocalyptic literature applied "to the godly who have already died" (*The Letter to the Hebrews*, 487). See also George H. Guthrie, *Hebrews*, NIVAC (Grand Rapids: Zondervan, 1998), 421.
24. O'Brien, *The Letter to the Hebrews*, 487.
25. Lane, *Hebrews 9–13*, 465.
26. Richard Bauckham, *Jude, 2 Peter*, WBC 50 (Nashville: Thomas Nelson, 2003), 254. (Bauckham himself does not hold this position, however; see below.) As Doug Moo explains it, "The ambiguity in the Greek lies in the participle *kolzaomenous*, 'being punished,' which modifies *terein*, 'to keep.' The NIV understands the participle to be denoting action taking place at the same time as the verb it modifies: 'keep while punishing.' The

words, this verse speaks not only of the future punishment of the wicked at the end of the age "but also a punishment that is already underway."[27] However, many commentators take issue with this rendering and the interpretations that follow from it. They claim that one should translate this verse, "to keep the wicked to be punished at the day of judgment." In this case, the punishment in question would not take place until the last day.[28] If these commentators are correct, then it is likely that the verse is not referring to the present punishment of the wicked in the intermediate state, but instead speaks of the certainty of the future punishment reserved for the wicked at the day of judgment. The passage, then, would not be addressing what punishment may or may not take place prior to that time.

It seems to me that there are good reasons to favor the NIV translation, which sees this punishment as presently in force. Moo cites the comparison to the rebellious angels, whom Peter says (v. 4) "have been put into gloomy dungeons 'to be held for judgment.'"[29] Granting that these unrighteous angels are *presently* in a state of punishment, even so would the wicked be, whom Peter mentions in verse 9. Moo, however, sees the punishment as inflicted on these rebellious humans during their earthly lives, along the lines of what one finds in Romans 1:18–32 (e.g., being "handed over" to various lusts and immorality). Regardless, Moo's arguments could apply with equal force to the wicked who have departed this life as they await the final judgment.

Some Concluding Thoughts on the Intermediate State

Granting its provisional, temporary, and incomplete nature, it is regrettable how often Christians misapply, confuse, and conflate descriptions of the intermediate state with our blessed hope (Titus 2:13), which we do not realize until our Lord returns. I find this especially true at funerals and in our hymnody.

Consider how frequently one hears little if anything said about the coming bodily resurrection at a funeral. Funerals typically focus on "heaven," and the preacher will comment about how the deceased is "in a better place,"

KJV, however, assumes that the participle has a future reference: 'keep to be punished'" (Douglas J. Moo, *2 Peter, Jude*, NIVAC [Grand Rapids: Zondervan, 1996], 106–7n14).

27. Moo, *2 Peter, Jude*, 106.

28. Bauckham, *Jude, 2 Peter*, 253–54. Gene Green renders the relevant part, "but keep the unrighteous for the day of judgment, when they will be punished" (Gene L. Green, *Jude and 2 Peter*, BECNT [Grand Rapids: Baker, 2008], 262). Davids, agreeing with this line of interpretation, prefers to translate it "to hold the unrighteous for the day of judgment, when they will be punished" (Peter H. Davids, *The Letters of 2 Peter and Jude*, PNTC [Grand Rapids: Eerdmans, 2006], 232). Schreiner likewise feels that the context demands a reference to future judgment only (Thomas Schreiner, *1, 2 Peter, Jude*, NAC 37 [Nashville: B&H, 2003], 344–45). Among eminent older commentators, Calvin adopts the deferred judgment view.

29. Moo, *2 Peter, Jude*, 107.

is experiencing "eternal rest," and is "free from suffering." True enough. However, it is very common for them to leave it at that, without explaining that this is not the *permanent* nor the *best* condition of the deceased Christian, which is to reside forever on a renovated, resplendent new *physical* earth in *physical,* glorified resurrection bodies.

REFLECTION QUESTIONS

1. What can we learn about the intermediate state from the story of the rich man and Lazarus in Luke 16:19–31? Does the fact that it employs figurative language preclude us from drawing conclusions from it about the nature of the intermediate state?

2. What are the three states of existence that 2 Corinthians 5:1–10 presents? Compare these three.

3. Discuss Paul's possible ambivalence about being disembodied or "unclothed" vs. continuing to live on in the flesh. What are the pros and cons, as far as he is concerned? How do you feel about this, in your own case?

4. What does the Bible teach about the punishment of the wicked during the intermediate state? In what ways might this differ from their *eternal* punishment?

5. Thinking back on your experiences from having attended memorial or funeral services, does it seem to you that there has been an excessive emphasis placed on "heaven" (i.e., the intermediate state) vs. the eternal, resurrected state?

What Happens to Infants Who Die?

In the previous question, we examined the fate of those who die in this present age. There, we considered the varied destinies of believers and unbelievers at the point of death. In that question, we simply assumed that we were dealing with those who were capable of belief or unbelief, which is to say, *adults*. We now turn our attention to the special and very important issue of what happens to infants who die. As parents who have lost a precious little one can attest, much more is at stake here than satisfying our academic theological curiosity. (Although this question focuses specifically on infants who die in infancy, most of the same considerations apply to those born with severely diminished mental capacity who die even after growing into physical adulthood.)

In this chapter, I shall argue the following:

1. We cannot answer this question from the Bible with certainty.

2. The most probable answer to this question, based on Scripture, is that all infants dying in infancy go to heaven.

3. According to the biblical doctrine of original sin, infants are both guilty and corrupt, and therefore require salvation through Christ's atoning work.

The Certainty with Which We Can Answer This Question

Many believe that the Bible is exceedingly clear on the salvation of infants and urge that there is no excuse for failing to pronounce a dogmatic answer on this question. Pastor John MacArthur relates a story about his participation on a panel of pastors in which this question came up. To his great "dismay," MacArthur says that three of the pastors admitted that they did not know the answer. "How can a person be a pastor and not have an answer to that question?" he chides.[1]

In reality, the answer to this question is not nearly so tidy. Spurgeon observed, "With regard to infants, Scripture saith but little, and, therefore, where Scripture is confessedly scant, it is for no man to determine dogmatically."[2] Webb, who wrote one of the best and most theologically sophisticated works on this subject, put it this way:

> When [the interpreter] has looked at them every one [i.e., of the Bible verses mentioning the word "child"] he will be surprised and disappointed to find that not a single text explicitly and dogmatically tells us what is the fate of infants dying in infancy.[3]

Even though the scriptural evidence may not allow us to answer this question beyond any possible doubt, the overall tenor of the Bible suggests that infants dying in infancy do go to heaven. Christendom generally has embraced this view, for reasons we shall now consider.

As with all such questions, the Bible must be our guide. We must not decide the matter based on emotion or sentimentality but on Scripture alone.

Scriptural Arguments That Favor Infant Salvation

2 Samuel 12:22–23

This is perhaps the most frequently cited text on the question of infant salvation.

In 2 Samuel 12:10–14, Nathan the prophet delivers the somber news of divine judgment against David for his adultery with Bathsheba and for the murder of her husband, Uriah the Hittite. Among the consequences God assigns for David's wickedness is the death of the child that David fathered by Bathsheba. The child became sick, and David engaged in prayer, fasting, and self-abasement, in hope that God would relent and spare the child's life. David's refusal to eat or even to pick himself up off the ground greatly concerned his servants. Nevertheless, despite David's penitence and spiritual exertions, on the seventh day the child did expire.

Given David's distress while the child was still clinging to life, David's servants feared that the child's death would push him over the edge and that

---

1. John MacArthur, *Safe in the Arms of God* (Nashville: Thomas Nelson, 2003), 13.
2. Charles Spurgeon, "Exposition of the Doctrines of Grace," Sermon 385 (preached April 11, 1861).
3. R. A. Webb, *The Theology of Infant Salvation* (Richmond, VA: Presbyterian Committee of Publication, 1907), 11.

he might actually harm himself (v. 18). But contrary to their expectations, on hearing the news of the child's death, David's attitude changed for the better: he arose, washed and anointed himself, changed his clothes, worshipped in the Lord's house, and ate (v. 20). The servants, puzzled, asked David why he fasted and wept while the child was yet alive but arose and ate food when the child died (v. 21).

David's answer contains information that many interpreters believe directly addresses the question of infant salvation:

> While the child was still alive, I fasted and wept, for I said, "Who knows whether the LORD will be gracious to me, that the child may live?" But now he is dead. Why should I fast? Can I bring him back again? I shall go to him, but he will not return to me. (2 Sam. 12:22–23)

The crux of this passage hangs on the meaning of the last sentence: "I shall go to him, but he will not return to me." What does David mean when he says, "I shall go to him"?

Those who cite this passage in proof of infant salvation take it to mean that David would one day see the child in the afterlife, when he would "go to him." Since there is no doubt that David, a man after God's own heart, went to heaven when he died, even so there can be no doubt that the infant preceded him there.[4]

Other interpreters argue that the expression "I will go to him" means simply that David would someday meet the same fate as the dead child, likewise "meeting him" in the grave.[5] In other words, David would go the way of all flesh when he, too, would die. They sometimes argue this based on the observation that the expression "I will go to him" is very naturally interpreted in that sense. Some further claim that such an interpretation would avoid the problem of reading into this passage an otherwise uncharacteristically developed view of the afterlife for the Old Testament. However, as we have already seen, the Old Testament view of the afterlife is more developed than some suggest.[6] More to the point, such an interpretation cannot easily account for

---

4. Commentators who take the passage in this sense include Cyril J. Barber, *The Books of Samuel*, 2 vols. (Neptune, NJ: Loizeaux, 1994), 2:193–94; Joyce G. Baldwin, *1 and 2 Samuel*, TOTC (Downers Grove, IL: InterVarsity, 1988), 241; and Robert D. Bergen *1, 2 Samuel*, NAC (Nashville: Broadman & Holman, 1996), 376. See also Webb, *The Theology of Infant Salvation*, 19–22.

5. Mary J. Evans, *1 and 2 Samuel*, New International Biblical Commentary 6 (Peabody, MA: Hendrickson, 2000), 187; David G. Firth, *1 & 2 Samuel*, Apollos Old Testament Commentary 8 (Downers Grove, IL: InterVarsity, 2009), 429; and Ben F. Philbeck Jr., *1–2 Samuel*, BBC (Nashville: Broadman, 1970), 114.

6. For example, see the discussion at Question 6.

the decidedly positive change in David's attitude upon the child's death. How would David's recognition that he, too, would someday go to the grave give him any relief? Webb observes:

> The idea of meeting his child in the unconscious grave could not have rationally comforted him; nor could the thought of meeting him in hell have cheered his spirit; but the thought of meeting him in heaven had in itself the power of turning his weeping into joy.[7]

At the same time, Webb—himself a proponent of the doctrine of infant salvation—laments:

> While I think the interpretation which I have given is more likely to be the true meaning, yet the observations of the critics make us long for some Scripture statement on the fate of dead infants more assuring and more dogmatic and less liable to criticism than this Old Testament incident.[8]

Texts Demonstrating That God Has a Relationship with Infants
Proponents of infant salvation often cite a class of texts indicating that God has a relationship with infants—sometimes while yet in the womb—and they with him. The general import of these texts is that God "knows" the infant, or "chooses" him or her for some kind of service, or that the infant "trusts" in God, etc.
Some of the passages cited are:

- Psalm 22:9–10, in which David declares that he "trusted" God while at his mother's breast (see also Ps. 13:13; 71:6).
- Jeremiah 1:4–5, in which the Lord, speaking of and to Jeremiah, states, "Before I formed you in the womb I knew you, and before you were born I consecrated you; I appointed you a prophet to the nations."
- Luke 1:15–16, which speaks of John the Baptist, who was "filled with the Holy Spirit, even from his mother's womb."
- Galatians 1:15–16, where Paul indicates that God had "set me apart before I was born."

The relevance of these passages to infant salvation is indirect at best. They do show that God chooses and relates to certain individuals, at least, even

---

7. Webb, *The Theology of Infant Salvation*, 21.
8. Ibid., 22.

before their birth and, in some sense, they to him. Whether these texts prove the eternal salvation of the individuals to whom they refer, much less the eternal salvation of all infants generally, is another matter.

Jesus's Statements about "Little Children" and the Kingdom of Heaven
Jesus's words on the relationship of little ones to the kingdom of heaven are among the most often cited passages on this question. The most relevant texts include Matthew 18:1–14; 19:14–15; Mark 10:13–16; and Luke 18:15–17. The nineteenth-century theologian Charles Hodge summarized well the argument drawn from such passages:

> The conduct and language of our Lord in reference to children are not to be regarded as matters of sentiment, or simply expressive of kindly feeling. He evidently looked upon them as the lambs of the flock for which, as the good Shepherd, He laid down his life, and of whom He said they shall never perish, and no man could pluck them out of his hands. Of such He tells us is the kingdom of heaven, as though heaven was, in great measure, composed of the souls of redeemed infants. It is, therefore, the general belief of Protestants . . . that all who die in infancy are saved.[9]

One need exercise caution in interpreting such texts, however. Observe that Jesus is citing, by way of analogy, certain specific childlike characteristics that need to apply to *adults*—or at least to those children who have reached an age of moral discretion or awareness.[10] Consider Jesus's statements in Matthew 18. Notice that the individuals in view are capable of belief (v. 6). But they also have the capacity to commit acts of sin, to succumb to temptation to sin (vv. 6–9), and—what amounts to the same thing—to wander from the true path (vv. 12–13). Indeed, this suggests the possibility of damnation and not automatic salvation. At any rate, the question we are discussing is what happens to literal infants who die, i.e., to those who have not yet reached an age where either personal belief or conscious acts of sin are possible for them (Rom. 9:11).

Passages That Show That the Final Judgment Is Based on Works
One of the stronger arguments in favor of infant salvation is the biblical teaching that the final judgment is based on works. Specifically, Scripture repeatedly and consistently ties the condemnation of sinners at the final judgment to evil works, or "deeds done in the body" (Matt. 16:24–27; Rom. 2:6–11;

---

9. Charles Hodge, *Systematic Theology*, 3 vols. (New York: Scribner's, 1871), 1:27.
10. See also Luke 10:21, in which he applies the term "little children" or "infants" (*nēpiois*) specifically to his *adult* disciples.

2 Cor. 5:10; Col. 3:5–9; see also Rev. 20:13). Yet, infants are incapable of committing acts of sin, as Romans 9:11 makes plain. Therefore, the basis on which God condemns the wicked to eternal punishment cannot apply to infants.[11]

For an extended discussion on the role of works at the final judgment, see Question 16, "On What Is the Final Judgment Based?"

Infant Salvation and the Doctrine of Original Sin

We cannot form a proper estimate of the truth of infant salvation without also taking into account the biblical doctrine of "original sin." We have already discussed this doctrine to some extent in Question 4, "Why Do People Die?"

The doctrine of original sin is the teaching that all of Adam and Eve's descendants (i.e., you and I) are born in a state of guilt and moral corruption, which results from Adam and Eve's first sin in the garden. By "guilt," I mean that all people—infants included—in and of themselves stand condemned before the bar of God's justice. And by "moral corruption," I refer to our natural bias or inclination to evil, present in the human heart from the earliest motions of life all the way through to life's end. Simply put, we are guilty for our first parents' first sin, and we inherit their morally depraved natures out of which our specific acts of sin flow.

The Bible teaches both of these facts, i.e., that we are born both guilty and corrupt because of Adam and Eve's sin. However, before we consider the scriptural basis for this teaching it is important for us to make a few observations about the logic of salvation generally, if we are to understand the significance of this doctrine for the issue of infant salvation.

The Logic of Salvation

Throughout this chapter, we have considered the question of whether infants who die in infancy "go to heaven." But this is not quite the same thing as asking whether infants who die are "saved."

When we speak of being "saved" in the biblical sense of salvation from sin, we are talking about deliverance from the judicial penalty of sin. As discussed elsewhere in this book, the ultimate penalty for sin is eternal, conscious punishment in hell. But the penalty for sin can only be in force where there is guilt (Gen. 18:25; Nah. 1:3). This is so by the nature of the case; without guilt, there can be no justly inflicted punishment. Furthermore, according to Scripture, the only way the guilty can avert punishment is through an atonement, which must be applied to the one receiving remission (Heb. 9:22). This is invariably true in terms of the biblical logic of how forgiveness works.

Now, if infants are innocent and bear no guilt for sin, then they require no salvation since there is nothing from which they must be saved. Neither is it relevant to speak of them receiving atonement for their sins, since again there

---

11. See Webb, *The Theology of Infant Salvation*, 42.

would be nothing for which they need to atone. God surely could take them to heaven when they die. Indeed, one might even argue that God would be obligated to do so, granting their innocence. But merely issuing them a one-way ticket to heaven would not be the same thing as *saving* them.

If, however, infants are guilty and corrupt, then it also follows that they need salvation. But it also follows that God would be under no obligation to save them any more than he is obliged to save any other sinner, be it an adult human or a fallen angel. Indeed, God made no provision whatsoever to redeem the angels who fell, and he is not unjust for failing to do so. Salvation from deserved punishment is always a gift. Therefore, any argument that would base infant "salvation" on their innocence would be a nonstarter, as would any position that would paint God as unjust, cruel, or heartless were he not to save an infant.[12]

Of course, the above conclusions about sin, guilt, punishment, and salvation are relevant to our question only if infants are in fact guilty and corrupt. Does the Bible actually teach this?

Biblical Proof for the Doctrine of Original Sin

Romans 5:12–21 furnishes the primary scriptural basis for the teaching that everyone is guilty for Adam's sin.[13] According to verse 18, Adam's "one trespass" resulted in "condemnation for all men." That Paul includes infants in his argument is clear from the fact that it speaks of "all" without limitation. In addition, the punishment for this sin is death (vv. 12, 14, 15, 17, 21), and it is undeniably true that infants die.[14]

The Bible attests not only to the guilt of all human beings in Adam—infants included—but also confirms the universal corruption of humankind, even from the dawn of our existence. Not only is our perversity evident from our youth (Gen. 8:21), but the moral disorder and uncleanness that underlie our specific, wicked acts are present from birth itself (Pss. 51:5; 58:3; Job 14:4; 15:14–16). The sinful acts that the child will someday commit flow from the child's inherited polluted nature (Eph. 2:3).

It is true that infants cannot commit acts of sin—or of righteousness, for that matter (Rom. 9:11). So in that sense, infants are *relatively* innocent in

---

12. Failure to keep straight the logic of salvation, as outlined in this section, has resulted in a hopelessly confused presentation on the doctrine of infant salvation in not a few popular treatments of the subject by evangelicals. Such books are replete with passages that speak of God's obligation to "save" infants because they are innocent, while declaring in the next breath that they are born in sin because of Adam and therefore require expiation through Christ's blood.

13. Though an older work, I think one can hardly do better than to study carefully Charles Hodge's *Commentary on Romans* for a fine treatment of this doctrine.

14. See also Question 4, "Why Do People Die?" for additional scriptural evidence that death is not natural but is specifically a punishment for sin.

comparison to adults, who are not only corrupt by nature but also have exercised their capacity to act out on that nature by committing specific acts of transgression. However, it does not follow that they are *absolutely* innocent, for they bear Adam's guilt and his corruption. Rather than confuse the issue by speaking of infants as "innocent," as one often finds in the many defective discussions of this topic, it is probably best to refer to them as simply "less guilty" than adults. Nevertheless, they are still guilty. The results of Adam's sin supply an ample basis for their condemnation, were God inclined to exact the deserved penalty. Yet, as we have seen, God bases actual condemnation solely on evil works, which would exclude infants. Webb summarizes the matter well:

> I think therefore that a study of the final judgment entitles us to infer that *actual condemnation* is always predicated upon *actual sin*. Original sin renders all the race—adults and infants—*damnable*; but the judgment scene shows us that *damnability* is converted into *damnation* only upon the ground of actual, personal, and conscious sins—a kind of sin which no infant dying in infancy could commit.[15]

Infants Are Saved through Christ's Atonement

Since original sin *is* sin and therefore punishable, on what basis does God remove the condemnation that otherwise would be chargeable to the infant? God saves infants on the same basis as adults, and that is through Christ dying for their sins on the cross and rising from the dead in order to impart new life to them.

As Augustine once well stated, "Jesus is Jesus even to infants," granting that his name means, "Jehovah saves."[16] Christ's death is the sole provision by which satisfaction to the divine wrath may be made for sin, whether for an infant or for an adult.

Conclusion

The question of infant salvation may not be one that we can answer definitively. The solution sketched here is plausible and even probable, though it still leaves unanswered a host of questions about which Scripture tells us little if anything. For example, granting that Adamic sin is in itself damnable, why does God choose to base the final judgment only on actual sins? Some have speculated that this is because a person dying in infancy would have

---

15. Webb, *The Theology of Infant Salvation*, 42. See also Ronald H. Nash, "Restrictivism," in *What about Those Who Have Never Heard?*, ed. John Sanders (Downers Grove, IL: InterVarsity, 1995), 119–20, who cites Roger Nicole as making this same point.
16. Augustine, *On Marriage and Concupiscence* 2.60.

no consciousness of either sin or righteousness, whereas at the final judgment everyone who is condemned will validate the rightness of that judgment in his or her own conscience, so that "every mouth may be stopped" (Rom. 3:19).[17] However, this answer, while intriguing, is admittedly somewhat speculative. Another question that Scripture does not answer is: How would an infant, who is incapable of faith, partake in Christ's atoning work, given that faith is what joins us to Christ? Again, on this point Scripture gives us little with which to work.

Regardless, what we *do* know beyond any doubt is that "the Judge of all the earth [shall] do what is just" (Gen. 18:25). Therefore, even if we do not have as much information on this topic as we might wish, we can be satisfied that we have a just and merciful God in whom we can place our absolute trust.

REFLECTION QUESTIONS

1. Considering this chapter as a whole, how strong do you think the evidence is for the salvation of infants who die in infancy? What argument(s) do you find to be the strongest, pro and con?

2. What do you feel is the most likely conclusion that we can draw, if any, about the fate of David's child who died, as recorded in 2 Samuel 12:22–23?

3. Do you believe that Jesus's statements about "little children" and the kingdom of heaven provide a basis for concluding the salvation of infants? Do you see any limitations to what we might be able to determine from such texts?

4. Granting that the final judgment is based on works, is this fact relevant for deciding the question of whether infants dying in infancy go to heaven?

5. Do you believe that God is obligated to save infants? Why or why not?

---

17. For a fascinating discussion of this point, see Webb, *The Theology of Infant Salvation,* 287–92.

Is It Possible for Us to Communicate with the Dead?

According to a 2003 survey performed by the well-known Barna Group, fully one third of Americans (34 percent) believe it is possible to communicate with the dead.[1] Furthermore, Barna states that this belief is "gaining traction" among the younger generations, with "nearly half of Busters" (48 percent) answering in the affirmative.[2]

Popular media well represents the fascination with the paranormal, including communicating with those who have passed to "the other side." Consider television psychic and medium John Edward, whose show *Crossing Over* enjoyed significant popularity from 1999 to 2004. In this show, Edward claimed to communicate with the dead relatives of people in the studio audience and reveal to them messages these loved ones have communicated to him from beyond the grave.[3] More recently, the TLC reality television series *Long Island Medium* (currently in its eighth season) features a medium named Theresa Caputo, "who conducts private readings with both believers and skeptics." This show has enjoyed enormous popularity, with some seasons registering well over 3 million viewers.[4]

The attraction of communicating with the dead is not difficult to understand. Emotionally, we miss the companionship of departed loved ones and long for the precious personal contact we once enjoyed. In addition, curiosity

---

1. Barna Research Group, "Americans Describe Their Views about Life after Death," October 21, 2003, https://www.barna.com/research/americans-describe-their-views-about-life-after-death/.
2. "Busters" refers to those born between roughly 1965 and 1983.
3. For an evaluation of Edward, see Joe Nickell, "John Edward: Hustling the Bereaved," *Skeptical Inquirer* 25, no. 6 (November/December 2001).
4. Wikipedia contributors, "Long Island Medium," *Wikipedia, The Free Encyclopedia*, accessed November 2, 2016, https://en.wikipedia.org/wiki/Long_Island_Medium.

about whether the afterlife is real and what it might be like can provide a powerful motivation to contact the deceased.

The main groups and individuals who advocate communicating with the dead are "Spiritualists" (sometimes also called "Spiritists") and adherents of the New Age who engage in a practice called "channeling." In this chapter, we shall focus on these two broad groups.

Spiritualism[5]

Definition of "Spiritualism"

Spiritualism, also known by some as "Spiritism,"[6] is an aspect of the "occult." Coming from the Latin word *occultus,* which means "hidden" or "secret," the occult focuses on that which is "beyond the realm of empirical knowledge; the supernatural; that which is secret or hidden."[7]

We may take the definition of Spiritualism as offered by the National Spiritualist Association of Churches (NSAC) as fairly representative of the entire movement:

> Spiritualism is the Science, Philosophy and Religion of continuous life, based upon the demonstrated fact of communication, by means of mediumship, with those who live in the Spirit World. . . . A Medium is one whose organism is sensitive to vibrations from the spirit world and through whose instrumentality, intelligences in that world

---

5. For compact summaries of Spiritualism's history, organizations, membership statistics, teachings, etc., see Robert S. Ellwood and Garcia Fay Ellwood, "Spiritualism," *Contemporary American Religions,* ed. Wade Clark Roof, 2 vols. (New York: MacMillan, 2000), 2:695–98; John Michael Greer, "Spiritualism," *The New Encyclopedia of the Occult* (Woodbury, MN: Llewellyn, 2003), 448–49; André Kole and Terry Holley, *Astrology and Psychic Phenomena,* Zondervan Guide to Cults and Religious Movements, ed. Alan W. Gomes (Grand Rapids: Zondervan, 1998), 41–55; James R. Lewis, "Spiritualism," *Encyclopedia of Afterlife Beliefs and Phenomena* (Detroit: Gale, 1994), 336–39; J. Gordon Melton, "Spiritualist, Psychic, and New Age Family," *EAR,* 153–62; Nigel Scotland, "Spiritualism," *New Religions: A Guide,* ed. Christopher Partridge (Oxford: Oxford University Press, 2004), 319–20; "Spiritualism," *EOP,* 2:1463–67; and "Spiritualism— United States," *EOP,* 2:1474–77. Melton provides stats and descriptions of various Spiritualist and New Age groups in *EAR,* 764–97.
6. Though some use these words interchangeably, the term "Spiritism" more technically refers to the teaching of Allan Kardec (1804–1869), a French medium who embraced certain views that were outside of mainstream Spiritualism, most notably reincarnation. Throughout this chapter, I shall refer to the movement as "Spiritualism" and its practitioners as "Spiritualists" (capital S) in keeping with their own usage.
7. George A. Mather and Larry A. Nichols, "Occult," *Dictionary of Cults, Sects, Religions and the Occult* (Grand Rapids: Zondervan, 1993), 212.

are able to convey messages and produce the phenomena of Spiritualism.[8]

The Phenomena of Spiritualism

The NSAC definition of Spiritualism given above speaks of the "phenomena" of Spiritualism. The most common phenomenon of Spiritualism is "trance mediumship," in which the spirit of the deceased takes control of the medium and speaks through him or her. The messages from these spirits tend to focus "largely [on] the conditions of life on the other side of the grave"[9] and on communicating messages to surviving loved ones. Spiritualists make much of the fact that such communications provide empirical evidence for life after death.

Besides the more common trance mediumship, Spiritualists also say that the dead sometimes communicate through a variety of physical manifestations, such as by producing rapping noises in order to tap out a kind of code. Other phenomena include moving physical objects through spiritual power alone, such as "table turning and tilting; playing musical instruments invisibly; spirit writing; bell ringing; levitation; [and] materialization of spirit hands."[10]

If the nineteenth century marked Spiritualism's golden age, the first quarter of the twentieth is what some call its "silver age."[11] Though Spiritualism boasted upward of two million adherents in the mid-nineteenth century,[12] participation in Spiritualism as an official movement, in the United States at least, appears to have waned considerably, as membership figures of the main groups show.[13] In Brazil, however, the movement still thrives, numbering around four million adherents.[14]

New Age Channeling

In the latter part of the twentieth century, New Age "channeling" largely supplanted Spiritualism as the more common form of alleged communication with the spirit world. Channeling "has no evident direct link to classic Spiritualism," historically speaking, and is more connected to Eastern teachings, including such doctrines as karma and reincarnation.[15]

---

8. Taken from the official website of the National Spiritualist Association of Churches, "Definitions," http://www.nsac.org/definitions.php.
9. "Medium," *EOP,* 2:1011.
10. "Spiritualism—United States," *EOP,* 2:1475. See also the NSAC website for a similar list.
11. Ellwood and Ellwood, "Spiritualism," 2:697.
12. "Spiritualism—United States," *EOP,* 2:1474.
13. Craig D. Atwood, Frank S. Mead, and Samuel S. Hill, *Handbook of Denominations in the United States,* 13th ed. (Nashville: Abingdon, 2010), 335–36. See also the stats given by Melton, *EAR,* 764–97.
14. "Spiritism," *EOP,* 2:1460. (Note: This is distinct from entries on "Spiritualism.")
15. Ellwood and Ellwood, "Spiritualism," 698.

Channeling is "an event or process in which a person called a channel is able to transmit information from a source, most often an incorporeal spirit." Channelers are very similar to "trance mediums," who "lose consciousness as a spirit takes over the channel's body and communicates through it."[16] The beings who communicate through channelers are often "evolved spirit entities," who may have been human at one time but who have "evolved and have access to higher levels of wisdom and knowledge."[17]

In contrast to Spiritualism, the messages that come through channelers often center on esoteric New Age teaching from exalted beings, ascended masters, and the like. These messages are replete with such New Age arcana as, for example, the need to recognize one's own divinity, the claim that all reality is one, the idea that we can create our own reality, etc.[18]

How Do We Account for Alleged Instances of Communication with the Dead?

The three main explanations that we shall consider are:

1. Fraud, deliberately perpetuated by the human medium/instrument.

2. Fraud, but practiced by demonic spirits (through the human medium), who impersonate the dead.

3. Real encounters with the dead, whether through the power of God or otherwise.

Option #1: Fraud Practiced by the Human Medium
Since its inception, fraud has rocked the Spiritualist movement, sometimes implicating the most prominent practitioners of the art. Melton observes, "The great problem that has hampered the development of Spiritualism is fraud. As soon as Spiritualism emerged, fraudulent practices by various mediums were uncovered."[19]

The Fox sisters, who virtually launched the modern Spiritualist movement in the late-nineteenth century, confessed to fraud in 1888. "Margaret reproduced 'spirit raps' for two thousand people at the Academy of Music using the first joint of her large toe on October 21, 1888, as her sister Kate looked on from a box adjacent to the stage." In a stunning reversal, however, Margaret

---

16. James R. Lewis, "Channeling," *Encyclopedia of Afterlife Beliefs and Phenomena* (Detroit: Gale, 1994), 68–69.
17. Melton, "Spiritualist, Psychic, and New Age Family," *EAR*, 157.
18. Ron Rhodes, *New Age Movement*, Zondervan Guide to Cults and Religious Movements, ed. Alan W. Gomes (Grand Rapids: Zondervan, 1995), 40–42, 58–59, 60.
19. Melton, "Spiritualist, Psychic, and New Age Family," *EAR*, 156.

rescinded her confession the following year. A well-placed source close to Fox claimed that she did so in order to recover her livelihood.[20]

Similarly, prominent medium Lamar Keene defected from the movement in 1976 and exposed the techniques used to dupe the unwitting. Keene "offered detailed information about a circle of churches operating what amounted to a confidence scheme to provide a constant stream of phenomena for their members."[21]

Besides the voluntary confessions of important mediums, investigators produced stunning exposés of pervasive legerdemain among the Spiritualists. Most noteworthy is the work of Harry Houdini, perhaps the most famous magician of all time, who was especially qualified to ferret out cunningly produced occurrences that seemed to defy natural explanation. Houdini concluded his investigations by writing, "I have not found one incident that savoured of the genuine."[22]

Option #2: Fraud Perpetrated by Demons Impersonating the Deceased

Certain Christian writers embrace this explanation. In this case, the medium may well believe that he or she is actually communicating with the dead, but the medium is actually contacting a demon impersonating the deceased. For instance, popular writer Neil T. Anderson writes, "The mediums and spiritists that God warned against in Leviticus and Deuteronomy were not con artists, but people who possessed and passed on knowledge which didn't come through natural channels of perception. These people have opened themselves up to the spirit world and become channels of knowledge from Satan."[23] Likewise, Mather and Nichols declare that, despite some instances of human fraud, "the authentic phenomena are attributed to the demonic and the Devil himself (John 8:44; 2 Cor. 4:4)."[24]

Option #3: Genuine Contacts with the Dead

The third explanation for claimed instances of contact with the "other side" is that such contact is in fact possible and that there are genuine cases of it. This is, of course, the position of Spiritualists and New Age channelers.

Evaluating the Options

As we shall see below, the Bible roundly condemns attempts to communicate with the dead. From this fact we can reject Option #3 as viable, at least

---

20. Kole and Holley, *Astrology and Psychic Phenomena,* 48.
21. Ibid.; "Spiritualism—United States," *EOP,* 2:1477.
22. Harry Houdini, *A Magician among the Spirits* (Cambridge: Cambridge University Press, 2011), xix.
23. Neil T. Anderson, *The Bondage Breaker* (Eugene, OR: Harvest House, 2000), 128–29.
24. George A. Mather and Larry A. Nichols, "Spiritualism; Universal Church of the Master (UCM) History," *Dictionary of Cults, Sects, Religions and the Occult* (Grand Rapids: Zondervan, 1993), 264.

in so far as the Spiritualists frequently claim that they are engaging in a God-empowered, God-sanctioned activity.

The Bible makes it clear that demons are real and are in the business of deceiving people through lying signs and wonders (2 Thess. 2:9). It is also true that demons, while far from omniscient, could possess knowledge of certain facts that they might employ in impersonating a deceased person when speaking through a medium during a séance. Therefore, it is entirely possible that some of these cases could involve demonic agency as their source. At the same time, the incidence of fraud in this movement is so widespread that this may be sufficient in itself to account for virtually all, if not all, of the Spiritualist and New Age phenomena.

It seems best, then, to accept fraud perpetrated by the human medium as the default explanation, retaining nevertheless the possibility of demonic activity.

The Biblical Prohibitions against Communicating with the Dead[25]

Regardless of how one accounts for supposed examples of contacting the dead, the Bible clearly and forcefully prohibits such attempts. While both testaments condemn occult practices, the main texts concerning contacting the dead occur in the Old Testament.

Leviticus 19:31; 20:6, 27

These verses contain stern prohibitions against consulting "mediums" and "necromancers."[26] Penalties include even capital punishment by stoning.

Deuteronomy 18:9–14

Here God emphatically commands the Israelites not to follow the abominable practices of the surrounding nations once they come into the land that God has promised to them. Verse 11 singles out specifically mediums, necromancers, and the practice of "calling up the dead."

2 Kings 21:2, 6 (cf. 2 Chronicles 33:6)

These texts catalog the apostasy of Manasseh in emulating the occult practices of his neighbors. Again, the text explicitly condemns mediums and necromancers.

---

25. For the specific Hebrew vocabulary used to describe mediumship and necromancy, with special reference to the use of these terms in 1 Samuel 28, see P. Kyle McCarter Jr., *1 Samuel*, AB (New Haven, CT: Yale University Press, 1980), 420–22; and David Toshio Tsumura, *The First Book of Samuel*, NICOT (Grand Rapids: Eerdmans, 2007), 617–22.
26. "Necromancy" refers to the practice of communicating with the dead, typically for divining hidden or future information.

1 Chronicles 10:13–14 (cf. 1 Samuel 15:23)
In the litany of Saul's disobedient acts, the writer of Chronicles highlights Saul's sin of consulting a medium for guidance rather than seeking his guidance from the God of Israel. Citing this passage, McCarter observes, "Later tradition came to regard [Saul's attempt to contact the dead through necromancy] as among the most heinous of Saul's crimes."[27]

Isaiah 8:19–20
This passage excoriates those who seek direction from mediums and necromancers "who chirp and mutter" rather than from God. Isaiah asks, "should not a people inquire of their God?"

How Are We to Evaluate Biblical Instances of Communicating with the Dead?

Despite the very clear biblical prohibitions against communing with the dead, one also finds specific and arguably genuine examples of this practice in Scripture, which Spiritualists seize upon to argue its legitimacy.

Indeed, Spiritualists have often claimed that "from cover to cover, the Bible is a psychic book"[28] and have pointed to Christ himself as "a master medium." Most notably, they cite the mount of transfiguration, which involved "the materialization of the spirits of Moses and Elias."[29] The other main passage they cite is 1 Samuel 28, in which, according to Spiritualists, "occurs one of the most famous single incidents of mediumship in the history of the West."[30]

Some General Thoughts about Biblical Instances of Communicating with the Dead
Before we look at the two main passages that Spiritualists cite, I shall stipulate a few points right at the outset.

First, there is no reason to conclude that it would be impossible *per se* for the dead to communicate with the living. Granting that the human spirit survives the death of the physical body, as we demonstrated in Question 6, God could, in his omnipotence, bring about such occurrences whenever he wanted to. Therefore, the question is not whether such is theoretically possible but whether God in fact ever does this.

Second, even if God were to bring about such contact on particular occasions, this would not demonstrate that it is standard operating procedure for him to do so, nor would it follow that it is legitimate for human beings to

---

27. McCarter, *1 Samuel*, 422. See also Tsumura, *The First Book of Samuel*, 616.
28. Melton, "Spiritualist, Psychic, and New Age Family," *EAR*, 153.
29. Atwood, Mead, and Hill, *Handbook of Denominations in the United States*, 335.
30. Melton, "Spiritualist, Psychic, and New Age Family," *EAR*, 155.

initiate such encounters—particularly when the Bible specifically condemns mediumship and necromancy, as we have already seen.

The Mount of Transfiguration (Matthew 17:1–9)

In this passage, Moses and Elijah did indeed "appear" to Jesus's astonished disciples Peter, James, and John. The text does not specifically say that the actual spirits of Moses and Elijah "materialized" but merely that these Old Testament personages "appeared" (Greek: *ōphthē*, from the verb *oraō*), which means nothing more than that Moses and Elijah had in some sense become "visible" to them. Perhaps this was an actual materialization of Moses and Elijah themselves. It is also possible that God at that moment simply peeled back the curtain of the spirit world, so to speak, to make Moses and Elijah visible to them (along the lines of 2 Kings 6:17). Based on the language of the text, either is possible.

Therefore, Elijah and Moses, through God's power, may have "materialized" forms before Jesus and his disciples, as the Spiritualists claim. But this occurrence took place at *God's* initiative and not by the man Jesus nor by his disciples conjuring them through a séance. Furthermore, God effected this altogether unique situation for a very specific reason, which was to validate before these specific, key apostles the truth of Jesus's message about the coming kingdom (Matt. 16:28) and about the crucial importance of submitting to him in all things (Matt. 17:5).

1 Samuel 28:5–20

This passage, containing the account of the so-called medium of Endor, is perhaps the single most important text in the Spiritualists' arsenal for establishing a biblical precedent for Spiritualism. Therefore, we must look at this particular passage in some detail.

A Brief Description of the Encounter

The occasion for this encounter is an impending battle that the Israelite king Saul was about to conduct against the Philistine armies. After the typical methods of inquiring of the Lord about the battle's outcome yielded no results, Saul then determined to seek the advice of the now-departed prophet Samuel through the agency of a medium. Saul was referred to a medium in Endor who, he hoped, could bring up the spirit of Samuel, and that Samuel in turn might tell him how the battle would play out.

Verses 12–14 describe the results of the medium's conjuring efforts, which read in part,

> When the woman saw Samuel, she cried out with a loud voice. . . . The king said to her, "Do not be afraid. What do you see?" And the woman said to Saul, "I see a god coming

up out of the earth."[31] He said to her, "What is his appearance?" And she said, "An old man is coming up, and he is
wrapped in a robe." And Saul knew that it was Samuel, and
bowed with his face to the ground, and paid homage.

In the verses that follow, Samuel pronounces a word of judgment against
Saul, announcing his rejection by the Lord and his impending defeat at the
hands of the Philistines.

Did the Medium Genuinely "Bring Up" the Spirit of Samuel?
Some commentators reject the notion that the medium actually brought
up the spirit of Samuel. For instance, Heidel characterizes the medium's efforts as a "demonic delusion," contending that a demon materialized and
spoke to Saul.[32] However, this seems unlikely. "Had this been some sort of
demonic delusion," Ferguson opines, "the narrator would certainly have been
obligated to call this to the attention of his audience."[33] For this same reason
it is even less likely that the medium faked the entire event, for example, by
using some kind of ventriloquism. Samuel's "'coming up from the netherworld' is 'presented as an actual event, not a dream or a vision, even though
dreams are explicitly mentioned by Saul.'"[34] That "the narrator also refers to
the apparition as 'Samuel,' not as 'gods' or a ghost" lends further support to the
encounter's genuineness.[35]

Granting that the actual spirit of Samuel appeared to the medium and to
Saul, does this validate the genuineness of her mediumistic powers? Quite
the opposite. The woman's shock at bringing up Samuel's spirit is difficult to
explain if this were something she did customarily. This suggests that the medium's normal *modus operandi* was fakery, whereas in this instance, and contrary to her own expectation, the spirit of the deceased actually did show up!
As Kole and Holley state, "The fact of her surprise lends further weight to the
idea that the woman knew full well that she had no power to communicate
with the dead."[36]

In this particular instance, then, God used the occasion of a medium's
attempted trickery to effect a genuine encounter with the deceased Samuel in

---

31. Commentators typically take the word translated "god" (*elohim*) in this passage as a "supernatural" or "preternatural" being. See McCarter, *1 Samuel*, 421; and Tsumura, *The First
Book of Samuel*, 624–25.
32. Alexander Heidel, *The Gilgamesh Epic and Old Testament Parallels* (Chicago: University of
Chicago, 1949), 189.
33. Paul Ferguson, "Death, Mortality," *EDBT*, 154–55.
34. P. D. Miscall, *1 Samuel: A Literary Reading* (Bloomington: Indiana University Press, 1986),
171.
35. Tsumura, *The First Book of Samuel*, 627.
36. Kole and Holley, *Astrology and Psychic Phenomena*, 35.

order to pronounce judgment against Saul. But whether or not one grants that the encounter was genuine, this passage hardly lends support to the practice of Spiritualism. Hitchcock summarizes the matter well: "In the only biblical case of communicating with the dead, the message was anything but positive. God told Saul he was a dead man."[37]

REFLECTION QUESTIONS

1. Does the fascination with the occult and with contacting the dead in our supposedly secular culture surprise you? What do you believe accounts for this renewed interest?

2. Have you ever watched any of the shows mentioned in the introduction or seen other shows of this type? What was your impression of them? Has anything changed in your thinking because of reading this chapter?

3. Of the various explanations given to account for Spiritualist/New Age phenomena, which one(s) do you find most compelling?

4. We noted the severe biblical prohibitions against necromancy in the Old Testament, including even capital punishment for occult practitioners. Based on the verses provided, reflect on why God would so strongly condemn this practice.

5. What do you think about the biblical case that Spiritualists attempt to make to justify their practice? Do you find it in any way plausible?

---

37. Mark Hitchcock, *55 Answers to Questions about Life after Death* (Sisters, OR: Multnomah, 2005), 72.

Is There Such a Place as Purgatory?

The doctrine of purgatory is most commonly associated with Roman Catholic theology, though there are a very small number of Protestants who affirm the concept as well.[1] Because of the complexity of the doctrine in Roman Catholicism, and because purgatory or purgatory-like positions have gained such little traction among Protestants, I shall confine this discussion to the Roman Catholic variety.

The Roman Catholic Definition of Purgatory[2]

The *Catechism of the Catholic Church* defines purgatory as follows:

All who die in God's grace and friendship, but still imperfectly purified, are indeed assured of their eternal salvation; but after death they undergo purification, so as to achieve the holiness necessary to enter the joy of heaven.

The Church gives the name Purgatory to this final purification of the elect, which is entirely different from the punishment of the damned.[3]

---

1. Certainly the most notable Protestant to advocate for a doctrine of purgatory is C. S. Lewis. See his *A Grief Observed* (San Francisco: HarperSanFrancisco, 2001), 42–43; and *Letters to Malcolm* (London: Harcourt, 1964), 107–9. Jerry Walls is a contemporary Protestant theologian holding the position (Jerry L. Walls, *Purgatory* [Oxford: Oxford University Press, 2012]). But again, the number of Protestants holding to purgatory is negligible.
2. For a good, concise discussion of the theology undergirding the doctrine of purgatory, see R. J. Bastian, "Purgatory: In Theology," *NCE,* 11:825–29.
3. *Catechism of the Catholic Church* (1997), par. 1030–31.

As the name implies, purgatory is a place or state of purification,[4] taking place during the intermediate state,[5] in which a Christian who is not yet ready for entrance into heaven is purged of his or her sins. This purgation occurs through intense suffering, which Catholic theologians call a "cleansing fire" (*ignis purgatorius*). This is often understood as "a physical phenomenon, whereby the fire attaches uniquely to the soul freed from the body,"[6] though some writers conceive of it more in terms of spiritual or psychological suffering arising from "the temporary deprivation of the beatific vision" (i.e., God's presence).[7] In addition, purgatory is also a place where one works off the remaining debt owed for sin and makes compensation for it, in order to satisfy the demands of punitive justice. Thus, in the Roman Catholic doctrine, purgatory has both purifying as well as punitive aspects.[8] At all events, one should not confuse purgatory with hell. Historically, Catholic theologians have taught that the sufferings in purgatory are greater than any suffering in the present life, though they are surely less than those of hell.[9] At the same time, knowing that everyone in purgatory eventually will make it into heaven greatly tempers this suffering. This is very different from hell, from which there is no escape.

In order to understand properly the Catholic doctrine of purgatory, we must first observe how it relates to the Catholic sacrament of penance, through which one receives the forgiveness of sins.

According to Catholic teaching, sin carries with it guilt (*culpa*) with a corresponding liability to punishment (*poena*). In turn, the punishment for sin that one can experience is of two kinds: eternal and temporal. Eternal punishment, as the name implies, is without end; this is the punishment of hell, which no one can pay off. On the other hand, a person *can* pay off the temporal punishments for sin, given enough time. Mortal sins, which are the most serious, carry with them the liability to undergo both eternal and temporal punishment, whereas venial sins accrue only temporal punishment. An example of a mortal sin would be deliberately breaking the Ten Commandments, such as

---

4. "The desire to provide a spatial symbol for the hereafter is so ambiguous that nowadays most Catholics concur in regarding purgatory as a condition rather than a place" (Henri Bourgeois, "Purgatory," *ECT,* 3:1323).
5. Question 10, "What Fate Awaits Those Who Die in This Present Age, Immediately upon Death?" discusses the intermediate state.
6. Josef Finkenzeller, "Purgatory," *Oxford Encyclopedia of the Reformation,* ed. Hans J. Hillerbrand, 3 vols., 3:363.
7. Bastian, "Purgatory: In Theology," 826. For example, "St. Catherine of Genoa wrote that the desire of the soul for God was an ardent fire more consuming and painful than any earthly fire."
8. Karl Rahner, "Purgatory," *DT,* 426; R.T.B., "Purgatory," *NDT,* 549.
9. So Aquinas and Bonaventure; see Bastian, "Purgatory: In Theology," 827.

blasphemy, adultery, or homicide. By contrast, a venial sin would be something like "thoughtless chatter or immoderate laughter."[10]

Those who die in a state of mortal sin go straight to hell, from which there is no release. However, Catholic theology offers a provision for dealing with the problem of mortal sin before one dies, namely the sacrament of penance. Through this sacrament, one can receive forgiveness for the guilt (*culpa*) and punishment (*poena*) of mortal sin. The sacrament requires contrition (sorrow for sin) and confession (verbally, to a priest), followed by priestly absolution. Although the sacrament of penance removes one's liability to eternal punishment, the requirement to pay off the temporal penalties connected with the mortal sin still remains.

If the above distinction between "eternal" and "temporal" penalties for sin seems confusing, that is because it is. However, perhaps the following analogy will prove illuminating: If a person were to murder someone deliberately with his car, he might get the penalty of life in prison. For the purposes of our analogy, this would be somewhat analogous to "eternal punishment," because one cannot fully pay this debt within one's lifetime and because there is no release from it. But the court might also charge the person with lesser violations connected with the crime, such as running a red light and side swiping another vehicle on the way to the murder. These latter offences, being much less serious than murder, carry lesser penalties. We may consider these lesser penalties as "temporal" in nature, granting that the offender *could* pay them off eventually. Now, if somehow the sentence of life imprisonment could be commuted, the liability to pay for the lesser offences might nevertheless remain.[11]

Granting that the sinner must pay off these "temporal penalties," how is he or she to do this? In the sacrament of penance, the priest prescribes certain works of "satisfaction" (also known as "penance"[12]) in order to pay off the remaining temporal debt. Such satisfactions might consist of praying certain prayers, performing works of charity, etc.

The Catholic Christian who has racked up temporal debt for sin—whether from venial sins or from mortal sins that have had the eternal penalty removed through the sacrament of penance—must pay off this debt either in this life or in the next. Thus, whatever balance remains when a person departs the present life is taken care of in the next (i.e., in purgatory).

The amount of time that one must spend in purgatory, then, will depend upon how much purification the person needs to experience to become morally fit for heaven, as well as how much of the temporal debt of sin yet remains

---

10. *Catechism of the Catholic Church* (1997), par. 1856.
11. Although the following is my own analogy, I believe it fairly represents the Catholic position.
12. Some confusion is due to the fact that one of the elements of the sacrament of penance is itself called "penance." It is simply that one of its prominent parts designates the sacrament as a whole.

to be paid. Some will die with no outstanding temporal debt and no need for additional purification; these will bypass purgatory altogether. Others, however, will spend varying amounts of time there.

Finally, the time that souls must abide in purgatory can be reduced in a few different ways. First, "the Church has authoritatively defined that the souls detained there can be helped by the prayers and other good works of the faithful on earth."[13] Most notably, the Church may remit, at its discretion, all or part of the time that the sinner would otherwise spend in purgatory. It does this by issuing an indulgence.[14] Specifically, God has authorized the Church to dispense pardons from its "treasury of merit" (*thesaurus meritorum*), consisting of the merits of Christ and of the saints. The saints purportedly possessed more holiness than they needed for their own salvation, and so the Church may dispense this excess, together with Christ's infinite merits, to deliver souls in purgatory.[15] Christ himself granted Peter the right to dispense this merit when he conferred upon him the authority to bind and loose sins (Matt. 16:18–19). This authority, in turn, passes on to the Pope as Peter's successor. Individuals may obtain indulgences for the remission of their own temporal debt or for the debt of their departed loved ones. The sale of so-called "apostolic pardons" (indulgences) was, of course, one of the key issues that sparked the sixteenth-century Protestant revolt. The Roman Catholic Church still issues indulgences today.[16]

Evidence Offered for Purgatory

Catholic theologians offer a number of proofs for the doctrine of purgatory. Some of these originate from books that Protestants consider apocryphal, while others come from the biblical books that Catholics and Protestants share in common.

First, consider arguments drawn from the Apocrypha. Catholics point to the practice of praying for the dead, which in turn suggests some kind of postmortem deliverance for which the dead need such prayers.[17] One important passage comes from the Apocrypha in 2 Maccabees 12:39–45.[18] Verse 46 states, "Therefore Judas Maccabeus made atonement for the dead, that they

---

13. Bastian, "Purgatory: In Theology," 826.
14. For a discussion of indulgences, see *Catechism of the Catholic Church* (1997), par. 1471–79.
15. Ibid., par. 1476–77.
16. For example, see "Decree of the Apostolic Penitentiary on Special Indulgences Conceded for the 20th World Youth Day in Cologne," August 2, 2005, http://www.vatican.va/roman_curia/tribunals/apost_penit/documents/rc_trib_appen_doc_20050802_decree-xx-wyd_en.html.
17. John P. Beal, "Purgatory," *EC*, 4:454.
18. For a brief discussion of this passage, see J. F. X. Cevetello, "Purgatory: In the Bible," *NCE*, 824–25.

might be delivered from their sin."[19] In addition to prayers, "the Church also commends almsgiving, indulgences, and works of penance undertaken on behalf of the dead."[20]

Catholics also cite certain verses from texts that all regard as authoritative. First Corinthians 3:11–15 is "the foremost reference" for the doctrine.[21] This passage speaks of a person being saved "but only as through fire"—here seen as a reference to the flames of purgatory. Next, they point to Matthew 12:32, which discusses the blasphemy of the Holy Spirit. According to this text, blaspheming the Holy Spirit is a sin that will "not be forgiven, either in this age or in the age to come." This implies, so the argument goes, that *some* sins *can be* forgiven in the next age. Another commonly used verse is Matthew 25:26, a parable in which Jesus speaks of the offender remaining in prison until he pays the last penny. This suggests that there are some sins from which release is possible, but only after the offender pays the debt in full. Such sins are distinct from the sins that cast a person into hell, from which no release is forthcoming.

Problems with the Doctrine of Purgatory

There are many problems with the Roman Catholic doctrine of purgatory, both biblical and rational.

Problems with the Texts Cited in Proof of Purgatory

Of all the texts cited, the one in 2 Maccabees 12 would appear on its face to furnish the most direct evidence for the doctrine, since it teaches explicitly the practice of praying for the dead in order to remit their sins. Protestants, with good reason, do not accept 2 Maccabees as an inspired book; and so for them that might well be the end of the matter, at least as far as that particular passage goes.[22] But even if one were to grant that 2 Maccabees is inspired and therefore deserves a place among the authoritative biblical books, the passage in 2 Maccabees 12 actually contradicts the Roman Catholic doctrine of purgatory in particular and the Catholic doctrine of the sacraments in general. Swain makes the following observations about the problems that this text presents for Catholic theology. First, the sin for which prayers were to be offered on behalf of the slain was the sin of idolatry, as 2 Maccabees 12:40–41 makes plain. However, according to Catholic theology, idolatry—being a direct violation of the Ten Commandments—is a mortal sin, not a venial one. Indeed, some Catholics even suggest that "considered in itself, idolatry is the

---

19. The *Catechism of the Catholic Church* (1997), par. 1032, cites this text in proof of purgatory.
20. Ibid.
21. Finkenzeller, "Purgatory," 363.
22. For a discussion of the Old Testament Apocrypha and why these books should be rejected, see the discussion in Norman L. Geisler and William E. Nix, *A General Introduction to the Bible* (Chicago: Moody, 1968), 170–77.

greatest of mortal sins."[23] If we are to believe the Catholic system of penance, these men, dying in a state of mortal sin, would not be eligible for purgatory but would be in hell, from which there is no release—whether through prayers or by any other means. Second, even if we could somehow grant that their idolatry did not send them to hell, those offering such prayers were not intending to deliver them from purgatory into paradise anyway. These prayers were for them to attain the resurrection of their bodies (2 Macc. 12:43–44), which would occur at the last judgment. Deliverance from purgatory into paradise, in contrast, happens during the intermediate state and before the final judgment.[24]

As for 1 Corinthians 3:12–15, the Catholic use of this passage does violence to Paul's argument. In context, Paul is discussing the different rewards that believers will receive for their service to Christ. It has nothing whatever to do with paying for the temporal penalties for one's sins, nor with one's purification through purgatorial fire. Since we shall consider this text in detail under Question 16 ("On What Is the Final Judgment Based?"), I shall defer more discussion of this passage to that place. For the present purpose, though, Pache's summary of the problems with using this passage to support purgatory will suffice. I condense and paraphrase his remarks as follows:

1. The fire mentioned here burns the works, not the people.

2. The fire does not improve us or make us suffer, but simply tests our past works to see which ones deserve recompense.

3. According to verse 13, this takes place on the day of judgment, whereas purgatory occurs during the intermediate state.

4. Finally, "this test is instantaneous," whereas purgatory takes place over a long period.[25]

Their use of Matthew 12:32 fares no better. It does not follow, either directly or by implication, that because the blasphemy of the Holy Spirit is not forgiven "either in this age or in the age to come" that some sins *are* to be forgiven "in the age to come." Matthew 12:32 is simply an emphatic way of saying that blasphemy of the Holy Spirit will never, ever be forgiven—not now, not later, not ever.

---

23. Josef Wilhelm, "Idolatry," *The Catholic Encyclopedia* (New York: Robert Appleton, 1910), http://www.newadvent.org/cathen/07636a.htm.
24. See James Swain, "The Perspicuity of 2 Maccabees 12 on Purgatory?," *Alpha and Omega Ministries Blog*, March 3, 2009, http://www.aomin.org/aoblog/index.php/2009/03/03/the-perspicuity-of-2-maccabees-12-on-purgatory/.
25. René Pache, *The Future Life* (Chicago: Moody, 1962), 237.

Besides the misinterpretation of the verses used to argue for purgatory, we should also observe that the Bible is altogether silent about such a place. As we have already seen, Scripture describes those who die in this present age as going to one of two possible destinations during the intermediate state: hades or paradise.[26] We simply find no passages in the Bible that describe a state lying somewhere in between these two. Though one might argue that this is an argument from silence, this is a very loud silence indeed. Considering how important such a fate as purgatory would be if it were true, it strains credulity to think that we would see nothing of it in either testament but find only indications of the opposite. Similarly, the Bible is altogether silent about the related issue of prayers for the dead. The Bible neither describes nor enjoins this practice in any of the truly canonical books of the Bible, nor do Jesus or his Apostles mention, much less urge, this practice. Considering the weighty issues that would be at stake, it is difficult to see how the doctrine of purgatory could have escaped conspicuous and frequent mention were it true.

A Logical Problem with the Catholic Doctrine of Purgatory
In so far as purgatory is about sanctifying the sinner, the amount of suffering the person must undergo depends upon how tweaked that person is, as it were. Consider a twisted piece of metal that requires straightening. One would not torque the metal straight in an instant without running the risk of snapping it. Rather, one would heat the metal carefully with a torch and straighten it slowly. Following this analogy, a greatly "bent" individual would require more time and heat to straighten out than someone who is only slightly "out of true."[27]

Well and good. But recall also that the sufferings in purgatory are not only for the purpose of purification but are also administered to satisfy justice (i.e., in payment for the temporal penalties remaining for sin). As far as the sufferings of purgatory are a punitive infliction to satisfy the debt of sin, the Church may remit this suffering by issuing an indulgence, which can reduce the time spent in purgatory or eliminate it altogether.[28]

But herein lurks a problem for the doctrine.

To the degree that one sees the sufferings of purgatory as satisfying a debt, the Catholic teaching of indulgence has a certain semblance of logic to it.

---

26. See Question 10, "What Fate Awaits Those Who Die in This Present Age, Immediately upon Death?"
27. Speaking of the necessity of purgatory, Rahner states, "The interior perfecting of man, who matures in genuinely creaturely time, is a temporal process and on account of the many levels of the structure of human nature cannot be thought to happen by some *fiat* which would accomplish everything at once" (Rahner, "Purgatory," 427). Bastian makes a similar point ("Purgatory: In Theology," 828).
28. A partial indulgence merely reduces the time in purgatory, whereas a plenary indulgence provides full remission.

That is because a creditor may remit part or even all of a monetary debt at his or her discretion. However, in so far as Catholics teach that the amount of time one must spend in purgatory must be proportioned to the degree of disorder still inhering in one's soul, it is difficult to see how this time could be reduced, much less eliminated altogether, without thereby short-circuiting the sinner's transformation unto holiness. This would be a bit like yanking a cake out of the oven while it is yet half-baked. Indeed, one could argue that far from being merciful, remitting a sinner's time in purgatory is actually positively harmful. Realize that such a remission would circumvent the suffering needed to effect the holiness of life that the sinner desperately needs in order to enjoy life in heaven.

I therefore find myself in hearty agreement with Catholic theologian J. Cevetello, who states, "In the final analysis, the Catholic doctrine of purgatory is based on tradition, not Sacred Scripture."[29]

REFLECTION QUESTIONS

1. What is "purgatory" in Roman Catholic teaching? How does it differ from hell?

2. What are the two purposes of purgatory, according to Catholicism?

3. How does the Roman Catholic doctrine of purgatory relate to its doctrine of the sacraments, particularly the sacrament of penance? Based on what you know from Scripture, what is your own estimate of this teaching?

4. Evaluate the scriptural evidence that Roman Catholics offer for the doctrine of purgatory. Do you find any of these passages convincing? Which ones and why?

5. What are some of the logical problems inherent in the doctrine of purgatory?

---

29. Cevetello, "Purgatory: In the Bible," 825. Catholic theologian Ludwig Ott makes this same point (Ludwig Ott, *Fundamentals of Catholic Dogma*, 5th ed., ed. James Canon Bastible, trans. Patrick Lynch [St. Louis: B. Herder Book Company, 1962], 484).

Does God Give People an Opportunity for Conversion after They Die?

In the after life God will put the screw on hard enough to make men want to change their ways.

—Nels Ferré[1]

Basic Statement of the Position

Traditionally, Christian theologians have held that death settles one's final destiny. Nevertheless, a small minority of Christian thinkers throughout history have taught that conversion to Christ is possible in the next life. Proponents of this position typically say that this happens through some kind of postmortem encounter with Christ, which presents the occasion for repentance and salvation. As Clark Pinnock describes it:

> Humanity will appear in its entirety before God and God has not changed from love to hate [after one dies]. Anyone wanting to love God who has not loved him before is certainly welcome to do so. It has not suddenly become forbidden.[2]

The teaching that individuals can convert in the afterlife goes by a variety of labels: postmortem evangelism, postmortem encounter (Pinnock), divine perseverance (Fackre), eschatological evangelism, future probation, and probation after death. In this chapter, we shall refer to the teaching as "postmortem evangelism," or PME.

---

1. Nels Ferré, cited in J. I. Packer, "All Men Won't Be Saved," *Eternity*, November 1965, 44. Packer does not provide a reference for this quote.
2. Clark Pinnock, *A Wideness in God's Mercy* (Grand Rapids: Zondervan, 1992), 171.

Variations within the Postmortem Evangelism Theory

A First Chance or Multiple Chances?
Some hold that there is PME only for those who never had an opportunity to hear the gospel during their lifetimes. So in their case, it is not a question of being given a second chance or a "do-over," but rather of "the universality of a first chance" to believe.[3]
Others, however, believe that even those who have heard and rejected the gospel in their lifetimes will be confronted with it again in the afterlife—perhaps repeatedly. Some go so far as to teach that individuals already consigned to hell may, at any time, repent and be transferred to heaven.

Postmortem Evangelism and Universalism
Some, though not all, universalists hold to PME, while some, though not all, who hold to PME also embrace universalism.[4]
Some universalists argue that it is necessary to profess Christ explicitly in order to be saved. PME purportedly solves the problem of those who never had a chance to make such a profession before they die. Of course, the universalist advocating PME must also assume that everyone who hears the gospel message—whether in this life or in the next—will repent and receive it. This is the position of Nels Ferré, as observed in the opening quote to this chapter.
Other PME advocates reject universalism, reasoning that just as some reject the gospel during their earthly sojourn, some will continue to exercise their freedom to reject it in the afterlife. Nevertheless, at that point God will have done everything that he can to save them, and no one will perish purely out of ignorance or for lack of opportunity.

Main Arguments Offered for Postmortem Evangelism

The Argument from Divine Justice/Fairness
PME adherents sometimes argue that God would not be fair or just if on the one hand, he required explicit faith in Christ for salvation, but on the other hand did not provide everyone with an opportunity to exercise such faith. As Fackre, one of the leading modern proponents of PME, states, "Since God is just as well as loving, no one will be denied the good news, no one excluded from hearing the saving Word and making a decision for Christ."[5]

---

3. Donald Bloesch, "Descent into Hell (Hades)," *EDT*, 340.
4. For a thorough discussion of universalism, see Question 33.
5. Gabriel Fackre, "Response to Nash," in *What about Those Who Have Never Heard?*, ed. John Sanders (Downers Grove, IL: InterVarsity, 1995), 153.

The Argument Based on Infant Salvation

Most Christian theologians have granted that God saves at least some if not all infants dying in infancy.[6] At the same time, the Bible also teaches that one must have faith in Christ in order to be saved. Since babies as babies do not have the capacity to exercise faith, God gives them this ability and opportunity in the afterlife. Now, if God gives infants a chance for postmortem faith, it is reasonable to extend this to adults as well.[7]

Christ's "Descent into Hell" Supports Postmortem Evangelism

Historically, many theologians have taught that between Christ's death and resurrection he descended into hell, where, among other things, he made some kind of proclamation to those who had died. One finds this "descent into hell" (DH) in the later versions of the historic Apostles' Creed, and in certain passages of Scripture that we shall examine below. Partisans of the PME position argue that Christ specifically gave a postmortem offer of salvation at this time.

1 Peter 3:18–22

This is one of the key texts offered in proof of PME. Lange, a prominent nineteenth-century biblical interpreter, argued that the language is clear in teaching that Christ's spirit literally went to "the spirits in prison"—i.e., to the abode of departed spirits—and there preached the gospel to them. He urges strongly that the verb for "preached" always and only refers to the preaching of the gospel.[8]

Leckie concurs with this view. In his opinion, Peter's meaning is clear: "St. Peter almost certainly meant to teach that Jesus in the interval between death and resurrection went down into the lower world and there proclaimed good tidings."[9]

1 Peter 4:6

Cranfield maintains that one ought to connect the verses from chapter 3 about the spirits in prison (discussed above) with Peter's continuing discussion in chapter 4, particularly with 4:6, which speaks about "the gospel being preached to those who are dead."[10] Likewise, Fackre avers, "These verses in 1 Peter 4 correlate exactly with those in 1 Peter 3."[11]

---

6. See Question 11.
7. Pinnock, *A Wideness in God's Mercy*, 171; John Sanders, *No Other Name: An Investigation into the Destiny of the Unevangelized* (Grand Rapids: Eerdmans, 1992), 191. Note that Sanders himself does not hold to PME.
8. John Peter Lange, "Peter," in *Commentary on the Holy Scriptures*, vol. 23, trans. Philip Schaff (1867; reprint Grand Rapids: Zondervan, 1950), 68–70.
9. J. H. Leckie, *The World to Come and Final Destiny* (Edinburgh: T. & T. Clark, 1922), 91.
10. C. E. B. Cranfield, *I & II Peter and Jude* (London: SCM, 1960), 109–10.
11. Gabriel Fackre, "Divine Perseverance," in *What about Those Who Have Never Heard?*, ed. John Sanders (Downers Grove, IL: InterVarsity, 1995), 84.

John 5:25–29
These verses say that the dead will hear the voice of the Son of God and will be made alive. Commenting on verse 25, Fackre claims this text in support of PME: "In John a firm no is said to all our delimited maps and timetables."[12]

1 Corinthians 15:19
Fackre cites this verse in proof that the hope of salvation extends beyond this present mortal life: "If in this life alone human beings have hope, then we are miserable indeed (1 Cor 15:19). But such is not the lot of those born out of time or place. To them also comes the good news of Jesus Christ."[13]

Revelation 21:25
Some PME adherents hold that the door to salvation is always open, even to those who find themselves initially in hell. One commonly cited text is Revelation 21:25, which speaks of the gates to the New Jerusalem as "never shut." Universalist Rob Bell suggests this position when he opines, "If the gates are never shut, then people are free to come and go."[14]

Rissi, in his scholarly monograph *The Future of the World,* teaches the same thing. According to him, conversions will take place out of the lake of fire and into the New Jerusalem. For such, "the doors remain open! . . . Entry into the New Jerusalem means nothing less than being freed from the judgment of the lake of fire, the second death, and admission into God's world of the new creation."[15] Likewise, Vogelgesang states, "John evidently depicts a constant flow of the former outsiders and enemies of God from the lake of fire into the New Jerusalem after the final judgment of Rev. 20:11–15."[16] Bloesch has also argued along these lines, albeit tentatively.[17]

Refutation of Arguments Offered for Postmortem Evangelism

Response to the Argument Based on Divine Fairness
Underlying many of the PME arguments is the idea that God would not be fair if he did not give everyone an equal chance to be saved. Yet, these same

---

12. Ibid., 85.
13. Ibid., 84.
14. Rob Bell, *Love Wins* (New York: Harper Collins, 2011), 115. I say "suggests" because here, as throughout his book generally, Bell poses his view in the form of questions, to give the appearance of an open mind. Yet, he casts these questions in such a way as to make the view that he no doubt favors appear as the only attractive position.
15. Mathias Rissi, *The Future of the World,* Studies in Biblical Theology, Second Series 23 (London: SCM, 1972), 74, 78. See also 67–79.
16. Jeffrey Vogelgesang, "The Interpretation of Ezekiel in the Book of Revelation" (Ph.D. diss., Harvard, 1985), 104.
17. Donald Bloesch, *Essentials of Evangelical Theology,* 2 vols. (New York: Harper & Row, 1978), 2:226–27.

PME advocates would grant that salvation is by grace, because people are sinners and do not deserve salvation. But here their reasoning entails a deep inconsistency. If grace means anything, it must include a lack of obligation to extend it. Fairness or justice, on the other hand, has reference only to what is owed—that is, to "wages . . . due" (Rom. 4:4) and not to what is offered graciously and to the undeserving.

Response to the Argument Based on Infant Salvation
In Question 11 I observed that, although infants are sinners and do not deserve salvation, God regenerates them and applies Christ's atoning work to them without a conscious act of faith on their part. I further observed that God has determined to judge people for deeds done in the body (2 Cor. 5:10). This rules out infants, who are incapable of sinful acts. But one cannot generalize any of this to adults, who are capable of faith and who can and do commit sinful acts during their lifetimes.

Response to the Argument Based on the Descent into Hell
The later, modified versions of Apostles' Creed notwithstanding, we have excellent reasons for discounting the notion that Christ descended into hell. I have gone into considerable detail for why this is so in Question 39 and Question 40. Consequently, any argument for PME based on Christ's alleged descent into hell carries no force. Furthermore, many who do hold to a descent into hell strongly dispute that Jesus conducted a postmortem revival meeting there.

Response to the Argument Based on 1 Peter 3:18–22
In Question 39 and Question 40 I shall demonstrate that there is no good reason to take this passage as teaching that Christ preached the gospel to the unsaved in hell between his death and resurrection. For the present, we simply note:

1. This text speaks only of those who disobeyed in Noah's day. At most, one could only apply this PME, if indeed it were such, to these particular sinners; there is nothing in the passage that would allow us to generalize it beyond them. That in itself makes a PME interpretation of these verses suspect, since it would be difficult to understand why Christ would make such an offer only to them.[18]

---

18. Geerhardus Vos, cited in Robert Culver, *Systematic Theology: Biblical and Historical* (Fearn, Ross-shire, UK: Mentor, 2005), 1094. See also See Wayne Grudem, "He Did Not Descend into Hell: A Plea for Following Scripture Instead of the Apostles' Creed," *JETS* 34, no. 1 (March 1991): 109; and Karen H. Jobes, *1 Peter*, BECNT (Grand Rapids: Baker, 2005), 248.

2. Even if one were to assume against all probability that Christ conducted PME between his death and resurrection, "It is a question here of an action in the past; nothing in this text permits the interpretation that the gospel is being preached now to unbelievers in the other world."[19]

3. The word for "preach" (*ekēryxen*), on which Lange hangs so much of his argument, need not mean "preach the gospel," as most modern commentators would grant. The word can have a neutral or general sense of "announce" or "proclaim," including a message of condemnation just as well as of salvation.[20]

Response to the Argument Based on 1 Peter 4:6
Few modern commentators connect this verse with the earlier discussion in chapter 3.[21] It would not at all fit the context of Peter's argument to introduce, suddenly and as "a lightning bolt out of the blue," a discussion of Christ having preached the gospel to dead people.[22]

In addition, unlike with 3:18, the verb *euēngelisthē* does indeed refer to the preaching of the gospel. However, the reference to the "dead" has Christians in view who had heard and embraced the gospel *while they were yet alive* but who were *now dead* (i.e., at the time of Peter's writing). The NIV rendering of this verse makes this especially clear. Furthermore, as Schreiner points out, the verse does not say that Christ is the one doing the preaching, as would be expected by the PME theory.[23]

Response to the Argument Based on John 5:25–29
John 5:25–29 not only fails to prove PME but actually provides a very strong argument against it. Ronald Nash solidly refutes Fackre's interpretation:

> What did Jesus mean in John 5:25 when he said, "Very truly, I tell you, the hour is coming [a reference to a future event], and is now here [the present], when the dead will hear the voice of the son of God, and those who hear will live"? The present fulfillment of Jesus' words is found in the growing multitude of the spiritually dead who hear and accept the message of the Son of God and pass from spiritual death to

---

19. René Pache, *The Future Life* (Chicago: Moody, 1962), 315. See also Millard Erickson, *How Shall They Be Saved?* (Grand Rapids: Baker, 1996), 166.
20. John H. Elliott, *1 Peter*, AB (New Haven, CT: Yale University Press, 2000), 733, 660; Thomas Schreiner, *1, 2 Peter, Jude*, NAC 37 (Nashville: B&H, 2003), 189.
21. Elliott, *1 Peter*, 731; Jobes, *1 Peter*, 272.
22. Ronald H. Nash, "Restrictivism," in *What about Those Who Have Never Heard?*, ed. John Sanders (Downers Grove, IL: InterVarsity, 1995), 129. See also Schreiner, *1, 2 Peter, Jude*, 208.
23. Schreiner, *1, 2 Peter, Jude*, 207.

spiritual life (See John 5:24). The still future fulfillment is found in the coming bodily resurrection.[24]

Nash points out that Fackre's position becomes all the more untenable when one reads further and looks at verses 28 and 29, which Fackre fails to quote. Here we see the clear reference to the resurrection, not to some kind of postmortem encounter. Furthermore, these verses also show that the final judgment is based on works done while one is yet alive, in direct contradiction to the teaching of PME.[25]

Response to the Argument Based on 1 Corinthians 15:19

Fackre's paraphrase of 1 Corinthians 15:19 "does great violence to the text."[26] Here Paul teaches that if *we who are already Christians* have placed our hope in Christ only for this life—as would be the case if there is no resurrection—then *we Christians* are to be pitied above all men. The text has absolutely nothing whatever to do with the evangelism of unbelievers in the next life.

Response to the Argument Based on Revelation 21:25

The argument based on the "open gates" of the New Jerusalem allowing individuals to migrate from hell to heaven at their option is especially fanciful. I have dealt with the proper interpretation of this text in Question 23, "What Is the New Jerusalem?" Beyond my treatment there, it is enough to heed Beale's decisive refutation of this position:

> [Revelation] 21:7–8 contrasts the "overcomers" with false confessors in the Christian community, and such a contrast is likely to be seen as well in 22:14–15. This is supported by 22:11, which also contrasts ungodly people with godly people and views both as essentially permanently set in their respective ways (see on 22:11). Furthermore, the directly following 22:18–19 speaks of the judgment of the impious in definitive and absolute terms.[27]

Arguments against Postmortem Conversions

We have already seen that the arguments offered in support of PME do not even come close to making the case. Let us now consider verses that actually teach the opposite—namely, that one's destiny is fixed at the point of death.

---

24. Ronald H. Nash, "Response to Fackre," in *What about Those Who Have Never Heard?*, ed. John Sanders (Downers Grove: InterVarsity, 1995), 100.
25. Ibid.
26. Ibid., 98.
27. G. K. Beale, *The Book of Revelation: A Commentary on the Greek Text*, NIGTC (Grand Rapids: Eerdmans, 1999), 1098.

Luke 16:19–31

This is the parable of the rich man and Lazarus, a text that we have already considered from a variety of angles. Verse 26 records the key point of interest to us here, which is the great, fixed chasm, which keeps the rich man from passing from hades to "Abraham's side" or heaven.[28] That, and the parable taken as a whole, preclude the doctrine of PME.

Some have argued that we cannot derive our doctrine of the afterlife from a parable such as this (granting, as I do, that it is indeed a parable). For instance, Sanders claims that to conclude from this parable that our destinies become fixed at death is to engage in an overly "literalistic" interpretation, which misses the parable's point, which "is to instruct us about the use of wealth, not about eschatology."[29] However, Erickson is surely right when he points out that there is no reason that the parable cannot teach multiple truths. Furthermore, simply because it is a parable does not preclude it from teaching doctrine, eschatological or otherwise. As Erickson observes, "In Jesus' parables, even when the specific event referred to may not have been a historical occurrence, nothing in the details of the occurrence was untrue to life."[30] It is not surprising, therefore, that prominent modern evangelical commentators and theologians—such as Stein, Bock, Kistemaker, and Packer—conclude from this text the permanence of one's fate at the point of death.[31]

Hebrews 9:27

This text is perhaps the most oft-quoted against the idea of a second chance beyond the grave: "it is appointed for man to die once, and after that comes judgment." For instance, Phillips believes that this verse definitely rules out any sort of "second chance" theory.[32]

However, strictly speaking, the verse simply gives the relative order between death and judgment, namely that the former precedes the latter. Furthermore, if the author has in mind the final eschatological judgment that occurs at the end of the age—as opposed to a private judgment immediately occurring upon death—a great deal of time might intervene between the two events, providing what a PME advocate could argue is a window for repentance.[33]

---

28. See Question 7.
29. Sanders, *No Other Name*, 191n32.
30. Erickson, *How Shall They Be Saved?*, 172.
31. See Darrell Bock, *Luke 9:51–24:53*, BECNT (Grand Rapids: Baker, 1996), 1361; Simon E. Kistemaker, *Exposition of James, Epistles of John, Peter, and Jude*, NTC (Grand Rapids: Baker, 2002), 143; Packer, "All Men Won't Be Saved," 44; and Robert H. Stein, *Luke*, NAC 24 (Nashville: Broadman, 1992), 425.
32. Richard D. Phillips, *Hebrews*, Reformed Expository Commentary (Phillipsburg, NJ: P&R, 2006), 326. See also Packer, "All Men Won't Be Saved," 44.
33. Guthrie takes the "judgment" mentioned here as the final judgment at the end of the age (Donald Guthrie, *Hebrews*, TNTC [Grand Rapids: Eerdmans, 1983], 199). Attridge believes that the writer has in mind an "immediate post-mortem judgment" (Harold W.

While this text cannot prove conclusively that there is no postmortem chance at conversion, the overall tenor of the passage does seem to point to the notion that "the judgment of each human being reflects that person's standing with God at the moment of death."[34]

2 Corinthians 5:10
Paul states, "For we must all appear before the judgment seat of Christ, so that each one may receive what is due for what he has done in the body, whether good or evil." This verse shows that our judgment is based on what happens in this life, not in the next.

Paul's instruction here is entirely consistent with what Jesus declares in Matthew 25:31–46. There, our Lord teaches that judgment is based on deeds done in the present life. In the case of Christians, who are saved by grace through faith alone, their deeds provide evidence of salvation by Christ and furnish the basis for reward, whereas for those who do not believe, their works serve as the basis for their condemnation. Other passages that teach this same truth are Matthew 7:15–23; 13:24–30; 24:41–46; and Revelation 20:11–12.[35]

Revelation 22:11
This verse—speaking of events occurring at the end of the age as recorded in the very last chapter of the last book of the Bible—states, "Let the evildoer still do evil, and the filthy still be filthy, and the righteous still do right, and the holy still be holy." If PME were true, we would expect the verse to read, "Let the evildoer stop doing evil, for it is never too late to repent and be saved." This verse, however, tells us that by then it is too late: the die is cast, the decision made, the chance for salvation past. The words of this verse could not be more opposed to the idea that the wicked receive another chance to repent after death.

REFLECTION QUESTIONS

1. Do you think that God would be unfair if he did not allow people to convert after death?

2. Do you believe that the PME position has any implications for the urgency of missions and evangelism—whether positive or negative?

Attridge, *Hebrews*, Hermeneia [Philadelphia: Fortress, 1989], 265). Ellingworth holds that the author leaves the question "entirely open" (Paul Ellingworth, *The Epistle to the Hebrews*, NIGTC [Grand Rapids: Eerdmans, 1993], 486). On the distinction between immediate postmortem judgment and the final judgment, see Question 15.

34. Nash, "Restrictivism," 134.
35. See the discussion of the final judgment at Question 15.

3. Do you find the PME position to be a good answer to the question of how God will judge those who have never heard the gospel?

4. Do you believe that PME advocates have made a convincing case from the Bible for their position? What do you see as their strongest biblical evidence?

5. What do you regard as the greatest difficulties for the PME position?

PART 3

The Final Judgment

What Is the Final Judgment?

The author of Hebrews tells us that the doctrine of a final, eternal judgment is an "elementary" and "foundational" doctrine of the faith (Heb. 6:1–2). However "elementary" it may be in theory, we nevertheless find great confusion and misunderstanding about it, particularly when it comes to fleshing out the details of what this judgment entails.

We shall consider the following aspects of the final judgment (FJ) in this chapter:

1. What is the FJ?

2. Why will there be a FJ?

3. Who specifically shall be judged?

4. Who will do the judging?

5. When will the judging take place?

6. Where will the FJ take place?

Then, in some of the chapters that follow, I shall address the *basis* and the *results* of the FJ.

What Is the Final Judgment?

The FJ is the great time of reckoning, at the end of history and before the eternal state, when God will judge all of his moral creatures, whether men or angels, demanding of them an account of everything they have thought, said, or done. At the FJ, when God reveals his righteous judgment, he will render reward or punishment, as the case requires, to each according to his or her works.[1]

We should not confuse the FJ with more localized, temporal judgments that God has brought on the world throughout human history, such as the Babylonian captivity, the destruction of Jerusalem by the Romans, the annihilation of Sodom and Gomorrah, or countless other such divinely ordained events. Nor should one equate the FJ with what some theologians call a personal or private judgment that happens at the point of death, when the wicked and the righteous alike become aware of their final destinies in general (e.g., Luke 16:19–31).[2] Rather, the FJ occurs at the final phase of history, when God through Jesus Christ will "judge the living and the dead" (2 Tim. 4:1).

The Fact of a Final Judgment

Granting that the FJ is a basic, fundamental, undisputed fact of the Christian faith (Heb. 6:1–2), we are not surprised to find countless passages in Scripture that speak of it directly or by inference. To cite just a few passages from both testaments, consider Psalm 96:13; Ecclesiastes 12:14; Matthew 10:15; 12:36; 13:24–30, 36–43; Acts 17:31; Romans 2:5, 16; 14:12; 2 Corinthians 5:10; Hebrews 9:27; 2 Peter 2:9; 3:7; 1 John 4:17; Jude 6; and Revelation 20:1–15.[3]

Why Is There a Final Judgment?

There are at least two reasons for a FJ: to balance the scales of justice by avenging evil and rewarding good, and to display God's glory. These two purposes interconnect, since God glorifies himself by displaying his character in rendering to each person what his or her works deserve.

Scripture declares that God executes justice for the oppressed and brings the wicked to ruin (Ps. 146:7–9). It also tells us that each one will reap what he or she has sown (Gal. 6:7). Yet, it is clear that in this present life, the wicked often prosper at the expense of the righteous, and the moral universe remains out of kilter, as it were. The FJ sets all of that straight.

Our own moral intuitions attest to the need for a final day of reckoning. As I observed in the introduction of this book, we find ourselves vexed when moral degenerates who inflict unutterable suffering and ruin on innocent, helpless lives—such as drug lords and purveyors of sexual

---

1. For a discussion on the end of history and the movement into the eternal state, see Robert L. Saucy, *The Case for Progressive Dispensationalism* (Grand Rapids: Zondervan, 1993), 289–92.
2. On the distinction between the "private judgment at death" vs. the "public judgment at the last day," see W. G. T. Shedd, *Dogmatic Theology,* ed. Alan W. Gomes (Phillipsburg: P&R, 2003), 878.
3. Note that the terms, "that day," "the day of the Lord," "a day," and so forth could refer to a period of time, but they would in most instances doubtless include the FJ.

trafficking—prosper, live to a ripe old age, and then die peacefully in their sleep. We know deep down that something would be terribly askew if the story ended here. Who cannot relate to Jeremiah's anguish when he cries out in bitter complaint, "Why does the way of the wicked prosper? Why do all who are treacherous thrive?" (Jer. 12:1).

At the FJ, God will glorify himself by demonstrating his magnificent, praiseworthy attributes of mercy and justice. He will display his mercy in pardoning those who have repented of their sins and have received the forgiveness grounded in Christ's atoning work, which satisfied divine justice through his death on the cross. Moreover, in punishing the finally unrepentant, he will reveal his righteousness, and "by no means clear the guilty" (Nah. 1:3). Truly, this will be a cause of great delight and satisfaction, both for God and for his saints.[4]

Who Shall Be Judged?

The FJ will include every moral creature whom God has ever made. This includes men and angels, whether wicked or righteous, believers and unbelievers alike.

Given the fact of a FJ, the notion that God will judge unbelievers is uncontroversial and borne out in numerous passages such as Revelation 20:11–15.[5] However, some might question whether Christians will be judged, granting that Jesus says that the one who believes in him "does not come into judgment, but has passed from death to life" (John 5:24).[6] At the same time, verses such as Romans 14:10 show that the FJ is a comprehensive judgment of everyone who has ever lived, which means it would include Christians as well. Furthermore, we have passages that seem to focus on the judgment of believers specifically.[7] One of the most notable verses is 2 Corinthians 5:10, which states, "For we must all appear before the judgment seat (Greek: *bēma*) of Christ, so that each one may receive what is due for what he has done in the body, whether good or evil." The word *bēma* refers to a "judicial bench" or "tribunal," where the judgment administered by a magistrate takes place.[8] From the entire context of 2 Corinthians 5, and even in the verses preceding it in chapter 4, Paul undoubtedly is addressing believers and (most likely)

---

4. See Question 38.
5. Similarly, see the description of the new earth in Revelation 21 and 22, which depicts "the faithless" who lie outside (21:8).
6. See also John 3:17–18; Romans 5:8–9; 8:1; 1 John 4:17.
7. E.g., Matthew 18:23; 25:19; Romans 2:6–7, 16; 14:10–12; 1 Corinthians 3:11–15; and 2 Corinthians 5:10.
8. Murray J. Harris, *The Second Epistle to the Corinthians*, NIGTC (Grand Rapids: Eerdmans, 2005), 406. See also J. Dwight Pentecost, *Things to Come* (Grand Rapids: Zondervan, 1958), 221.

only them.[9] In Question 16, I shall reconcile the apparent tension between the fact that Christians "do not come into judgment" but nevertheless will stand before Christ's judgment seat.

Angels also will stand before God's tribunal on the last day (1 Cor. 6:3; 2 Peter 2:4; Jude 6), preeminently Satan himself (Rev. 20:10). This is entirely fitting, since angels are personal moral beings who render either obedience or disobedience to their creator.

Who Will Do the Judging?

Certain passages depict God as the judge,[10] while other passages point to Christ as the one who will pass judgment.[11] There is no contradiction here because it is God who "appointed" Christ to execute judgment at his behest (Acts 17:31), having "given all judgment to the Son" (John 5:22). Consequently, one may speak of "the judgment seat of Christ" (2 Cor. 5:10) and "the judgment seat of God" (Rom. 14:10) with complete consistency.

Perhaps more unexpected and even startling are passages that point to believers serving as judges in the final assize. For instance, Jesus informs his apostles that they will participate in judging the twelve tribes of Israel (Matt. 19:28).[12] Revelation 20:4 speaks of "thrones" (plural) and those seated on them, "to whom the authority to judge was committed."[13] This verse appears in the context of the "great white throne" judgment (v. 11), in which all the dead, "great and small," receive judgment "according to what they had done" (v. 12). Not only will believers participate in the judgment of wicked human beings, but in 1 Corinthians 6:2–3 Paul declares the remarkable fact that they will assist in rendering a verdict on angels as well.[14]

When Will This Judging Take Place?

Until now, we have spoken of the FJ as taking place "on the last day" or "at the end of the history." However, the relative timing of crucial events in this judgment is a complex and sometimes difficult interpretive issue that requires careful scrutiny. In untangling some of these details, we find that Bible interpreters often disagree on some of the specifics.

---

9. Harris, *The Second Epistle to the Corinthians*, 406.
10. Genesis 18:25; Psalms 82:8; 94:2; 96:13; 98:9; Romans 2:16; 3:6; Hebrews 12:23; Revelation 6:10.
11. Matthew 25:31–46; John 5:22, 27; Acts 17:31; Romans 2:16; 14:10; 2 Thessalonians 1:7–10; 2:8; 2 Timothy 4:1; Revelation 19:11–21; 22:12.
12. This judging "also conveys the idea of ruling or governing" (Saucy, *The Case for Progressive Dispensationalism*, 267, 273).
13. Note the similarity with Daniel 7:9, which also speaks of "thrones" at the final judgment.
14. See René Pache, *The Future Life* (Chicago: Moody, 1962), 276; and Robert Culver, *Systematic Theology: Biblical and Historical* (Fearn, Ross-shire, UK: Mentor, 2005), 1070.

What All Christians Hold in Common about the FJ
Let us first consider what all orthodox Christians believe about the FJ:

- There will be a FJ, preceding the eternal state (ES), in which God will judge both the saved and the unsaved.
- The FJ takes place in the embodied state, not a disembodied state. This means that the resurrection of the physical body, both for the just and for the unjust, precedes the FJ.
- After receiving their respective verdicts at the FJ, the wicked and the righteous go into the ES to experience their varied rewards or punishments, as the case may be.

Points about Which Christians Sometimes Disagree
The disagreements that one finds among Christians on the FJ mostly concern issues of timing, not about the fact of a judgment nor especially about what the judgment itself entails. These differences are in no way tests of orthodoxy. Nevertheless, we shall consider them in order to set forth a comprehensive picture of biblical teaching. I shall present what I believe to be the most likely position, realizing that many fine interpreters may see matters differently. These timing differences fall primarily into two categories.

First, is the FJ a single event that happens on a single occasion, or is it a phased event consisting of multiple components spread out over a space of time? So, for example: Is there only a single resurrection that includes both the wicked and the righteous, occurring at the same time and immediately preceding a FJ for both that happens on a single occasion? Alternatively, does the FJ occur in different stages, in which God resurrects the righteous and the wicked at separate times, followed by their own distinct judgments?

Second, what is the timing of the resurrection (or resurrections) and the final judgment (or judgments) relative to other possible events at the end of history? For example, is there a literal one-thousand-year reign of Christ on this present earth preceding the ES? If so, what is the timing of the aforementioned judgment(s) and resurrection(s) in relation to it?

What Is the Millennium?
Revelation 20 speaks of a thousand-year period during which Christ rules over this earth, before transitioning to the ES in Revelation 21. According to Revelation 20:2, God binds Satan throughout this time, during which God restrains him from deceiving the nations. Meanwhile, believers—whom God had raised from the dead before these millennial events—reign with Christ (vv. 4–6). At the end of the thousand years, God releases Satan (v. 7), who then incites certain nations to make war against the saints (vv. 8–9). God decisively crushes this final rebellion when fire from heaven consumes these enemies (v. 9). Then God casts the Devil into the lake of fire (v. 10). In addition, God

resurrects wicked humans, who had remained in their graves throughout this millennial period, to face their sentence of doom (vv. 11–13). Upon receiving their verdict, they join the Devil who deceived them in the lake of fire (vv. 14–15). God follows this with the creation of a new heavens and a new, glorified, literal earth on which believers will dwell forever (chapter 21).

Good, Bible-believing Christians differ as to how this thousand-year "millennial" reign of Christ ought to be understood.

Some hold to the position as depicted above in a literal sense, believing that Christ returns to inaugurate an actual thousand-year period of rule on this present earth. Note that this is not the new earth spoken of in Revelation 21:1 but is our present earth, albeit significantly (though not completely) enhanced. At the end of the thousand years, God establishes his everlasting rule on the newly constituted, literal, perfect, and glorified earth mentioned in 21:1. Those who hold this position are called "premillennialists" because Christ returns before and in order to establish his thousand-year reign.

Others hold that the millennium of which these verses speak does not refer to a future reign of Christ on this earth but rather is a figurative way of picturing his reign with the saints in heaven throughout this present age. Alternatively, some believe that this millennium refers to the church's reign with him on earth, again during this present age. According to these figurative understandings, the "first resurrection" in Revelation 20:4 that takes place at the beginning of this millennium is a *spiritual* resurrection that happens when one is made alive spiritually (i.e., born again) at salvation. The resurrection at the millennium's end (v. 5), on the other hand, is acknowledged to be the literal bodily resurrection at the end of the age for all human beings. These positions are commonly held versions of what is known as "amillennialism," because they aver that there is "no millennium," i.e., in a literal sense.

I am convinced that the premillennial position is correct, and in some of the points I will make below I will lay out matters from that perspective— recognizing, of course, that not all will agree with this position.[15]

One Literal Resurrection or Two?
Revelation 20:4–6 is the classic passage most explicitly teaching two resurrections: one for the righteous just before the millennium, and another for the wicked[16] at the millennium's close. This is certainly the most straightforward reading of the passage, as adherents of both positions agree. The point in

---

15. For an article that presents a position contrary to the view I argue below, see Benjamin L. Merkle and W. Tyler Krug, "Hermeneutical Challenges for a Premillennial Interpretation of Revelation 20," *Evangelical Quarterly* 86.3 (2014): 210–26.
16. Or at least primarily for the wicked. See the discussion on the great white throne judgment below.

dispute, though, is whether both resurrections are literal or whether the first one of these is merely spiritual, as the amillennialist contends.

The evidence points to a literal, physical resurrection for both. First, when the ancients spoke of resurrection, it "referred specifically to something that happened to the body," not to the spirit.[17] But second, even granting that one could speak of a spiritual renewal as a "resurrection," the immediate context rules that out in this passage. Verse 4 says that those who partake of the "first resurrection" (v. 5, *anastasis ē prōtē*) are those who had been physically beheaded and come back to physical life in order to reign with Christ. Furthermore, the coming to life for the "rest of the dead" (v. 5) has to be physical, granting that the "rest of the dead" in this passage are primarily (if not entirely) *unbelievers*, who certainly cannot be characterized as having experienced any kind of spiritual renewal or resurrection.

Other passages of Scripture suggest—some strongly—that the wicked and righteous receive separate resurrections. In Luke 14:14, Jesus refers to the "resurrection of the just," which implies a distinct resurrection from that of the wicked. Consider also Philippians 3:11, which also points to a different resurrection for the righteous. Paul speaks here of an *exanastasis tēn ek nekrōn* for believers, which we might translate (rather woodenly) as an "out-resurrection out *from among* the dead ones." In framing it this way, Paul may be distinguishing the resurrection *from among* the dead (*anastasis/exanastasis tēn ek nekron*)—which represents the resurrection of but a subset of humankind, i.e., of believers—from the resurrection *of* the dead (*anastasis nekrōn*), which refers to the resurrection of all human beings without distinction. Furthermore, Paul here states that he hopes that he "may attain" to this former resurrection. This shows that he cannot have in mind merely resurrection in general, since all will be raised whether they hope for it or not.[18] Note also that elsewhere in the Bible, the phrase "resurrection from the dead" [lit., "out of the dead ones"] is always and only used of believers (e.g., Luke 20:35; Acts 4:2).[19]

The Timing of the First Resurrection
According to Revelation 20:4–6, God raises the righteous first, while the wicked receive their resurrections later. When, however, does this "first resurrection" occur in relation to other end-time events?

As described above, Christ returns before the millennium, which he will inaugurate, and raises from the dead departed believers at that time. However, here again we encounter a myriad of complexities if we factor into our consideration the tribulation period (Dan. 7:24–27; 9:24–27; Matt. 24:15–33;

---

17. N. T. Wright, *Surprised by Hope: Rethinking Heaven, the Resurrection, and the Mission of the Church* (New York: HarperOne, 2008), 36. See also the discussion in Question 19.
18. Saucy, *The Case for Progressive Dispensationalism*, 287.
19. Ibid., 286.

2 Thess. 2:1–4; Rev. 7:14), which also occurs before the millennium, and attempt to situate the first resurrection with respect to it.

The tribulation is a period in which God pours out his wrath upon the earth in an unprecedented way. Some believe that Christ will return at the commencement of this tribulation to rescue his saints from it, "rapturing" them from earth to heaven (1 Thess. 4:16–17), where they will abide safely while these horrific events play out. According to this schema, known as a pretribulation rapture model, the first resurrection would take place at the time of this rapture: All believers who had died would be raised with glorified, immortal bodies, while those who find themselves alive at his coming simply would be transformed on the spot. At the end of the seven-year tribulation Christ would return from heaven with these glorified saints in tow, in order to usher in his millennial reign.

Others dispute the pretribulational chronology. Among the alternatives suggested, some premillennialists hold to a posttribulational position. According to them, Christians will go through the entire seven-year period of unprecedented distress, followed by Christ's return at the close of this tribulation. At his posttribulational return, Christ will effect the first resurrection (i.e., of believers), and then will usher in the millennium.

Not surprisingly, a number of subvariations of these views exist as well. Regardless, all of those who take a premillennial perspective hold that Christ returns before his millennial reign, and the first resurrection (i.e., of believers) takes place in anticipation of this reign. Those raised in this first resurrection stand before the judgment seat (*bema*) of Christ (2 Cor. 5:10), where Christ determines, among other things, the degree of reward that each shall receive for his or her earthly service.[20]

The Resurrection of the Wicked and the Great White Throne Judgment
The resurrection of the wicked takes place at the end of the millennium (Rev. 20:5). They shall then stand before God at the great white throne (GWT) judgment (Rev. 20:11–15). Here "the lost of all the ages will appear before the Lord to be judged for their sins."[21]

Some hold that the resurrection at the end of the millennium and immediately preceding the GWT judgment includes only unbelievers, with all believers having been raised and judged at the earlier, premillennial *bema* judgment (2 Cor. 5:10).[22] Others, though, point to the fact that at least some

---

20. See Question 17, "Will God Assign Rewards to Christians at the Final Judgment?"
21. Mark Hitchcock, *55 Answers to Questions about Life after Death* (Sisters, OR: Multnomah, 2005), 147.
22. Charles L. Feinberg, *Premillennialism or Amillennialism?*, 2nd ed. (Wheaton, IL: Van Kampen, 1954), 350; Hitchcock, *55 Answers,* 147; Erich Sauer, *From Eternity to Eternity,* trans. G. H. Lang (London: Paternoster, 1954), 80; John Walvoord, *The Millennial Kingdom* (Grand Rapids: Zondervan, 1959), 332.

believers entering the millennium, as well as those people born during the millennium, will not yet have received their resurrected bodies; some of these evidently will die before the millennium is over (Isa. 65:20). Consequently, such individuals would require a resurrection that, presumably, would or could take place at the millennium's close.[23] It seems reasonable to conclude that the GWT judgment would serve this function for them. Revelation 20:15 implies (or is certainly consistent with) the notion that at least some standing before the GWT will be believers, i.e., found to have their names written in the book of life.[24]

After the Great White Throne Judgment: The Eternal State
Following the GWT judgment is the eternal state. God casts the wicked into the lake of fire (or *gehenna;* Rev. 20:15), while the righteous experience glorious life on a newly renovated earth (Isa. 65:17; 2 Peter 3:10–13; Rev. 21:1).

Where Will This Judgment Take Place?

Scripture is unclear on where the judgments discussed earlier take place. Some suggest that the GWT judgment depicted at the end of Revelation 21 takes place "in space,"[25] or "somewhere in between [heaven and earth]"[26] after the existing heaven and earth have "fled away" (21:11) but before the creation of the new heaven and new earth (21:1). However, the chronology of these events is not altogether clear.

As for the so-called *bema* judgment of believers, it seems that most (all?) who hold to a pretribulational rapture believe that this judgment occurs in heaven, while the tribulation plays out on earth below.[27] Alternatively, and regardless of one's view of the rapture, one could place this judgment after Christ returns from heaven to earth at the end of the tribulation, perhaps at

---

23. Just who these saints are who enter the millennium in natural bodies is a matter of some speculation. Assuming the truth of a pretribulational rapture, with the first resurrection occurring at that time, the saints in question would come from conversions taking place during the tribulation period. Since they were not yet believers at the time of the rapture, they did not experience the transformation that living believers did at this time (1 Thess. 4:16–17). These as yet untransformed saints, converted during the seven-year tribulation, would enter the millennium upon Christ's return from heaven in their natural bodies, joining his previously raised and glorified saints. During the thousand-year reign, these tribulation saints would continue to exist in natural bodies, and many of them would produce offspring (Jer. 30:19–20) and eventually die (Isa. 65:20).
24. For an excellent discussion of this point, see Henry W. Holloman, "Resurrection," *Kregel Dictionary of the Bible and Theology* (Grand Rapids: Kregel, 2005), 464.
25. Walvoord, *The Millennial Kingdom,* 332.
26. Pentecost, *Things to Come,* 423.
27. E.g., Walvoord is representative (Walvoord, *The Millennial Kingdom,* 276). Pentecost gives some of the reasons for this view (*Things to Come,* 220–21).

the beginning of the millennium.[28] In this latter scenario, the *bema* judgment would take place on this earth.

REFLECTION QUESTIONS

1. How do you feel about the fact that there will be a future FJ? Do you eagerly await it or fear its arrival?

2. Do you agree that a FJ is necessary? Explain.

3. What is your reaction to the idea that we as Christians will participate as "co-judges" in the FJ? That we will judge angels as well as fellow human beings?

4. Do you find it unsettling that there are some points of disagreement among Christians related to the FJ? Compare these with the points about which all Christians agree, and consider how serious such differences of opinion really are in the big scheme of things.

5. What is your opinion about the millennium? Do you think it makes the most sense to interpret it literally or figuratively? What arguments do you find most persuasive for the position you have adopted?

---

28. George Eldon Ladd, *The Blessed Hope* (Grand Rapids: Eerdmans, 1956), 103.

On What Is the Final Judgment Based?

In the previous question, I defined the final judgment (FJ) as "the great time of reckoning, at the end of history and before the eternal state, when God will judge all of his moral creatures, whether men or angels, demanding of them an account of everything they have thought, said, or done." I also laid out the rationale for such a judgment and discussed some differing viewpoints about the timing of it.

The FJ has two major outcomes: (1) God's final declaration of whether he pronounces a person "not guilty" (justified) or condemned; and (2) the bestowal of specific rewards or punishments, as God deems appropriate.[1] In this question, we shall consider the basis for these two major outcomes. Since every one of us will stand before God at this judgment, there is no matter of greater practical importance than for us to know the ground on which God will render his verdict. A proper understanding of the basis for God's final reckoning can and should affect how we live here and now.

To answer this question, I shall demonstrate the following:

1. The verdict at the FJ is based on a person's works.

2. Even though the FJ is based on works, one is nevertheless saved by faith alone in Christ alone.

The Final Judgment Is Based on Works

The consistent witness of Scripture in both testaments is that a person's deeds or works determine the outcome of the FJ. Scripture attests to this so pervasively that we need only consider a representative sampling here. We shall consult briefly our Lord's teaching in the Gospels and the apostles'

---

1. I cover this point specifically in Question 17 and Question 18.

teaching in the Epistles. Finally, we shall look at a few passages in Revelation, the Bible's closing book.

The Biblical Witness

Direct Statements of Our Lord
Our Lord had much to say about the final judgment—some of it stark and terrifying. For instance, in Matthew 7:15–23 Jesus warns of false prophets, who are known by the evil fruit of their lives. These rotten trees, he tells us, will be "cut down and thrown into the fire" (v. 19) and will be banished from Christ's coming kingdom (v. 21). In Matthew 16:27 our Lord flatly states that at his return he "will repay each person according to what he has done." And in Matthew 25:31–46, Jesus makes it plain that he will separate the sheep from the goats based on what they did while on earth, concluding, "And these will go away into eternal punishment, but the righteous into eternal life."

The Epistles
The Epistles offer teaching consistent with the Lord's own. Second Corinthians 5:10 speaks of the "judgment seat of Christ," which, as we observed in the previous chapter, has the judgment of Christians primarily if not exclusively in view. Note particularly that Paul states directly what will serve as the basis of this judgment, namely "what he has done in the body." This expression is but another way of designating the works that people have done in this present life.

Romans 2 also stresses that the FJ will be according to works. In verse 6, Paul testifies that in that day God "will render to each one according to his works." Those who persevere in doing good will receive eternal life (v. 7), whereas those who disobey the truth and serve unrighteousness instead will incur divine wrath (v. 8).

In Galatians 5:19–21 Paul presents a list of certain abominable practices that he calls "deeds of the flesh," including immorality, impurity, sensuality, angry outbursts, and drunkenness. At the end of this list, he offers the stern warning that "those who do such things will not inherit the kingdom of God" (v. 21). Notice that Paul has in mind those who *practice* such behaviors as the overall habit pattern of their lives. Similarly, he admonishes the Corinthians, "do you not know that the unrighteous will not inherit the kingdom of God?" (1 Cor. 6:9).[2] Again, the "unrighteous" are those for whom such practices characterize their habitual orientation. (See the further elaboration of this point below.)

Peter's teaching is entirely consistent with Paul's. He, too, states that God will judge "according to each one's deeds" (1 Peter 1:17), and that the

---

2. See also Ephesians 5:5–6.

practices of godly virtue will result in the "entrance into the eternal kingdom of our Lord and Savior Jesus Christ" (2 Peter 1:11). Peter does not wish us to confound these godly virtues with mere outward moralism or simply "being good." Rather, Peter has in mind the genuine fruits of a transformed, godly life, present in those in whom God's divine power is operative (2 Peter 1:3).

Revelation
The book of Revelation, quite appropriately, contains some key passages about the FJ, including the basis upon which it will proceed. Revelation 20:11–15 depicts the great white throne judgment, where the dead, "great and small," stand before the throne to await their awesome verdict. In verse 12, we read that God judges the dead "according to what they had done," which the next verse repeats for emphasis. In 21:7–8 we find a list of specific sins that exclude a person from eternal life. Then, in 22:12, Jesus states that he is "coming soon" to bring reward in order "to repay each one for what he has done."

Just What "Works" Does God Take into Account?
Until now, we have spoken generally of "deeds" or "works" that form the basis of the FJ. However, it is important to note that these "deeds" include also the words we say as well as the thoughts and inclinations of our hearts. Concerning our words, Jesus declared forcefully in Matthew 12:36–37:

> I tell you, on the day of judgment people will give account for every careless word they speak, for by your words you shall be justified, and by your words you shall be condemned.

Our innermost thoughts likewise fall under the all-encompassing divine scrutiny. First Corinthians 4:5 tells us that when the Lord returns he "will bring to light the things now hidden in darkness and will disclose the purposes of the heart." Similarly, Paul speaks of one's inward, secret thoughts that will excuse or accuse "on that day when . . . God judges the secrets of men" (Rom. 2:15–16).

Whose Works Will God Scrutinize at the Final Judgment?
In Question 15, we observed that the FJ will include every person who has ever lived, unbeliever and believer alike. However, we must address two issues.

First, how can God fairly judge the works of those unbelievers who never received an opportunity to put faith in Christ? Granting that millions have never heard of Christ and his offer of salvation, how would such a judgment on God's part be fair? Second, does not the teaching that the Christian is saved by faith and not by works (Eph. 2:8–9) contradict the idea that Christians will be judged by their works at the FJ?

How Can God Fairly Judge Those Who Have Never Heard the Gospel?

Those who reject Christ as savior will not escape condemnation at the FJ. As John states, "Whoever believes in him is not condemned, but whoever does not believe is condemned already, because he has not believed in the name of the only Son of God" (John 3:18). Deliverance from wrath is only for those who are in Christ, for whom there is no condemnation (Rom. 8:1). I shall demonstrate this in the next section of this chapter.

Nevertheless, how can God fairly judge those who never received an opportunity to hear the gospel, and therefore, had never received an opportunity to put their faith in Christ?

Whether or not a person has heard the gospel, God has endowed all human beings with a sufficient knowledge and revelation of himself to render them morally accountable. God has furnished all human beings with conscience (Rom. 2:14–15) and with an awareness of himself through nature, which leaves them without excuse (Rom. 1:19–20). Holloman states,

> Even if one is without direct knowledge of God's will and law, God can equitably judge thought, word, and deed in light of the individual's natural sense of right and wrong (Ezek 7:3, 27; 24:14; Mt 7:2; Lk 12:46–48; Rom 2:1, 14–15; Jas 3:1).[3]

In Romans 2:12–16, Paul teaches that those who sin without having received any special revelation (specifically the law) will perish for their sins based on the light they do have (i.e., conscience and God's revelation from creation) but nevertheless reject. On the other hand, those who have received special revelation of God's will shall be judged by it and condemned if they reject it. Indeed, their punishment will be even greater for having rejected the greater light.[4]

Even Though the Final Judgment Is Based on Works, We Are Nevertheless Saved by Grace

In John 5:24 Jesus says that the one who believes in him "does not come into judgment, but has passed from death to life."[5] At the same time, as we have already seen in the previous question, verses such as Romans 14:10 show that the FJ is a comprehensive judgment of everyone who has ever lived, including Christians. Indeed, in John 5:29, only five verses after saying that believers do not come into judgment, Jesus also declares that it is only "those who have

---

3. Henry W. Holloman, "Judgment," *Kregel Dictionary of the Bible and Theology* (Grand Rapids: Kregel, 2005), 263.

4. See Question 18, "Will There Be Degrees of Punishment Assigned to Unbelievers at the Final Judgment?"

5. See also John 3:17–18; Romans 5:8–9; 8:1; and 1 John 4:17.

done good" who will attain to the resurrection of life, whereas "those who have done evil" will face a resurrection unto judgment. Would this not imply that Christians are saved by what they do (i.e., by their works) and not by grace through faith?

The Fact and Necessity of Salvation by Grace

We begin first by emphasizing the biblical truth that no one will escape condemnation at the final judgment because his or her works can merit such deliverance. As the psalmist cries out, "If you, O LORD, should mark iniquities, O LORD, who could stand?" (Ps. 130:3). The answer, of course, is no one, including even the most holy saint of God.

Paul tells us that we cannot be justified by law keeping. In Romans 3:20 he informs us that "by works of law no human being will be justified in his sight."[6] To be "justified" means, among other things, to be declared "not guilty." Moreover, by "works of law," Paul is not limiting himself merely to the Mosaic Law—as if some other law might do the job where the Mosaic Law failed. Rather, he is talking about *any* attempt to make oneself right before God based on "law method" (i.e., by commandment keeping, regardless of what specific commandments one has in mind).[7] Paul removes all doubt about this when he proclaims, "if a law had been given that could give life, then righteousness would indeed be by the law" (Gal. 3:21).

The truth of Romans 3:23, then, is that all people, including believers, "have sinned and fall short of the glory of God." Note that Paul here surely has believers in mind when he says that even as we believers continually fall short, we are at the very same time being "justified by his grace as a gift, through the redemption that is in Christ Jesus."[8]

It is for this reason that salvation must necessarily be by grace through faith alone in Christ alone (Eph. 2:8–9).

The Role of Works as Evidence of Salvation

If we cannot be saved by our works for the reasons stated above, then in what sense are we judged by our works at the FJ? Simply stated, works provide the *evidence* that a person has been saved by grace alone through faith alone

---

6. See also Galatians 2:16.
7. The fact that the word "law" (*nomos*) is anarthrous (i.e., lacks the definite article) is consistent with the idea that Paul here rules out justification by *anything* which is of the nature or essence or character of law keeping.
8. My translation and conclusion take into account the following points of the Greek grammar: The verb translated "falling short, lacking" is *ysterountai*, which is a present indicative. The present tense can carry the sense of an ongoing or durative action. Then, the word that I have translated as "while being justified," is *dikaioumenoi*, which is a present passive participle. This participle takes its time from the main verb "falling short," with the sense that even as we are falling short, we are being justified freely (*dōrean*) through grace.

in Christ alone. Schreiner states, "It seems legitimate to say that works are the necessary evidence and fruit of a right relation with God. They demonstrate, although imperfectly, that one is truly trusting in Jesus Christ."[9]

So, then, the Christian is justified (declared "not guilty") by faith alone (Eph. 2:8–9), with good works serving as the evidence that this justification has in fact taken place (James 2:18). As Stott succinctly explains, "Works are never the ground or means of salvation, but they are the evidence of it, and therefore they constitute an excellent basis for judgment."[10]

A Few Observations about James 2:14–26

A few observations about James 2:14–26 are in order, since this passage has an important bearing on the role of works in salvation and therefore on the outcome of the FJ.

Some have pointed to verses 22 and 24 of this important chapter to argue that we are not justified by faith alone. Indeed, verse 24 states explicitly, "You see that a person is justified by works and not by faith alone." From this, some have concluded that we escape condemnation at the FJ because of our good works and not because of faith alone in Christ alone, as argued above. Furthermore, some have even tried to set what James teaches here against Paul's teaching of justification by faith alone, suggesting that they are at odds with one another.

James's teaching is entirely consistent with Paul's teaching that we are justified by faith alone. The apparent problem or contradiction disappears when we understand that Paul and James are writing for somewhat different purposes and use certain key terms with a bit of a different emphasis.[11]

First, James sometimes uses the term "faith" in this passage to refer to mere intellectual assent as opposed to genuine, saving belief. Note verse 14, where he says *that* faith (i.e., *that kind of* faith) cannot save; even the demons have that sort of faith (v. 19).

Second, when Paul says that we are not justified by works of law (Rom. 3:20; Gal. 3:21), he is talking about works through which one attempts to gain

---

9. Thomas Schreiner, "Justification Apart from Works: At the Final Judgment Works Will Confirm Justification," in *Four Views on the Role of Works at the Final Judgment*, eds. Alan P. Stanley and Stanley N. Gundry (Grand Rapids: Zondervan, 2013), 97.

10. John R. W. Stott, *What Christ Thinks of the Church* (Grand Rapids: Eerdmans, 1972), 80. Note that elsewhere, Schreiner eschews speaking of works as the "basis" for the FJ, while Stott speaks of works as forming "an excellent basis for judgment." Though their language is different, they are affirming the same truth. There is no reason one cannot speak of works as the "basis" for judgment if by that one means that works furnish the *evidential basis* on which one can discern and declare that salvation is a genuine, living reality for the one being judged.

11. In the discussion that follows, I am indebted to my colleague Robert Saucy and I have drawn upon some of his unpublished notes. I have condensed, summarized, and paraphrased some of his important thoughts on this in the next three paragraphs.

merit before God. James, on the other hand, is talking about works that express the genuineness of one's faith and are faith's natural outcome, which in a real sense "completed" it (v. 22).

Finally, Paul is using the term "justification" in the sense of a judicial or legal declaration of "not guilty." James places an emphasis on a declaration of righteousness that is based on the proof of faith as demonstrated in a person's works. Here the word "to justify" carries also the nuance of "*showing* to be righteous," as it arguably does in such passages as Matthew 12:37 and Luke 10:29. This is a bit of a different emphasis than in Paul's predominant use of the term, though one sees this sense of the word in Paul as well (Rom. 2:13, 15; 3:4).

A Word about Assurance at the Final Judgment
Since we are justified by faith alone, from this it follows that we can know even now how we will fare at the FJ, at least in terms of whether we will be condemned or delivered from condemnation on the last day. We have already seen throughout this chapter that the one who puts his or her faith in Christ does not come into judgment but has eternal life; I shall not rehearse those verses here.

Furthermore, just as works will serve as evidence at the FJ that we are truly children of God, even so they can serve that evidential function for us here and now. To cite but one example, John tells us,

> We know that we have passed out of death into life, because we love the brothers. Whoever does not love abides in death. (1 John 3:14)

John is surely not arguing that we always and perfectly love other Christians, for "If we say we have no sin, we deceive ourselves" (1 John 1:8). John's view, rather, is that the fundamental orientation of a genuine Christian is not to practice sin as the overall habit pattern of one's life, but to pursue a life of holiness from the heart (1 John 3:9).[12] Furthermore, John tells us in 1 John 3:14 that the outward evidence of this fundamental orientation, such as our love for the brethren, can provide us with assurance about our standing with God.

The flip side is that those who live in a way that seems fundamentally contrary to God's commands need to take seriously Paul's admonition, "Examine yourselves, to see whether you are in the faith" (2 Cor. 13:5). While Christians certainly do sin (1 John 1:8; 2:1; etc.)—sometimes to such an extent that God must chastise them even with physical death (e.g., 1

---

12. See the extended treatment of 1 John 3:9 in Question 27, "Will It Be Possible for Us to Sin in the Eternal State?"

Cor. 11:27–32)—it is also true that such a lifestyle may indicate a lack of true conversion to Christ, however loud and earnest one may protest to the contrary (Matt. 7:21–23).

REFLECTION QUESTIONS

1. We observed above that God takes into account not only our deeds but also our thoughts and words. How does the comprehensiveness of the FJ influence the way you live your life as a Christian?

2. Do you believe that it is fair for God to judge the works of those who have never heard the gospel? Reflect on the brief discussion given in this chapter, in formulating your answer.

3. How is a FJ based on works consistent with the teaching that we are saved by grace alone through faith alone in Christ alone?

4. Does James 2:14–26 contradict the teaching that we are saved by faith alone? Harmonize James's teaching with Paul's.

5. Discuss whether we can have assurance in this life that we will not be condemned at the FJ. If such assurance is possible, on what do we base it?

Will God Assign Rewards to Christians at the Final Judgment?

In this chapter, we shall focus on the rewards that God will bestow on believers at the final judgment (FJ), leaving for the next chapter the question of what punishments God will assign to unbelievers on that great day of reckoning.

The Fact of Rewards for Christians at the Final Judgment

Some of the verses that we have already considered in the previous two chapters point to the fact that God will reward believers at the FJ for their service. However, to establish this point firmly, we shall provide a quick overview of New Testament teaching, followed by a more detailed consideration of 1 Corinthians 3:8–15, which is one of the key passages on reward.

A Brief Overview of Reward in the New Testament

Our Lord himself had much to say about the bestowal of rewards for faithful service. He exhorts his disciples to stand firm in persecution, in the knowledge that their reward in heaven will be great.[1] He tells them not to invest their lives in the cares and pursuits of this world but to lay up for themselves imperishable treasure in heaven.[2] The most seemingly minor and trivial acts of service will not escape his notice, and even for these he shall compensate his children richly.[3] Moreover, he promises his disciples inexpressible delights, employing the figure of a banquet celebration to convey his point.[4]

---

1. Matthew 5:11–12; Luke 6:23.
2. Matthew 6:20; 19:21; Mark 10:21; Luke 12:33; 18:22.
3. Matthew 10:41–42.
4. Matthew 8:11; 22:1–10; 25:10; 26:29; Mark 14:25; Luke 13:28–29; 14:16–24; 22:16, 29–30.

The two very similar parables of the "talents" (Matt. 25:14–31) and the "minas" (Luke 19:12–26) contain important teaching about the rewards that our Lord will bestow in recompense for faithful service.

Turning to the epistles, Paul makes considerable reference to the rewards that Christians will receive at the FJ. He provides an extended discussion of this topic in 1 Corinthians 3:8–15 (see below). In 2 Timothy 4:7–8, Paul looks forward to being awarded what he calls "the crown of righteousness" as recompense for having "fought the good fight" and "finish[ing] the race."

Moving outside of Paul, we see that the author to the Hebrews declares that God "rewards those who seek him" (Heb. 11:6). He cites the example of Moses, who "considered the reproach of Christ greater wealth than the treasures of Egypt, for he was looking to the reward" (Heb. 11:26). Peter as well tells his readers of the imperishable, undefiled, and unfading inheritance that God has reserved for us in the life to come (1 Peter 1:4).

The theme of bestowing reward for faithfulness is dominant in Revelation. For instance, in Revelation 2:10 the Lord exhorts his persecuted saints not to fear suffering and even death, for he will award them "the crown of life." Moreover, in 22:12, speaking of his return, he promises to bring his recompense with him, "to repay everyone for what he has done."

1 Corinthians 3:8–15: An Extended Discussion on Reward

Because this passage is Paul's most detailed discussion on reward, we do well to consider it separately and in some detail. Verses 12–15 in particular read:

> Now if anyone builds on the foundation with gold, silver, precious stones, wood, hay, straw—each one's work will become manifest, for the Day will disclose it, because it will be revealed by fire, and the fire will test what sort of work each one has done. If the work that anyone has built on the foundation survives, he will receive a reward. If anyone's work is burned up, he will suffer loss, though he himself will be saved, but only as through fire.

Commentators point out that the context of Paul's remarks is the day of judgment, which he calls simply "the Day."[5] Thus, this passage is highly relevant for our purposes here. The "foundation" of which he speaks is the gospel of Christ—indeed, Christ himself—which Paul faithfully set forth and upon which others have built.

5. Roy E. Ciampa and Brian S. Rosner, *1 Corinthians*, PNTC (Grand Rapids: Eerdmans, 2010), 154; Gordon Fee, *First Epistle to the Corinthians*, NICNT (Grand Rapids: Eerdmans, 2014), 154; David E. Garland, *1 Corinthians*, BECNT (Grand Rapids: Baker, 2003), 117.

Some commentators say that Paul has in mind primarily leaders who have labored with varying degrees of effectiveness in building up the church.[6] On this reckoning, Paul is admonishing these leaders to build well upon the foundation in their work of the ministry, employing materials suitable for the purpose and executing their responsibilities with appropriate skill. However, commentators also point out that Paul's exhortation has a more general applicability, which "is signaled with the words, *if anyone builds*."[7] This is because "each member has an assignment in this building project."[8]

We note that Paul clearly has Christians in view here, including even those who build poorly on the foundation. He distinguishes these workers— even the sloppy ones—from the false teachers who have "another Jesus" (2 Cor. 11:4) and who actively attempt to *destroy* the building (1 Cor. 3:17).[9]

Considering the various building materials that Paul lists, we should not parse these too specifically but see them rather as falling into one of two categories: durable materials that can withstand the test by fire, and those that cannot and will be consumed by it.[10] The "gold, silver, [and] precious stones" characterize the former, while the "wood, hay, [and] straw" represent the latter (v. 12). The point is, the wise worker will "use fit materials and follow the plans of the architect (who is God, not Paul) and the building code,"[11] which would be fidelity to the teaching of Christ and him crucified. As for the shoddy materials specifically, Paul hints at what these might be in the verses that follow. In the context of the passage, it appears that "the building materials that will be *burned up* are those in keeping with human wisdom instead of the wisdom of God, which is the fullness of the message of the cross."[12]

Depending upon the quality of the work performed and in keeping with the materials employed, God will scrutinize the work and bestow reward upon it accordingly. It is very important to observe that what is "assayed in a divine firestorm" in this passage is the quality of the Christian's work and not the Christian him or herself.[13] Specifically, and as virtually all evangelical commentators acknowledge, the issue is not about whether one will be saved but rather about whether the Christian's work of service will merit reward: "What is consumed is the building, not the workers as evil doers. . . . The fiery

---

6. Ciampa and Rosner, *1 Corinthians*, 153, 155; Fee, *First Epistle to the Corinthians*, 156.
7. Ciampa and Rosner, *1 Corinthians*, 154.
8. Garland, *1 Corinthians*, 115. See also Blomberg, who argues against limiting these admonitions to church leaders or the work to "doctrine or teaching" or "to working specifically for the church" (Craig Blomberg, *1 Corinthians*, NIVAC [Grand Rapids: Zondervan, 1994], 74 n5; see also 79).
9. Garland, *1 Corinthians*, 115–16; Blomberg, *1 Corinthians*, 81.
10. Anthony C. Thiselton, *The First Epistle to the Corinthians*, NIGTC (Grand Rapids: Eerdmans, 2000), 311.
11. Garland, *1 Corinthians*, 115.
12. Ciampa and Rosner, *1 Corinthians*, 156. See also Fee, *First Epistle to the Corinthians*, 151.
13. Garland, *1 Corinthians*, 117.

test exposes what has lasting value."[14] Here the "fire" is not the fire of hell, which punishes the finally impenitent, but is the fire that tests what is of permanent value of a Christian's earthly service. This should not in any way be confused with salvation by works, but speaks "instead to Christ's assessment of the way Christians have lived their lives subsequent to salvation. . . . These works flow from faith and include everything that pleases God, aligns itself with kingdom priorities, and advances his purposes in the world."[15]

God will reward the one who builds well and whose work survives (v. 14). Paul does not specify just what this reward entails in the immediate context, though in 4:5 he says that at the judgment, "each one will receive his commendation from God." Thus, the reward consists, at least in part, in the inexpressible joy of receiving the master's praise for a job well done.

As for the "loss" that one will suffer if his or her work is burned up (v. 15), Paul does not elaborate on this. We know that this is not the loss of salvation, since the same verse states explicitly that such a one will be saved, but "only as through fire." Commentators frequently liken Paul's expression to the English idiom "being saved by the skin of one's teeth"—that is, that one escapes, as if from a burning building, but narrowly.[16] At all events, what is lost is the prospect of reward; and, most likely, such a Christian will experience chastisement and a sense of shame at Christ's return. Sproule, in an interesting article on the judgment seat of Christ in 2 Corinthians 5:10, makes this observation, which is equally relevant here:

> At the *Bema* [judgment seat] believers will be rewarded for lives of faithful service and obedience. . . . However there is strong evidence to indicate that believers, at the judgment seat of Christ, will suffer some kind of divine chastisement for slothful, careless lives. This involves more than simply the loss of reward. Concerning details, the Bible is silent.[17]

John may have the same idea in mind when he exhorts his "little children" to "abide" in Christ, so that at his appearing they "may have confidence and not shrink from him" (1 John 2:28). The chastisement here is considerable: the shame of having failed their master in the important tasks he entrusted them to do, whether through selfish ambition, laziness, or other moral failings. This is the opposite of the joy of those who hear the much-coveted accolade, "Well

---

14. Ibid., 118. So Fee: "It is the work and not the worker that is burned up" (Fee, *First Epistle to the Corinthians*, 155).
15. Blomberg, *1 Corinthians*, 74.
16. Ibid., 75; Ciampa and Rosner, *1 Corinthians*, 157; Fee, *First Epistle to the Corinthians*, 156; Thiselton, *The First Epistle to the Corinthians*, 315.
17. J. A. Sproule, "'Judgment Seat' or 'Awards Podium,'" *Grace Theological Journal*, 13, no. 1 (Spring 1974): 4–5.

done, good and faithful servant" (Matt. 25:21). Furthermore, if the parable of the stewards in Luke 12:41–48 includes in its description genuine Christians who have nevertheless been unfaithful to varying degrees in discharging their leadership responsibilities, it provides additional proof of chastisement, possibly even in the form of a "severe beating" at the FJ.[18]

Navigating this issue of a seemingly fruitless life resulting in a loss of reward but nevertheless obtaining final salvation is admittedly a bit tricky. On the one hand, we saw earlier that good works provide evidence of a genuinely regenerated life, and in that sense the FJ for Christians is based on works.[19] We shall again confront this fact below, when we consider the parable of the talents in Matthew 25. On the other hand, Paul's teaching in this passage also shows that it is possible for a genuine Christian to do shoddy work and have his or her work burned up while at the same time being saved, i.e., making it into the kingdom smelling a bit like smoke.

One factor to keep in mind is that Paul is probably characterizing the person's life overall, but does not intend his description to be absolute. Just as Christians who live a productive, godly life are not without flaws, even so the generally "fruitless" Christian may have *something* to show for his or her service to Christ.[20] Regardless, what we can say is that the Lord is able to search the heart and know those who are truly his children, rewarding or chastising them as appropriate for each case, while punishing those who fundamentally oppose him with eternal separation from him. In any case, a genuine Christian inclined to lackadaisical living should take seriously the warnings of Scripture, for whatever having one's works burned to the ground may mean exactly, it is not something the wise Christian will want to experience.

Verses That Show Varying Degrees of Reward

The verses considered above demonstrate the fact of reward for faithful service. However, we also find verses that, in addition to establishing the mere fact of reward, also demonstrate that Christians will receive different degrees of reward. God bases the degree of reward upon the quality and extent of service for him. At the same time, all Christians receive the fundamental reward of eternal life as their base pay, so to speak. Considering specifically Paul's teaching, Geerhardus Vos observes,

> With Paul the judgment is an event that will make discrimination as to future rank and enjoyment in the life to come between individual Christians. The differences established may

---

18. See the detailed discussion of this parable in Question 18.
19. See Question 16, "On What Is the Final Judgment Based?"
20. I am indebted to my colleague Henry Holloman for this insight.

and will be great, but the range covered by them lies within the realm of salvation.[21]

The parable of the laborers in Matthew 20:1–16 well illustrates the latter part of Vos's observation. Here, all of the laborers received the same wage, regardless of when they began their work. Following on the heels of his discussion in Matthew 19 about inheriting eternal life in the kingdom, we may reasonably conclude that all of God's servants in one sense receive the same reward, which is everlasting life. That said, we also see indications that "within the realm of salvation" the Lord indeed rewards his servants variously.

Matthew 25:14–30

In Matthew 25:14–30, Jesus presents a parable of the talents, in which a master entrusts his servants with varying sums of money, apportioned according to their managerial skills, to invest for the master's benefit. Depending upon the acumen and care with which the servants managed the money, they received varying degrees of reward in the form of greater responsibility to manage an even greater share of the master's assets in the future.

Though the exact value of a talent is difficult to pin down, particularly when trying to correlate it with modern values of currency, one finds general agreement that "the sums are vast."[22] The slave to whom the master entrusted five talents received an overwhelming sum with which to work. But even the slave who was to manage but one talent was still responsible for a huge amount.

Although Carson cautions against attempting to identify too specifically just what these "talents" represent,[23] they "probably symbolize personal gifts and abilities."[24] Morris is likely correct when he says that this parable "starts with the fact of the different gifts to be found in God's servants and brings out the way they use (or do not use) those gifts."[25]

Even though the first two slaves are both given "many things" in recompense for their wise investing, some commentators, such as Carson, believe that rewards bestowed are likely not identical. Rather, each servant experiences "increased responsibility and a share in the master's joy to the limits of each faithful slave's capacity."[26] However, even though "the reward of earnings

---

21. Geerhardus Vos, *The Pauline Eschatology* (Grand Rapids: Eerdmans, 1961), 270.
22. Donald A. Carson, *Matthew,* EBC (Grand Rapids: Zondervan, 2005), 579. See also Leon Morris, *The Gospel according to Matthew*, PNTC (Grand Rapids: Eerdmans, 2000), 627; Michael J. Wilkins, *Matthew*, NIVAC (Grand Rapids: Zondervan, 2004), 806.
23. Carson, *Matthew*, 580.
24. Donald A. Hagner, *Matthew 14–28*, WBC (Dallas: Word, 1995), 734.
25. Morris, *The Gospel according to Matthew*, 626.
26. Carson, *Matthew*, 580.

bestowed may differ," Wilkins observes, "Both servants received identical joy in the presence of their master."[27]

The third servant in this parable clearly is not saved. In that regard the parable differs from Paul's discussion in 1 Corinthians 3, in which all of the builders in question are Christians and therefore saved—albeit with the loss of reward for those whose work is slovenly. We observe the third servant's lack of salvation from the following: (1) his malignant attitude toward the master (vv. 24–25); (2) his characterization by the master as "wicked" (v. 26); and (3) the statement that he, unlike the others, will not enter into the joy of his master but be cast "into the outer darkness" where there will be "weeping and gnashing of teeth" (v. 30), which is an unmistakable reference to eternal punishment.

Luke 19:12–26

Luke 19:12–26 presents a very similar parable to the one just considered in Matthew—so similar, in fact, that some believe these to be simply different versions of the same parable. However, they are different enough for us to consider them distinct teachings that Jesus probably presented on different occasions.[28] One of the key differences is that Jesus expressly teaches that there are varying degrees of rewards bestowed, whereas in the similar account in Matthew such differences may be only implied.

In this account, the master entrusts each slave with one "mina," which is perhaps equivalent to four months' wages.[29] While this sum is significant, it is not as vast as in the previous parable. Nevertheless, the basic point is essentially the same: The master assigns considerable resources to his servants and expects them to invest these resources well.

When the master settles accounts with his servants, they report on how much of a return they have to show for their efforts. Here Jesus very explicitly presents different degrees of reward in the form of "a prominent administrative role in the kingdom,"[30] expressed as having jurisdiction over a number of cities commensurate with the number of minas their investment returned. As Green observes, "In this parable, 'more' turns out to be not only more in terms of the original distribution of money, but also a share in the newly secured imperial rule."[31]

Of what does this "imperial rule" and "prominent administrative role in the kingdom" consist? Could Jesus be speaking here of leadership over literal cities, or do the cities represent some other sort of responsibility or service? Here we ought not to be too dogmatic. Most commentators would probably

---

27. Wilkins, *Matthew*, 807.
28. Darrell Bock, *Luke 9:51–24:53*, BECNT (Grand Rapids: Baker, 1996), 1529, 1534.
29. Ibid., 1533.
30. Ibid., 1536.
31. Joel B. Green, *The Gospel of Luke*, NICNT (Grand Rapids: Eerdmans, 1997), 680.

take the cities as symbolic. However, assuming a literal millennium, the presence of literal cities over which the saints will reign seems likely.[32] Even if one does not hold to a literal millennium, there is every reason to grant the presence of literal cities on the new earth—the New Jerusalem being preeminent among them.[33] Regardless of whether one takes these "cities" as literal or figurative, the point is the same: Jesus will reward his followers in accordance with how faithful they were in this life in their service for him, and this reward will consist, at least in part, in further opportunities for continued service.[34]

Though not stated as explicitly as the parable in Matthew, we have good reason to conclude that the third servant in this parable is not genuinely saved, either. Bock opines,

> The third servant represents people who are related to the king in that they are associated with the community and have responsibility in it. Nevertheless their attitude shows that they do not see God as gracious and that they have not really trusted him.[35]

The Nature of the Reward

Is there anything more that we can say about the nature of the reward that we shall receive?

Scripture only gives us some hints about the nature of the reward that believers may expect. Perhaps this is because the joys awaiting us are beyond anything we could presently conceive anyway (1 Cor. 2:9). Yet, God has revealed to us something of these matters by his spirit (v. 10), even if we now can only understand such matters in a glass, darkly (1 Cor. 13:12).

Perhaps we may best consider our eternal reward by examining what we shall do in the eternal state. I treat some of the most important of these activities in Question 25, "What Will We Do in the Eternal State?"

Does "Earning" Reward Contradict Salvation by Grace?

Some may question how it is possible for us to "earn" reward if salvation is by grace, as the Bible repeatedly states (e.g., Eph. 2:8–10). Our Lord himself admonishes us, "So you also, when you have done all that you were

---

32. Bock suggests that this text indicates "full participation in the exercise of the kingdom's authority in the consummation (cf. 1 Cor. 6:2–3)," in which "the kingdom is not to be equated with the eternal state or the church," but, presumably, the millennium (*Luke 9:51–24:53*, 1536; see also Bock, *Luke 9:51–24:53*, 1180). See the earlier discussion on the millennium in Question 15.

33. See Question 23, "What Is the New Jerusalem?"

34. For a further discussion of this point, see Question 25, "What Will We Do in the Eternal State?"

35. Bock, *Luke 9:51–24:53*, 1542.

commanded, say, 'We are unworthy servants; we have only done what was our duty'" (Luke 17:10). How, then, is it possible for us to merit anything at all before God?

It is certainly true that salvation is by grace and that God is under no obligation to bestow reward for our works, even if they were perfect works, which of course they are not. As Jesus makes clear in the above parable, God owes us nothing. We are his creatures in his universe and we are obligated to keep his moral law perfectly as our duty and without the slightest requirement on his part to reward this in any way. At the same time, God freely chooses, as a matter of grace, to reward our service for him, purely out of the bounty of his love. This graciousness becomes all the more incomprehensible when we stop to consider that any truly good works that we perform are themselves the result of his grace enabling us to perform them (John 15:5; Phil. 2:13). So here, God in effect rewards us for his own good work in us!

Furthermore, even if one were to argue that we somehow deserve something from God for our efforts, what God bestows upon us is entirely out of proportion to any service we may have performed. The parable of the minas, examined earlier, shows a huge disproportion between the work tendered to the master and the reward he bestows upon his servants.[36] Even the worst trials in this life that we steadfastly endure for our Lord's sake are but "light momentary affliction," which are "preparing us for an eternal weight of glory beyond all comparison" (2 Cor. 4:17).

REFLECTION QUESTIONS

1. Discuss the ways in which the knowledge that the Lord rewards faithful service affects (or should affect) your daily decisions, such as how you spend your time, money, energies, etc.

2. Reflecting on 1 Corinthians 3:8–15, consider what practical steps you can take to "build on the foundation" with the proper building materials.

3. React to the idea that there will be varying degrees of reward in the eternal state. Do you find this encouraging? Comforting? Unsettling?

4. In what sense do we "earn" reward? How does this fit with God giving us salvation by grace?

5. Contemplate the possibility of loss at the FJ. Does this prospect cause you concern? How ought you to respond to this concern?

---

36. Robert H. Stein, *Luke*, NAC 24 (Nashville: Broadman, 1992), 473.

Will There Be Degrees of Punishment Assigned to Unbelievers at the Final Judgment?

In the previous question, I demonstrated that God will bestow rewards on Christians at the final judgment (FJ). I also showed that the amount of reward bestowed will vary from Christian to Christian, depending upon the quality and effort expended in "building on the foundation" of Christ.

In this chapter, we shall consider the flip side of God's recompense for believers at the FJ, which is the punishments that God will assign to unbelievers who have finally rejected him and his offer of salvation. In Question 30 and Question 31 I shall discuss at length the *nature* of punishment in hell, and so I shall say only a little about that here. Instead, this chapter shall focus more narrowly on the issue of whether there are *degrees* of punishment in hell, and if so, just what this entails.

Verses That Show Varying Degrees of Punishment

Several passages lead us to conclude that the wicked will not all be punished exactly alike.

Matthew 10:15; 11:20–24; Luke 10:12–16

In these passages, Jesus commissions his disciples to preach in the surrounding towns ahead of him. He instructs them on how to handle both acceptance and rejection by those who hear the message. Concerning those who may prove hostile to their preaching he declares, "I say to you, it will be more bearable on the day of judgment for the land of Sodom and Gomorrah than for that town" (Matt. 10:15).

Likewise, in Matthew 11:20–24, Jesus "began to denounce the cities where most of his mighty works had been done, because they did not repent" (v. 20), specifically Chorazin, Bethsaida, and Capernaum. He draws a comparison to the ancient judgments against Tyre and Sidon, and again against Sodom, and declares that "in the day of judgment" it will be "more tolerable" for these exceedingly wicked cities than it shall be for the cities in which Jesus performed his many and convincing signs.

These verses make two facts clear: (1) There will be degrees of punishment for sin on the day of judgment; and (2) the reason for these differences lies in the heinousness of the sins committed—which, in turn, relates to the degree of light that they had received. As debauched and wicked as, for example, Sodom may have been, God holds the cities in which Jesus performed his miracles to an even greater level of accountability, because of the clarity of truth that he had revealed to them. Here they had the Son of God himself, performing miracles in their midst, and yet stubbornly persisted in unbelief. Amazingly, Jesus states that even a city as wicked as Sodom would have repented had they witnessed the signs that he performed. This highlights the incredible degree of hardness and depravity of the towns that Jesus excoriates, accounting for the greater severity of the sentence that he will pronounce against them on the last day.

Luke 12:41–48

Luke 12:41–48, known as the parable of the stewards, is an oft-cited passage used to demonstrate that God assigns degrees of punishment in hell.[1] Verses 45–48 in particular seem to make this point:

> But if that servant says to himself, "My master is delayed in coming," and begins to beat the male and female servants, and to eat and drink and get drunk, the master of that servant will come on a day when he does not expect him and at an hour he does not know, and will cut him in pieces and put him with the unfaithful. And that servant who knew his master's will but did not get ready or act according to his will, will receive a severe beating. But the one who did not know, and did what deserved a beating, will receive a light beating. Everyone to whom much was given, of him much will be required, and from him to whom they entrusted much, they will demand more.

---

1. Some scholars who use this text to demonstrate this are Robert Culver, *Systematic Theology: Biblical and Historical* (Fearn, Ross-shire, UK: Mentor, 2005), 1078; Henry W. Holloman, "Judgment," *Kregel Dictionary of the Bible and Theology* (Grand Rapids: Kregel, 2005), 264; Robert A. Morey, *Death and the Afterlife* (Minneapolis: Bethany, 1984), 250; Roger Nicole, "Universalism: Will Everyone Be Saved?" *Christianity Today*, March 20, 1987, 38; and Robert Reymond, "Dr. John Stott on Hell," *Presbyterion* 16 (Spring 1990): 49.

This passage unquestionably teaches that there are degrees of punishment. What may not be so clear, however, is whether it teaches about degrees of punishment *in hell*. That is, in order to cite this text as direct evidence for this purpose, one must first establish that the beatings of which Jesus speaks are the infernal torments of the damned. However, this, according to some of the best commentators on Luke, is unlikely.

Bock says that this parable presents "stewards" as falling into "four categories in two classes." In the first class we have one faithful steward (vv. 42–44), whom the master rewards appropriately for his efforts. But in the second class we have "three types of unfaithful stewards (12:45–48)." The first of these is "blatantly disobedient, where what is done is the opposite of what is commanded" (vv. 45–46). He receives the horrific punishment of being "cut into pieces." The second unfaithful steward (v. 47) is guilty of "conscious disobedience" but is not as debauched as in the first case. The master beats him severely, but not as badly as the first. Finally, Jesus presents the third unfaithful steward (v. 48a), who commits "disobedience in ignorance." This third steward, while still deserving and receiving chastisement, incurs a notably lighter sentence than the second, and one far less severe than the first.[2]

The first unfaithful slave seems clearly not to be saved, as seen by his description as "unbelieving" (*apistos*) in verse 46 and by the extreme severity of his punishment.[3] Bock takes issue with the RSV's weak rendering of "punish" for the Greek word *dichotomēsei*, pointing out that this word is more properly rendered, "to dismember, to cut in two."[4] Further, as Stein comments, "The parallel in Matthew 24:51 makes clear that the servant receives an eternal punishment because he goes with the hypocrites to the place 'where there will be weeping and gnashing of teeth.'"[5] Bock likens this servant to Judas, as well as to the Jewish leaders who rejected Jesus—individuals for whom perdition was assured.[6]

Thus far, the parable would seem to be relevant for our purposes. However, these same commentators doubt that the remaining two unfaithful slaves are unsaved, and these interpreters do not take the lighter punishments to be the punishments of hell. On this point, Stein avers:

> Whereas the evil servant of 12:45–46 seems to receive eternal punishment, the evil servant of 12:47 is given "many blows" but not, apparently, eternal punishment. He appears rather to be "saved, but only as through fire" (1 Cor. 3:15, RSV).

---

2. Darrell Bock, *Luke 9:51–24:53*, BECNT (Grand Rapids: Baker, 1996), 1180.
3. Ibid., 1182. Bock argues for taking *apistos* as "unbelieving" rather than simply as "unfaithful."
4. Ibid.
5. Robert H. Stein, *Luke*, NAC 24 (Nashville: Broadman, 1992), 362; cf. 359.
6. Bock, *Luke 9:51–24:53*, 1185–86.

> Although he knew better (was wise), he did not prepare him-
> self (was not faithful) and so will be severely punished. The
> one who was unprepared due to ignorance of these teachings
> will be treated less severely, for the guiding principle is that
> judgment is dispensed according to the knowledge that one
> possesses.[7]

It is true, according to Bock, that the second category of unfaithfulness, which consists of "ignoring Jesus' instruction," is serious enough to merit "a severe beating" (*darēsetai*), which "refers to harsh discipline."[8] This servant's guilt is greater than that of the third unfaithful servant due to the degree of knowledge that carries with it increased responsibilities. At the same time, Bock thinks it possible that this "less disobedient slave is disciplined but does not lack a relationship to the master (i.e., is grouped with the unbelievers)— unlike the previous servant," i.e., the one who is cut into pieces.[9] If the second unfaithful servant does not lack a relationship to the master, then this certainly would be true of the third unfaithful steward as well, whose punishment is even lighter than the one received by the second.

If these commentators are correct and only the first of the three disobedient slaves receives eternal punishment, then there would be no direct evidence from this particular parable that there are degrees of punishment in hell. Rather, what it would prove *directly* is that unfaithful Christians— specifically those in positions of leadership (as the context seems to indicate)—will receive degrees of *chastisement* in recompense for varying degrees of unfaithfulness, specifically because of their failure to discharge properly their leadership responsibilities among God's people.

That said, it is surely appropriate to make a broader application of the principles from this text to the question before us. This text shows that "knowledge influences the severity of the punishment, which in turn is meted out with various intensities."[10] Stein concurs, concluding that "the guiding principle" that one gleans from this parable is "that judgment is dispensed according to the knowledge that one possesses."[11]

These commentators have correctly identified a key point. However, can we use this principle to argue for degrees of punishment specifically in hell? I fail to see why not. Why would God not apply this principle to the wicked

---

7. Stein, *Luke,* 359. On the chastisement of unfaithful Christians at the *bema* judgment, see the discussion in Question 17.
8. Bock, *Luke 9:51–24:53*, 1184.
9. Ibid.
10. Ibid.
11. Robert H. Stein, *Luke*, NAC 24 (Nashville: Broadman, 1992), 359.

in hell every bit as much as he would to Christians at the final judgment?[12] It seems eminently reasonable that he would, and it would be special pleading to conclude otherwise.

Hebrews 10:26–31

This passage speaks of those who at one time professed the faith but deliberately and willfully have come to reject and profane it. Specifically, it addresses the sin of willful and blatant apostasy. The key portion of the passage in relation to our question is verse 29, which reads, "How much worse punishment, do you think, will be deserved by the one who has trampled underfoot the Son of God, and has profaned the blood of the covenant by which he was sanctified, and has outraged the Spirit of grace?" Not surprisingly, some have cited this text in proof of degrees of punishment in hell.[13]

The author specifically compares the greatly more serious offence of rejecting Christ's forgiving and sanctifying work under the new covenant with violating the Mosaic Law under the old. Those who commit the former offence will receive "much worse punishment" than the latter. The greater degree of light that they have rejected greatly multiplies their guilt and corresponding punishment. Having at one time associated themselves with the Christian community, these have now "profaned the blood of the covenant" that in some sense had at one time "sanctified" or set them apart, and they have "outraged the Spirit of grace," the influences of whom they had tasted firsthand. These are the same sorts of persons whom the author had already mentioned in 6:4–8[14] (i.e., individuals who had hardened themselves to such a degree that repentance no longer remained even a possibility).

As with our previous consideration of the parable of the stewards, it may be that this passage does not directly demonstrate degrees of punishment in hell. That is because the author seems to be drawing the contrast between punishment in the form of an earthly death penalty for Mosaic violations, as contrasted with eternal punishment for spurning the new covenant. As Lane explains the argument's logic, "If disregard for the Mosaic Law was appropriately punished, neglect of the salvation announced in the gospel must inevitably be catastrophic."[15] This is not to deny that "the faithfulness or disobedience of OT people had eternal consequences."[16] Rather, the point is that the author may be focusing simply on the temporal and earthly consequences

---

12. On the question of whether some Christians will experience some form of chastisement at the FJ, see Question 17.
13. E.g., Morey, *Death and the Afterlife*, 154.
14. William L. Lane, *Hebrews 9–13*, WBC 47B (Dallas: Word, 1991), 291.
15. Ibid., 293.
16. Gareth Lee Cockerill, *The Epistle to the Hebrews*, NICNT (Grand Rapids: Eerdmans, 2012), 488.

of violating the law under the old covenant and then contrasting that with the far graver eternal consequences for blatant apostasy under the new.

Nevertheless, and as we saw in the case of the parable in Luke, we may use this passage to show degrees of punishment in hell, albeit indirectly. It, too, firmly establishes that the greater degree of light and spiritual influences one has received, the greater degree of responsibility that comes packaged with it. The particular species of unbelief cataloged here is beyond typical or garden variety unbelief, as it were. As Lane explains,

> The heinous character of this offense resides in the fact that it occurred after the reception of *tēn epignōsin tēs alētheias*, "the full knowledge of the truth." . . . The term *epignōsis* implies "a penetrating and certain knowledge," a clear perception of the truth. . . . The measure of privilege distinguishing the new covenant from the old necessarily defines the extent of the peril to which those who spurn its provisions expose themselves.[17]

From the foregoing, it is clear that there are degrees of guiltworthiness in rejecting God's provision of salvation in Christ. From this, it is entirely reasonable to conclude that there would be degrees of punishment in hell corresponding to this.

How Might the Punishments of Hell Differ?

In what sense might someone's punishment in hell be "worse" or "lighter" than another's? How are degrees of punishment even possible, if suffering in hell is as bad as it gets? Besides, hell's punishment is eternal in any case, so duration cannot be a distinguishing factor. Is it a matter of intensity? The kind of punishment? Some combination of these?

The nature of hell's punishment is important enough to merit two questions in this book.[18] These chapters provide an overall treatment of what hell is like, and one should consult them for more details. Without repeating the details laid out in those chapters, I will simply note that whatever else hell may entail, a key aspect of eternal punishment is God "giving up" the sinner to himself or herself. Such suffering will take place from the inside out, as it were. The wicked will suffer the natural consequences of rejecting God and his goodness toward them. They will experience the pain of complete abandonment, remorse unmingled with comfort, and the relentless torments of their own consciences, which will burn forever but never finally consume them. This cup they will drink to the full, experiencing unmitigated pain in body and soul.

---

17. Lane, *Hebrews 9–13*, 292, 294.
18. See Question 30, "What Is Hell Like?" and Question 31, "Are the Fires of Hell Literal?"

At the same time, it seems likely that not all people will experience in the same way what is in one sense the identical condition of complete abandonment. That is, the peculiar moral condition of the sinner, which does vary from individual to individual, will affect directly the intensity and quality of suffering that each person feels. Erickson states the matter well:

> To some extent, the different degrees of punishment reflect the fact that hell is God's leaving sinful man with the particular character that he fashioned for himself in this life. The misery one will experience from having to live with one's wicked self eternally will be proportionate to his degree of awareness of precisely what he was doing when he chose evil.[19]

There is, we should observe, good reason to think that our enjoyment of eternal reward will work in analogous fashion. That is, while everyone on the new earth will in one sense be rewarded identically with the divine presence, and therefore be as blessed as he or she can possibly be, we may also differ in our capacities for enjoying God, based upon our character that we have formed in this present life.

How Will God Punish Those Who Never Heard the Gospel?

One of the most commonly asked questions in relation to the fate of the unsaved is: How could God punish those who have never heard the gospel? We have already addressed that issue sufficiently in Question 16. Here again, we note that everyone will be judged based upon what they do with the light that they have. Those who have no special revelation from God nevertheless have the light of conscience and creation, and God will punish them for violating that light. On the other hand, as we have seen, greater light carries with it greater responsibility, together with more severe punishment for repudiating that light.

REFLECTION QUESTIONS

1. Of the biblical arguments presented at the beginning of this chapter, which do you consider the strongest for making the case that there are degrees of punishment in hell? Do you believe that any of the verses put forth in support of this conclusion fail to do so?

2. In the parable of the stewards, do you agree with commentators (such as Bock) who say that two of the three disobedient servants are actually

---

19. Millard Erickson, *Christian Theology* (Grand Rapids: Baker, 1985), 1240.

believers? If so, what is your reaction to what Jesus says will happen to them?

3. Discuss this statement of Erickson: "To some extent, the different degrees of punishment reflect the fact that hell is God's leaving sinful man with the particular character that he fashioned for himself in this life." What are the implications of this for how we live our lives now?

4. Have you encountered in popular preaching or in your discussions with other Christians statements such as, "sin is sin" and "all sins are the same"? Do you agree or disagree with this, and why?

5. Are you troubled over the question of how God can punish those who never heard the gospel? Does the notion that different degrees of light carry different degrees of responsibility clarify any aspect of this issue for you?

What Will the Resurrection Body Be Like? (Part 1)

> And so the King Christ Jesus was put to death in the flesh and was resurrected an invisible spirit creature.[1]

> Whether [the body of Jesus] was dissolved into gasses or whether it is still preserved somewhere as the grand memorial of God's love . . . no one knows.[2]

> There is no article of the Christian faith which has encountered such opposition as that of the resurrection of the flesh. (St. Augustine)[3]

We are not surprised when a cult of Christianity, such as the Jehovah's Witnesses (cited in the first two quotes above), vehemently denies the doctrine of Christ's bodily resurrection. However, as we observed in Question 2, a declining number of Americans in general believe in Christ's bodily resurrection, and far fewer still hold out hope for the resurrection of their own bodies. Sadly, these numbers include many who profess to be Christians.

The resurrection of the body—both Christ's and ours—is a foundational teaching of Christianity and central to the Christian's "blessed hope." With so many conflicting and confused voices, it is more critical than ever to

---

1. Watch Tower Bible and Tract Society, *Let God Be True* (Brooklyn: Watch Tower Bible and Tract Society, 1946), 122.
2. Charles Taze Russell, *Studies in the Scriptures,* 2:129, cited in Ron Rhodes, *Reasoning from the Scriptures with the Jehovah's Witnesses* (Eugene, OR: Harvest House, 1993), 175.
3. Augustine, *Exposition on Psalm 89,* 32.

understand what the Bible teaches about the resurrection. In fact, this issue is so important that we shall devote two questions to it.

In this question, I shall demonstrate the following:

1. Christ's resurrection body establishes the pattern for ours.

2. The resurrection body of Christ, and therefore of believers, is a *body of literal flesh*.

Then, in the next question, I shall establish these truths:

3. The resurrection body is a *glorified* body of literal flesh.

4. The resurrection body is a glorified version of the *same* body that died and was buried.

5. The wicked will likewise have resurrected bodies of flesh, but unlike those of believers, these will not be glorified.

Christ's Resurrection Body Is the Pattern for Ours

Scripture teaches clearly that Christ's resurrection is the pattern for ours. Consider Philippians 3:21, in which Paul declares that the Lord Jesus "will transform our lowly body to be like his glorious body, by the power that enables him even to subject all things to himself." In 1 Corinthians 15:49, where Paul is specifically discussing the nature of Christ's resurrection body and of ours, he states, "Just as we have borne the image of the man of dust, we shall also bear the image of the man of heaven." The apostle John makes the same point in 1 John 3:2.

What this means is that when we examine the biblical descriptions of Christ's postresurrection body, we may take them as specifying what our own resurrection bodies will be like. Now, at this point Jesus is the only human being who has a resurrected body.[4] Therefore, if we want to know what a resurrection body will be like, it makes sense for us to look at his. As we ponder the characteristics of Christ's body as detailed in the gospel accounts, coupled with the descriptions of the resurrection body found elsewhere in Scripture, we can discover all that God has seen fit to reveal about the redemption of our own bodies.

---

4. While it is true that others died and were raised before Christ—such as the widow's son (Luke 7:12–15), Jairus's daughter (Luke 8:41–42, 49–56), and Lazarus (John 11:41–44)— these resuscitations were not to immortal life but to "natural life," and the individuals so raised went on to die again. See Robert Culver, *Systematic Theology: Biblical and Historical* (Fearn, Ross-shire, UK: Mentor, 2005), 1052.

The Resurrection Body Is a Literal Body of Literal Flesh

Despite the claims of some, Jesus Christ rose from the dead in a literal body of literal flesh. Consequently, we, too, shall rise in a body of literal flesh.

Biblical Evidence for the Resurrection of the Flesh

Luke 24:39

Several passages clearly establish that Jesus rose in a body of flesh. However, Luke 24:39 is sufficient all by itself to remove any doubt about this.

In one of Jesus's appearances to his disciples after his resurrection, they were frightened and supposed that they were seeing a spirit or ghostly apparition. Jesus disabuses them of this notion, saying, "See my hands and my feet, that it is I myself. Touch me, and see. For a spirit does not have flesh and bones (*sarka kai ostea*) as you see that I have." The word "flesh" translates precisely the Greek word *sarka* used in this passage. That Jesus meant literal flesh by this word is clear from its juxtaposition with the word "bones." It is interesting that Jesus did not say that a spirit lacks "flesh and *blood*"—a common enough expression—but rather used the words "flesh and *bones*." Schep insightfully observes that Jesus spoke of his "flesh and bones" to emphasize the body's "most solid parts; they give shape to the body, can be seen, touched, and handled, whereas the blood cannot."[5]

Notice that what Jesus presents is his own body and not merely a form that he manifested. After saying that it is "I myself," he states that a spirit does not have flesh and bones "as you see that I have (lit., 'am having,' *echonta*)." Then, in verse 40 (emphasis added), the text says, "he showed them *his* hands and *his* feet."

John 2:19–21

> Jesus answered them, "Destroy this temple, and in three days I will raise it up." The Jews then said, "It has taken forty-six years to build this temple, and will you raise it up in three days?" But he was speaking about the temple of his body.

The word translated "body" in verse 21 is a form of the Greek word *sōma*. This word is used to designate a body of flesh. The facts themselves bear this out: the Jews and Romans did indeed destroy Jesus's body of flesh through crucifixion. However, Jesus raised up this selfsame body of flesh, i.e., the "it" of verse 19. (In the next question, we shall explore the identity between the body that dies and the one that God raises.)

---

5. J. A. Schep, *The Nature of the Resurrection Body* (Grand Rapids: Eerdmans, 1964), 132.

Historical and Linguistic Evidence

Here we note simply that when the ancients spoke of "resurrection" (Greek *anastasis*)—whether pagan or Jew—they had something other in mind than the ongoing existence of one's soul or spirit. Rather, for them the word "resurrection" always designated the raising of the physical body that had died. N. T. Wright makes the point forcefully:

> When the ancients spoke of resurrection, whether to deny it (as all pagans did) or to affirm it (as some Jews did), they were referring to a two-step narrative in which resurrection, meaning new bodily life, would be preceded by an interim period of bodily death. Resurrection wasn't, then, a dramatic or vivid way of talking about the state people went into immediately after death. It denoted something that might happen (though almost everyone thought it wouldn't) sometime after that. . . . In content, resurrection referred specifically to something that happened to the body; hence the later debates about how God would do this—whether he would start with the existing bones or make new ones or whatever. One would have debates like that only if it was quite clear that what you ended up with was something tangible and physical. Everybody knew about ghosts, spirits, visions, hallucinations, and so on. Most people in the ancient world believed in some such things. They were quite clear that that wasn't what they meant by resurrection.[6]

Thus, in keeping with the uniform usage of the word, whenever the Bible speaks of "resurrection"—whether Christ's or ours—it has in view the raising of the fleshly body.

Answering Arguments against the Resurrection of the Flesh

Some deny that the Bible teaches a resurrection of the flesh. Those who reject the doctrine sometimes cite certain biblical texts that they say teach a "spiritual" resurrection instead. This "resurrection" may be seen either as the ongoing life of the person's spirit, or as a resurrection in the form of some kind of nonfleshly, immaterial or quasi-material "spirit body" (whatever exactly that is supposed to mean).

There are two reasons for rejecting such interpretations. First, as we have already seen, the Bible clearly and explicitly teaches that the resurrection body

---

6. N. T. Wright, *Surprised by Hope: Rethinking Heaven, the Resurrection, and the Mission of the Church* (New York: HarperOne, 2008), 36. See also Schep, *The Nature of the Resurrection Body*, 63.

is a body of literal flesh; we have it on no less authority than Jesus himself that he was raised in a body of flesh and bones (Luke 24:39). Second, when we actually examine the passages marshaled against a fleshly resurrection, we see that they do not teach this.

1 Corinthians 15:44[7]

In this verse, Paul compares the body that dies or is "sown" into the ground with the future resurrection body: "It is sown a natural body (*sōma psychikon*); it is raised a spiritual body (*sōma pneumatikon*)." From this, some conclude that we shall be raised as spirits, or perhaps with a body composed of intangible, spirit-like material. The RSV translation of this verse appears to lend credence to this general position by rendering *sōma psychikon* as "physical body," thus setting up a supposed contrast between a body that is physical vs. one that is non-physical.

However, this is to misunderstand the adjective "spiritual" (*pneumatikon*) in the expression "spiritual body." To have a "spiritual body" is *not* to have a body made out of some kind of "spiritual stuff," much less to be raised as a disembodied spirit. Rather, to have a "spiritual body" is to possess a body controlled or directed by God's Spirit. The idea behind the word "spiritual" is that of *control,* "not substance or matter."[8]

N. T. Wright provides an excellent discussion of the Greek words *pneumatikon* and *psychikon* that appear in this verse. As Wright observes, "The contrast is not between a body made out of physical stuff vs. one made out of spiritual stuff. Rather, the contrast is between the present body, corruptible, decaying, and doomed to die, and the future body, incorruptible, undecaying, never to die again."[9] This is shown by the meaning of the words themselves, for as Wright points out, "Greek adjectives ending in -ikos describe not *the material out of which things are made, but the power or energy that animates them.*"[10]

As for the translation of *sōma psychikon* as "physical body," few commentators and Bible translations support this rendering. That is because the contrast here is not between a physical and a nonphysical body, but between two kinds of physical bodies. A "natural" or "soulish" principle of life animates the first kind of physical body (Adam's as first created), while a higher kind of spiritual, incorruptible, and immortal principle of life animates the second kind of physical body (such as Christ's body at his resurrection).[11]

---

7. On the use of the adjectives "soulish" and "spiritual," see the earlier discussion in Question 5.
8. Culver, *Systematic Theology*, 1064.
9. Wright, *Surprised by Hope*, 155.
10. Ibid. (emphasis original).
11. Gordon Fee provides an excellent discussion of this, showing that the word "spiritual" in this context does not refer to the "stuff" of the body but rather to the new, material body's supernatural and heavenly properties (see Gordon Fee, *First Epistle to the Corinthians,* NICNT [Grand Rapids: Eerdmans, 1987], 786).

1 Corinthians 15:45

Here Paul states, "'The first man Adam became a living being (*psychēn zōsan*)'; the last Adam became a life-giving spirit (*pneuma zōopoioun*)." Some conclude from this verse that Jesus rose as a spirit and not in a body of flesh. Moreover, since Jesus's resurrection forms the pattern for ours, one might further conclude that we, too, shall rise as spirits.

It is important, however, to read verse 45 within the context of Paul's overall argument. This verse follows on the heels of verse 44, which we just considered. Paul develops his argument by contrasting the life of the first Adam with that of the resurrected Christ (the last Adam). He does so by providing a somewhat loose quotation from Genesis 2:7. In that verse, Adam received natural life from the breath of God, becoming a "living soul" or "living creature."[12] There, the life Adam received was mere "natural" or "soulish" life. In contrast, Christ became a "living spirit," meaning that he received a Spirit-energized quality of life at his resurrection.

But why does Paul say that the last Adam actually *became* a life-giving spirit? I believe that he speaks somewhat figuratively, doing so to maintain the literary form or pattern dictated by Genesis 2:7—the pattern being, "Adam became this, Christ became that."[13] Just as Adam "is" or "became" a living soul by virtue of having received a soulish-quality of life, even so Christ "is" or "became" a life-giving Spirit by virtue of having received a Spirit-empowered principle of life, which he in turn grants to others in their resurrections.

1 Corinthians 15:50

This verse states that "flesh and blood cannot inherit the kingdom of God." Since the context of this passage is on the resurrection, those opposing a resurrection of flesh believe this directly proves their position.

The key to understanding this verse is the meaning of the expression "flesh and blood." As many commentators point out, the expression "flesh and blood" does not have primarily the physical substance of the human body in view. Rather, "flesh and blood" refers to human beings in their own inherent, natural, this-worldly life—with all of its weakness and frailty—as opposed to human beings as empowered by God's Spirit. As Culver notes, "The term in then-current rabbinic vocabulary always denoted the whole man with all his functions, with particular emphasis on man's earthly condition as a frail and perishable creature in contrast to the eternal and Almighty God."[14] Therefore,

---

12. See the earlier discussion of the biblical usage of "soul" in Question 5.
13. So Fee: "A considerable amount of scholarly energy has been expended on both vv. 45 and 47 in terms of the Christological implications. But these are quite beside Paul's point, which, as in vv. 21–22, has to do with Christ's *resurrection* being the ground of ours. The *language* has been dictated by the argument itself, especially the use of Gen. 2:7" (*First Epistle to the Corinthians*, 787n 7 [emphasis in the original]).
14. Culver, *Systematic Theology*, 1064.

when Paul says, "flesh and blood cannot inherit the kingdom of God," he means that humans in their present weak and corruptible condition cannot go there without first undergoing a transformation. "What man needs is a change in the *conditions* of his body and of his *whole humanity.*"[15]

That the expression "flesh and blood" cannot refer primarily to physicality as such is evident from Jesus's statement in Matthew 16:17. When Jesus says that "flesh and blood" did not reveal to Peter the truth of Jesus's divine Sonship, he could not possibly have had in mind the blood in Peter's veins nor the outward flesh of his body. Rather, Jesus's point is that this truth was revealed to Peter by divine power and not through feeble human reasoning or calculations.[16]

Verses That Appear to Show "Flesh" or the Body as the Seat of Sin
There are many verses that some believe identify the "flesh" (Greek *sarx*) or the body (Greek *sōma*) as the source or seat of sin. To consider but a few, note Paul's statements about the "flesh" in Romans 7:14; 13:14; Galatians 5:16, 24; and Ephesians 2:3. He speaks of the "body" in similar terms in Romans 6:6, 12; 8:13. From this, some conclude that God cannot possibly resurrect us in a body of "flesh," granting that "Those who are in the flesh cannot please God" (Rom. 8:8).

But ought we to conclude from these verses that the body as such is evil, or perhaps the source of evil per se? There are several reasons to think otherwise.

First and most importantly, God created Adam with a body of flesh (e.g., Gen. 2:23). Adam had this body of flesh (Hebrew *basar*) from the very moment of creation, before sin, as did Eve, whose body God fashioned from Adam's (v. 21). From the start, God pronounced this creation "very good" (Gen. 1:31). We may conclude from this that whenever the Bible connects "flesh" with "sin," it is only fallen or sinful flesh that is in view, not flesh per se. But in the resurrection, our flesh will no longer be fallen but glorified flesh. Note, too, that in our sinful state the Bible describes our spirits as defiled as well (2 Cor. 7:1), but in the resurrection this will no longer be so. Therefore, if one were to reason that God will not resurrect our bodies of flesh because they are presently defiled by sin, one must equally reject a resurrection of our spirits because they, too, are defiled by sin. But at the Lord's coming he will sanctify the whole person in his or her entirety (1 Thess. 5:23).

Second, while some "works of the flesh" (Gal. 5:19–21), such as sensuality and sexual immorality, may arise, at least in part, from the physical cravings of a corrupt bodily constitution, it is also clear that quite a few vices in Paul's list have no such connection. For example, it is difficult to see how enmity, strife, rivalries, and divisions have any special tie to the body. These

---

15. Schep, *The Nature of the Resurrection Body*, 204.
16. See ibid., 201.

are preeminently sins of the spirit or heart and not of the body.[17] Indeed, as Charles Hodge observed, such "sins of the flesh" typify fallen angels (i.e., demons and Satan) at least as much as they do human beings, and these have no physical bodies in which to root such sins.[18]

Granting that certain "works of the flesh" have no particular connection to the physical body—though others surely do—why would Paul use the word "flesh" to describe the entire list? I think Schep gives a reasonable account:

> Though . . . Paul does not regard the flesh-substance and the physical body as evil in themselves, it cannot be denied that he connects them very closely with sin. The very fact that "flesh," "body," and "members" are used to denote sinful human nature points in this direction. And with good reason: man on earth is always man-in-the-flesh, in the literal sense of the word. It is by means of his flesh, his biological body, that man expresses himself, whether in his sinfulness or in his holiness. Even merely "spiritual" sins such as hatred and pride express themselves in the way a man looks, bears himself, and acts. Even unbelief, the most "spiritual" sin, expresses itself this way. The physical body, therefore, as man's instrument of expression, certainly has a part in his sinning, just as it plays a part in his living by faith.[19]

REFLECTION QUESTIONS

1. A Jehovah's Witness comes to your door and you have a discussion. At one point in your discussion this person states, "Although Christ Jesus was resurrected as an invisible spirit creature, we believe that we will have resurrected bodies and live on a paradise earth." Based on what you learned in this chapter, how would you respond to this statement?

2. You attend the funeral for your uncle Fred and the preacher at the graveside service says, "Today we are laying Fred's earthly body into the ground. But even though his body of flesh will soon be no more, we know that his spirit will live forever in heaven." Evaluate these statements based on what we discussed in this chapter.

---

17. Ibid., 99.
18. Charles Hodge, *Systematic Theology*, 3 vols. (New York: Scribner's, 1871), 2:142. Augustine also makes this point (Augustine, *City of God* 14.3).
19. Schep, *The Nature of the Resurrection Body*, 101.

3. Before reading this chapter, did you tend to think of your eternal existence in more "spiritual" and less "fleshly" terms? After reading this chapter, has your thinking changed?

4. How do you feel about the thought of having a literal body of literal flesh and bones for all eternity? Does this make the eternal state seem more or less inviting to you?

5. What does the resurrection of the body of flesh tell us about the value that God places on our physical bodies? Do you think that Christians sometimes tend to elevate the importance of the spirit and ignore or denigrate the body? Discuss the ways in which you may have observed this tendency and consider how the material presented in this chapter might promote a more balanced view.

What Will the Resurrection Body Be Like? (Part 2)

In Part 1 of this issue, which we treated in the previous question, I demonstrated that Christ's resurrection body establishes the pattern for ours, and that this body will be a body of literal flesh. In this question, I shall show that the resurrection body is a glorified body of literal flesh, and that the body that God glorifies is the same body that died and was buried. I shall also make a few observations about the resurrected bodies of the wicked.

The Resurrection Body Is a *Glorified* Body of Literal Flesh

As we observed in Part 1 of this topic (i.e., the previous question), the resurrection body, though a physical body of flesh, is animated by a new spiritual principle of life, made alive by the Holy Spirit himself (Rom. 8:11). Consequently, Paul speaks of it as a "spiritual body," in contrast to the "natural body" that Adam received at his creation, which he then defiled through sin. This spiritual body has certain remarkable properties that distinguish it from a natural body, which we shall now consider.

The Resurrection Body Is Glorified and Resplendent

A number of biblical texts characterize the resurrection body with words and expressions such as "shine like the sun" (Matt. 13:43); "glory" and "glorious" (1 Cor. 15:43; Phil. 3:21); "shine like the brightness of the sky above" (Dan. 12:3); and so forth.

What exactly do the biblical writers mean when they describe the resurrection body in such "luminous language" or "glowing terms"? Do they have in mind a literal, physical brightness similar to when Jesus stood transfigured before Peter, James, and John (Matt. 17:2)? Perhaps. We do note, however, that when Jesus appeared to his disciples after his resurrection his appearance was, for the most part, unremarkable. "Indeed, he appears as a human being with a body that in some ways is quite normal and can be mistaken for a gardener or a fellow traveler on the road."[1]

Could it be that Jesus veiled the glory of his body specifically for those postresurrection appearances? Or does the "glory" consist primarily in some of the other features of the body that I shall discuss below—such as incorruptibility, immortality, a newly energized and dynamic spiritual power, and things of this sort?

The Resurrection Body Is "Immortal," "Incorruptible," and "Imperishable"

A central feature of the resurrection body is that "incorruptibility/imperishability" (*aphtharsia*) and "immortality" (*athanasia*) characterize it. As Paul states in 1 Corinthians 15:53–54:

> For this perishable body must put on the imperishable (*aphtharsian*), and the mortal body must put on immortality (*athanasian*). When the perishable puts on the imperishable (*aphtharsian*), and the mortal puts on immortality (*athanasian*), then shall come to pass the saying that is written: "Death is swallowed up in victory."

The meaning of these words is clear. The resurrection body will be free from and impervious to all disease, defect, corruption, dissolution, or death. It will be a body full of health, life, and energy, empowered by the Spirit of God. It will be indestructible. As Hodge put it, "There is to be no decrepitude of age; no decay of the faculties; no loss of vigor; but immortal youth."[2]

Compare this body to our present, natural body. The bodies we now possess are greatly inferior even to Adam's body when God first created him, before he sinned. Adam, created a "living being" (1 Cor. 15:45), enjoyed perfect natural, animal life. He was free of all sickness and disease. God provided him with the tree of life, which would stave off the ravages of aging and corruption—a kind of fountain of youth, so to speak. As long as Adam had access to this tree, he could remain in this state.[3] Yet, once sin entered the picture, it defiled Adam both in body and in spirit. Furthermore, God banished him from the garden. Without access to the life-sustaining properties of the tree of life, he began his inexorable march toward death (Gen. 3:22). And so it is for us, his posterity.

---

1. N. T. Wright, *Surprised by Hope: Rethinking Heaven, the Resurrection, and the Mission of the Church* (New York: HarperOne, 2008), 55.
2. Charles Hodge, *Systematic Theology*, 3 vols. (New York: Scribner's, 1871), 3:782.
3. Augustine, *City of God* 13.23; 14.26; *On the Merits of Forgiveness of Sins, and on the Baptism of Infants* 2.35.

Yet, we would greatly err were we to conclude that in the resurrection God simply puts matters back to the state they were at Adam's initial creation, before sin's entrance into the world. Paul makes this clear in 1 Corinthians 15:45, where he compares Adam's pre-fall "soulish" or natural animal life to the Spirit-energized resurrection life that is to come. Our resurrection bodies will be far superior to the original bodies of Adam and Eve, even before their fall into sin.[4]

Can the Resurrection Body "Defy the Laws of Physics"?
Some of the events connected with Jesus's postresurrection appearances are quite baffling. When Jesus encounters two of his disciples on the road to Emmaus, they do not recognize him at first (Luke 24:16). Their failure to do so was not because he was inherently unrecognizable but because "their eyes were kept from recognizing him." Indeed, that God had to prevent them from recognizing him tells us that they would have otherwise identified him as the Jesus that they knew. But what is especially surprising about this account is what we find in the latter part of verse 31: "And their eyes were opened, and they recognized him. And he vanished from their sight." Taking this text at face value, it seems that Jesus simply disappeared from where he was and, presumably, went somewhere else; he was there one moment and gone the next.

Equally mysterious are the accounts given in John 20:19–30. On two separate occasions, Jesus appeared in a room with the doors locked (vv. 19, 26). Though some have suggested that the miracle consisted in Jesus forcing the locked door open "by the power of his will,"[5] this is hardly the most natural reading of the text.[6] It seems rather that Jesus simply appeared inside of the room, despite the fact that the doors were locked and continued to be so.

What, if anything, can we conclude about the nature of the resurrection body from these texts? It is difficult to say. Perhaps the resurrection body has special properties that allow it to violate the normal laws of physics as we know them, enabling it to appear and disappear at will. Perhaps it can also pass through solid objects. However, this is not certain.

For one thing, the text does not say that Jesus "passed through the closed door"; it merely states that he appeared inside the room with the doors locked. That he may have passed through the closed door or solid wall is an assumption drawn from the fact that he was not in the room and then suddenly was. This might suggest that in transiting from point A (outside the room) to point B

---

4. Augustine, *City of God* 13.20.
5. J. A. Schep, *The Nature of the Resurrection Body* (Grand Rapids: Eerdmans, 1964), 142.
6. Had that been the case, it is much more likely that John would have recorded something along the lines of what we find in Acts 5:19, where God miraculously opened the locked prison doors through angelic agency.

(inside the room) he would have gone through the wall or door somehow. The text, however, does not state that.

Consider, too, that we have another "physics-defying" event in Matthew 14:25, 29. Here Jesus walks on water, as does Peter—at least for a time. This, however, is before Jesus received his glorified body and well before Peter will receive his. Therefore, however this miracle took place, it had nothing to do with any inherently new properties in our Lord's or Peter's body.

Therefore, it may not be possible to determine from these texts whether Jesus could perform these feats because he had a body with new properties, or because he simply performed specific miracles unique to those particular situations.[7]

The Resurrection Body Is the *Same* Body That Died and Was Buried

God is in the business of redeeming his fallen and broken creation, not annihilating and replacing it with something made from scratch. This is certainly so where our resurrection bodies are concerned. The body that God raises and exalts is the numerically same body that went into the grave.[8]

Biblical Evidence

Several biblical texts identify the body that dies with the one that is raised.

From the Biblical Texts Describing Jesus's Resurrection

Many biblical texts describing Jesus's own resurrection tell us that the body that was placed in the tomb is the same one that was raised.

First, Jesus himself predicted that it would be so. In John 2:19–22 he stated that in three days he would raise "it" up. The "it" he clearly identifies as the body that would be slain.

Next, we have the fact that Jesus's body miraculously did not experience the ravages of corruption, as Acts 2:27 makes plain. Granting that the body that died did not "dissolve into gasses," as the Jehovah's Witnesses wrongly

---

7. Out of curiosity, I asked my friend and colleague at Biola University, Dr. John Bloom, who has a Ph.D. in Biophysics from Cornell, if there is anything from our knowledge of modern physics that might shed some light on the ability of Jesus to walk through a wall—assuming that this is what took place. He replied as follows:

   "As far as the physics goes, atoms and molecules are mostly empty space . . . the atomic nuclei are about 100,000 times smaller than the space that the electron cloud surrounding the atom takes up. So in theory, if one ignored/over-rode the electrical forces, two atoms could go through each other. But that's a lot to ignore.

   "Quantum tunneling is another possibility, but for macroscopic objects (a person) going through a fairly thick wall, this would be so statistically unlikely that one is justified in calling it a miracle, especially if it can be done at will" (John Bloom, email message to author, April 8, 2015).

8. By "numerically same," I mean it is not an unrelated body created from scratch, but is in some sense a version, development, or modification of the original body.

suggested, then what became of it if, in fact, God created a new, unrelated body for Jesus at his resurrection? The only reasonable conclusion is that God raised the very same body that was placed in the tomb—or, as N. T. Wright put it, that Christ's resurrection body "uses up (so to speak) the matter of the crucified body."[9]

Third, consider the evidence that Jesus himself offered to demonstrate the continuity between the body that died and the one that was raised. Especially important is his display of the nailprints and scars, which were the marks of his crucifixion (John 20:24–29). Schep correctly observes, "The scars made it clear, more than anything else could do, that the crucified and buried Master was standing before them in the very same body in which they had seen him suffer."[10]

Isaiah 26:19
This verse reads, "Your dead shall live; their bodies shall rise. You who dwell in the dust, awake and sing for joy!" The most straightforward reading of this text is that God will raise the very bodies that died.

Romans 8:11; Philippians 3:21
In Romans 8:11, Paul states that the same Spirit that raised Jesus from the dead "will also give life to your mortal bodies." The reference to our "mortal bodies" obviously has our *present* bodies in view, which the Spirit will bring back to life in the resurrection.

Similarly, consider Philippians 3:21, which states that the Lord "will transform our lowly body to be like his glorious body." Note that this text does not say that he will simply replace our present bodies with a new one created from scratch, but that he will *transform* our *existing* lowly bodies.

1 Corinthians 15
1 Corinthians 15, the most extended treatment of the nature of the resurrection body, makes it plain that there remains an organic, physical continuity between the body that dies and the one that is raised.

We see this first in the analogy of the seed that Paul gives in verses 36–44. Paul likens the mortal body that is buried in death to a seed of wheat or grain that is sown into the ground. The resulting plant maintains an organic connection to the seed that is sown, but at the same time is different from it. While we ought not to press every aspect of this seed analogy, what is clear is that there is both continuity and discontinuity between the seed and the resulting plant, just as there is between the natural body that dies and the resurrection body that results from it.

---

9. Wright, *Surprised by Hope*, 55.
10. Schep, *The Nature of the Resurrection Body*, 131.

Next, consider specifically the "it" of verses 42–44 (KJV, emphasis added): "*It* is sown in corruption; *it* is raised in incorruption: *It* is sown in dishonor, *it* is raised in glory: *it* is sown in weakness; *it* is raised in power: *it* is sown a natural body; *it* is raised a spiritual body" (emphasis added). The same "it" that is "sown" (i.e., buried at death) is the "it" that is raised.[11] It is clear from the back-and-forth contrast that Paul has in view the same body in both instances.

Must the Resurrection Body Contain the Identical Molecules of the One That Died?

If we grant that the resurrection body is the same body as the mortal one that dies, but yet is also different in so many ways, this raises the question of what it means for a body to be the "same" body.

Some have suggested that in order to be the same body, the new body must contain exactly the same particles and molecules as the old one. According to this view, at the resurrection God will gather up all of the particles of our bodies, which had dissolved in death, and reassemble them into our new bodies. Consider the following quote from Spurgeon:

> . . . at the blast of the archangel's trumpet, every separate atom of my body will find its fellow; like the bones lying in the valley of vision, though separated from one another, the moment God shall speak, bone will reconnect to bone; the flesh will come upon it, the four winds of heaven will blow, and the breath will return.
>
> So let me die, let beasts devour me, let fire turn this body into gas and vapor, all its particles shall yet again be restored.[12]

This position is highly unlikely, and in any event is not required in order for us to consider the body to be the same body.

Bear in mind that our physical bodies are in a constant state of flux, losing cells and gaining others. Probably not a single cell of my sixty-three-year-old body was in it when I was fifty-two or fifty-three. Yet, despite these changes over time, I still have the same body, which has been my body throughout that entire period—and indeed, throughout my whole life. As Perowne observed,

---

11. The Greek text does not contain a separate word "it," such as we find in all English translations of these verses. Rather, the subject "it" in Greek is built into the verbs themselves, which in all of these instances are third person singular, present passive indicatives. So, for instance, *speiretai*, taken by itself, could be translated as "he/she/it is sown." Whether "he," "she," or "it" is chosen for the translation depends upon the subject in question. Since the subject is "the body," the pronoun "it" is the correct English rendering.

12. Spurgeon, sermon entitled "I Know that My Redeemer Liveth." Augustine also apparently held this extreme view. See Hodge, *Systematic Theology*, 3:775–76.

it therefore seems arbitrary to require that the resurrection body must contain all of the identical particles with the body that existed right at the time of death. Why not reassemble all of the particles from my body at age thirty, or age forty-five, or from when I was an infant? These are as much "my body" as any of the others.[13]

Besides, such a view appears to be at odds with Paul's analogy of the seed, which we considered above. All of the particles that may have been in the seed do not find their way into the new plant, and there are many in the new plant that were not present in the original seed. Nevertheless, *some* of the substance of the seed is present in the new plant, at least at its inception.

Therefore, one need not anxiously inquire as to how God will reclaim for our resurrection bodies the particles of our body that have entered the food chain and become parts of other animals, which then other humans eat and in turn become parts of their bodies, etc. Even if we were to grant that God in his omnipotence could disentangle all this, it appears to be a nonproblem, since exact identity of molecules is not what accounts for bodily identity anyway. At the same time, and in keeping with Paul's analogy, there does appear to be *something* of the original body that dies that finds its way into the glorified resurrection body.

What Is the Principle of Continuity between Our Present Body and Our Resurrection Body?[14]

Granting that there is continuity of identity between the body that dies and the one that is raised, what is the principle that underlies this continuity? The answer, stated simply, is that the same spirit, i.e., *our own* spirit, animates and "informs" both bodies.

As we noted in our earlier discussion of the constitution of the human person in Question 5, the human spirit is not merely the seat of the intellect, emotions, will, reason, self-consciousness, and all of the other mental functions of the person. The spirit also is the principle of life that animates the body on the biological level (e.g., so that the lungs breathe air and the heart beats and circulates blood). The spirit maintains the body's outward form as well as its internal workings. This is why the body literally falls apart and turns to dust when the spirit departs from it (James 2:26).

Consequently, for our present bodies, our spirit underlies and manages the continuity amid all the fluctuations and variations in our physical constitution. But our spirit will also be what maintains continuity *between* our old and new body, and also *within* our new resurrection body for all eternity. Just

---

13. W. G. T. Shedd, *Dogmatic Theology,* ed. Alan W. Gomes (Phillipsburg: P&R, 2003), 876, Supplement 7.3.6.

14. For excellent discussions of this question, see Hodge, *Systematic Theology,* 3:775–80; and Shedd, *Dogmatic Theology,* 869–73, 875–77.

as our present body is the same body from year to year because our spirit that governs it is the same, even so our glorified body will be the same body as our present body because of the presence of our spirit—the same spirit—in it. In turn, the reason our resurrection body is the same body one million years after we first obtain it is, again, that our spirit continues to animate it.

We observed earlier that a new, vital principle of spiritual life energizes the resurrection body; this vital principle is the Spirit of God himself (Rom. 8:11). This does not contradict what I have said above. God's Spirit will indeed be the root, foundation, and ultimate source of this new resurrection life. Nevertheless, it is best to see this power as operating from the inside out, in concert with our own spirit. God's Spirit will so vitalize our spirits with heretofore-unknown capacities of life that the body in which our spirits dwell will truly be what the Apostle calls "a spiritual body." God's Spirit does not replace our spirit in our personal makeup but empowers and invigorates our spirit in new and remarkable ways. This will manifest itself not only in our spirit-empowered mental and spiritual life but in the glorification of our bodies as well.

The Wicked Will Have Resurrected but Unglorified Bodies of Flesh

Scripture teaches that not only the just but also the wicked will be raised bodily from the dead (Dan. 12:2; John 5:28–29; Acts 24:15; Rev. 20:5, 12–13). However, Scripture does not provide us with much information about the nature of the bodies of the damned.

What we can say is that the wicked will be raised in a body of flesh. We have already seen in Question 19 above that this is the meaning of the word "resurrection." Daniel 12:2 testifies to this truth when it says that the wicked, as well as the righteous, will be raised "from the dust of the earth." Again, Jesus states directly that those who are cast into gehenna will be dispatched there bodily (Matt. 10:28).

We may also conclude that the bodies of the wicked will be capable of feeling pain (see Question 31). Nor will they be glorified, for that description applies only to those who are in Christ, as we have already observed.

Beyond this, it is probably best to take Augustine's wise counsel and "not weary ourselves speculating about their health or their beauty, which are matters uncertain, when their eternal damnation is a matter of certainty."[15]

---

15. Augustine, *Enchiridion* 92.

REFLECTION QUESTIONS

1. As you think about the resurrection body as a glorified body of flesh, does this increase your desire to have one? Which of the characteristics of that body discussed in this chapter do you find the most attractive?

2. Why do you think that God raises the same body that died instead of simply creating a new, unrelated one for us from scratch? Hint: Think about the difference between God replacing his fallen creation vs. redeeming it.

3. Deal with the following objection based on what you learned in this chapter: "There is no way that God can raise the same body that died. After all, the body eventually decays, is eaten by worms that are in turn eaten by other animals, and some of these animals are then eaten by other people, etc."

4. Respond to this statement: "In order for the body that is raised to be the same as the one that died, the new body must contain all of the same particles and molecules as the old one."

5. What is the relationship between our own spirits and the Holy Spirit in the resurrection body? Does the Holy Spirit replace our spirit? If not, then what is the connection between them?

PART 4

The Eternal State

The Eternal State for Believers

We begin this section by examining the key truth through which we must understand the eternal state for believers: the creation of a new heavens and a new earth (NHNE). This truth is so critical and central that we shall devote three entire questions to examining crucial facets of the NHNE: what they are, how they come about, and how the New Jerusalem relates to them.

Having thus established the NHNE as the foundation on which we should build our understanding of the eternal state for believers, we shall then consider some additional issues that often come up when we contemplate the believer's life in eternity.

What Are the New Heavens and the New Earth?

This world is not my home, I'm just a-passin' through.
My treasures are laid up somewhere beyond the blue.
The angels beckon me from heaven's open door.
And I can't feel at home in this world anymore. . . .

Oh Lord, You know I have no friend like you.
If heaven's not my home then Lord what will I do?
The angels beckon me from heaven's open door.
And I can't feel at home in this world anymore.

The Physicality of the Eternal State

Earlier in the book, I made a claim that many will find shocking: that "heaven" is not the believer's "eternal home."[1] There I mentioned that we will spend eternity on a recreated, physical earth in physical, resurrected bodies. It is now time to unpack this claim.

Our Design as Physical Beings

It is no accident that God created the first man and woman as physical beings, and that every child produced since then comes into this world with a physical body. Nor is it by chance that Jesus, the "last Adam," took on real flesh in the womb of the virgin (John 1:14), when he was "made like his brothers in every respect" (Heb. 2:17). It is no mere coincidence that God raised Jesus with a body of real flesh and bones (Luke 24:39), and that he will give life to our mortal bodies as well (Rom. 8:11).

---

1. See Question 7, "What Does the Bible Mean When It Speaks of 'Heaven'?"

And yet, we have observed that the conventional wisdom is that we will spend all eternity in "heaven," in either a nonphysical or a quasiphysical state, sitting on fluffy clouds and strumming harps. How far this is from the true and much richer biblical picture of the eternal state for believers! Robert Culver correctly admonishes, "We greatly err when we ignore the biblical emphasis on the Ascension of Christ in a physical body and of our coming back with Him to earth, at the resurrection, in glorified but physical bodies, to inhabit an earthly (not etherial) earth."[2] As Ladd cogently observed, the Bible "always places man on a redeemed earth, not in a heavenly realm removed from earthly existence."[3]

Illustrating the Confusion

We can most easily illustrate this confusion by looking at some of our most cherished Christian songs and hymns.

We began this chapter with some snippets from the famous song, "This World Is Not My Home." If we are to believe this song, we shall live "eternally" in heaven—described also as "glory land"—positioned "somewhere beyond the blue." Not to be outdone, the song "Do Lord," popularly sung by Johnny Cash, likewise places us in our "glory land home," which is not merely "beyond the blue" but "*way* beyond the blue." Then we have the words to the much earlier and more soberly expressed hymn, "Jesus Thy Blood and Righteousness." The lyrics, written by Nicolaus von Zinzendof, contain this line: "When from the dust of death I rise to claim my mansion in the skies. . . ." Note that this hymn is not talking about the disembodied intermediate state but speaks instead of the eternal state, i.e., after the resurrection. Consider also the Christmas carol "Away in a Manger," which implores God to "fit us for heaven to live with thee there." Absent from this Christmas favorite, Wright observes, is any mention of resurrection, new creation, or God dwelling with his people on a renovated earth.[4]

Accounting for the Confusion

The source of this confusion is no doubt manifold. Some writers point to the influence of Greek dualism infecting the church, "in which salvation consists of the flight of the soul" from the "earthly or transitory" to the "eternal

---

2. Robert Culver, *Systematic Theology: Biblical and Historical* (Fearn, Ross-shire, UK: Mentor, 2005), 1098.
3. George Eldon Ladd, *A Commentary on the Revelation of John* (Grand Rapids: Eerdmans, 1972), 275.
4. For an interesting discussion of other problematic lyrics on the afterlife in Christian music, old and new, see J. Richard Middleton, *A New Heaven and a New Earth* (Grand Rapids: Baker, 2014), 27–30.

spiritual world."[5] Perhaps the main factor, though, is a simple failure to attend carefully to what the Bible has to say about the eternal state.

Often people just assume that the many references to heaven describe our "eternal home," and then, almost as an afterthought, "the language of resurrection, and of the new earth as well as the new heavens, must somehow be fitted into that."[6] Writers frequently conflate descriptions of "heaven"—such as we find in the book of Revelation—with those of the eternal state, which will actually be on a new earth. We also find the reverse, where people take passages that describe the new earth as referring to "heaven." The result is a hopeless muddle.[7]

The Results of This Confusion

This mixed up thinking on the eternal state has practical implications. I am convinced that one tragic result is that Christians often remain overly attached to this present world, despite what they may say about looking forward to "the joys of heaven." They think that they are supposed to regard heaven as their "true eternal home" but really cannot get too excited about it. In one sense, it is difficult to fault them. The traditional picture of the eternal state as an ethereal, floaty, intangible, interminable church service is frankly a bit weird and unappealing.

I believe we may attribute this faulty thinking to two factors. First, Christians often have a distorted view of what heaven—i.e., the intermediate state between death and resurrection—really is. As discussed in Question 10, "What Fate Awaits Those Who Die in This Present Age, Immediately upon Death?" the disembodied intermediate state *does* represent a superior

---

5. Ibid., 275. Likewise, concerning the afterlife, Culver states, "A large incubus of medieval, mystical, neo-Platonic, ascetic thinking has carried over among many Christians into modern times" (*Systematic Theology*, 1098).

6. N. T. Wright, *Surprised by Hope: Rethinking Heaven, the Resurrection, and the Mission of the Church* (New York: HarperOne, 2008), 19.

7. Here are but a few of the countless examples I could cite—and these are from academic sources: "All believers will ultimately dwell in heaven in their resurrection bodies, which they will receive when the Lord comes for them from heaven" ("Heaven," *BEB*, 2:941). "Heaven is the abode of God and of God's angels, the just, and the holy. It is the real home of Christians on earth . . . the ultimate home of Christ's disciples" (Cheryl A. Kirk-Duggan, "Heaven," *EDB*, 564). "[According to Paul, heaven is] the eternal home of the believer: 2 Cor. 5:1, 2; Phil. 3:20; cf. Gal. 4:26" (J. F. Maile, "Heaven, Heavenlies, Paradise," *DPL*, 381). Commenting on Revelation 21:1–22:5—the text that explicitly discusses the new heavens and the new earth—Osborne states that this passage provides us with "the only extended description of 'heaven' in the Bible." And again, "Heaven in 7:9–17 is almost certainly the same place as the renewed earth of 21:1–22:5" (Grant R. Osborne, *Revelation*, BECNT [Grand Rapids: Baker, 2002], 742; see this confusion generally throughout 732–43). Then there are the popular-level books by Randy Alcorn on heaven, in which "he still uses the word heaven when what he emphatically talks about throughout is the new heavens and new earth" (Wright, *Surprised by Hope*, 298–99).

situation for the Christian when compared to the present life. That is because of the direct sense of God's presence and the corresponding absence of any mental distress caused by sin. Therefore, if the choice were between heaven, where we enjoy God's direct presence, and our present earthly existence, where we do not, then heaven is clearly the superior choice. Christians may fail to grasp that superiority—again, when the choice is only between heaven vs. life in this present age. But second, Paul also expresses a decided disinclination to be disembodied (i.e., "unclothed") and shrinks back from it as an unnatural condition, despite the positives about being with Christ in heaven ultimately outweighing this in his mind. Paul is not alone in this: I believe the natural inclination of most people is to find the idea of disembodied existence, considered by itself, undesirable as well. We were never designed to live without bodies; we know that intuitively, and so it is difficult for many people to get beyond that fact.

Contrast this, on the other hand, with the true biblical picture. Who would not want to live someday on a magnificently beautiful and lush earth, free of all pollution, floods, earthquakes, harsh climate extremes, decay, and everything else about this world that brings us dissatisfaction and pain? What if we could pursue activities that are similar in many ways to what we do now, only vastly better and purged of all defect and disappointment, including physical undertakings that allow us to work with our hands as well as with our minds?[8] And, best of all, who would not long to have unbroken, perfect, and direct fellowship with God, and ideal relationships of consummate joy and love for one another, in this idyllic setting!

Stated simply, I am convinced that one of the main reasons Christians do not find the idea of "heaven" especially desirable or compelling is because, as typically presented, it differs from our present experience in ways that violate our true nature as complete human beings. While there will be much different about the eternal state compared to now, in certain key and fundamental respects there is far more continuity between it and our current mode of existence than we often realize.

The Fact of a New Heavens and a New Earth (NHNE)

Both testaments mention the NHNE as such—specifically in Isaiah, 2 Peter, and Revelation.[9] Peter tells us, "But according to his promise we are waiting for new heavens and a new earth in which righteousness dwells" (2 Peter 3:13). John depicts the fulfillment of that promise in the final two chapters of Scripture, in which he "saw a new heaven and a new earth, for the first heaven and the first earth had passed away" (Rev. 21:1).

---

8. I shall discuss this more in Question 25, "What Will We Do in the Eternal State?"
9. See Isaiah 65:17; 66:22; 2 Peter 3:13; and Revelation 21:1.

In the next question, we shall explore in what way the old heaven and earth go out of existence and how the new ones come to take their place. For now, we shall simply stipulate the NHNE as a fact, and consider some of their most salient features.

What Will the NHNE Be Like?

Though the Bible is not exhaustive in its description, it nevertheless provides us with some key information about the new earth and life on it.

The NHNE Are Qualitatively New and Different from Our Present Universe

As many commentators observe, the NHNE are a new *kind* of heaven and earth. The Greek word translated "new" is *kainos*, which stresses the newness of quality and not just something that is more recent in time.[10] (The word *neos* emphasizes the temporal sense of "new."[11]) The NHNE are built to have a more "permanent and enduring" character to them, as opposed to the first heaven and earth, which were "impermanent and temporary."[12]

Though I have made much of the fact that we ought not to confuse the NHNE with "heaven," there is a genuine sense in which we should acknowledge that the NHNE will be imbued with a "heavenly" character.[13] By "heavenly," I do not for a moment mean intangible, nonphysical, or ethereal. The NHNE will be "heavenly" in the sense that they will reflect and embody perfectly God's presence and the complete execution of his will in all things. They will reflect his heavenly glory. And yet, these heavenly properties will operate in the material sphere of the NHNE.[14]

The New Earth Is Where God Will Be Specially Present with Us

The most amazing and central characteristic of the new earth is God's presence there with his people. No verse expresses this key facet of the new earth better than Revelation 21:3:

> And I heard a loud voice from the throne saying, "Behold, the dwelling place of God is with man. He will dwell with them, and they will be his people, and God himself will be with them as their God."

---

10. See, for example, G. K. Beale, *The Book of Revelation: A Commentary on the Greek Text*, NIGTC (Grand Rapids: Eerdmans, 1999), 1040; and Bradford A. Mullen, "Heaven, Heavens, Heavenlies," *EDBT*, 334; Osborne, *Revelation*, 729.
11. Beale, *The Book of Revelation*, 1040.
12. Ibid.
13. For this line of thinking I am indebted to my colleague Robert Saucy.
14. This, I might add, is analogous to how we may speak of the resurrection body as "spiritual" without it being a spirit. That is, it is a tangible, physical body imbued with certain spiritual properties.

Now, it is certainly true that as Christians we already experience God's presence in our lives. Nevertheless, our sense of God is dim, as if seen "through a glass, darkly" (1 Cor. 13:12, kjv). However, in the eternal state we shall have an unattenuated, perfect, and clear apprehension of God. The barriers of sin, weakness, and corruption will no longer hinder our perfect fellowship with God. While it is true that we will directly experience God's presence at death (i.e., in the intermediate state), it is not until we reside on the new earth that we will do so as complete human beings. There, with our resurrected, glorified bodies, we will enjoy God's presence as he designed us to experience it: both in body and in spirit. It is then and only then that we shall enjoy God completely.

Many scholars—wrongly, in my view—speak of this intimacy of God dwelling with humans on the new earth in terms of a "merging" of heaven and earth, such that there will no longer remain any real distinction between the two.[15] For instance, Culver endorses the following statement by Schilder, in which he declares, "Man will inhabit the new earth—and also heaven—physically. Heaven also, because heaven then will unite itself with earth (Rev. 22:1ff.)."[16] Mullen expresses the same thought when he states, "The sharp distinction between heaven and earth will be removed when God makes all things new."[17] Osborne speaks of "heaven as an earthly reality,"[18] in which "heaven will be brought down to earth."[19] He cites Revelation 7 as teaching that "the saints will spend eternity in heaven," whereas in Revelation 21 and 22 they will abide in "the final Eden" on a new earth. "In other words," Osborne concludes, "heaven and earth will be united into a larger reality"[20] in which "heaven has now become the 'new earth.'"[21]

Is it true that heaven and earth will collapse into one another in this way?

I do believe these commentators are partially correct in so far as we can describe the new earth as having "heavenly" qualities. There also is a very real sense in which we can say that heaven will invade earth, as it were, because God's reign throughout it will be complete; his will shall then be done "on earth as it is in heaven." Nevertheless, it does not follow from this that heaven *becomes* earth or earth *becomes* heaven, nor are they melded or blended into some composite entity that is both at the same time. Heaven remains heaven and does not become earth, despite imparting certain of its qualities to it.[22]

---

15. Here and throughout the present discussion I am of course speaking of the third heaven, i.e., heaven as God's abode.
16. Culver, *Systematic Theology*, 1101.
17. Mullen, "Heaven, Heavens, Heavenlies," 335.
18. Osborne, *Revelation*, 727.
19. Ibid., 732.
20. Ibid., 730.
21. Ibid., 743.
22. Sauer is quite incorrect when he states, "Not only to heaven will the perfected come (John 14:2, 3) but the heaven [sic] will come to the earth; indeed, the new earth will itself be

Simply because God abides with human beings on a new earth does not mean that he ceases to be in the third heaven. God is omnipresent, which means that when his presence fills the new earth it does not cease to fill the highest heaven as well. Moreover, God is transcendent, which means that however much he will abide with us on a new earth, he will not cease to exist beyond it as well. God will continue to transcend the earthly sphere and abide in heaven together with his angels, just as he did before. As an analogy, think of God's special presence in the Holy of Holies under the old covenant. Despite his special presence there, God was not contained therein, and continued to fill all heaven and earth (1 Kings 8:27).[23]

In the eternal state, there is no reason to think that we will reside in heaven, nor in a heaven merged with earth, nor divide our time "commuting" between heaven and earth. The Bible says that we will spend eternity on a new earth. Even a moment's reflection shows that this makes perfect sense. What possible reason would we have for existing in heaven? It could not be to experience God's presence more fully, for God will have made his dwelling with us on earth. Nor could it be that heaven provides an especially suitable habitat for resurrected human beings, for God designed a renovated, material earth precisely for that purpose.

As I shall argue in Question 23, the New Jerusalem is a literal city that God will situate on the new earth (Rev. 21:2). However, the text says that this city comes *out of* heaven to reside on the earth, not that it takes all of heaven down with it.

The New Earth Will Be Free of Suffering and Full of Joy

The Bible presents many of the joys of the new earth to us in symbolic language. We shall see this particularly when we examine the New Jerusalem in the next question. No doubt one of the reasons for this is because our language is too feeble to communicate directly the glories of the age to come. As Paul put it, "Eye hath not see, nor ear heard, neither have entered into the heart of man, the things which God hath prepared for them that love him" (1 Cor. 2:9, KJV).

At the same time, one of the ways we can get a good idea of what the new earth will be like is by considering what it is not. As Thomas observes, "The negative description of future conditions is in a sense easier."[24] That is because we already know all too well the pains of this present life, such as sorrow, crying, disappointment, sickness, decay, and death. None of these has any

---

heaven; for where the throne of God is, there is heaven" (Erich Sauer, *The Triumph of the Crucified* [Grand Rapids: Eerdmans, 1952], 180). Alcorn falls into this same error in his popular book *Heaven* (Randy Alcorn, *Heaven* [Wheaton, IL: Tyndale House, 2004], 45).

23. I am indebted to my colleague Robert Saucy for this helpful illustration. See also my discussion of this passage in Question 7.

24. Robert L. Thomas, *Revelation 1–7: An Exegetical Commentary* (Chicago: Moody, 1992), 445.

place in the new earth. As Revelation 21:4 reads, "He will wipe away every tear from their eyes, and death shall be no more, neither shall there be mourning, nor crying, nor pain anymore, for the former things have passed away."

Considered positively, in some places Scripture compares the new earth to the original garden of Eden, using figures and pictures directly reminiscent of it.[25] "It is especially noteworthy to observe how the closing chapters of Revelation reflect the motifs of Genesis 1–3."[26] Most telling are the several references to the "tree of life" (Rev. 2:7; 22:2, 14, 19) and the "river of the water of life" (Rev. 22:1–2). Though analogous to the original Edenic Paradise, the new earth will be superior to it in every way, preeminently in its permanence and inviolability; within it, sin and its corrupting effects are no longer even a possibility.[27]

The New Earth Will Be a Place of Joyous Relationships

The new earth is a place of community and relationships. I shall defer a more in-depth discussion of this for Question 23, "What Is the New Jerusalem?" and Question 24, "What Will We Know in the Eternal State?" For now it is sufficient to note that in the eternal state there will be national entities and literal cities—preeminently the New Jerusalem (Rev. 21:1–22:5). This indicates that some kind of social structure and organization, so characteristic of human life in this age, will carry over into the next. I agree with Middleton:

> The reference to kings and nations in the new creation is a telling signal that cultural and even national diversity is not abrogated by redemption. Salvation does not erase cultural differences; rather, the human race, still distinguished by nationality, now walks by the glory or light of the holy city, which is itself illuminated by the Lamb (Rev. 21:24).[28]

Because there we will be completely holy and in tune with God's purposes, we shall experience none of the strife and disappointment that characterize our relationships in this present age. We will love one another supremely and enjoy delightful and utterly satisfying fellowship with our brothers and sisters for all eternity.

---

25. See, for example, Gary T. Meadors, "New Heavens and New Earth," *EDBT*, 563; Robert H. Mounce, *The Book of Revelation*, rev. ed., NICNT (Grand Rapids: Eerdmans, 1998), 379.
26. Meadors, "The New Heavens and New Earth," 563.
27. See the discussion in Question 27, "Will It Be Possible for Us to Sin in the Eternal State?"
28. Middleton, *A New Heaven and a New Earth*, 173–74.

REFLECTION QUESTIONS

1. How does our creation as physical beings relate to the biblical teaching of the NHNE?

2. This chapter cites the rampant confusion that exists about the eternal state in teaching, hymns, etc. Discuss the ways in which you may have observed this confusion before reading this chapter.

3. Do you find the prospect of a NHNE more inviting and attractive than remaining in "heaven" for all eternity? Why?

4. In what ways will God's presence in the NHNE differ from the way in which we experience it now?

5. What activities do you think will be the most exciting on the new earth? What aspects of life there do you look forward to the most? (Note: You may wish to revisit this question after you read Question 25, "What Will We Do in the Eternal State?")

How Will the New Heavens and New Earth Come About?

The Bible makes it clear that the present order of the universe is transitory. Jesus himself declared, "Heaven and earth will pass away" (Matt. 24:35). The writer of Hebrews describes heaven and earth "wear[ing] out like a garment" (Heb. 1:11), an idea already present in the Old Testament (e.g., Ps. 102:26; Isa. 51:6). Isaiah 34:4 expresses a similar thought, stating, "All the host of heaven shall rot away, and the skies roll up like a scroll." Describing his vision of God seated on the great white throne, John states, "From his presence earth and sky fled away, and no place was found for them" (Rev. 20:11).

Peter offers an even more dramatic and breathtaking depiction of the coming cosmic conflagration:

> But the day of the Lord will come like a thief, and then the heavens will pass away with a roar, and the heavenly bodies will be burned up and dissolved, and the earth and the works that are done on it will be exposed. Since all these things are thus to be dissolved, what sort of people ought you to be in lives of holiness and godliness, waiting for and hastening the coming of the day of God, because of which the heavens will be set on fire and dissolved, and the heavenly bodies will melt as they burn! But according to his promise we are waiting for new heavens and a new earth in which righteousness dwells. (2 Peter 3:10–13)

What exactly will God replace when he establishes this new heavens and new earth? And how will he bring this about? We shall address both of these issues here, the former briefly and the latter in some detail.

The NHNE: A Literal Replacement of the Entire Physical Universe

The "heaven" and "earth" that are replaced refer to the entire created universe—in other words, not only the earth but the atmospheric (first) and celestial (second) heavens. The Hebrew Old Testament has no word for "universe" as such, and the expression "heaven and earth" serves that function.[1]

Heaven as God's abode (the third heaven) will not experience renovation or replacement, for there is no need for that. We need a NHNE because of the corruption sin caused in the old ones, from which the necessity of their renovation arises (Rom. 8:19–22). But that is inapplicable to heaven in the sense of God's abode, which is a place untouched by sin and where even now his will is already carried out perfectly (Matt. 6:10). What sort of "renovation" could possibly improve it?

I therefore agree with the statement in the *Baker Encyclopedia of the Bible*: "The heaven that will be renewed is not the heaven of God's presence, but the heaven of human existence, the starry expanse which constitutes the universe."[2]

The NHNE: Created from Scratch or Renovated and Redeemed?

One of the major questions surrounding the NHNE is how the old one goes out of existence and the new one comes to be. Does God annihilate the old heavens and earth and then replace them with new ones that he creates *ex nihilo*, i.e., from scratch? Or does God radically renew and renovate the existing ones?

Much hinges on how one interprets the language in Revelation 20:11 and 2 Peter 3:10–13, which we cited above. How should we understand words and expressions such as "set on fire and dissolved," "pass away with a roar," "melt," and "fled away"?

Commentators are divided in answering this question. Some opt for the annihilation and replacement model,[3] others favor the renewal position,[4]

---

1. Gary T. Meadors, "New Heavens and New Earth," *EDBT*, 563; Bradford A. Mullen, "Heaven, Heavens, Heavenlies," *EDBT*, 332.
2. "New Heavens and New Earth," *BEB*, 3:1547.
3. For example, among more recent commentators taking the annihilation and replacement view we have Osborne (whose language, despite some ambiguous disclaimers, seems to support the replacement view in fact) (Grant R. Osborne, *Revelation*, BECNT [Grand Rapids: Baker, 2002], 730; cf. 736–37). See also David E. Aune, *Revelation 1–5*, WBC 52 (Dallas: Word, 1997), 1117; and Robert L. Thomas, *Revelation 1–7: An Exegetical Commentary* (Chicago: Moody, 1992), 439–40. I believe Osborne incorrectly places Aune in the "renovation" camp (Osborne, *Revelation*, 736).
4. Richard Bauckham, *Jude, 2 Peter*, WBC 50 (Nashville: Thomas Nelson, 2003), 326; G. K. Beale, *The Book of Revelation: A Commentary on the Greek Text*, NIGTC (Grand Rapids: Eerdmans, 1999), 1040; Peter H. Davids, *The Letters of 2 Peter and Jude*, PNTC (Grand Rapids: Eerdmans, 2006), 284–87; Gene L. Green, *Jude and 2 Peter*, BECNT (Grand Rapids: Baker, 2008), 334; and Gale Z. Heide, "What Is New about the New Heaven and the New

and yet others admit their uncertainty.[5] According to Gouvea, those in the Reformed tradition tend to favor renewal, while Lutherans gravitate toward replacement.[6] The answer to this question, though, certainly crosses denominational lines.

The Argument for Annihilation Followed by a New Creation from Scratch

Those who argue for the replacement view place significant weight on the language both in 2 Peter 3 and in Revelation 20. Moo, himself undecided on the correct position, admits that the language of 2 Peter, taken alone, could readily imply annihilation followed by replacement.[7] Thomas, a strong proponent of the annihilation position, remarks, "The language of 20:11 which depicts an entire dissolving of the old, a vanishing into nothingness followed by a new creation in 21:1 without any sea is the decisive contextual feature that determines this to be a reference to an entirely new creation."[8]

Proponents of the annihilation/replacement position do not limit their argument merely to 2 Peter 3 and Revelation 20, however—critical as those passages may be to their view. Thomas urges that "the theory of a complete disappearance of the old before replacement by a new creation" boasts many verses in support besides these two classic texts, particularly Psalm 102:25–26; Isaiah 34:4; 51:6; and Matthew 24:35.[9] Aune would add Matthew 5:18; Mark 13:31; and Luke 16:17; 21:33 to this list.[10]

The Argument for Renewal/Renovation of the Present Earth

Others hold that the present earth will experience a massive and radical transformation without experiencing total eradication. Boring, in an interesting turn of phrase, puts it this way: "God does not make 'all new things,' but 'all things new.'"[11] They base their position both on an understanding of the biblical language discussing this transformation, and on certain larger theological considerations.

Earth? A Theology of Creation from Revelation 21 and 2 Peter 3," *JETS* 40, no. 1 (March 1997): 37–56, teach a renovation of the old earth.

5. Douglas J. Moo (*2 Peter, Jude*, NIVAC [Grand Rapids: Zondervan, 1996], 202), Robert H. Mounce (*The Book of Revelation*, rev. ed., NICNT [Grand Rapids: Eerdmans, 1998], 380), and Thomas Schreiner (*1, 2 Peter, Jude*, NAC 37 [Nashville: B&H, 2003], 392) present the pros and cons clearly enough but finally confess uncertainty as to whether we can determine the matter. Though Osborne places Mounce in the "replacement" camp, Mounce himself states, "Neither the language employed nor rabbinic commentary on relevant passages such as Isa 65:17ff. will supply a definitive answer" (*The Book of Revelation*, 380).

6. F. Q. Gouvea, "New Heavens, New Earth," *EDT*, 829.

7. Moo, *2 Peter, Jude*, 201.

8. Thomas, *Revelation 1–7*, 440.

9. Ibid., 439–40.

10. Aune, *Revelation 1–5*, 1132–33.

11. M. Eugene Boring, *Revelation*, Interpretation (Louisville: John Knox Press, 1989), 220.

Arguments for Renewal Based on the Language

One line of argument is that the Bible mentions a "regeneration" of the present cosmic order. Jesus himself speaks of "the regeneration" (*palingenesia*) that will occur when the Son of Man will sit on his glorious throne (Matt. 19:28). *Palingenesia* can be translated "regeneration" or "renewal."[12] Advocates of the renewal position say this word carries the sense of transforming or renovating something, not annihilating and then replacing it.[13]

As for taking the passage in 2 Peter 3 as teaching the annihilation and then replacement of the present earth, one need not take Peter's language as teaching annihilation followed by replacement. As I will show later in the context of the annihilationist theory of eternal punishment, when the wicked are said to be "consumed," "destroyed," and the like, such language does not mean that the wicked are removed from all existence.[14] Rather, the meaning is that they are "destroyed," "demolished," or otherwise rendered unfit for their intended purpose. Peter, in describing the earth's coming renewal, uses language very similar to this, in fact drawing upon related Greek vocabulary in verse 6.[15] Therefore, even though the earth and the celestial realm are "destroyed" in the sense that Peter describes, it would not follow that the constituent materials pass out of existence altogether but that God raises up something new and marvelous from the rubble, or at least from part of the rubble.

Argument for Renewal Based on the Analogy of Redemption

Moving beyond an examination of the specific language of key passages such as those mentioned above, we also have broader theological considerations and analogies that would cause us to lean toward a renovation model over the annihilation/replacement position.

Consider the parallel between the coming cosmic destruction and the Noahic flood. Peter himself, in the same epistle we have been considering, draws precisely this comparison.[16] But in the case of the flood, God did not annihilate and then recreate the earth from scratch, even though he judged, decimated, and cleansed it. Likewise, we should not see a complete annihilation as taking place here, either.[17]

Another analogy that points to a regeneration of the existing earth is the comparison Scripture makes between the redemption of creation and our own redemption from sin, and that seen preeminently in the bodily resurrection.

---

12. The ESV renders *palingenesia* as "new world." The KJV and ESV have "regeneration." See BDAG, "παλιγγενεσία" 752; Friedrich Büchsel, "παλιγγενεσία," *TDNT* 1:686–89.
13. See the discussion of this word in Moo, *2 Peter, Jude,* 201; and Meadors, "New Heavens and New Earth," 564.
14. See Question 34.
15. I.e., *apōleto,* which is a form of *apollumi.*
16. I.e., 2 Peter 2:5 and 3:6–7.
17. See Gene L. Green, *Jude and 2 Peter,* BECNT (Grand Rapids: Baker, 2008), 334.

In Romans 8:19–23, Paul depicts a creation that is "groaning" and in the "pains of childbirth" (v. 22), just as we, too, "groan inwardly as we wait eagerly for adoption as sons, the redemption of our bodies" (v. 23). Now, from a spiritual perspective, in our own redemption there is not an annihilation of who we are as individuals but a radical renovation and cleansing. When we become "a new creation" in Christ (2 Cor. 5:17), we do not become different people *numerically* speaking, but renewed and transformed creatures *qualitatively* speaking. In other words, when you become a "new creation," you are still you (i.e., the same person numerically), but you are just a "whole lot better of a you" (i.e., qualitatively). Likewise, and from a physical perspective, Scripture makes it clear that God will transform our mortal bodies, not create new ones for us from scratch (Phil. 3:21; 1 Cor. 15:44).[18] At the same time, there is also a destruction (though not an annihilation) of the old entailed in the bringing forth of the new in both aspects of our renewal. Even so, the new earth will not be numerically different from the old but will retain some continuity of identity with it, even though the transformation will be dramatic.[19] Ladd correctly summarizes the matter when he states, "The redemption of the natural world from evil and decay is the corollary of the redemption of the body."[20]

REFLECTION QUESTIONS

1. What will be replaced when the NHNE comes into being? Will this include "heaven" in the sense of God's abode? Why or why not?

2. After reading this chapter, do you favor the annihilation and replacement model or the renovation and redemption model for understanding how the NHNE comes into being? What do you see as the strongest arguments for each?

3. When you consider the awesome way in which the NHNE comes into being—on either view—how does this make you feel? Reflect on Peter's statement in 1 Peter 3:11–12.

4. In what way does the destruction of Noah's flood point toward the renovation model and not the annihilation/replacement model?

---

18. For more discussion, see Question 19, "What Will the Resurrection Body Be Like?"
19. As Meadors states, "The term *kainos*, 'new,' in contrast to *palaois*, 'old,' may mean new in character rather than substance (cf. 2 Cor. 5:17; Heb. 8:13)" ("New Heavens and a New Earth," 564). See also the discussion in Question 21 on the meaning of the word "new" in the expression "new heavens and new earth."
20. George Eldon Ladd, *Theology of the New Testament* (Grand Rapids: Eerdmans, 1993), 613.

5. Consider the doctrine of the resurrection of the flesh that will take place at the final judgment. Is there anything about this doctrine that lends support to either the annihilation/replacement or the renovation/redemption model?

What Is the New Jerusalem?

> The one who conquers, I will make him a pillar in the temple of my God. Never shall he go out of it, and I will write on him the name of my God, and the name of the city of my God, the new Jerusalem, which comes down from my God out of heaven, and my own new name. (Rev. 3:12)

> And I saw the holy city, the new Jerusalem, coming down out of heaven from God, prepared as a bride adorned for her husband. (Rev. 21:2)

The Bible mentions the "New Jerusalem" (NJ) as such in only two New Testament passages: one toward the beginning of the book of Revelation (3:12) and the other toward the end (21:2). However, the concept expressed by the term is broader, with aspects of it attested elsewhere.[1]

The ancient city of Jerusalem was, of course, a place of great significance for God's covenant people. In the Old Testament, Jerusalem was "the place where God's rule over his people and his presence among them was centered."[2] This key aspect of Jerusalem carries over in the case of the New Jerusalem as well, and no doubt figures significantly in the continuing use of this name even into the eternal state.

The Heavenly Jerusalem in Relation to the New Jerusalem

Besides the two references to the NJ cited above, Hebrews 12:22–24 also speaks of the "heavenly Jerusalem" (HJ). This text reads:

---

1. For example, Isaiah 65:18 most likely refers to the same thing.
2. Michael J. Wilcock, "Jerusalem, New," *BEB*, 3:1135.

> But you have come to Mount Zion and to the city of the
> living God, the heavenly Jerusalem, and to innumerable an-
> gels in festal gathering, and to the assembly of the firstborn
> who are enrolled in heaven, and to God, the judge of all, and
> to the spirits of the righteous made perfect, and to Jesus, the
> mediator of a new covenant, and to the sprinkled blood that
> speaks a better word than the blood of Abel.

When we examined this text earlier, I noted that the reference to "the spirits of righteous men made perfect" shows that the HJ is the abode where de-ceased believers presently reside, i.e., in the intermediate state, awaiting the resurrection of their bodies.[3] It is the place that Jesus said he would prepare for his disciples—his Father's house in which are many rooms (John 14:2). In this present age, the HJ is located in heaven, and the saints who abide in it do so awaiting the resurrection of their bodies. At the end of the age, God will relocate the HJ to the earth as the NJ.[4]

A closely related passage is Galatians 4:26, in which Paul refers to "the Jerusalem above." Though Paul does not discuss heaven as such in this text, there is nothing to preclude identifying the "Jerusalem above" with the HJ, and the expression itself strongly suggests that they are equivalent.

Is the New Jerusalem a Literal City?

Some argue that the NJ is not a literal city but that we should under-stand it as pointing symbolically and figuratively to certain other truths. The point here in dispute is not whether John may have used figurative language to describe a literal city, for at least some of the language describing the NJ is almost certainly figurative. Rather, the question is whether Revelation 21 is describing—figuratively or otherwise—a literal city, or whether it is using the figure of a city to describe something else.

One View: The New Jerusalem Is Not a City but the People of God

Some believe that the NJ is not a city at all but is simply a metaphor for the people of God. Gundry, in an oft-cited article devoted to this subject, states flatly, "John is not describing the eternal dwelling place of the saints; he is de-scribing them, and them alone."[5] According to Gundry, the NJ is a "dwelling

---

3. See discussion of this text in Question 10.
4. I believe Ladd gets the connection exactly right. See George Eldon Ladd, *A Commentary on the Revelation of John* (Grand Rapids: Eerdmans, 1972), 276.
5. Robert H. Gundry, "The New Jerusalem: People as Place, Not Place for People," *Novum Testamentum* 29, no. 3 (1987): 256. While Gundry does admit that a city can stand both for its inhabitants and for its location, his point is that here it stands for the people only and not a location.

place" but only in the sense that "it is God's dwelling place in the saints rather than their dwelling place on earth."[6]

Gundry believes that many factors point to this identification. Preeminently, in 21:2–3 and 21:9–10, "the earlier hints turn into a virtually explicit personal identification of the New Jerusalem with the saints."[7] Verse 2 describes the NJ as a "bride adorned for her husband." Then in verse 9 the angel says that he will show John "the Bride, the wife of the Lamb," which in verse 10 appears as the NJ coming down out of heaven.

It is important to note that Gundry does believe that the saints will dwell on a literal, physical new earth as their eternal abode. He has no doubt that the saints' "dwelling place is the earthly part of the new universe (21:1), down to which part they descend to take up their abode (21:2)."[8] However, he simply rejects the idea that it will be in a particular "localized city," no matter how capacious.[9]

Gundry is not the only scholar to embrace this line of argument. Beale, too, believes that to take this as speaking of a literal city "is to miss its fundamental symbolic nature."[10] For him, the "holy Jerusalem" is identical with "God's true people."[11] For that matter, they are not only the city but also the temple, "in which God's presence resides."[12] At the same time, Beale, like Gundry, affirms that there will be a "literal new cosmos"; he argues merely that here "the point of the vision is the focus on the exalted saints as the central feature of the new order."[13] Other scholars, such as Mounce and Aune, follow suit.[14]

The New Jerusalem as a Literal City (The Preferred View)

It is best to understand the NJ both as a literal city and as a reference to the people of God.

These are certainly not mutually exclusive ideas. Many commentators point to the parallel between Babylon and the NJ as illustrative. Osborne observes, "Babylon was both a people and a place, and that is the better answer

---

6. Ibid., 256.
7. Ibid., 257.
8. Ibid.
9. Ibid., 256.
10. G. K. Beale, *The Book of Revelation: A Commentary on the Greek Text*, NIGTC (Grand Rapids: Eerdmans, 1999), 1064.
11. Ibid., 1066.
12. Ibid.; see also 1070.
13. Ibid., 1065. It is interesting that Beale does not seem to be entirely consistent in his interpretation of the NJ as the people of God. Later, he states that it is "plausible" to regard the "city-temple" (i.e., the NJ) to be "equated with" the NHNE itself (1109). This would represent a shift in his earlier view that the NJ and the temple imagery point to the people and not to the place where they dwell.
14. See David E. Aune, *Revelation 1–5*, WBC 52 (Dallas: Word, 1997), 1187; Robert H. Mounce, *The Book of Revelation*, rev. ed., NICNT (Grand Rapids: Eerdmans, 1998), 382.

here."[15] The particular emphasis may vary, depending upon the point that the author is attempting to illustrate. So, the NJ refers to the people in 21:9–10, when the angel shows John the NJ as a bride. But it is a place in 21:3, which speaks of God as dwelling there; in 21:24, 26, when people "inherit" it; and in 21:24, 26, when the text describes nations as entering it.[16]

Thomas strongly urges that we should not see the NJ as "merely an ideal and fantastic city, but a true, real, substantial, and eternal one."[17] He, too, agrees that the bride refers both to "the people of God and [to] the seat of their abode."[18] According to him, "The figure of a bride-city captures two characteristics of the New Jerusalem: God's personal relationship with His people (i.e., the bride) and the life of the people in communion with Him (i.e., the city, with its social connotations)."[19] Boring makes this same point, saying, "A city is the realization of human community, the concrete living out of interdependence as the essential nature of human life."[20]

Interpreting the Language: Symbolic or Literal?

Is Any or All of the Language Used to Describe the New Jerusalem Symbolic?
Though the NJ is a literal city, the Bible nonetheless describes it using figurative and symbolic language. I believe Culver is correct when he urges, "Great care as well as caution must characterize our effort to distinguish literal and figurative elements."[21]

The issue here, I hasten to note, is not whether the Bible is trustworthy, reliable, or accurate. Nor is it a question of whether we can interpret the Bible "literally," for a "literal" interpretation of the Bible takes into account the use of figures of speech, metaphors, symbols, and the like where the context requires it. That the book of Revelation contains a good deal of symbolism is a point beyond dispute.

Some, especially popular writers, tend to take all or nearly all of the details given for the NJ in 21:11–27 literally.[22] Indeed, many of the common attributes associated with "heaven" in the common imagination—such as

---

15. Grant R. Osborne, *Revelation*, BECNT (Grand Rapids: Baker, 2002), 733. See also Craig S. Keener, *Revelation*, NIVAC (Grand Rapids: Zondervan, 2000), 486.
16. Osborne, *Revelation*, 733, 747. But in what may be a possible contradiction to this, see Osborne's discussion on 767.
17. Robert L. Thomas, *Revelation 1–7: An Exegetical Commentary* (Chicago: Moody, 1992), 461.
18. Ibid., 460.
19. Ibid., 442.
20. M. Eugene Boring, *Revelation*, Interpretation (Louisville: John Knox Press, 1989), 219.
21. Robert Culver, *Systematic Theology: Biblical and Historical* (Fearn, Ross-shire, UK: Mentor, 2005), 1108.
22. For example, Hitchcock appears to take all of the elements as literal, including the city's dimensions, materials, etc. Randy Alcorn's popular book on heaven also does this.

"pearly gates" and "streets of gold"—come from a literal understanding of this passage. However, it is highly questionable which elements one should take literally here. For example, Thomas, a scholarly writer who tends to be one of the more literal interpreters of the city's characteristics, admits, "The dimensions and layout design of the Jerusalem descending from heaven are an accommodation to finite minds, so a complete comprehension of the new creation is not the expected result." At the same time, Thomas believes that the text "does give architectural information about the city, and is not merely theologically symbolic of the fulfillment of all God's promises."[23] On this latter point he could well be correct, though it may be difficult to tease out the literal from the figurative. For example, if one takes the dimensions of the walls literally, they are "hopelessly out of proportion for a city some 1,400 miles high!"[24]

Examples of Some of the Symbols Employed

The features of the NJ are described primarily in 21:11–27. An exhaustive consideration of what these descriptions might symbolize is not necessary here, even if it were possible to determine them all. We shall consider a few of some of the more commonly discussed ones, just for the sake of illustration.

The City's Shape and Measurements

The dimensions of the city, if taken literally, would make it a massive cube 1,400 to 1,500 miles high. However, as noted, it is questionable whether we should take these dimensions literally. Regardless, the city's massive measurements mean "that all the saints, whom the city represents, will amount to an astronomically high number."[25] The city's dimensions speak not only of its immense capacity but also reflect its "perfect symmetry" and "splendor."[26]

Commentators note the parallel here with the cube-shaped Holy of Holies in 1 Kings 6:20 and 2 Chronicles 3:8–9.[27] This is singularly appropriate in as much as the Holy of Holies was "the place of divine presence" under the old covenant.[28] There God especially manifested his glory, thus foreshadowing one of the key aspects of the eternal city.

---

23. Thomas, *Revelation 1–7*, 460–61.
24. Mounce, *The Book of Revelation*, 392. Beale (*The Book of Revelation*, 1074) and Osborne (*Revelation*, 753) make this same point. There is some dispute whether the 144-cubit (216-foot) dimension of the wall refers to its width or its height. Osborne takes it as referring to the width, but concludes, "Either way, the wall is terribly small for a city 1,500 miles high (an argument for taking the description as more symbolic than literal)." Taking it as reference to the wall's width, Thomas (*Revelation 1–7*, 468) does not regard it as out of proportion to its height.
25. Gundry, "The New Jerusalem," 260.
26. Mounce, *The Book of Revelation*, 391.
27. E.g., Gundry, "The New Jerusalem," 261; Keener, *Revelation*, 494; Mounce, *The Book of Revelation*, 392; Osborne, *Revelation*, 753; Thomas, *Revelation 1–7*, 444.
28. Mounce, *The Book of Revelation*, 392.

The act itself of measuring the city (21:15–17) is designed to highlight certain key truths about it. The process of measuring it "connotes God's ownership and protection of his people."[29] It points to the "security of its inhabitants against the harm and contamination of unclean and deceptive people."[30]

The City's Foundation, Walls, and Gates
The NJ, being a literal city, could be surrounded by a literal wall with twelve literal gates. Of course, such a wall and gates would not be required for the function typically assigned to them in the ancient (or even the modern) world, which was to keep out potential enemies and invaders.

If symbolic, perhaps the reason for mentioning the twelve gates is to stress the "abundant entrance" to the city.[31] The names of the twelve tribes are on the gates because Israel, through whom the Messiah came, served as the channel of blessing to the entire world. Moreover, the fact that there are gates on all sides of the city shows that it "welcomes people from all directions."[32]

While the names of the twelve tribes are inscribed on the gates, the foundations contain the names of the twelve apostles. One might question why the imagery was not reversed, granting that the twelve tribes are chronologically prior, and so in a certain sense the old covenant was foundational for the new. However, as some commentators argue, the apostles are more appropriately placed here, for they preached Christ and the church is built on their foundation (Eph. 2:20). Taken together, the text makes plain the continuity and unity between God's people in both dispensations.

As for the walls, their enormous height demonstrates safety and the "inviolable nature of fellowship with God," which cannot be broken.[33]

The Gold, Pearls, and Precious Stones
It may be that the city has literal gates and literal streets paved with material gold, whose literal foundations are bedecked with literal jewels, and whose actual gates sport physical pearls. Some, such as Gundry, take these as references to material wealth, and argue that we ought not to spiritualize them.[34] This is certainly possible, especially if we grant that the NJ will be a literal city. Perhaps, though, some or all of these items are figurative. Regardless, all of these elements, whether literal or figurative, point to the city's real beauty and splendor.

29. Osborne, *Revelation*, 752.
30. Beale, *The Book of Revelation*, 1072.
31. Mounce, *The Book of Revelation*, 390.
32. Keener, *Revelation*, 492.
33. Beale, *The Book of Revelation*, 1084.
34. Gundry, "The New Jerusalem," 261.

The Presence of Nations outside of the New Jerusalem

One point that has occasioned some difficulty for interpreters is the mention of nations apparently situated outside of the NJ. Revelation 21:24 states that "the kings of the earth will bring their glory into [the NJ]," while 21:26 indicates that these kings "will bring into it the glory and the honor of the nations." Who are these nations, where did they come from, and why are they outside the city?

What further complicates the matter is that after 22:14 refers to the blessed who have the right to enter the city by the gates, verse 15 declares, "*Outside* are the dogs and sorcerers and the sexually immoral and murderers and idolaters, and everyone who loves and practices falsehood" (emphasis added). If these nations reside "outside" the city—which they must, if the text says that they "enter" it—would not this list have them in mind? But how could such people be "blessed" and given access to the city? Furthermore, 21:8 clearly describes these same immoral individuals as consigned to the lake of fire and therefore not as residing on the glorious new earth at all!

While there are many details connected with this issue, for now a few observations may suffice.

First, it does appear that the NJ and the new earth are not exactly coextensive. The NJ is a city that resides on the new earth but it is not the only city. The fact that nations enter and exit it demonstrates that, per se. Nevertheless, there is a real sense in which we may consider even those dwelling outside the city limits to be citizens of that city in a larger, more profound sense. This becomes evident when one examines Psalm 87, which is highly relevant to this question. Here, the redeemed from nations such as Babylon, Philistia, Tyre, and Cush are "given a Zion-birth status,"[35] and in verse 6 are described as being formally registered among its citizens by God himself. This is because the city of Jerusalem is "the world center of Yahweh worship, which will be for all peoples" and "the 'mother city' in a universal worship of Yahweh."[36] Accordingly, "The Lord counts them not as so many Egyptians or Babylonians, Philistines, Tyrians, or Ethiopians, but as sons and daughters of Zion,"[37] despite the varied geographical locations in which they may reside physically. This is because "God calls Zion the place of their spiritual birth and the religious mother of His people who dwell in those lands."[38] "It is," in short, "Yahweh's intention to make peoples from nations far and wide to be citizens of Zion, joining with those native to the city."[39]

---

35. Marvin E. Tate, *Psalms 51–100*, WBC 20 (Dallas: Word, 1990), 386.
36. Ibid., 387, 389.
37. Elmer. A. Leslie, *Psalms: Translated and Interpreted in the Light of Hebrew Worship* (Nashville: Abingdon Press, 1949), 35.
38. Ibid.
39. Tate, *Psalms 51–100*, 392–93. See also Ross's comments on this psalm. Allen P. Ross, *A Commentary on the Psalms*, 2 vols. (Grand Rapids: Kregel, 2013), esp. 2:796–99.

Second, it is evident that the nations mentioned in Revelation 21 are not hostile to God in any way but are redeemed believers. Clearly, dogs, sorcerers, idolaters, and the like could not possibly bring "glory" or "honor" into the city! Besides, 21:27 explicitly says that nothing unclean will enter the city, but only those whose names are written in the book of life. This must characterize the nations in 21:24, 26, since they have free access to it. Consequently, these nations no doubt comprise true followers of God, whoever exactly they may be.

Third, the apparent problem of 22:15 hinges on the meaning of "outside." Here two considerations come to mind. The first is that the text says only that the reprobate listed in verse 15 are outside the city, not that they reside on the new earth. Nor is there any implication that they do. Granting that the focal point of chapters 21 and 22 has been on the NJ in particular, it is hardly surprising that the passage would indicate those who have no right to abide in the city. This in no way implies that the wicked will have any portion in the "suburbs" of the new earth, as it were, even if not in its main city. Second, and consistent with our discussion of Psalm 87 above, being "inside" or "outside" of the city can refer to something other than geographical or spatial location. While the wicked are indeed "outside" of the city spatially—and outside of the entire new earth, for that matter—they find themselves especially excluded in a spiritual sense. Given that the NJ stands for the center of the universal worship of Yahweh, the reprobates remain "outside" of this, regardless of where they may abide physically.

REFLECTION QUESTIONS

1. What was the significance of the ancient city of Jerusalem in the Old Testament? What aspects of that significance carry over into the NJ in the eternal state?

2. Is the "heavenly Jerusalem" (HJ) the same as the NJ? Where is it located now? Where will it be in the future?

3. Should we understand the NJ literally or figuratively or both?

4. Does the fact that the NJ is discussed primarily in books that are often highly symbolic suggest that we cannot really understand anything about it? What extremes ought we to avoid when interpreting the NJ and concepts like it?

5. Reflect on the presence of nations outside of the NJ. Does this suggest that literal, national entities may carry over into the eternal state? How do you feel about this?

What Will We Know in the Eternal State?

> Now I know in part; but then shall I know even as also I am known. (1 Cor. 13:12b, KJV)

When we pass from this present life, what will we know in the next? Will we remember our previous earthly experiences? Will we recognize our loved ones and other acquaintances? Will we know more than we do now—perhaps even knowing everything like God does? Will we continue to learn new things? People often ask questions such as these, and with good reason. Since what goes on in our minds is the most important part of our present life, why would this not be true in our future life as well?

We can state the following about what we will know in the age to come:

1. Our knowledge in the afterlife will be much greater than it is now.

2. We will never be omniscient.

3. We will continue to learn and grow in our knowledge for all eternity.

4. We will remember our past experiences.

5. We will recognize one another.

Our Knowledge in the Afterlife Will Be Much Greater Than It Is Now

There is every reason to think that we will possess greatly expanded knowledge and consciousness in the next life. For one thing, we will not have the degrading effects of sin that diminish our mental powers. Though we have no direct scriptural evidence about what Adam's mental capabilities might have been like before the fall, we may safely infer that they were greater than afterwards. Scripture does clearly mention the damaging effects of sin on Adam's body; we have examined this to some degree already.[1] But this degradation of Adam's body suggests immediately a similarly degrading effect on his mind. We all know that bodily weaknesses and defects may affect adversely the operations of our minds. For instance, even in an otherwise healthy person, bodily fatigue harms mental concentration. Even more seriously, the ravages of diseases that afflict the brain, such as Alzheimer's, ruin memory and mental acuity.

None of these bodily defects will have any place in the afterlife. In the intermediate state, we lack a physical brain through which cognition takes place, so there can be no impairment of our thought processes through that bodily organ. Moreover, in the eternal state, our new, resurrected bodies will be full of life and utterly incorruptible. So assuming that thought operates in conjunction with some kind of physical brain there, it will be a flawless brain, matching the rest of our body's perfections.

Just as our physical bodies in the resurrection will be superior even to Adam's body before he fell into sin, even so, our minds will be greater than Adam's, even before he fell. Though we do not have explicit verses to prove this directly, I do think it reasonable to assume, for example, that we will have perfect memories, with absolute and instant recall of all that we have learned. Perhaps, too, our other senses will be enhanced and sharpened, and we will possess superior agility and speed of movement.[2] If our bodies will take on heretofore unimagined properties, we may reasonably conclude that our minds will also.

We Will Never Be Omniscient

While our knowledge in the eternal state will be much greater than it is now, it does not follow that we will know everything there is to know. In other words, we will not become omniscient. Shedd's observation is correct:

> We are not to understand that the creature's knowledge, in the future state, will be as extensive as that of the Omniscient One; or that it will be as profound and exhaustive as His. The infinitude of things can be known only by the Infinite Mind.[3]

But what about Paul's statement in 1 Corinthians 13:12 (KJV): "For now we see through a glass, darkly; but then face to face: now I know in part; but then shall I know even as also I am known"? Shedd suggests that we ought not

---

1. See, for example, Question 20, "What Will the Resurrection Body Be Like? (Part 2)."
2. Charles Hodge, *Systematic Theology*, 3 vols. (New York: Scribner's, 1871), 3:783.
3. W. G. T. Shedd, *Sermons to the Natural Man* (New York: Scribner's, 1871), 23–24.

to take this statement absolutely, as if referring to all knowledge about everything, but only relatively. "Upon certain moral subjects," Shedd states, "the perception of the creature will be like that of his Maker and Judge, so far as the kind or quality of the apprehension is concerned."[4] For example, we shall comprehend sin, righteousness, and the glories of redemption with an immediacy and directness impossible in this present life. Though now we possess only a very limited understanding of these matters, then we shall know the whole story because we shall see it directly or "face to face," i.e., by sight. Nevertheless, the immediacy and clarity of such knowledge is not the same as God's infinite and exhaustive knowledge of all things. It remains adapted to what we can comprehend as glorified creatures, for creatures we are and creatures we remain.

We Will Continue to Learn and Grow in Our Knowledge for All Eternity

Related to the finitude of our knowledge is our continued growth in it. What we know and experience in the eternal state will not be static but ever increasing.

As created and therefore finite beings, we are mutable. This means that we are subject to change. Change, however, is not necessarily a bad thing if the direction in which we are changing is for the better. As we grow, we develop, enlarge, and actualize our capacities for enjoying God and his creation—from "glory to glory" (2 Cor. 3:18, kjv), so to speak.

But are we not perfect in the eternal state? And if we are perfect, then how can we grow in knowledge or in any other way? Well, the good angels are already perfect, and yet it is clear that their knowledge of the plan of redemption was limited (1 Peter 1:12). Angels no doubt understand more now about God's magnificent plan than they did before the coming of Messiah, meaning that they have increased or grown in their knowledge. Yet, there was and is no flaw in these ministering spirits.

Perhaps it is helpful to distinguish between perfect knowledge and exhaustive knowledge. We can know something perfectly to the degree that we are capable of knowing it, without thereby knowing it exhaustively. Our knowledge may be "perfect" in the sense that it is fully true as far as it goes, without any admixture of error. Nevertheless, we may still be able to learn even more about the subject, or to develop an appreciation for it in new and different ways. This is especially so if our capacity for understanding expands with further experience and use.

What we are saying here about growth in the eternal state should in no way discourage us but rather be cause for great excitement. Simply because growth in our present state of existence is frequently painful does not mean it will always be so. Far from being a defect, growth is the glory of the mutable

---

4. Ibid., 24.

creature. God made us for growth and we will revel in it. Learning new things about God, his creation, and one another for all eternity is truly a thrilling prospect. Imagine the anticipation and delight that each day will hold!

We Will Remember Our Past Experiences

Memory is an essential part of our personhood. Without memory, there could be no psychological continuity of personal identity or sense of the self. We can only know who we are today by our connection with who and what we were yesterday.

If we were to enter the eternal state with our mental "hard drives" erased of all their data, this would be more like the creation of an altogether new person than the redemption and glorification of an existing one. Without such memory, how could we appreciate the splendor of our redemption? The book of Revelation shows that the saints in heaven remain fully aware of their redemption and they praise God for it.[5] But absent their memories of the past, "all the songs of heaven would cease. There could be no thanksgiving for redemption; no recognition of all God's dealings with us in this world." Hodge concludes that, far from losing our memories, "the records of the past may be as legible to us as the events of the present."[6]

If we retain our memories of the past, including all the trauma and heartache we experienced in this life, then how could we be supremely happy? Would not our memory of those painful events generate renewed hurt and anguish? How could God "wipe away every tear from [our] eyes" (Rev. 7:17; 21:4) without also wiping out our memory of what caused those tears in the first place? Furthermore, did not God himself say that on the new earth there would no longer be weeping and sadness, but that "the former things shall not be remembered or come into mind" (Isa. 65:17)?

Sometimes when the Bible speaks of "forgetting" it is not talking about forgetting in the literal or absolute sense, but rather "forgetting" in the sense that a negative situation or action will no longer bring about its harmful effects. Consider the case of sin. When the Bible says that God will not "remember" our sins (Isa. 43:25; Jer. 31:34; Heb. 8:12; 10:17), we should not take this to mean that God literally no longer remembers the *facts* about our sins, such as what they were, when we committed them, etc. Were that so, then God would cease to be omniscient. Furthermore, since we most certainly recall these details, we would have to draw the absurd conclusion that we would know certain things that God does not, which is of course impossible.[7]

---

5. E.g., chapters 4–6. Though not all of the beings in these chapters are human (e.g., angels), some are.

6. Hodge, *Systematic Theology*, 3:782.

7. Indeed, since God knows perfectly our thoughts, even if he somehow *could* literally forget the details of our sin, his ignorance would be quite short lived, granting that he would be reminded of these details the instant he read our thoughts about them (Heb. 4:13)!

Rather, God no longer "remembers" our transgressions in the sense that he forgives them, treating us as if we had never committed them; he no longer "brings them to mind" in order to punish us for them. Similarly, in the eternal state we will so see things from God's perspective that we will no longer remember our past hurts and pain as we experienced them, but will see all from the divine vantage point. We will remember *that* these hurts occurred, but they will no longer bring us pain but rather praise, as we contemplate how God has worked all for good (Rom. 8:28) and brought us "beauty for ashes" and "the oil of joy for mourning" (Isa. 61:3, KJV).

We find a clear example of this in Revelation 6:9–11, which depicts the souls under the altar, who were martyred for their testimony to Jesus. This scene occurs in the intermediate state in heaven, and the "souls" thus depicted are disembodied at this point. These individuals demonstrate a vivid recollection of their martyrdom, even crying out for God to avenge their deaths. In one sense, their happiness is not yet complete because they await God's justice for their deaths, which has yet to take place. Yet, though they long for God to exact justice on his enemies and theirs, it is also clear from this text that God has given them peaceful repose when he tells them to "rest (*anapausontai*) a little longer" before he grants their request (v. 11).[8]

We Will Recognize One Another

One of the most frequently asked questions about the afterlife is whether we will recognize our loved ones there. The answer is definitely yes!

If we retain our memories of our (present) earthly life in general, why would that not include the most important facet of our earthly lives, which is our interpersonal relationships? As Hodge put it, "If men are to retain in heaven the knowledge of their earthly life, this of course involves the recollection of all social relations, of all the ties of respect, love, and gratitude which bind men in family and society."[9]

Beyond this general conclusion, we find passages in the Bible that teach or at least suggest that we will recognize the identities of others in the afterlife. This is so both in the intermediate and in the eternal state.

Jesus's Postresurrection Appearances to His Disciples

In Question 20, in our consideration of the resurrection body, we observed that Christ's disciples recognized the resurrected Christ as the Jesus that they knew. Indeed, on the road to Emmaus, the noteworthy case where they did not recognize him, it took a special miracle of God to prevent them

---

8. The verb translated "rest" here means more than simply to bide one's time but can also carry the sense of regaining one's strength after arduous labor; to experience refreshment. See the discussion of this text in Question 38.
9. Hodge, *Systematic Theology*, 3:782.

from identifying him, thus showing that would have otherwise perceived who he was (Luke 24:16, 31).

Luke 16:19–31
The story of the rich man and Lazarus, which is set during the disembodied intermediate state, shows recognition of one's former earthly relations. Lazarus and the rich man clearly identify one another and have complete recollection of their former interactions. Furthermore, the rich man recalls his five brothers who were yet alive on earth (v. 28). Though this account may well be a parable, we may nevertheless use it to derive truths about the afterlife, as I have urged earlier.[10] For this reason, not a few interpreters use this verse to demonstrate precisely this point.[11]

Matthew 8:11
In this verse, Jesus said that we shall sit down with Abraham, Isaac, and Jacob in the kingdom of heaven. If we will recognize them for who they are, having never met them prior, how much more will we recognize those whom we have already known?

1 Thessalonians 4:13–18
These verses teach that when the Lord returns to earth, he will have in his train an entourage of believers who have previously passed away. Paul presents this to the Thessalonians to comfort them (vv. 13, 18), since some of them were harboring doubts about the fate of their previously deceased loved ones. But what comfort would this be apart from a definite recognition of these saints?

To Be Gathered to One's Fathers/One's People
Quite a few Old Testament verses speak of an individual as being "gathered to one's people,"[12] or "gathered to one's fathers" at death.[13] Some prominent Old Testament scholars have made a strong case that such expressions refer to more than simply the common fate of death that befalls all mortals, but point rather to ongoing existence in the afterlife with one's deceased but still conscious family members. As Delitzsch states, "Union with the fathers [is] not a union merely of corpses but of persons."[14] Similarly, Heidel observes:

---

10. See the discussion in Question 6, "Does Our Soul or Spirit Survive the Death of Our Body?"
11. E.g., René Pache, *The Future Life* (Chicago: Moody, 1962), 8; W. G. T. Shedd, *Dogmatic Theology*, ed. Alan W. Gomes (Phillipsburg: P&R, 2003), 875n7.3.5.
12. E.g., Genesis 25:8, 17; 35:29; 49:29, 33; Numbers 20:24; 27:13; 31:2; Deuteronomy 32:50.
13. E.g., Genesis 15:15; 2 Kings 22:20; 2 Chronicles 34:28; Judges 2:10.
14. Franz Delitzsch, *A New Commentary on Genesis*, trans. Sophia Taylor, 2 vols. (New York: Scribner & Welford, 1889), 2:121.

> . . . the expressions under consideration cannot mean anything else than that the soul or spirit of a certain person leaves this world at death and enters the afterworld, in which his fathers or certain of his kindred already find themselves.[15]

Now, if these expressions do indeed point to the conscious existence of one's family members beyond the grave, and further indicate that we shall join them there upon our own earthly demise, it must certainly follow that we will recognize these family members upon being "gathered" to them.

REFLECTION QUESTIONS

1. Does the thought of having greatly enhanced mental capacities in the eternal state excite you? Try to imagine for a moment what it might be like to have perfect memory and other greatly expanded mental powers.

2. Does the thought that you will not be omniscient even in the eternal state bother or disappoint you? Why or why not?

3. How do you feel about the idea that you will continue to learn new things in the eternal state? Had you ever thought about this before? Do you see this as exciting or discouraging?

4. Are you concerned that you might be sad if you remember your past in the eternal state? Consider how seeing your past from God's perspective, including even the painful events, might lead to joy and praise.

5. Do you look forward to being reunited with your loved ones in the eternal state? How does this provide comfort for the pain you may now be experiencing over the loss of those with whom you had been close?

---

15. Alexander Heidel, *The Gilgamesh Epic and Old Testament Parallels* (Chicago: University of Chicago, 1949), 188. Heidel makes the case for this understanding on 186–89.

What Will We Do in the Eternal State?

Sitting on a heavenly cloud, strumming a golden harp or polishing a halo. An interminable church service, where people sing psalms without respite. A semiconscious slumber in which our disembodied soul forever "rests in peace." There you have some of the common, popular conceptions of our everlasting life "in heaven." It is small wonder that many professing Christians remain so firmly attached to this present life, despite what they may tell their Sunday school teachers.

I am convinced that one of the main reasons people may not be excited about "dying and going to heaven forever" is that the usual picture of life after death is so unnatural, weird, and utterly unlike anything they really enjoy. But what if our activities in the eternal state actually look more like the most enjoyable things we do in this life, only vastly better in every way?

As I have already demonstrated,[1] the notion of spending eternity in heaven in a kind of disembodied or semi-embodied, ethereal, floaty, and slumberous existence must go. For one thing, such a view of heaven is in some ways skewed to begin with. However, more to the point, heaven is not the believer's eternal home anyway; a new earth is. We will enjoy our lives on this physical new earth in new *bodies*—as fleshly and tangible as the ones we have now. Moreover, we will continue to do many of the kinds of activities we do here, minus all the suffering, pain, and disappointment that often taints even our best experiences.

If the eternal state is not so much about giving up our legitimate and God-honoring joys in the present life as it is about enjoying them perfectly and in right relationship with the giver of all perfect gifts (James 1:17), why would we want to cling to the inferior version? At the same time, there will be some surprises in store for us, too. In the eternal state, we shall enjoy new

---

1. See especially Question 7 and Question 21.

adventures awaiting us that never have or could have entered our minds until we get there (1 Cor. 2:9).

Based on Scripture, we can affirm the following about our activities in the eternal state (i.e., on the new earth):

1. We will revel in God's direct presence and worship him supremely.

2. We will experience joyful rest.

3. We will engage in physical activities with physical bodies.

4. We will enjoy social interactions with one another.

5. We will exercise responsibility and service.

We Will Revel in God's Direct Presence and Worship Him Supremely

By far the best thing about the eternal state is that God is there!

Revelation 21:3 speaks of the new earth as follows: "Behold, the dwelling place of God is with man. He will dwell with them, and they will be his people, and God himself will be with them as their God." God's direct, unfiltered presence is by far the best and most exciting aspect of life on the new earth. This truth is so important that we cannot begin to do justice to it in many volumes, much less as a brief subpoint of the larger question we are considering here.

Now, one might well ask, "Is not God with us already? After all, God is omnipresent, is he not? So how could God be any more 'present' with us than he already is?" Of course God is omnipresent. However, our weakness and sin greatly cloud and diminish our *sense* of God's presence in this life. In the eternal state, on the new earth, we shall have a greatly enhanced capacity for experiencing God, and we shall enjoy his presence to a degree that we simply cannot yet imagine.

Why would contemplating God and experiencing his full presence be something we would want to do? What fun is that? Well, for the Christian, we do enjoy God's presence, even in this present life. God is, as the psalmist David makes clear, the object of ultimate beauty. David exclaims that he eagerly desires to "gaze upon the beauty of the LORD" and to "dwell in the house of the LORD" all the days of his life (Ps. 27:4).[2] The biblical writers often speak of their longing to "see" God and enjoy him as their most ardent object of desire. A psalm of Asaph declares, "[T]here is nothing on earth that I desire besides you. My flesh and my heart may fail, but God is the strength of my heart and my portion forever" (Ps. 73:25–26). Yet, the degree to which we can and do delight in God now is limited, spasmodic, and feeble. How much more

---

2. See also Psalms 17:15; 42:2; and 65:4.

will we revel in the contemplation of the Divine when that which beclouds our vision is removed and we see him "face to face" (1 Cor. 13:12)?

Our immediate vision of God leads directly to our spontaneous worship of him. Revelation 19:1–8 depicts a heavenly scene, describing the worship of a great multitude that includes both angels and the church. Revelation 15:2–4 portrays those who had withstood the beast, worshipping God with exclamations of praise and song. Other scenes of worship include Revelation 7:10; 11:16–18; and 15:2–4. Although these particular scenes take place in heaven, such worship and praise of God certainly will carry over into life on the new earth, since the reasons for such praise—the greatness of God and his works, and our capacity for marveling at them—will be just as true then.

I agree with Culver, who states, "*Worship* is the primary activity of saints in glory."[3] However, it is important to see this worship in a holistic way, realizing that all of our life in the eternal state is worship. Everything we do there—whether praising God in song, exploring the unfathomable beauties and mysteries of the new earth, engaging in exciting occupations of creativity and service, or enjoying supremely satisfying social interactions with one another—will redound to the praise and glory of our Creator. Consequently, worship is not so much a specific "activity" on the new earth but is more like the oxygen that fuels all of what we do there.[4]

We Will Experience Joyful Rest

The Bible describes the state of the redeemed in the afterlife as one of "rest." For instance, Revelation 14:13 declares as "blessed" those "who die in the Lord from now on." This is because "they may rest from their labors." A major theme in the book of Hebrews, particularly the fourth chapter, is entering into God's heavenly Sabbath rest. Paul likewise speaks of the "relief" or "rest" that God will grant believers at our Lord's second coming (2 Thess. 1:6–7).

We should not see the "rest" here as one of inactivity, much less as the semiconscious, shadowy slumber that those who speak of the dead as "resting in peace" (R.I.P.) typically have in mind. Rather, the idea is one of relief from burdensome or painful labor or suffering or affliction. This is immediately clear in the context in 2 Thessalonians 1:6–7, for example. Erickson correctly observes that the Christian's rest is not an absence of activity but "the completion of the Christian's pilgrimage, the end of the struggle against the flesh, the world, and the Devil. There will be work to do, but it will not involve fighting

---

3. Robert Culver, *Systematic Theology: Biblical and Historical* (Fearn, Ross-shire, UK: Mentor, 2005), 1106.
4. I agree with Middleton: "We should not reduce human worship of God to verbal, emotionally charged expressions of praise. . . . Rather, our worship consists in all that we do" (J. Richard Middleton, *A New Heaven and a New Earth* [Grand Rapids: Baker, 2014], 40).

against opposing forces."[5] This is so not only during our temporary heavenly sojourn that occurs immediately upon leaving this life but also on the new earth. In both places, we shall be refreshed continually in all of our occupations and pastimes, whatever they may be.

We Will Engage in Physical Activities with Physical Bodies

This particular point, of course, applies only to the eternal state on the new earth and not to the intermediate state, i.e., in heaven. Our resurrection bodies, as we have demonstrated at length, are physical, tangible bodies of flesh and bones.[6] Likewise, the new earth will be a literal, physical earth.[7] Consequently, it follows that we shall engage in physical activities. Why would God furnish us with a body, complete with physical limbs, and set us on a new earth with physical properties, if we are not going to put that physical body to good use?

What sorts of activities will we actually do with our new bodies? Here we need to keep our speculation within proper bounds, because Scripture tells us very little about day-to-day life on the new earth.

Some verses speak of eating and drinking in the kingdom of God (e.g., Luke 14:15; 22:16, 30),[8] while other passages present the imagery of a marriage supper (e.g., Rev. 19:9). Though it is possible that these references are to be understood figuratively, we do know that Jesus was able to eat after his resurrection and actually did so (Luke 24:41–43). Jesus surely did not need this or any other food to stay alive, and may have eaten in this instance simply to impress the truth of his physicality upon his astonished disciples. Also, we have the fruit trees mentioned in Revelation 22:1. Here again, this may be figurative but perhaps not. Who can say whether eating and drinking—something that brings us much pleasure in this present life—will continue in the resurrected state? Note that in this life, the sharing of a meal is often connected with our enjoyment of fellowship with one another (e.g., Acts 2:42), and surely that fellowship will continue in the eternal state (see the next point below). In any case, if we do eat food on the new earth it will not be because we have to but because we want to.

What about other physical activities, such as sports? One sometimes hears homey reflections at memorial services that depict, for example, "Cousin Joe

---

5. Millard Erickson, *Christian Theology* (Grand Rapids: Baker, 1985), 1229–30.
6. See Question 19 and Question 20.
7. See Question 21.
8. Some premillennial interpreters see these verses as referring specifically to the time of the millennium, which is the literal, thousand-year rule of Christ on this present earth, occurring before the new heavens and new earth in the eternal state. Those who do, myself included, also hold that (most) believers will already have received their new resurrected bodies at that time, in which they will also enjoy the eternal state. Thus, the verse may be relevant to the point being made here either way.

up there playing golf with the angels." While such a notion may bring an odd comfort to the bereaved, it is surely false, granting that golf requires a physical body to swing a physical club in order to whack a physical ball. However, on the new earth we will have physical limbs that we could use to swing an actual club. Who can say what the physics of the new earth will be like, and whether we would find activities like golf fun? Though we do not know, it is not impossible.

How about creating works of art or composing and performing music, which in our present experience involves the body as well as the mind? Again, there is every reason to think this is possible. Certainly, music continues beyond this present life in the worship of God, as we noted in our discussion above. The heavenly scenes in Revelation 5:8 and 15:2 depict harps—surely figurative language there, granting that these passages describe events taking place in the disembodied state. But might there not be literal, physical instruments on which musicians will make music on the new earth? Or will we convey the beauty of music in some other way? And does not the Bible talk about new songs (Rev. 5:9; 14:3), suggesting that composers will still have much to do? Might it be that the media through which they create and perform their music involves something physical?

Though we cannot know the specifics of what physical undertakings will occur on the new earth, we need not fret. We may safely say that we will be able to do anything that we want to do that involves a tangible body. Therefore, no one will be disappointed there in any way.

We Will Enjoy Social Interactions with One Another

As we observed in Question 24, we will remember our past relationships and continue to recognize one another in the eternal state. Since this is so, it makes sense that we will do more than merely recognize one another but will also enjoy blessed fellowship together.

As noted above, the primary activity in the afterlife—whether in heaven or on the new earth—will be to worship God. However, notice how those verses show the communal aspects of that worship. We will worship God not merely as solitary individuals but together, which will make our enjoyment of that worship even sweeter.

When you are passionate about something—a hobby, a new car, a great piece of music—you enjoy it even more when you share your enthusiasm with likeminded people who enjoy the same thing. For example, I love sailing. When I am not writing books about the afterlife, I spend time on some of the Internet forums or down at the marina talking with others who love the hobby as I do. We extol the virtues of this boat or that slick new piece of marine hardware. We simply love to laud what we find praiseworthy about these things, and we especially enjoy doing so with others who share the same passion. This is because human beings were made to praise that which is praiseworthy.

Now, I think there is nothing wrong with "praising," so to speak, a beautiful, well-designed sailboat. I find few objects lovelier than a sailboat hard on the wind,[9] gracefully slicing through the water, and I love to share my excitement and enthusiasm about sailing with others. Well, if my buddies and I can take a certain legitimate delight in "praising" a sailboat—which from another perspective is but a piece of wind-propelled, fiberglass-reinforced plastic—how much infinitely greater delight is there in praising the God of the Universe, who is beautiful and lovely and desirable beyond all description! To sing his praises with others multiplies exponentially our joy in him.

Further, we observe the reality of social interactions in the eternal state in the persistence of national entities that will carry over into life on the new earth. I take passages like Revelation 21:24–27, for instance, as specifying literal nations.[10] The Bible gives us little detail about these nations, other than to make clear that they worship God along with the inhabitants of the New Jerusalem. But the mere fact that these groupings continue to subsist as "nations" suggests that there may be some kind of social structure or identifiable organization that so constitute them even in the eternal state. This further would show that we shall not spend eternity as isolated individuals but in relationship with one another, in community.

We Will Exercise Responsibility and Service

Quite a few passages state or strongly suggest that God shall invest us with various responsibilities in the kingdom. The Bible speaks of this in terms of serving (Rev. 7:15); exercising authority (Luke 19:17, 19); ruling or being put in charge (Matt. 25:21, 23); and reigning (Rev. 5:10; 22:5), to name some of the expressions used.

Of what do these responsibilities consist? Smith is correct when he says that "we must acknowledge that we do not really know specifically how the servants of the Lord will exercise the authority here spoken of."[11] Viewed generally, N. T. Wright is safe in saying, "The redeemed people of God in the new world will be the agents of his love going out in new ways, to accomplish new creative tasks, to celebrate and extend the glory of his love."[12] Just what will that look like in view of the passages cited above? Much of the problem lies in determining how literally or figuratively to understand the few descriptions that we do have.

Take ruling, for example. In the parable of the minas, those who have been deemed faithful in managing the master's money receive greater areas

---

9. I.e., with the boat's bow pointing as closely as it can into the direction of the oncoming wind.

10. See the earlier discussion toward the end of Question 23.

11. Wilbur Smith, *The Biblical Doctrine of Heaven* (Chicago: Moody, 1968), 193.

12. N. T. Wright, *Surprised by Hope: Rethinking Heaven, the Resurrection, and the Mission of the Church* (New York: HarperOne, 2008), 104–6.

of responsibility, including exercising authority over cities (Luke 19:17, 19).[13] Are we to take this reference to "cities" literally, or do these "cities" merely stand for some other kind of responsibility or service, the nature of which Jesus leaves unspecified? Despite being a parable, I nevertheless see no reason that this could not apply to rulership over literal cities. If national entities continue on the new earth, might not some form of government continue?

Now, one might object that governmental authority will have no place in the eternal state, as human government is only required because of the need to restrain sin and punish evil (Rom. 13:1–5), which will have no place on the new earth. While surely the governmental functions related to sin—such as the need for a police force or army—would have no role on the new earth, perhaps the positive ways in which we will serve one another and even serve God himself might involve some kind of hierarchy with differing degrees of authority.

How can there be a hierarchy in the eternal state? Would that not mean that there is inequality between believers? Yes, it would. But why should we assume that believers are "equal" there? As we have already seen in Question 16, Scripture makes it plain that there are degrees of rewards in the eternal state. The texts we are considering here demonstrate this, at least in part.[14]

One might ask, "If there is not complete equality in the eternal state, would this not lead to jealousy and strife?" I believe Kreeft answers this well enough:

> Why is there no jealousy in this hierarchical, aristocratic, nonegalitarian Heaven of authority and obedience? Because all are cells in the same body. The kidney does not rebel because it is not an eye. Jealousy is the principle of Hell. There is no Hell in Heaven.[15]

REFLECTION QUESTIONS

1. Before you read this chapter, what did you think life in the eternal state would be like? Has your view changed because of anything you read here?

---

13. Again, some interpreters see Jesus's words here as applying to the millennial age. Nevertheless, it seems to me that the role of stewardship over cities would not have to be limited only to this time, if one grants that cities themselves persist into the eternal state.

14. Note that the issue of inequality shown in these passages is one quite separate from the question of whether one takes the "governing" over "cities" literally or figuratively. Either way, the inequality of reward shown in these texts remains a key feature of them.

15. Peter Kreeft, *Everything You Ever Wanted to Know about Heaven . . . but Never Dreamed of Asking* (San Francisco: Ignatius Press, 1990), 31.

2. The chapter points out that that our activities in the eternal state are in many ways similar to what we enjoy in this present life. Had you ever thought about this before now? Does the eternal state seem more or less desirable to you, in light of this?

3. Respond to this statement: "The eternal state sounds so boring! I mean, who would want to sit around all day just worshipping God?"

4. Think about the kinds of social interactions that may be possible on the new earth. Describe what you would find enjoyable and satisfying about these.

5. Does the idea of exercising new responsibilities on a new earth sound attractive or burdensome to you?

Will There Be Marriage and Sex in the Eternal State?

One of the central doctrines of Mormonism is that marriages may be made everlasting, or "sealed for time and eternity." According to official Mormon teaching, only those whose marriages are "sealed" in a Mormon temple may attain the exaltation to god- or goddesshood in the highest, "celestial" level of heaven. Such a husband and wife (or wives) will continue to have an "eternal increase" of spirit babies, which they will procreate through literal sexual intercourse, performed on the planet over which they rule. These spirit babies eventually receive bodies on an earth, through the agency of parents there who procreate physical bodies or "tabernacles" for them to inhabit. These now-embodied spirit babies, in turn, have the potential to grow up and achieve exaltation through celestial marriage. And so the cycle continues, without end.[1]

Mormonism is not the only non-Christian religion to teach the continuation of marriage into the afterlife. Consider Islam. The Qur'an makes it clear that earthly spouses will reside together in paradise.[2] Muslim commentators hold that the virtuous Muslim woman "will meet her husband in Paradise and become again his legal wife . . . while polygamous husbands will be allowed to keep all their earthly wives."[3] The Qur'an also teaches that Allah will furnish

---

1. The Mormon doctrine of celestial marriage is treated particularly in Doctrine and Covenants 131–32. See also the discussion in Mormon Apostle Bruce McConkie's *Mormon Doctrine* (Salt Lake City: Desert, 1966), 85–86, 105, 173–74, 185, 197, 285, 301, 400, 410, 434, 480, 481, 545.
2. Qur'an 13:23; cf. 36:56; 40:8.
3. A. J. Wensinck and Ch. Pellat, "Hūr," *Encyclopaedia of Islam,* 2nd ed., ed. P. Bearman et al. (Leiden: E. J. Brill, 2012), Brill Online Reference Works, http://dx.doi.org/10.1163/1573-3912_islam_SIM_2960.

"houris" as additional spouses. These "fair women with large, beautiful eyes,"[4] are, according to some Muslim authorities, nonhuman partners described as "virgins, devoted to their husbands,"[5] with "swelling breasts."[6] The houris will serve the faithful Muslim man as "purified wives,"[7] which Muslim scholars have understood as being "free alike from bodily impurity and from defects of character."[8]

But is this so? Fortunately, the Son of God himself answered this question as clearly and simply as anybody could. And his answer is a resounding "no."

There is one incident in the life of our Lord that bears directly on our question, and that is his debate with the Sadducees. All three Synoptic Gospels carry the account,[9] but we shall examine the relevant portion of this encounter as found in Luke.

The Passage Stated

> There came to him some Sadducees, those who deny that there is a resurrection, and they asked him a question, saying, "Teacher, Moses wrote for us that if a man's brother dies, having a wife but no children, the man must take the widow and raise up offspring for his brother. Now there were seven brothers. The first took a wife, and died without children. And the second and the third took her, and likewise all seven left no children and died. Afterward the woman also died. In the resurrection, therefore, whose wife will the woman be? For the seven had her as wife." And Jesus said to them, "The sons of this age marry and are given in marriage, but those who are considered worthy to attain to that age and to the resurrection from the dead neither marry nor are given in marriage, for they cannot die anymore, because they are equal to angels and are sons of God, being sons of the resurrection." (Luke 20:27–36)

Background to the Sadducees' Argument

In order to understand what is going on in the passage above, we must first delve into some background issues.

---

4. Qur'an 44:54; 52:20.
5. Qur'an 56:34–40.
6. Qur'an 78:33
7. Qur'an 2:25; 3:15; 4:57.
8. Wensinck and Pellat, "Hūr."
9. Matthew 22:23–33; Mark 12:18–27; and Luke 20:27–40.

Who Were the Sadducees and What Did They Believe?

According to Bock, the Sadducees were "priestly and lay aristocrats" who arose in the second century BC. "They were somewhat rationalistic, tended to be wealthy, rejected oral tradition, and desired to preserve the status quo."[10] The Jewish historian Josephus refers to them in his *Jewish Wars* and in his *Antiquities,* giving certain details about their beliefs, practices, and other characteristics.

The Sadducees' rejection of the spiritual world, personal immortality, divine providence, angels, and the bodily resurrection demonstrate their rationalism.[11] They denied the authority of oral tradition and only accepted the five books of Moses (the Pentateuch) as authoritative.[12]

Concerning the resurrection, the issue treated in this passage, the Sadducees denied its possibility on materialistic grounds. According to them, the soul dies with the body,[13] thus ruling out the resurrection, hell, or any kind of afterlife, whether embodied or disembodied.

What Is the Logic of the Sadducees' Argument?

Underlying the hypothetical case study presented by the Sadducees is a provision in the Mosaic Law known as "levirate marriage,"[14] based on Deuteronomy 25:5–10. As Osborne neatly summarizes:

> The purpose of levirate marriage was to protect the name of a deceased brother without children and to guarantee that he would have legal heirs and thus the ancestral lands would continue in the family, as well as to take care of the widow who would often be left destitute. So when a man died childless, his brother was supposed to marry his wife and bear children in his name. In Deut 25:7–10 the brother could refuse but would be publicly shamed for doing so. We do not know how extensively this was practiced in Jesus' time (no instance is recorded), but the point of law was well known.[15]

---

10. Darrell Bock, *Luke 9:51–24:53,* BECNT (Grand Rapids: Baker, 1996), 1616.
11. See J. E. H. Thompson, "Sadducees," *International Standard Bible Encyclopedia,* 4 vols., ed. James Orr. (Grand Rapids: Hendrickson, 1956), 4:2660. On their theology, see Rudolf Meyer, "Σαδδουκαῖος," *TDNT* 7:46–50.
12. There is some disagreement among scholars as to whether the Sadducees absolutely rejected all biblical books outside of the Pentateuch. Regardless, as a practical matter they gave supreme authority to the Pentateuch alone.
13. Josephus, *Antiquities* 18.1.4 (16); *Jewish Wars* 2.8.14 (164).
14. "Levirate" comes from the Latin "levir," which refers to a wife's husband's brother.
15. Grant R. Osborne, *Matthew,* ZECNT 1 (Grand Rapids: Zondervan, 2010), 816.

The Sadducees exploit the fact that these marriages, while legitimate when contracted successively, now pose a problem when they are to exist simultaneously, which would happen if the resurrection were true.[16]

The Sadducees employ a *reductio ad absurdum* form of argument against Jesus. They try to make the doctrine of the resurrection appear absurd by illustrating certain ridiculous consequences that could follow if one were to affirm it. According to the situation they have devised here, the individuals depicted in this account find themselves caught on the horns of a dilemma. Either the woman would arbitrarily become the wife of only one of the men, thereby abandoning the other six, or she would be the wife of all seven of them, which would be incestuous and polyandrous (i.e., one woman with multiple husbands).[17] Thus, the Sadducees believe that they have placed Jesus in a no-win situation in which he is forced to choose between these unpalatable options, or else abandon the doctrine of the resurrection altogether.

Jesus's Refutation of the Sadducees

According to Plummer, the dilemma posed to Jesus was a well-known problem that the Sadducees had used against the Pharisees, who were also proponents of the resurrection.[18] The typical answer was to say that in the resurrection she would become the wife of only the first brother. This response, however, is weak and unsatisfying, as it does not do justice to the underlying problem that this scenario exposes. If her marriages to all seven of these brothers were lawful and legitimately contracted, on what ground could they be dissolved arbitrarily for all but one of them?

Jesus takes an altogether different approach. The Sadducees, and for that matter the Pharisees, simply assume that marriage continues in the resurrected state. Jesus refutes this very premise, and thus cuts off their argument at the knees. If there is no marriage in the resurrection, then the dilemma posed by the Sadducees no longer exists; it becomes a nonissue. And that, Jesus informs them, is precisely the truth of the matter.

What Does Jesus's Argument Tell Us about Marriage in the Eternal State?

Jesus's argument settles absolutely and completely the question of whether there is marriage in the eternal state. However, notice that Jesus does more than simply answer the question "no" and leave it at that: He also provides a

---

16. Alfred Plummer, *A Critical and Exegetical Commentary on the Gospel According to St. Luke*, 6th ed., ICC 42 (New York: Scribner's, 1903), 228.
17. Although the Jews allowed for polygamy, such as one finds throughout the Old Testament, there was no provision for polyandry. See Leon Morris, *The Gospel according to Matthew*, PNTC (Grand Rapids: Eerdmans, 2000), 559.
18. Plummer, *Luke*, 468.

rationale for *why* marriage does not continue. Although Matthew and Mark do not recount that rationale, it does appear in Luke, which is why we are examining that version of the encounter.

In Luke's account, Jesus tells us that there is no marriage in the resurrection because there is no death (20:36), which renders further procreation unnecessary. In this sense, he compares the righteous who experience resurrection to the angels, who are likewise impervious to death.[19]

In the case of the angels, God created the full extent of their number initially and in a single creative act. No more angels will come into existence, whether through some kind of angelic procreation or in any other way. Nor will their number decrease through death. The angelic population is forever stable; it is now what it was from the start and always will be that. This is not so for human beings, however.

For humans, a key purpose of marriage is the expansion and perpetuation of the race. While this is not the only purpose, it is one of the central ones. God made this clear to the first human pair in Genesis 1:28 with the command, "Be fruitful and multiply and fill the earth." Now, God gave the command to populate the earth before the fall into sin, and hence before the entrance of death into the world (Rom. 5:12). But in the fallen world in which death reigns, there is the added need to replenish the population to make up for those who are lost to human society by death. At the time of the resurrection, however, the new earth will have sufficient population to fulfill God's purposes for it. Since there will be no attrition through death, this ideal population will remain stable. Consequently, there is no need for procreation, thereby eliminating one of the key purposes for marriage.

Additional Considerations about Marriage in the Eternal State

In the passage we just examined, Jesus asserts that there is no need for marriage in the eternal state because the need to procreate offspring no longer exists. Nevertheless, one might reply, "Are there no other reasons for marriage to continue in the next life that have nothing to do with procreation? For example, what about sex, which married couples enjoy even apart from producing children? Moreover, how about the intense emotional closeness of the marital bond? Should not that closeness continue forever?"

---

19. Note that in comparing human beings to angels, Jesus is *not* suggesting that we, like angels, will be disembodied spirits. The point of comparison here is strictly one of immortality, not incorporeality. Consequently, Dorothy Sayers's understanding of this passage could not be further from the truth when in one of her plays she has Jesus replying to the Sadducees, "Do you think the resurrection will be just this world all over again? Blessed spirits neither marry nor are given in marriage—any more than the angels of God" (Dorothy L. Sayers, *The Man Born to Be King* [London: Victor Gollancz, 1943], 224).

I believe these considerations are not compelling, and the fact that God did not establish marriage as a perpetual institution tells us as much in and of itself. But how might we address these concerns?

Sex in the Eternal State

Though we have been considering more narrowly the question of whether the marriage bond persists into the eternal state, an issue closely related to it is whether sexual intercourse would continue as well. Now, one might argue that there is no reason that the sex act could not continue even if marriage does not. However, we may safely conclude that if marriage does not continue then neither will sexual intercourse. That is because the "one flesh" sexual bond is not merely one of the purposes of marriage (as, for example, procreation is), but the sexual union is central to the very definition of marriage itself (Gen. 2:24). In other words, the "one flesh" union within marriage is much more than just something that married couples *do*: It rather lies at the heart of what marriage *is*—at least if one is looking at God's definition and not at the many human, sinful perversions of it. Therefore, to say that marriage will not continue in the eternal state is to say that sexual intercourse will not continue either.

It does not follow from this that we will be genderless in the eternal state. Males will still be male and females female. There is more to being male and female than one's physical organs or the sexual act. The differences between male and female run much deeper than that, and lie at the core of who we are.[20] Note, by the way, that the resurrected Jesus is still a man and not a genderless "it" (1 Tim. 2:5).

Granting that sex is one of the most pleasurable experiences we know in this life, some doubt that we could be supremely happy in the afterlife without it. One finds this view, for example, in Islam:

> For a normal human being the concept of an everlasting reward without the satisfaction of his most pressing desires is obviously incomplete. The Qur'an has recognized this fact, as all realistic views should. Only an ascetic, incomplete and unnatural view of life with arbitrary concepts of reward and punishment can refute this fact.[21]

---

20. John Coe, "Being Faithful to One's Gender: A Biblical Theology of Masculinity and Femininity," in *Women and Men in Ministry*, eds. Robert L. Saucy and Judith K. TenElshof (Chicago: Moody, 2001), 185–228.
21. See Guided Ones, "The Islamic Paradise: What's in It and for Whom?," http://www.guidedones.com/metapage/frq/islamicpar.htm.

While sex within the bounds of the marital union is a good gift from the creator in the present order of things, we need not worry that we will be disappointed without it. Even the best and most wholesome sex life in this present age cannot fully satisfy the deepest longings of body and soul. We can be confident that we will not pine after whatever does not carry over from the old order, for in the eternal state we shall be fully satisfied, lacking nothing we desire. If something we enjoyed in this life does not carry over into the next, it is only because God will replace it with something much better. Peter Kreeft provides this interesting and rather humorous analogy:

> I think there will probably be millions of more adequate ways to express love than the clumsy ecstasy of fitting two bodies together like pieces of a jigsaw puzzle. Even the most satisfying earthly intercourse between spouses cannot perfectly express *all* their love. If the possibility of intercourse in Heaven is not actualized, it is only for the same reason that lovers do not eat candy during intercourse: there is something much better to do. The question of intercourse in Heaven is like the child's question whether you can eat candy during intercourse: a funny question only from the adults' point of view. Candy is one of children's greatest pleasures; how can they conceive of a pleasure so intense that it renders candy irrelevant? Only if you know both can you compare two things, and all those who have tasted both the delights of physical intercourse with the earthly beloved and the delights of spiritual intercourse with God testify that there is simply no comparison.[22]

Will We Not Miss the Closeness of the Marriage Bond?
What about the intense emotional closeness that characterizes a happy marriage? If marriage will be no more, then will we not miss that intimacy?

Again, the answer here is similar to what we just observed. God takes nothing away from us in the eternal state except to replace it or enhance it with something better. In this instance, it is not that we will love our earthly spouse any less in the eternal state than we do now, but that we will love *everyone* in the eternal state to a degree unfathomable and unattainable at present.

---

22. Peter Kreeft, *Everything You Ever Wanted to Know about Heaven . . . but Never Dreamed of Asking* (San Francisco: Ignatius Press, 1990), 131 (referring to a comment by C. S. Lewis in his book *Miracles*). Although Kreeft speaks here of "heaven," he clearly has in mind the eternal state, so I believe his point still stands.

As we observed in Question 24, we will surely recognize and remember one another in the eternal state, and our social relationships will continue there. We will know our former spouse as having been our spouse. We shall likewise recognize our children, other family members, friends, etc. for who they were to us. But in the eternal state, our relationships with everyone will be satisfying beyond anything we can presently conceive. Bock puts it well:

> But we must remember that the quality and purity of relationships will extend far beyond what marriage provides today. Sin will no longer cloud our relationships, and the quality of personal interaction in a world [sic] will be directed fully by the presence of God. The absence of evil and the presence of God make marriage as a supportive and protective institution superfluous. For those who hesitate at this remark because their marriage has been good, just remember, heaven will be better.[23]

REFLECTION QUESTIONS

1. What does Mormonism teach about marriage in the afterlife? How does this relate to their view of salvation? Compare this with the biblical view.

2. Muslims argue that we could not be fulfilled in paradise without sexual relations (see the quote given earlier). What is your response to that statement?

3. Outline the argument the Sadducees used against the resurrection. What is the logic of their argument? What assumptions do they make as far as marriage is concerned?

4. What lies at the heart of Jesus's argument against the Sadducees for why marriage will not continue in the eternal, resurrected state?

5. Does the thought that marriage does not carry over into the eternal state cause you concern? For example, do you think it might diminish your happiness there? Explain.

---

23. Darrell Bock, *Luke*, NIVAC (Grand Rapids: Zondervan, 1996), 520.

Will It Be Possible for Us to Sin in the Eternal State?

Many Christian thinkers have argued that one of the supreme blessings of the eternal state (ES) is knowing that we will not and cannot ever lose this happiness. The blessedness of heaven and, finally, of the new earth is an *eternal* blessedness, characterized by joy without end. But how can we be certain of this if we retain an ability to sin even in the afterlife? Is there a chance that we could sin and thereby spoil it all?

The question of whether we will be able to sin in the ES presents us with some interesting and also difficult and complex theological and philosophical problems.[1] Roman Catholic philosopher Peter Kreeft describes the conundrum in these terms:

> Here is another dilemma. If we answer no [i.e., that we cannot sin in heaven], we seem to lack something: free will. If we answer yes, we lack something else: moral perfection. The Heavenly question thus lands us squarely into an earthly and present issue concerning the nature of freedom and of morality.[2]

I believe that the problem is actually more difficult than Kreeft's statement of it would suggest.

---

1. This question focuses strictly on the issue of whether *believers* can sin in the ES. I am not considering unbelievers, who no doubt will persist in their rejection and hostility to God for all eternity.
2. Peter Kreeft, *Everything You Ever Wanted to Know about Heaven . . . but Never Dreamed of Asking* (San Francisco: Ignatius Press, 1990), 39.

Adam and Eve *were* created morally perfect (Gen. 1:31; Eccl. 7:29) and placed in the perfect environment of paradise (Gen. 2:8). Yet, this same morally perfect Adam and Eve exercised their free wills to rebel against God. Might this not suggest that we, too, when we are made morally perfect (1 Thess. 5:23) and placed in the pristine environment of paradise in the ES (Rev. 2:7; cf. 22:1–2), could do the same? And if so, is this not a cause for concern? What would happen if we, like Adam and Eve, chose to fall into sin? Might we then face the prospect of being kicked out of paradise, even as Adam and Eve were (Gen. 3:23–24)?

There Will, in Fact, Be No Sin in the Eternal State

Although the issue before us is whether believers can sin in the ES, the question of whether or not a believer ever will in fact sin in the ES is certainly relevant. If, on the one hand, the Bible were to provide us with evidence that there will be believers sinning in the ES, then that would obviously prove that there *can* be and there would be no need of further discussion. On the other hand, if we can prove from the Bible that believers will not sin in the ES, then this might at least suggest that they could not, even in theory.[3]

Biblical Evidence That There Will Be No Sin in the Eternal State

It is not difficult to show that there will be no sin in the ES. Certainly, there will be no sin at the beginning of the ES, for Revelation 21:27 makes plain that "nothing unclean will ever enter [the New Jerusalem]." Therefore, the ES starts out with a clean slate.

But what if someone were to sin perhaps a million years into the ES? A few verses later, we find that the same saints who enter in a holy state will "reign forever and ever" (Rev. 22:5). First Thessalonians 4:17 likewise asserts that "we will always be with the Lord." Such declarations are impossible to square with the idea that some percentage of the saints will defect down the road and, therefore, get themselves kicked out of the new earth.

One might counter by suggesting that perhaps someone might sin in the ES but also repent and receive forgiveness, based on Christ's atoning work.[4] Being forgiven, God would not banish them from his presence. However, Revelation 21:4 tells us that there will be no sorrow in the ES. This means that there will be no repentance there, either, granting that repentance entails sorrow for sin (2 Cor. 7:10).

---

3. Warfield, addressing a related but slightly different issue, put it well: "A universal will-not, like this, has a very strong appearance of a can-not. A condition in which a particular effect follows with absolute certainty, at least suggests the existence of a causal relation; and the assertion of the equal possibility of a contrary effect, unsupported by a single example, bears the appearance of lacking foundation" (Benjamin B. Warfield, *Perfectionism* [Philadelphia: P&R, 1958], 177).

4. I thank my friend Kathy Olson for pointing out this hypothetical objection.

It Will Be Impossible to Sin in the Eternal State

Armed with biblical proof that there *will not* be sin in the ES, we now move to the stronger claim there *cannot* be, i.e., that it is inherently impossible.

Biblical Proof That Sin Is Impossible in the Eternal State

We shall consider two key texts that demonstrate the impossibility of sin in the ES.

Luke 20:35–36

Jesus states:

> . . . but those who are considered worthy to attain to that age and to the resurrection from the dead neither marry nor are given in marriage, for they cannot die anymore, because they are equal to angels and are sons of God, being sons of the resurrection.

In this passage, Jesus declares that believers will become like (good) angels in the resurrection because they, like angels, will be unable to die. From this truth we can also conclude that it will be impossible for believers to sin, once we properly understand the necessary connection between sin and death.

The angels that Jesus has in mind are the good angels that chose not to fall and join in Satan's rebellion. This is surely so because the angels that did fall (i.e., demons) will in fact experience the "second death" in the lake of fire (Rev. 20:10, 14), which is eternal separation from God.

Now, the Bible teaches that there is an inexorable connection between sin and death (e.g., Gen. 2:17; Ezek. 18:20; Rom. 6:23; James 1:15, etc.). If a good angel absolutely cannot die, then we may conclude that a good angel absolutely cannot sin. This shows us that the angels who did not follow Satan in his rebellion have become confirmed in their holiness. By "confirmed in holiness" I mean that even the possibility of rebellion—and death, which would be the necessary effect of that rebellion—can no longer occur.

Jesus's point is that our natures will become equal to the angels in the critical respect of being utterly impervious to death. This will be so because we, like the angels, will be confirmed in holiness without the slightest possibility of committing sin.

1 John 3:9

> No one born of God *makes a practice of sinning,* for God's seed abides in him, and he *cannot keep on sinning* because he has been born of God. (emphasis added)

Notice that this verse contains the requisite "cannot" needed to answer our question: One who is born of God *cannot* (*ou dynatai*) "keep on sinning" (*amartanein*). The NIV renders this as "continue to sin," while the ESV (quoted above) has "keep on sinning."[5] To "keep on sinning" is equivalent in meaning to "make a practice of sin" (*amartian poiei*). This verse tells us that not only will a true Christian not "keep on sinning," but that a true Christian *cannot* do so.

On the face of it, however, it might seem that this verse does not help us to answer our question because: (1) John is talking about what is *presently* true of Christians and not what will be true of them in the ES; and (2) the verse says only that Christians cannot *practice* sin—whatever that may mean—but not that they cannot sin at all, as John makes clear in 1:8, 10 and 2:2. (We shall consider what it means "to practice sin" in a moment.) Nevertheless, while it is true that this verse does not prove directly what we are after, it is possible to leverage the truths it does contain to answer our question about whether sin in the ES is possible.

First, notice that this verse shows that even in this present life there are certain moral actions that are simply impossible for a Christian. Specifically, it is morally impossible for one to be a genuine Christian and at the same time to "practice sin" or "keep on sinning." By "practice sin" or "continue to sin," John has in mind the wanton, continuous commission of sin as reflecting one's overall habit pattern and orientation. "Although the Christian still falls prey to sinful acts, John insists that it is *impossible* for sin to become a believer's pattern of life."[6] This fact in itself sufficiently explodes the premise underlying the notion that sin might be possible in the ES, and that premise is a particular and faulty understanding of free will. Specifically, those who would suggest the possibility of sinning in the ES understand free will to consist in the power of contrary choice, which means being able both to sin and not to sin. However, if this understanding of free will were correct, then Christians, who certainly have free will, should be "able to

---

5. As is commonly known, many Greek grammarians teach that the present tense may carry the sense of an ongoing or continuous action. Nevertheless, some Johannine scholars would not agree with the NIV or ESV rendering here. However, at the same time, even some of these same scholars still grant, based on other contextual factors, that John's point is contrasting sin as a habitual pattern or overall orientation of life as opposed to discrete or specific acts of sin. (Refer to some of the commentators referenced in the footnotes to follow.)

6. Daniel L. Akin, *1, 2, 3 John*, NAC (Nashville: Broadman & Holman, 2001), 150 (emphasis added). A good many commentators understand John's meaning in this way. See also Gary M. Burge, *Letters of John*, NIVAC (Grand Rapids: Zondervan, 2000), 157; Kerry Inman, "Distinctive Johannine Vocabulary and the Interpretation of 1 John 3:9," *WTJ* 40 (1977–78): 136–44; Simon J. Kistemaker, *James, Epistles of John, Peter, and Jude*, NTC (Grand Rapids: Baker, 2002), 303; and Colin G. Kruse, *The Letters of John*, PNTC (Grand Rapids: Eerdmans, 2003), 124.

practice sin and able not to practice sin." Yet, here John teaches precisely the opposite. I will say more about the true nature of free will below. But for now it is sufficient to note that even this side of eternity, Christians have absolute limits placed on their ability to sin, i.e., that "sinning as an ongoing action . . . [is] *impossible* for those born of God."[7]

Next, it is important for us to observe why the Christian, even in this life, not only does not but also cannot "practice sin." John tells us that the Christian has been "born of God," which is to say "God's seed abides in him." It is *for this reason* (Greek *hoti*) that the Christian is unable to practice sin: The presence of God's "seed," implanted in us at regeneration, makes the ongoing practice of sin (as previously defined) an absolute impossibility.[8] Now, if the seed planted in us by the Spirit at regeneration precludes us from having sin as our fundamental, overall orientation, how much less will sin be a possibility in the ES when that seed has blossomed fully?

Consider it this way. Being born of God (regeneration) in this life means that a fundamental change has taken place in one's heart, such that one is now oriented toward holiness and away from sin.[9] But even though this foundational change has occurred, it is also an incomplete change that has yet to permeate every aspect of our lives due to the continuing presence of indwelling sin (Rom. 7:14–25). The seed for our total and complete transformation is already present and has begun to show itself, just as the young shoots of a newly planted tree orient themselves relentlessly skyward toward the sunlight. But in the ES, the transformation that has begun here will find completion in all of its particulars; the acorn will become the fully grown oak. Therefore, if a fundamental yet partial transformation means that we cannot sin as the overall habit pattern of our lives even now, then a complete transformation will mean that we will be unable to sin at all.[10]

Responding to the "Free Will" Argument

The Argument from "Free Will" Fully Stated
Some may question how the biblical position as outlined above can be true in light of certain other biblical and philosophical considerations. As I have already suggested, the reason for affirming that sin will be possible in

---

7. Kruse, *The Letters of John*, 124 (emphasis added).
8. "The word *seed* has a figurative connotation: 'God's nature' or 'God's principle of life.' God guards the new life he planted in the heart of the believer and causes it to develop. The Christian, then, will not and cannot yield to sin because of that divine principle in his heart" (Kistemaker, *James, Epistles of John, Peter, and Jude*, 303). See also I. Howard Marshall, *The Epistles of John*, NICNT (Grand Rapids: Eerdmans, 1978), 186.
9. Robert L. Saucy, *Minding the Heart* (Grand Rapids: Kregel, 2013), 107–17.
10. See Augustine's excellent discussion in his *On the Merits and Forgiveness of Sins, and on the Baptism of Infants* 2.10.

the ES boils down to a certain view of free will. I shall now fully state this particular understanding of free will and then see whether it holds up.

This view of free will sees the essence of moral freedom as the power of contrary choice. Accordingly, a moral agent, such as an angel or a human being, is called "free" when he/she/it is able to sin and also able not to sin. In any given circumstance, the person is free to choose righteousness or wickedness, holiness or sin. Indeed, if we could *only* act in a certain way, such as *always* to obey and love God, then this would show that our "obedience" and "love" are but preprogrammed illusions. In that case, our actions would be no more moral or immoral than a robot's. On the other hand, if we choose to obey and love God when we might not have, then our choice is morally significant, free, and genuine.[11] Granting that our genuine obedience to God and our love for him continues throughout the ES, it must be that the power of contrary choice carries over to then as well.

Though the simplicity of this reasoning may appear attractive on its face, several considerations unmask its fatal flaws.

The Case of God

The argument based on this particular understanding of free will most obviously breaks down when we apply it to God. God is surely a free moral agent—indeed, the most free moral agent of all (Dan. 4:35; Eph. 1:11). Yet, it is impossible for God to sin (e.g., Heb. 6:18; James 1:13). Now, granting that God created us in his image, God himself provides the pattern for understanding personhood, including the moral freedom that is essential to it. That God is unable to sin suggests that we look somewhere other than the power of contrary choice for our understanding of what it means to be free.

Therefore, we start with God, who is both free and unable to sin. *Why* is God unable to sin? He cannot sin because of what he *is*. Specifically, God is, by nature, infallibly holy. Moreover, God always acts in accordance with what he is. For example, God is love (1 John 4:16); therefore he acts in a loving way. God is holy (Isa. 6:3); therefore he acts in a holy way (e.g., Hab. 1:13). Yet, God in his actions is also freely loving and freely holy because he is not under any outside compulsion or coercion to act in a loving or holy way. Rather, his holy actions are *self-determined,* based upon the kind of "self" he is—which in God's case is an infallibly holy self (James 1:17).

That may be well and good for God, one might say, but how about for us? Well, the principle I have described is just as true for us as it is for God, and indeed is so for all moral agents. That principle is simply this: *To be a free moral agent is to determine one's own actions based upon one's nature,*

---

11. For instance, Trevor Hart states that genuine love "presupposes the genuine possibility of rejection of love" ("Universalism: Two Distinct Types," in *Universalism and the Doctrine of Hell,* ed. Nigel M. de S. Cameron [Grand Rapids: Baker, 1991], 31).

unfettered or unencumbered by external constraint. Now, if a (free) being is infallibly holy by nature then that being will freely, though necessarily, only choose the good. He or she will invariably choose the good because he/she *is* good, and infallibly so. We have already seen that God falls into that category. The angels in heaven and human beings in the ES are/will be in that category also. On the other hand, if a being is infallibly unholy,[12] then such a being will only and always—yet freely—desire and do what is contrary to God's law. This applies to fallen angels (including Satan) and to fallen human beings, apart from a regenerating work of God's grace (1 Cor. 2:14; Eph. 2:3; Heb. 11:6). If a being is fallibly holy, then such a being is able to defect or fall away from his/her/its holiness; such a being is able to sin and able not to sin. This applies to Adam and Eve before the fall, to the angels (including Satan) before some of them chose to fall, and also applies (to a certain degree, as qualified earlier) to Christians in this life, in whom the work of grace is yet in process.

But Could We Not Sin in the Eternal State If We Wanted To?

One might still object to the above, saying, "Now wait a minute! How can this be true? Do you mean to tell me that we couldn't sin in the ES *even if we wanted to?* That sure sounds like our free will has been taken away!"

Well, it is certainly true that we "*could* sin *if* we wanted to." But this highlights a very critical point, and that is that sin and holiness are fundamentally about the "want to." The desire to sin is itself sin,[13] while the desire for holiness is itself holiness. The desires, or inclinations of the heart, are the root from which specific behaviors of sin or holiness proceed.

Therefore, the question "Could we sin if we want to sin?" actually reduces to this: "Could we sin if we sin?" The answer is, of course, "yes," but this kind of statement or question is what we call a tautology—sort of like asking, "Could it rain today if it rains today?"

In the ES, when we shall be infallibly holy, we will never, ever, ever want to sin. This is not because God has done some kind of "will-ectomy" on us, whereby he amputates our wills so that we lose our ability to make choices. Our willing faculty remains fully intact, and we will continue to make choices for all eternity. Rather, it is our natures—both body and spirit—that will be so transformed in the glorified ES that the desire to sin would be so repugnant to us that we would never, ever exercise our choices contrary to God's will. We will surely make choices in the ES, but these will only be holy choices, as we choose to obey him, choose to love him, and choose to enjoy him eternally. The fact that we will make these choices certainly and invariably in no way renders them less real or significant.

---

12. That is to say, a being that cannot fail to be anything but unholy.
13. Consider, for example, that God not only prohibits actual theft (Exod. 20:15) but even the *desire* to take what is not one's rightful possession (Exod. 20:17).

But What about Adam and Eve in Paradise?

We still have not accounted for Adam and Eve, however. God created them holy, and yet they could and did sin in paradise. Why not us, then, in the ES?

Why Adam and Eve, as holy beings, chose to throw away their holiness and trade it in for sin is truly a difficult question to answer. While it is true that Satan tempted them, they had full ability to withstand that temptation and could have repelled it easily. I personally do not believe that we can answer fully why they would choose to rebel.[14] We can say this much: Though God created Adam and Eve holy (Gen. 1:31; Eccl. 7:29), they were *fallibly* holy, with the ability to throw it all away—as the "facts on the ground" make clear. We, however, will possess glorified natures in the ES, superior to Adam's at his creation. Not only will our bodies be superior to those of pre-fall Adam and Eve,[15] but our spirits will be as well. I can do no better than to present Augustine's summary of the matter, in which he contrasts the nature of Adam's freedom at his creation with ours in the new creation:

> Now it was expedient that man should be at first so created, as to have it in his power both to will what was right and to will what was wrong. . . . But in the future life it shall not be in his power to will evil; and yet this will constitute no restriction on the freedom of his will. On the contrary, his will shall be much freer when it shall be wholly impossible for him to be the slave of sin. We should never think of blaming the will, or saying that it was no will, or that it was not to be called free, when we so desire happiness, that not only do we shrink from misery, but find it utterly impossible to do otherwise. As, then, the soul even now finds it impossible to desire unhappiness, so in the future it shall be wholly impossible for it to desire sin.[16]

REFLECTION QUESTIONS

1. Before reading this chapter, had you ever wondered about whether it might be possible to sin in the ES? Has your conclusion changed due to anything you have read here?

---

14. Observe that this conundrum applies just as well to Satan, who was created holy (Ezek. 28:13–15) but discarded his righteousness in an act of willful rebellion. Moreover, in his case, there was no external temptation.
15. See Question 19 and Question 20.
16. Augustine, *Enchiridion* 105.

2. Do you believe that the inability to sin in the ES infringes on your freedom? How do you feel about that?

3. Reflect on God's inability to sin. Do you derive any comfort from this fact?

4. What was your understanding of free will before reading this chapter? Has anything here challenged or modified your previously-held assumptions?

5. Compare our freedom in the ES with that of Adam and Eve's in paradise. In what ways are they similar and different? Which do you prefer?

Will There Be Animals in the Eternal State? (Part 1)

A mericans are crazy about their pets—more than ever. Nearly two-thirds of all homes in the US have pets, and most of these have more than one.[1] More than half of US households have a dog, and more than forty percent have a cat. The total number of pets, including also reptiles and fish, is just shy of 400 million.

The economics of pet ownership testifies to this love affair. In 2014, Americans lavished $58 billion on their beloved animals. Twenty-two billion dollars of this went to food and $15 billion to the vet, with the remainder spent on a variety of pet-related items. These jaw-dropping figures exceed the entire GDP of most countries throughout the world, and well outstrip what even a highly prosperous nation like Germany spends on its entire annual defense budget.

These enormous dollar amounts, breathtaking as they are, only give us part of the picture. We must also consider the increasingly extravagant treatment that much of this spending represents. Consider food. Specialty pet foods are now a booming industry. Animal bakeries do a brisk business in pet birthday cakes, gourmet carob chip cookies, "pup tarts," and "pup cakes."

---

1. I have culled the statistics and other data in the following paragraphs from a number of news sources, including (but not limited to) the following: Lindsey Adkison, "Pampering Pets Pumping Cash into Growing Niche," *The Brunswick News*, February 11, 2008; "Americans Spend $56 Bil. a Year on Pets," *Korea Times*, March 16, 2014; John Reid Blackwell, "Pets Rate at Cash Register," *Richmond Times Dispatch*, June 6, 2010; Stephanie Bouchard, "Lucky Dog," *Portland Press Herald (Maine)*, December 14, 2003; Sue Manning, "Americans Are Spending Big to Pamper Pets," *The Vancouver Province*, March 9, 2015; Wendy McLellan, "Extravagant Animal Lovers Spend Billions on Pet Care," *Edmonton Journal (Alberta)*, March 2, 2005; Adam Tschorn, "The Pets Issue: By the Numbers," *Los Angeles Times*, June 20, 2015.

More health-conscious owners fête their four-legged friends with gluten-free, wheat-free, reduced-sugar, reduced-calorie, and low-carb fare—not to mention such exotic treats as 100% salmon dog chews. Pet accessories have also taken on a new level of elegance, including memory foam and micro-velvet Bowser Beds, animal strollers, and stylish tuxedo bandannas for those dapper canine ring bearers at animal-friendly weddings. And finally, we must not omit the growing number of "pet hotels," equipped with flat-screen TVs for the animals and webcam access that lets anxious owners keep tabs on their tabby. It has not always been this way.

Changes in How People View Animals

This lavish treatment of animals has developed mostly in the last twenty to twenty-five years. During this time, there has been an increasing tendency for people to regard their pets as literal family members. Several sociological factors have led to this development. One is that people are having fewer children. Amy Chaitoff, an attorney specializing in animal law, observes, "As people work more, they have fewer kids. So they have animals as substitutes."[2] At the other end of the age spectrum, older Americans, particularly baby boomers whose own children have left the nest, seek to fill that void with "companionship in the form of loveable dogs and cats."[3]

Directly related to the view of pets-as-kin is an increasing inclination to blur the distinction between pets and humans, and to see the animal as a person. University of California Berkeley anthropologist Stanley Brandes remarks, "It is the marked prevalence and intensity of the family bond with animals, together with the near obliteration of classificatory distinctions between animals and humans among growing segments of society, that characterize present-day pet ownership in America."[4]

Animals as Endowed with "Immortal Souls"

Nowhere do we more clearly see the shift to viewing animals as persons than in how people deal with their pets' demise. There are currently more than six hundred pet cemeteries in the US, with the oldest dating back over one hundred years. Originally for the rich, these cemeteries now inter the deceased pets of owners from all social strata.[5]

Brandes performed a fascinating study of the gravestone inscriptions at Harsdale Pet Cemetery in New York. Established in 1896, Harsdale is the oldest pet cemetery in the United States, containing the remains of more than

2. Claude Solnik, "The Woof of Wall Street," *Idaho Business Review,* October 30, 2014.
3. David Berman, "Pet Food Retailers Deserve a Pat; Baby Boomers Fuel Fat Profits at PetSmart, Pet Valu," *National Post's Financial and FP Investing (Canada),* July 5, 2007.
4. Stanley Brandes, "The Meaning of American Pet Cemetery Gravestones," *Ethnology* 48, no. 2 (Spring 2009): 116.
5. Ibid., 100–1.

70,000 animals. Based on these inscriptions, Brandes observed marked differences in the view of animals over the last several decades. He documents the growing tendency to speak of the deceased pet in ways formerly reserved for blood relations, using such familial terms as "son," "daughter," "child," "baby," and the like. Coupled with this is an increasing number of inscriptions that show "an enhanced religious and ethnic identity bestowed upon pets."[6]

A key element of this "religious identity" is the notion that animals are endowed with immortal souls. Since the 1990s, Brandes notes, the gravestone inscriptions often "express the owner's belief in an afterlife for the pets, as well as the expectation, or at least the hope, that owners and pets will be reunited in the afterlife." By contrast, before the 1980s "almost no monument inscriptions indicate the belief that pets are equivalent to kin. Nor do they show evidence that owners consider animals to be endowed with souls."[7]

The Importance of This Question

From what we have seen above, I am not surprised to learn that the question of animal immortality is now one of the most frequently asked when people turn their attention to the afterlife. As popular author Mark Hitchcock relates:

> In my own ministry, I've been asked that same question time and again—by people of all ages. In fact, it probably rates up at the top of the most-asked questions about life after death. And you have to be careful how you answer! This issue stirs up a great deal of emotion for those who deeply love their pets.[8]

Personally, I have not found this question especially urgent, nor has the Christian tradition generally.[9] While I am modestly fond of my parakeet Scupper—that is, when he is not biting me or stealing the scrambled eggs off my breakfast plate—I have never been much concerned about whether I will see him in the next life. Emotionally speaking, I really do not have a dog in this fight, you might say.

However, what I *am* passionate about is *how we go about answering this question.* This is arguably more important than the answer itself. What are the arguments for animal immortality? Are they sound? On what are they based?

---

6. Ibid., 99.
7. Ibid., 102, 110.
8. Mark Hitchcock, *55 Answers to Questions about Life after Death* (Sisters, OR: Multnomah, 2005), 229.
9. Paul J. Griffiths, *Decreation: The Last Things of All Creatures* (Waco, TX: Baylor, 2014), 273.

How Can We Answer This Question?

As we urged strongly in Question 3, the only things we can know for certain about the afterlife are what God has seen fit to reveal to us in Scripture. It is not our place to make this stuff up as we go, such as what we find in a popular children's book like Cynthia Rylant's *Dog Heaven*. It might please us to no end to believe that "dogs can eat ice-cream biscuits, sleep on fluffy clouds, and run through unending fields." But the issue is not what we find pleasing but what is *true*. While one might urge that the author of this book may not intend for us to take such fanciful descriptions seriously—she wrote it for children, after all—it is also true that the portrayals of "animal heaven" sometimes offered by adults in all seriousness deviate little from this.

After surveying the most commonly offered arguments for animal immortality, I place them into two broad categories: those with absolutely nothing to commend them, and those that suggest that there might be animals in the eternal state (ES).

Commonly Offered yet Flawed Arguments

Although the following arguments do not help us to answer our question, we must consider them because of how often one encounters them in treatments of this subject.

The Argument from Desire/Wish Fulfillment

Perhaps the most common "argument" advanced for animals in the ES is based on nothing more than the desire for it to be true. The reasoning, if we may call it that, runs along these lines: "I love my parakeet Scupper and cannot imagine life without him. Therefore, Scupper will be with me in heaven."

Evangelical Christians are not immune from this faulty way of thinking. For example, consider bestselling children's author Nancy Tillman, whose book *The Heaven of Animals* informs children, "When dogs get to heaven they're welcomed by name, and angels know every dog's favorite game."[10] In a *New York Times* interview, Tillman explains how she got the idea for her book, when she was observing her own dog and cat:

> "They were gazing off into the distance," Ms. Tillman said. "And I thought, 'What a lovely thought if they see heaven. And wouldn't that comfort children if they lost a pet?'"[11]

---

10. Nancy Tillman, *The Heaven of Animals* (New York: Feiwel and Friends, 2014).
11. Mark Oppenheimer, "Fascination Persists Over Pets and the Afterlife," *New York Times*, January 16, 2015.

A lovely thought indeed! But surely we cannot determine the truth of an idea based on whether we find it "lovely" and "comforting." We can, however, grant this much: Scripture does tell us that we will be supremely happy in the ES. There will be nothing of sadness there, only perfect joy (1 Cor. 2:9; Rev. 7:17; 21:4, etc.). From this we may conclude that God will furnish us with whatever we need to be happy. Therefore, *if* we cannot be happy in the ES without our pets, then we will have our pets. However, that is a very big "if." We cannot reason from what we may believe we need for our happiness now and conclude, necessarily, that we will require it then.

For example, consider marriage. A man might conclude that because his marriage is so foundational to his happiness here, that surely this marriage bond must carry over into the next life. Yet, as we have already seen, Jesus tells us explicitly that marriage does not continue in the ES.[12] Since we know that we will be perfectly happy in the ES, we can conclude that marriage, however wonderful it may be in the present order of things, is unnecessary for our supreme happiness in the afterlife. That may be hard for some to imagine now, but it will be true then nonetheless.

The Argument Based on Animals Having "Souls"

As we observed in our introductory remarks, there is a growing belief, especially in the last twenty years, that animals have "souls." Many conclude from this that animals consciously survive the death of their bodies, and further surmise that we shall be reunited with them in the afterlife.

This reasoning entails a logical fallacy known as "begging the question," in which the argument simply assumes as true the very assertion that requires proof. Even if we were to grant that animals have "souls"—and I do think there is every reason to grant this, when properly understood—it would not automatically follow that the animal's "soul" survives its bodily death, which is the very point in dispute.

To address the question of animal souls, we must consider at least the following: (1) Do animals have a soul? (2) If they do, what is the nature of that soul? and (3) What happens to the animal's soul after the animal dies?

The Nature and Fate of Animal "Souls"

In Question 5, we discussed at length what the Bible means when it talks about the soul. Though we focused on what this means for human beings, we did note briefly how this applies to animals. There, we observed that according to the Old Testament, both animals and humans *are* "living souls" (Hebrew: *nefesh khayah*), i.e., living beings, made alive by virtue of the presence of "spirit" (Hebrew: *ruakh*) within them.[13]

---

12. See Question 26.
13. Robert L. Saucy, *Minding the Heart* (Grand Rapids: Kregel, 2013), 32–33.

Well and good. But does this mean that there is no difference between an animal and a human? Not at all. As we also noted in Question 5, the animal's spirit lacks the personal capacities of the human spirit. This includes the faculty of reason, which animals do not possess (Jude 10). Accordingly, there are entire forms of consciousness lacking to them that depend upon rational reflection, such as the ability to make ethical and aesthetic judgments and the like. Significantly, God created man alone, and not animals, in his own image (Gen. 1:26); it is man alone into whom God directly breathed his own spirit (Gen. 2:7). On the other hand, a purely material principle of life animates or enlivens an animal, as the language of Genesis 1:24 suggests.[14] As prominent nineteenth-century Old Testament scholar E. W. Hengstenberg correctly observed, "According to Genesis 2:7, two elements are united in man, an earthly and a divine, which latter no other creature shares with him."[15]

The key question, then, is what becomes of the nonpersonal animal spirit upon its death? The biblical text that seems to deal with this issue most directly is Ecclesiastes 3:18–22. We observe the especially relevant part in verse 21:

> Who knows whether the spirit of man goes upward and the
> spirit of the beast goes down into the earth?

As is often the case with the book of Ecclesiastes, this text is notoriously difficult and commentators understand the flow of the argument (in the verses leading up to it) variously. Taken at face value, it might appear that Solomon is agnostic about the fate both of animals and of humans after their deaths. However, this seems unlikely, particularly in light of 12:7 in that same book. There, Solomon flatly declares that for human beings, "the spirit returns to God who gave it."

In Ecclesiastes 3, it seems preferable to understand the author as speaking in terms of how matters seem outwardly or "under the sun"—an expression frequently appearing throughout the book. From all outward appearances, man and beast both meet a common fate: They die and go to the grave. But who knows—again, based on appearances alone—whether there is anything beyond that?

---

14. So Aquinas: "For the souls of brutes are produced by some power of the body; whereas the human soul is produced by God" (St. Thomas Aquinas, *Summa Theologica* 1.75.6). See also W. G. T. Shedd, *Dogmatic Theology*, ed. Alan W. Gomes (Phillipsburg: P&R, 2003), 179–81, 430.

15. E. W. Hengstenberg, *Commentary on Ecclesiastes* (Edinburgh: T. & T. Clark, 1860), 120–21. By "divine" Hengstenberg does not mean that our spirit is identical in substance to God's. Rather, he has in mind the fact that our human spirit, while created and finite, nevertheless reflects God's image in a way that animals do not, as mentioned earlier in this paragraph.

The point of Solomon's argument is to question whether man sustains any advantage over a mere animal, as reckoned by our senses and apart from faith. He takes as a given that the spirit of the animal perishes with its body when it goes "down into the earth" from where it came. Does man fare any better? Certainly, man and beast share the same *bodily* fate when they die: They both return to dust (v. 20). But is that true for their spirits as well? Viewed outwardly, who can say whether the human spirit returns to its creator or whether it "goes down into the earth" like the beast's?

Thus, Solomon is not wrestling with whether an animal's spirit might return directly to God, for it certainly does not. The animal's spirit, like its body, is a product of the earth (Gen. 1:20, 24) and returns to it at death. Solomon's only question is whether man has an advantage over the beast in this regard.[16] And certainly there is no strictly empirical way to settle the matter.

Consider it this way: Taken together, the books of Genesis and Ecclesiastes articulate and illustrate the principle that at death, the substances that God provided return to their immediate points of origin (Gen. 3:19). The bodies both of animals and of men originate from the earth, and so return there (Eccl. 3:20). The spirit of a human originates directly from God (Gen. 2:7) and so returns to him (Eccl. 12:7). But the spirit of an animal originates from the earth (Gen 1:20, 24) and so returns to the earth from which it came (Eccl. 3:21).

If this understanding of the issue is correct, it appears that no part of the animal survives its bodily death. Now, this in itself would not preclude the possibility of animals in the ES, though it probably would mean that they would not be the *same* animals that existed here on earth; God would have to create essentially new animals from scratch.

Recall that in Question 20 I demonstrated that it is the persistence of the same human spirit that accounts for the continuity of identity: from our present existence in our earthly body, to our disembodied state (in heaven), and then on into the ES (on a new earth) in our resurrected bodies. There would be no such continuity for the animal, however, since it perishes completely at death—body and spirit alike—without a trace. Therefore, while God might well create a new parakeet for me in the ES, it would be a new one and not a resurrection of my old one. It might be a Scupper-like "knock-off"— with a long yellow tail feather and an affinity for scrambled eggs—but it would not be Scupper himself. That is because Scupper's spirit would no longer even exist in order to be "put into" an immortal parakeet body.

---

16. See Hengstenberg, *Commentary on Ecclesiastes*, 118–19. See also Craig G. Bartholomew, *Ecclesiastes*, Baker Commentary on the Old Testament Wisdom and Psalms (Grand Rapids: Baker, 2009), 178; and Iain W. Provan, *Ecclesiastes, Song of Songs*, NIVAC (Grand Rapids: Zondervan, 2001), 94.

Animals Are Saved "in" Their Human Masters

An oft-repeated argument, derived from C. S. Lewis, runs like this: Whereas humans are saved "in" Christ, animals in turn are saved "in" their human masters.

According to Lewis, the "good homestead" comprises both the animals and children who are part of it, a "body" over which the husband and his wife rule. "And how much of that 'body' may be raised along with the goodman and the goodwife, who can predict?" Lewis concludes, "In this way it seems to me possible that certain animals may have an immortality, not in themselves, but in the immortality of their masters."[17]

Such ideas admittedly possess a certain charm, especially as narrated by a master wordsmith like Lewis. I am not surprised that these musings have taken such firm root in popular treatments of animal immortality,[18] given the generally uncritical approval among evangelicals of all things Lewis. Its imaginative charm notwithstanding, it is difficult to identify any cogent reason—scriptural or otherwise—to embrace such a position.

The Bible Depicts Animals in Heaven

There are certain passages, particularly in the book of Revelation, that some offer as direct proof of animals "in heaven." For instance, popular author Randy Alcorn points to the "living creatures" who praise God in Revelation 4:6–9. John described these as winged creatures with features like a lion, an ox, an eagle, and a man. The Greek word translated "living creatures," Alcorn tells us, is "*zoon*," which is used in many places in the Bible (e.g., in the Old Testament Septuagint) for literal animals.[19] Based on this, Alcorn concludes, "The primary beings shown articulating God's praise in Heaven, along with angels and humans (the elders), are animals!"[20] Couple this with the heavenly armies that ride upon horses in Revelation 19:11–14 and 2 Kings 6:17, and—on Alcorn's reckoning—we have all the proof we need that animals populate heaven.[21]

But is this so? First, one can arrive at such conclusions only through an oddly literal method of interpretation that must completely ignore the obviously symbolic and visionary nature of such passages. No doubt John actually saw living creatures and horses in his vision, and they appeared to him as he described them. However, this does not mean that we should take these creatures to be literal animals, any more than we should regard Jesus as a seven-eyed animal with horns (Rev. 5:6).

---

17. C. S. Lewis, *The Problem of Pain* (New York: Macmillan, 1962), 139–40.
18. E.g., Wesley Smith, "Do Pets Go to Heaven?," *Christianity Today*, April 2012, 66–67.
19. Randy Alcorn, *Heaven* (Carol Stream, IL: Tyndale House, 2004), 392–93.
20. Ibid., 393.
21. Ibid., 394.

Speaking of the "living creatures" of Revelation 4 specifically, it is probably safe to say that no serious interpreter of the book understands these as referring to literal animals. Rather, as virtually every commentator attests, the living creatures point to the seraphim of Isaiah 6:1–3 and the cherubim of Ezekiel 10:14.[22] But cherubim and seraphim are not animals but *angels*. Furthermore, Revelation 4 clearly portrays these creatures (*zōa*) as rational and therefore as (angelic) persons. This rules out classifying them with animals, whom Jude describes as "unreasoning" (*aloga zōa*) (Jude 10) and therefore not persons.[23]

REFLECTION QUESTIONS

1. What was your reaction to the information about pet ownership in the United States presented in the introduction to this chapter?

2. How do you feel about the growing tendency to equate animals with human beings?

3. What is the proper approach that we should take in attempting to answer the question of whether there are animals in the ES?

4. Do animals have "souls"? If so, what would this prove about whether there are animals in the ES—if anything?

5. Do the biblical passages that depict animals in heaven (e.g., in the book of Revelation) prove that there are actual animals there? Why or why not?

---

22. See George Eldon Ladd, *A Commentary on the Revelation of John* (Grand Rapids: Eerdmans, 1972), 77. Even the most literal interpreters of the book, such as Thomas and Patterson, concur with this identification. See Robert L. Thomas, *Revelation 1–7: An Exegetical Commentary* (Chicago: Moody, 1992), 357–58; Paige Patterson, *Revelation*, NAC (Nashville: Broadman & Holman, 2012), 153–56. John Walvoord, also among the more literal interpreters, does not see the living creatures as angels but as symbolic of various attributes or qualities of God (*The Revelation of Jesus Christ* [Chicago: Moody, 1966], 109–10). As far as I know, *no* scholarly commentator regards these as literal "animals."

23. Richard Bauckham, *Jude, 2 Peter*, WBC 50 (Nashville: Thomas Nelson, 2003), 63; Peter H. Davids, *The Letters of 2 Peter and Jude*, PNTC (Grand Rapids: Eerdmans, 2006), 63; Gene L. Green, *Jude and 2 Peter*, BECNT (Grand Rapids: Baker, 2008), 85; and Michael Green, *2 Peter and Jude*, TNTC 18 (Downers Grove, IL: InterVarsity, 2007), 185.

Will There Be Animals in the Eternal State? (Part 2)

In this part, we shall examine some biblical arguments that suggest that there might be animals in the ES. Whereas the arguments treated in Part 1 have nothing to commend them, these at least lend some credence to the idea that there may be animals in the afterlife.

Biblical Arguments That Suggest the Possibility of Animals in the Eternal State

Isaiah 11:6–9; 65:25 Point to Animals in a Future Age

The two passages above use similar language to discuss a future age in which animals experience transformation, their natural ferocity removed, and wildlife normally at enmity will live in harmony. Consider Isaiah 65:25:

> "The wolf and the lamb shall graze together; the lion shall eat straw like the ox, and dust shall be the serpent's food. They shall not hurt or destroy in all my holy mountain," says the LORD.

Then, in an oft-quoted passage from Isaiah 11, we see a more expansive statement of these ideas, mentioning also the friendly relations that these predatory animals will have even with small human children:

> The wolf shall dwell with the lamb, and the leopard shall lie down with the young goat, and the calf and the lion and the fattened calf together; and a little child shall lead them. The cow and the bear shall graze; their young shall lie down together; and the lion shall eat straw like the ox. The nursing

child shall play over the hole of the cobra, and the weaned child shall put his hand on the adder's den. They shall not hurt or destroy in all my holy mountain; for the earth shall be full of the knowledge of the Lord as the waters cover the sea.

Now, these events point to a future age for their fulfillment. In Isaiah 11, the expression "in that day" refers to this coming epoch (vv. 10–11). Even aside from this phrase, it is clear that many of the events discussed in this chapter remain unfulfilled. Similarly, in Isaiah 65 we find a number of future allusions that point to a time beyond this present age, including an explicit reference to "a new heavens and a new earth" that stands in contrast to "the former things" (65:17).

In order to determine whether we can adduce these texts as proof of animals in the ES, we must answer two questions about them: (1) Are we to take the references to animals in these texts literally? (2) Is the age to which these passages refer the ES or some other time?

First, not all interpreters take these references to tame animals literally. For instance, while Oswalt does see these passages as pointing to a future age, he believes that these bucolic scenes merely express, in a figurative way, the security and freedom from harm that will characterize the ES.[1] While it is not impossible that such references are purely figurative, I see no reason for taking them so. The matters about which Isaiah speaks make perfectly good sense when understood as having a literal fulfillment, for the most part yet future, as many commentators believe.

Granting that these texts refer to a transformation of animals at a time yet future, the question is whether these scenes take place in the ES. This is doubtful. It seems better to take these descriptions as occurring during the time of the millennial kingdom—the thousand-year reign of Christ on this present earth—which precedes the new heavens and new earth of the ES. (I discussed the millennium in Question 15.)

The Relevance of the Millennium for Interpreting These Passages
Why is the millennium relevant to whether we can cite these passages in support of animals in the ES? Very simply this: If the premillennial position is true (which I accept), and if these verses should be situated as taking place during the millennium and not during the ES, then these verses would not constitute direct evidence for animals in the ES. On the other hand, if there is good reason to see these verses as pointing to events transpiring on the new earth, then these passages would be the biblical smoking gun, so to speak, that

---

1. John N. Oswalt, *The Book of Isaiah: Chapters 1–39*, NICOT 23 (Grand Rapids: Eerdmans, 1986), 283.

would prove definitively that there will be animals in the ES—assuming, of course, that we also take the animal references literally.

Some commentators, such as Motyer, place these verses in the ES.[2] He takes verses 17–25 as a unit and as referring to the same period. Since verse 17 explicitly speaks of the new heavens and the new earth, the events of verse 25 likewise occur there. From this, one may conclude that there are animals on the new earth.

On the other hand, some commentators find certain characteristics in these verses that they regard as incompatible with the ES. For instance, though these verses describe vastly improved conditions over the present age, 65:20 tells us that there will still be death during this period, as well as the presence of sinners.[3] This fits with the somewhat "mixed" character of the millennium, in which there is a foretaste of what life on the new earth will be like but in which defects and blemishes of the old still inhere.[4] As for the fact that 65:17 specifically mentions the new earth in such close proximity to verse 25, a common characteristic of this type of prophecy is that it rarely presents such material in a strict chronological order. That is, verses right next to one another—and even material within the same verse—may point to different periods for their fulfillment.[5]

---

2. Alec Motyer, *Isaiah: An Introduction and Commentary* (Downers Grove, IL: Inter-Varsity, 1999), 398–400.

3. Recognizing this problem, Motyer takes the references to sinners and death in this passage as metaphorical: "It simply affirms that, over the whole of life, the power of death will be gone. . . . We are again dealing with metaphor: even if, *per impossible,* a sinner were to escape detection for a century, the curse would still search him out and destroy him. In reality, just as death will have no more power, so sin too will have no more place" (*Isaiah,* 399). This ad hoc explanation is unconvincing. It is best to take this as referring to literal death and actual sinners in the millennial age.

    Though resurrected saints rule with Christ during the millennium (Rev. 20:6), there are also unresurrected humans there with natural bodies, who are capable of committing sin and experiencing death. Presumably, these individuals were alive at Christ's coming to usher in the millennium, or are the descendants of these individuals born during the thousand years. It is from within the ranks of these that sinners would be found in the millennial kingdom, including those who would side with Satan in his final attempt at overthrowing Christ's rule (Rev. 20:7–9).

4. So Grogan: "We can of course be sure that when a promise is made of conditions that fall short of perfection—as for instance when life is lengthened but death is not abolished (65:20)—this does not apply to the perfected church but is best related to millennial conditions. . . . On the other hand, references to 'new heavens and a new earth' (65:17; 66:22) presuppose the advent of God's new order, where all will be perfect and which, according to Revelation 21–22, lies beyond the millennium" (Geoffrey W. Grogan, "Isaiah," *The Expositor's Bible Commentary,* 12 vols., ed. Frank E. Gaebelein [Grand Rapids: Zondervan, 1986], 6:15).

5. Citing specifically the case of Isaiah 65, John Walvoord states the matter well: "Only a few other passages in the Bible deal with the subject of the new heaven and the new earth, and these are often in a context dealing with the millennium. . . . It is a common principle in

So What Can We Prove from Isaiah 11 and 65?

It seems best to take these texts as pointing to a time in which there will be a literal transformation of the animal kingdom. But it also seems most likely that this time is the millennium and not the ES.

At the same time, the millennium is in a sense the "front porch" of the eternal kingdom, since it provides a foretaste of the conditions that are to come.[6] Therefore, one might argue that these verses suggest the presence of animals in the ES. Grogan's observation is worth bearing in mind: "The millennium itself is earthly, and passages that relate primarily to it may also point beyond themselves to the ultimate divine order in the new creation."[7] Therefore, while these verses cannot serve as direct evidence for animals in the ES, they do suggest it.

The General Redemption of the Creation May Include Animals

The Bible speaks much of the disorder that sin has introduced into our world and the way in which God plans to remedy it. Paul described this vividly in Romans 8:19–22:

> For the creation waits with eager longing for the revealing of the sons of God. For the creation was subjected to futility, not willingly, but because of him to subjected it, in hope that the creation itself will be set free from its bondage to corruption and obtain the freedom of the glory of the children of God. For we know that the whole creation has been groaning together in the pains of childbirth until now.

From this passage, it is clear that humankind is not alone in suffering the ravages of sin. When Adam introduced sin and death into the world (Rom. 5:12) he wreaked havoc on the entire created order. This includes the animal kingdom, which became subject to death and decay, as well as the inanimate creation, which storms, floods, dissolution, and corruption mar at every turn. At the same time, this passage also speaks of a glorious liberation of the entire created order that will take place when human beings experience their own deliverance, at "the revealing of the sons of God" (v. 19).

Paul also touches on this theme in Colossians 1:20. Here he states that God, through Christ, will "reconcile to himself all things, whether on earth

---

prophecy to bring together events that are distantly related chronologically, such as frequent reference to the first and second comings of Christ, actually separated by thousands of years (Isa. 61:1–2; cf. Luke 4:17–19)" (John Walvoord, *The Revelation of Jesus Christ* [Chicago: Moody, 1966], 311).

6. Mark Hitchcock, *55 Answers to Questions about Life after Death* (Sisters, OR: Multnomah, 2005), 231.

7. Grogan, "Isaiah," 6:16.

or in heaven, making peace by the blood of his cross." What exactly does the expression "all things" include? Might this liberation also include animals? Commentator Robert Wall suggests that it could:

> In a passage that explores the importance of Christ in terms of God's creation, I am led to understand God's reconciliation of *all things* as encompassing the nonhuman and inanimate worlds. . . . While I think it unwise to speculate how God might restore each part of the natural world or whether there are animals in heaven, I also think it unwise to limit God's reconciliation to the human order of creation, for that denies grace its unconditional and universal character.[8]

John Wesley was much less tentative. He argued vigorously that God redeems the entire created order, citing among other passages Revelation 21:5 ("Behold, I am making all things new"), which he believes must surely include animals. He also points to the text in Isaiah 11, which we have already considered.[9]

Though this reconciliation of the animal order may be sufficiently accomplished in the millennial kingdom, it is certainly plausible that a complete restoration of the creation would point to animals in the ES.

Argument Based on Human Stewardship over Animals

The argument based on human stewardship over animals is, in a sense, a variant of the one based on the redemption of the creation. The basic thesis of this position is that God gave human beings charge over the animals, as shown in Genesis 1:26, 28 and Psalm 8:6–8, to name a few such passages. As such, humans were to be a conduit of blessing to the animal world.[10] As John Wesley put it:

> Man was God's vicegerent upon earth, the prince and governor of this lower world; and all the blessings of God flowed through him to the inferior creatures. Man was the channel of conveyance between his Creator and the whole brute creation.[11]

---

8. Robert W. Wall, *Colossians and Philemon*, IVP New Testament Commentary Series 12 (Downers Grove, IL: InterVarsity Press, 1993), 77.

9. John Wesley, Sermon 60, "The General Deliverance," http://wesley.nnu.edu/john-wesley/the-sermons-of-john-wesley-1872-edition/sermon-60-the-general-deliverance/.

10. At first blush, this may appear to be the same as C. S. Lewis's argument, which I rejected in Part 1 of this discussion. However, the details of this argument and basis for it are actually significantly different.

11. Ibid.

Unfortunately, due to the introduction of sin into the world, human beings have not properly fulfilled their role in stewarding animals.[12] But just as there will be a renovation that will fulfill creation's original design, even so will human beings fulfill their obligations to the animal world by carrying out the original mandate entrusted to them. This will happen, so the argument goes, in the ES, on the new earth.

This argument has a certain plausibility to it. However, it may be that humans will fulfill this mandate during the millennium, to which the passages in Isaiah 11 and 65 (considered above) most likely point. Indeed, a number of theologians argue that the rationale for a thousand-year reign of Christ before the ES is precisely so that human beings will fulfill all of the original responsibilities entrusted to them at the original creation. That is, God's plan for humans to rule over *this* earth will find fulfillment before God moves on to the next and final epoch in the ES. The man Christ Jesus, the last Adam descended from the line of David, will accomplish on this earth what the first Adam did not. We, too, shall participate with Christ in this rulership during the millennial kingdom.[13] Now, if this is the overall divine rationale for a millennium, then the question of human stewardship over animals would be but one of a number of specific areas of rulership folded into the larger goal of humankind ruling this present world for God.

This is not to say that such dominion over animals might not carry over into the ES. It might. But the point is, the argument based on human stewardship would not require animals in the ES for its fulfillment if that fulfillment could be realized before that time, i.e., during the millennium.

The Bible Shows Explicitly That God Cares for and Delivers Animals

A number of texts show God's providential care for animals, including specifically his deliverance of them in this life. Psalm 145:9 tells us that God's "mercy is over all that he has made." Moreover, Psalm 36:6 states that God delivers both man and beast.

The Bible presents us with certain striking instances of God delivering animals together with humans from impending judgment.

Noah's flood is a clear example of this. God preserved at least some animals from destruction by placing two of each type in the ark (Gen. 6:19–21). In Genesis 8:1, the text tells us that God not only "remembered Noah" but also "all the beasts and all the livestock that were with him in the ark." After the flood, God vowed never again to destroy "every living creature" off the face of

---

12. Peter Kreeft, *Everything You Ever Wanted to Know about Heaven . . . but Never Dreamed of Asking* (San Francisco: Ignatius Press, 1990), 45–46.
13. See Erich Sauer, *The King of the Earth* (Grand Rapids: Eerdmans, 1962), 92–100; Erich Sauer, *The Triumph of the Crucified* (Grand Rapids: Eerdmans, 1952), 151; and Robert L. Saucy, *The Case for Progressive Dispensationalism* (Grand Rapids: Zondervan, 1993), 283–84; cf. 289–92.

the earth (Gen. 8:21). It is also significant that in 9:9–17 God makes multiple and explicit references to animals being included in his covenant with Noah.

Might these texts, showing as they do that God delivered animals from judgment and destruction in this life, point toward some kind of deliverance in the next?

Conclusion on Animals in the Eternal State

Taking Parts 1 and 2 of this topic together, we may conclude the following about whether there are animals in the ES:

1. The Bible contains no verses that disprove that there will be animals in the ES.

2. The Bible contains no verses that prove conclusively that there will be animals in the ES.

3. Some verses and biblical themes imply that there may well be animals in the ES.

4. If there are animals on the new earth, it is unlikely that they would be the same animals that existed on this earth. That is, God would create new animals, not resurrect previously existing ones.

Let us close by reconsidering and emphasizing an important point that I made in Part 1. While we may not know whether there will be animals on the new earth, we do know that we will be supremely happy there. God will provide us with whatever we need to make sure this is so. Therefore, we need not agonize over this issue. If we need animals on the new earth to be completely happy, then we can be sure that they will be there. But the reverse is also true: If no animals will be there, it will not bother us one bit when the time comes. Probably the best thing one can do is to not be anxious about this question but rest in knowing that we shall be satisfied, however it turns out.

REFLECTION QUESTIONS

1. Reread Isaiah chapters 11 and 65. Do you believe the references to animals are literal or figurative? Of what period or age do you believe these passages speak?

2. What is the rationale for a literal, thousand-year reign of Christ on this earth prior to the ES? How might the presence of animals during the millennium fit into that rationale?

3. Of all the arguments presented in favor of animals in the ES, which one(s), if any, do you find the most compelling?

4. After reading both Parts 1 and 2 on this subject, do you believe there will be animals in the ES? Has your opinion changed in any way, compared to what you thought about this before reading these chapters?

5. How do you feel about whether there will be animals in the ES? Do you think that the presence of animals will be necessary for your complete happiness in the ES?

The Eternal State for Unbelievers (Hell)

What Is Hell Like?

The Bible teaches that the finally impenitent will experience eternal, conscious punishment for their sins. This is the eternal hell or lake of fire, of which Scripture speaks.[1] In other words, this conscious punishment is true not only during the temporary intermediate state in hades, which we examined in Question 10 (and elsewhere). It is also true of the permanent, eternal, *embodied* state of existence in the lake of fire, taking place after the resurrection of the wicked that occurs on the day of judgment, as discussed in Part 3, "The Final Judgment."

In this question we are not considering the duration of the punishment; I shall deal with that in Question 32 below. Nor, strictly speaking, are we here considering the degree of that punishment or whether such punishment may admit of varying degrees for different individuals; we have already considered that in Question 18 above. Rather, the issue before us is: What is the nature of hell, *qualitatively* speaking? The simple answer is that the nature of hell is punishment consciously felt.

Even after narrowing the issue as I have done, there are still too many pertinent Scriptures to allow a detailed consideration of them all. However, I believe that two sets of texts answer this question conclusively. One set of verses is in Matthew 25. The other verses come from the book of Revelation. While I could offer many other texts to defend the orthodox position, these are the clearest. Therefore, I will treat these two sets of texts in detail.

---

1. See Question 8, "What Does the Bible Mean When It Speaks of 'Hell'?"

The Nature of Hell from Matthew 25:41, 46

This text reads:

> Then He will also say to those on His left, "Depart from me, accursed ones, into the eternal fire (*to pyr to aiōnion*) which has been prepared for the devil and his angels." (Matt. 25:41, NASB)

> And these will go away into eternal punishment (*kolasin aiōnion*), but the righteous into eternal life (*zōēn aiōnion*). (Matt. 25:46)

Observe that the wicked share the same fate as Satan and his demonic hosts. Indeed, this text tells us that God created hell specifically for Satan and his angels. As followers of Satan, the impenitent will receive the same fate as he. This is significant, because when we look at other passages in the book of Revelation that speak of the Devil's fate (see below), we may justly ascribe this same fate to unredeemed human beings.

Also, notice that this passage describes hell as a place of "eternal fire." Should we understand this to mean literal, material, physical fire? Alternatively, should we regard the expression as metaphorical language, designed to convey an awful spiritual reality through physical language? This is important enough of an issue that I have chosen to deal with it in its own right; see Question 31 below. It is enough for now to observe that whether one understands the fire—or any of the other words employed to describe hell's suffering—figuratively or literally, the experience entails *pain*. Granting that being burned by fire is among the most excruciating pains in our earthly experience, Jesus sought to impress upon his hearers the awfulness of eternal punishment by comparing hell's sufferings to it.

In the verses before us, Jesus describes the final state of the wicked as one of everlasting *punishment* (*kolasin aiōnion*).[2] From this, it follows that God does not remove the wicked from existence or annihilate them, but they experience conscious suffering in the afterlife. (I shall deal with the arguments offered by the annihilationists in Question 34 below.) That is because punishment, by the nature of the case, must be consciously felt in order for it to be truly a punishment. As Shedd cogently argues, "the extinction of consciousness is not of the nature of punishment."[3] If suffering is lacking, so is punishment; punishment entails suffering. But suffering, in turn, requires

---

2. BDAG, "κόλασις," 555; J. Schneider, "κολάζω, κόλασις," *TDNT* 3:814–17.
3. W. G. T. Shedd, *The Doctrine of Endless Punishment* (1886; repr., Minneapolis: Klock & Klock, 1980), 92.

consciousness. "If God by a positive act extinguishes, at death, the remorse of a hardened villain, by extinguishing his selfconsciousness, it is a strange use of language to denominate this a punishment."[4] Indeed, as Shedd notes, those who are experiencing severe punishment would actually long for an extinction of their consciousness. Luke 23:30–31 and Revelation 9:6 talk about the wicked experiencing the intense wrath of God, begging in vain to have the mountains fall on them so as to put them out of their misery; they would clearly prefer unconsciousness to their continuing torment. As Shedd observes, "The guilty and remorseful have, in all ages, deemed the extinction of consciousness after death to be a blessing."[5]

The punishment of the wicked entails separation from God as a key component. Notice that Christ banishes them forever from his presence. As Guthrie observes, "When we penetrate below the language about Hell, the major impression is a sense of separation."[6] Even those who do not follow Christ in this lifetime are still recipients of his goodness (Matt. 5:45), even if they do not acknowledge this. In the final state, it will not be so.

At the same time, there is also a sense in which God is *present* to the sinner in his/her punishment. This is a wrathful presence, such as one finds depicted in Revelation 14:10: "He will be tormented with fire and brimstone in the presence of the holy angels and of the Lamb." This is not a contradiction but two sides of the same coin. In hell, God is completely absent in terms of his presence to bless, but is only present to impart suffering and pain to the sinner.

The Nature of Punishment in Revelation 14:9–11; 20:10

These passages read:

> If anyone worships the beast and his image . . . he will be tormented (*basanisthēsetai*) with fire and brimstone in the presence of the holy angels and in the presence of the Lamb. And

---

4. Ibid.
5. Ibid., 94. One might object that if the doctrine of hell that I am advancing here is true, then the wicked mentioned in this passage would gain nothing by seeking death. Indeed, by dying they would exchange their present form of suffering for an even greater one. However, such an argument has no real force. The wicked depicted in this verse are simply seeking escape from their suffering and death seems, to them at least, to offer the prospect of respite from it. In addition, this objection assumes that the wicked themselves hold to an orthodox view of eternal, conscious punishment rather than the expectation that death ends it all. Regardless, at the moment of their intense suffering, they would rather seek the extinction of their *present* painful consciousness than the ongoing experience of their torment.
6. Donald Guthrie, *New Testament Theology* (Downers Grove, IL: InterVarsity, 1981), 889–90. So, too, Morey: "Hell is described by many different figures of speech, each emphasizing a different aspect of ultimate alienation from God" (Robert A. Morey, *Death and the Afterlife* [Minneapolis: Bethany, 1984], 31).

the smoke of their torment (*basanismou*) goes up forever and ever (*eis aiōnas aiōnōn*), and they have no rest, day or night, these worshipers of the beast and its image. (Rev. 14:9–11)

And the devil who deceived them was thrown into the lake of fire and brimstone, where the beast and the false prophet are also; and they will be tormented (*basanisthēsontai*) day and night forever and ever (*eis tous aiōnas tōn aiōnōn*). (Rev. 20:10, NASB)

These texts describe the nature of the punishment as "torment." The words used in these verses are forms of the Greek word *basanizō*. As Thayer states, *basanizō* means "to vex with grievous pains (of body or mind), to torment."[7] Likewise, Arndt and Gingrich say that *basanizō* means "to torture, torment," and may apply to either physical or mental pain or distress.[8] When we examine the uses of the verb *basanizō* and its various noun forms throughout the New Testament, we see that great pain and conscious misery are in view, not annihilation or cessation of consciousness. For example, the centurion's sick servant is grievously tormented (*deinōs basanizomenos*) by his palsy (Matt. 8:6). Revelation 12:2 uses the verb to describe the pains of childbirth. Second Peter 2:8 describes righteous Lot as tormented (*ebasanizen*) in his soul by the Sodomites' wicked deeds. Luke 16:23, 28 uses the plural noun "torments" (*basanoi*) to describe the rich man's conscious suffering in hades. Indeed, verse 28 depicts hades as "this place of torment" (*ton topon touton tēs basanou*).[9]

One might object that these passages do not specify whether the torment is "conscious." Are we not smuggling in the word "conscious" here?[10] But what other kind of torment is there besides conscious torment? Torment, by the nature of the thing, demands a sentient (i.e., feeling) subject to experience it. A rock or a tree cannot be tormented. Moreover, if the annihilationists are correct and the wicked pass out of existence altogether, how much less could a nonentity experience torment?

One might also object that these passages in Revelation do not say that humans are tormented—just the Devil, the beast, and the false prophet. Are

---

7. Joseph Henry Thayer, *A Greek–English Lexicon of the New Testament* (New York: Harper, 1887), 96.
8. BDAG, "βασανίζω," 168.
9. While I realize that Luke 16 has the intermediate state and not the eternal state in view, I cite the passage here simply in reference to the language of conscious torment that it employs.
10. Clark Pinnock makes precisely this accusation against adherents of the traditional doctrine. See Clark Pinnock, "The Destruction of the Finally Impenitent," *CTR* 4, no. 2 (Spring 1990): 256. In context, his reference is to the traditional understanding of Matthew 25.

we justified in jumping from the Devil's torment to the torment of wicked humans? As we already observed from Matthew 25, the fate of the wicked is the same as the Devil's fate. Other passages affirm the same fact (e.g., Rev. 20:15).

REFLECTION QUESTIONS

1. Regardless of whether one should take the fires of hell literally or figuratively, what is the key idea expressed by hell as a place of "eternal fire"?

2. Can a punishment rightly be considered a punishment if it is not consciously felt? What is the significance of one's conclusion on this for the position known as "annihilationism"? (see Question 34).

3. Does God cut off his presence from sinners in hell, or do they experience his presence? Reconcile these two concepts in light of this chapter.

4. What can we conclude about the nature of eternal punishment from Matthew 25, and Revelation 14 and 20?

5. How does the Devil's punishment in hell compare or contrast to that of unrepentant human beings? In what way is correlating the Devil's punishment with that of human beings significant when it comes to the interpretation of certain key biblical texts?

Are the Fires of Hell Literal?

Probably the most striking image of hell is as a place of everlasting flames. Popular depictions of hell—whether mocking and humorous, as in Gary Larson's cartoons, or devout and serious, as in the lurid images of the fifteenth-century artist Hieronymus Bosch—portray its victims being roasted alive, as if on a barbecue. The more fanciful portrayals throw in for good measure boiling cauldrons and demons prodding their victims with pitchforks.[1] Not a few people, repulsed by such imagery, reject the notion of hell altogether on this basis alone.

Nevertheless, we have observed a number of biblical passages that do use the language of fire to describe hell's awful reality. What should we make of such expressions? Should we understand this to mean literal, material, physical fire? Or, should we regard such expressions as metaphorical language, designed to convey an awful spiritual reality in physical terms?

The Argument for Literal Fire

Let us consider some arguments for understanding the flames of hell as literal, physical, material fire.[2] [Note: Although this is not the position I hold, throughout this section I am arguing for it as someone would who does embrace it.]

---

1. Incidentally, the notion that Satan himself or even his demons will preside over humans' torment in hell is utterly without foundation and far wide of the mark. The Devil and his angels will themselves be consigned to the gehenna of fire, not as jail wardens but as fellow sufferers. Indeed, their suffering will be the worst of all! (See Matt. 8:29; 25:41; Rev. 20:10.)
2. One of the more recent advocates of this position is John Walvoord, who contributed a chapter defending the "literal view" of hell (John F. Walvoord, "The Literal View," in Four Views on Hell, ed. Stanley N. Gundry [Grand Rapids: Zondervan, 1996], 11–39). For the most part, I am presenting the main lines of argument that he offers, while also supplementing them with some arguments that I think he could have but (for whatever reason) did not use.

The Literal Interpretation Is the Most Straightforward
The Bible describes hell as a place of fire. Why not simply take the Bible on its face and let it speak for itself? Given "the frequent mention of fire in connection with eternal punishment," it becomes difficult to escape the conclusion that literal fire "is what the Scriptures mean."[3]

For example, the case of the rich man and Lazarus in Luke 16:19–31 shows that we are to understand the fire literally. "The rich man in Hades asked father Abraham to cool his tongue with water because, 'I am in agony in this fire' (v. 24). Thirst would be a natural reaction to fire, and the desire to cool his tongue would be in keeping with this description."[4] Indeed, "Scripture never challenges the concept that eternal punishment is by literal fire. Objections have to be on philosophic or theological grounds rather than on exegetical ones."[5]

A Figurative Interpretation Undermines Biblical Authority
"The main argument against accepting literally the doctrine of hell is that the idea of eternal punishment by fire is repulsive to many people."[6] By making hell fire into a figure or a metaphor, proponents of the figurative interpretation believe that they are able to "alleviate some of the suffering of eternal punishment."[7] Indeed, an apologetic motivation may be at work here: Perhaps the desire is to make the Christian threat of hell less jarring to those who might otherwise reject it and the entire Christian message along with it.

However well-intentioned such people may be, so the argument goes, the figurative approach seriously undermines Scripture's absolute authority. Allowing our own sensibilities and desires free rein, we effectively set ourselves over Scripture as its judge. But who are we "to interpret a Scripture in a way other than its literal meaning simply because we do not like what it says?"[8] Walvoord admonishes:

> If the Bible describes this afterlife, as far as the lost are concerned, as a place of unending punishment characterized by fire, are we free to question it? And if so, on what basis? Though the accuracy of scriptural revelation has often been questioned in modern times on the basis that it was written in a different culture and a different time and, therefore, has to be revamped to fit our current situation, the idea that the

---

3. Ibid., 28.
4. Ibid.
5. Ibid.
6. John F. Walvoord, "Response to William V. Crocket," in *Four Views on Hell*, ed. Stanley N. Gundry (Grand Rapids: Zondervan, 1996), 79.
7. Walvoord, "The Literal View," 28.
8. Walvoord, "Response to William V. Crocket," 79.

Bible is antiquated and out of date leads to total rejection of the accuracy of biblical revelation for today.[9]

Simply stated, those who reject a literal understanding of hell's fire do so because "they find it impossible to reconcile this concept with their idea of a loving God who is indulgent and forgiving,"[10] not because it is the most straightforward reading of Scripture.

Many Eminent Christians in Church History Have Held to a Literal View
Some of the greatest Christian luminaries throughout the history of the church have taken the literal position. To name but a few, we have a large number of thinkers in the early church, including the greatest church father of western Christendom, St. Augustine. Turning to the medievals, we may number Thomas Aquinas among the literalists. More recently, we can add Jonathan Edwards, considered by many to be America's greatest theologian, and Charles Haddon Spurgeon, "the prince of preachers."[11] If this position was good enough for them, it should be good enough for us as well.

The Case for a Figurative Understanding of Hell's Flames
Probably most conservatives—that is, most theologians who also affirm the doctrine of eternal, conscious punishment—urge that we should understand the flames of hell metaphorically. This includes such eminent theologians as John Calvin, Charles Hodge, W. G. T. Shedd, and a host of others. In my view, this is the correct position, notwithstanding the arguments already raised to the contrary. Several solid reasons underlie this conclusion.

Flames Cannot Harm a Disembodied Spirit
If the flames of hell refer to literal, material fire, then they can only literally burn a corporeal (i.e., embodied), physical object. Consequently, the flames of gehenna (also known as the lake of fire) could be literal, in principle—at least for humans. This is because human sinners in gehenna have already been reembodied at the resurrection, which takes place before God casts them into gehenna's fires.

The problem, though, is that the Bible also applies the description of "fire" to disembodied human beings in the intermediate state. Recall that Jesus described the rich man in Luke 16:24 as being in agony in the flames. Jesus also described

---

9. Ibid., 78.
10. Ibid., 80.
11. For instance, in one of his sermons Spurgeon states, "You have seen asbestos lying in the fire red hot, but when you take it out it is unconsumed. So your body will be prepared by God in such a way that it will burn for ever without being consumed; it will lie, not as you consider, in a metaphorical fire, but in actual flame" (Sermon 66, http://www.spurgeon.org/sermons/0066.htm).

him as having a tongue, and said that Lazarus has a finger. As we noted earlier,[12] this scene occurs in hades, not gehenna, and that is during the disembodied state between death and resurrection. Therefore, just as it is impossible for a nonphysical being to possess a literal tongue, even so, there is no way that literal, physical fire can torment him.[13] As Alfred Plummer noted long ago, "The properties of bodies are attributed to souls in order to enable us to realize the picture."[14]

Furthermore, consider the case of demons. Demons, being fallen angels, have no physical bodies; they are pure spirit (Heb. 1:13–14).[15] And yet, the Devil himself, the prince of fallen angels, will be "thrown into the lake of burning sulfur" (Rev. 20:9), which is gehenna.[16] Therefore, not only should we understand hades's fire to be nonliteral, but also gehenna's fire—in the Devil's case, at least.

The point in citing the passages above is to demonstrate that in at least *some* instances, the Bible describes the agony of fire affecting beings who simply cannot be touched by physical fire, granting that they themselves are not physical. This is true both for hades and for gehenna. Given this fact, the burden of proof lies with those who would make the flames of hell literal for resurrected unbelievers in gehenna, which is the only remotely possible case in which literal, material fire could exist.

Other Descriptions of Hell's Punishment Must Also Be Figurative

When we examine the other descriptions of hell, we see that some of these make no sense if taken literally. For example, the Bible describes a certain class of disobedient angels as "kept in darkness, bound with everlasting chains for judgment of the great day" (Jude 6).[17] However, just as literal flames

---

12. See Question 6.
13. See Roger Nicole, "Punishment of the Wicked," *Christianity Today*, June 9, 1958, 14. As noted above, Walvoord cites Luke 16 in proof that the fires of hades are literal, whereas this text is actually among those most devastating for his view.
14. Alfred Plummer, *A Critical and Exegetical Commentary on the Gospel according to St. Luke*, ICC 42 (New York: Scribner's, 1903), 393. See also Simon J. Kistemaker, *Exposition of the Second Epistle to the Corinthians*, NTC (Grand Rapids: Baker, 1997), 168–69.
15. While it is true that angels sometimes manifest themselves in physical form, they are not physical beings. Angels materialize these physical manifestations for specific purposes, so that they may appear to human beings who otherwise would be unable to perceive them. As to their own true nature, however, angels do not have physical bodies. This holds true equally for demons, who are simply angels who rebelled against God.
16. Hodge observes, "There seems no more reason for supposing that the fires spoken of in Scripture is to be literal fire, than that the worm that never dies is literally a worm. The devil and his angels who are to suffer the vengeance of eternal fire, and whose doom the finally impenitent are to share, have no material bodies to be acted upon by elemental fire" (*Systematic Theology*, 3:868).
17. Jude describes something presently true of these particular demons, and so the passage does not refer to the post-judgment gehenna of fire. Nevertheless, that fact has no bearing on the point that I am drawing from the language employed.

cannot harm a disembodied spirit, neither can a literal chain bind a spirit. The reference to "everlasting chains" is therefore metaphorical, the meaning of which is quite clear: the fate of these wicked spirits is sealed and, just as for a prisoner bound by an unbreakable chain, there is no escaping it.

Consider also that some of the depictions are mutually exclusive if taken as literal, physical realities. For example, flames give off light, but at the same time hell is also presented as a place of complete darkness (Matt. 8:12; 22:13; 25:30; 2 Peter 2:17; Jude 6). How both can be literally true is difficult to see. There is no contradiction involved, however, when we recognize that these are all figures of speech that get at some important underlying realities about the nature of eternal punishment. Consequently, we need not concoct some kind of new, exotic physics to reconcile such discrepancies.

The Awfulness of Hell Requires Figurative Language

We have considered at some length the objection that those who deny the literal character of hell's flames are attempting to water down, so to speak, the awfulness of hell's reality. This is certainly Walvoord's view, and no doubt others of his persuasion share it. Whether this motivation may drive some, I cannot say. But granting the large number of eminent conservative, orthodox, Bible-believing scholars who take this position, such a sweeping claim is an inexcusable slander. It strains credulity to think that any such motivations were at work in biblically faithful men such as John Calvin or Charles Hodge.

In fact, not a few conservatives who hold the figurative view argue that the opposite is the case. It is far more reasonable to take the language as symbolic because the actual horrors of hell far outstrip the competency of literal, physical expressions to describe them. By using the figure of unquenchable fire, undying worms, etc., Jesus selected the most horrific descriptions that earthly language would allow. Culver observes, "When the subject matter of revelation transcends anything of direct human experience, when even direct analogies break down, God teaches us by symbols and figures. The literal realities represented by the symbols will be immeasurably more meaningful than the symbols. Hence to employ the symbols is in no wise to degrade or depreciate the realities."[18] Calvin summarizes the matter bluntly: "Let us lay aside speculations, by which foolish men weary themselves to no purpose, and satisfy ourselves with believing, that these forms of speech denote, in a manner suited to our feeble capacity, a dreadful torment, which no man can now comprehend, and no language can express."[19]

---

18. Robert Culver, *Systematic Theology: Biblical and Historical* (Fearn, Ross-shire, UK: Mentor, 2005), 1081.
19. John Calvin, *Commentary on a Harmony of the Evangelists, Matthew, Mark, and Luke*, trans. by William Pringle, 3 vols. (Grand Rapids: Baker, 1979), 1:201.

What, then, do metaphors such as fire, worms, outer darkness, and the like actually tell us about hell if we should not understand them literally? I believe Powell captures the matter well, and merits quoting in full:

> Although the biblical descriptions of Hell are stated in very physical and literal terms, the essential character of Hell should not be conceived in or limited to designations such as the worm that devours, the stripes that are inflicted, the burning or being consumed by fire. This affirmation does not detract from the horror or the gravity of the situation in Hell, because nothing could possibly be worse than separation from God and the torment of an evil conscience. Hell is Hell for those who are there essentially because they are completely alienated from God, and wherever there is alienation from God there is always estrangement from one's fellows. This is the worst possible punishment to which anyone could be subject: to be totally and irrevocably cut off from God and to be at enmity with all those who are around oneself. Another painful consequence of such a condition is to be at odds with oneself, torn apart from within from an accusing sense of guilt and shame. This condition is one of total conflict: with God, one's neighbor, and one's self. This is Hell! If the descriptions of Hell are figurative or symbolic, the conditions they represent are more intense and real than the figures of speech in which they are expressed.[20]

So, for instance, "The 'undying worm' has often been interpreted as the soul's internal torment, coveting and grieving what has been lost (Mark 9:48)"—a regret that "is compounded, since the reprobate are not penitent but locked into their rebellion."[21] The fire represents the pangs of one's conscience, and the burning is a destructive sense of remorse.

The Sense in Which Hell Does Entail Physical Punishment
If Walvoord and other literalists choose to mitigate the horrors of hell by making its fire physical and material, they are certainly free to do so but should realize that they have fallen into the very snare they wish to avoid. The worst suffering that we experience in this life is of a mental, spiritual, and psychological character. Consider the following two options: (1) the choice of a debilitating physical disease but joyous fellowship with Christ and our loved ones; or (2) a robust, healthy physical constitution but complete enmity with God and our family and friends. If forced to pick between one of these two options, which would you

---

20. Ralph E. Powell, "Hell," *BEB*, 2:953.
21. Timothy R. Phillips, "Hell," *EDBT*, 339.

choose? The decision would be immediate and clear. There is no doubt but that suffering in one's soul is by far worse than any and every malady of body.

At the same time, the choice as I have presented it above is in a certain sense unrealistic and represents a false alternative. That is because for human beings, mental suffering almost invariably results in bodily suffering. As I discussed earlier and at some length, the Bible depicts human beings holistically, as psycho-physical unities.[22] Our own experience amply bears this out. When we are distraught, grieved, vexed, and so forth, our bodies suffer as well.

Bear in mind that in the gehenna of fire, the wicked will not suffer as disembodied spirits but as complete (though corrupt) human beings, having body and spirit. There is therefore every reason to expect the wicked in hell to suffer great bodily pains there.[23] This suffering will take place from the inside out, as it were. It will not arise from God boiling sinners in a cauldron or turning them over slowly on a rotisserie spit, as vulgar, cartoonish depictions would have it. Rather, they will suffer the natural consequences of rejecting God and his goodness toward them, in which they will experience the pain of complete abandonment, remorse unmingled with comfort, and the relentless torments of their own consciences, which will burn forever but never finally consume. This cup they will drink to the full, experiencing unmitigated pain in both body and spirit.

REFLECTION QUESTIONS

1. After reading this chapter, do you think that we should understand the fires of hell literally or figuratively? What are the strongest arguments for each position?

2. Do you believe that those who take the flames of hell as figurative necessarily undermine biblical authority (whether they realize it or not)? Why or why not?

3. In what way does the fact that the Devil and his angels (demons) will be cast into the "lake of fire" suggest that the fires of hell might be metaphorical?

4. Assuming that the language of eternal fire is figurative, why might Jesus have spoken figuratively rather than literally?

5. In what sense do the fires of hell involve physical suffering, even on the metaphorical view?

---

22. See Question 5.
23. Pache correctly notes this physical element in eternal punishment as well (René Pache, *The Future Life* [Chicago: Moody, 1962], 287).

How Long Does Hell Last?

The question of hell's duration is not difficult to answer, as the Scriptures are clear on this point. The short answer is: the sufferings of hell are without end; they are in that sense "eternal."[1]

In saying that hell is without end we are not here considering the temporary period of punishment that the wicked endure during the disembodied, intermediate state in hades, which takes place between death and the bodily resurrection at the final judgment. The sufferings of hades indeed will end, just as the intermediate state is itself but a temporary condition. Rather, we are here addressing the eternal state that continues unabated, long after hades itself is "cast into the lake of fire" (Rev. 20:14).

Some dispute the eternality of hell. For example, both universalists and annihilationists deny the orthodox understanding of hell as eternal, conscious punishment. As we shall see, the universalists argue that everyone makes it into heaven in the end. The annihilationist, on the other hand, teaches that God removes the incorrigibly wicked from any existence at all, though he may punish them for a finite period first. In either case, no one suffers the pains of hell for all eternity, if at all. We shall explore both of these suggested alternatives in Question 33 (universalism) and Question 34 (annihilationism) respectively. In the present question, however, I shall confine myself to presenting the positive case for the eternality of hell's duration, as taught in the Bible. Then, in Question 35 I shall also consider some arguments drawn from the inherent logic of guilt and punishment. Additionally, when we look at the arguments that the universalists and annihilationists

---

1. Though we often speak loosely of "eternal punishment," it may be more precise, as W. G. T. Shedd observes, to designate the sufferings of hell as "endless" rather than "eternal." As Shedd states, "The absolutely eternal has no beginning, as well as no ending; it is the eternity of God. The relatively eternal has a beginning but no end; it is the immortality of man and angel" (W. G. T. Shedd, *The Doctrine of Endless Punishment* [1886; repr., Minneapolis: Klock & Klock, 1980], 80–81).

marshal against the biblical view, I shall highlight the flaws specific to those arguments at that time.

The Biblical Argument for the Eternality of Hell

Daniel 12:2
Speaking of the final judgment on the last day, Daniel 12:2 declares, "And many of those who sleep in the dust of the earth shall awake, some to everlasting (*olam*) life, and some to shame and everlasting (*olam*) contempt." The Hebrew word translated "everlasting" is *olam*. Since the meaning of this word is critical to the point in question, I shall make a few observations about its use not only here but also in other Old Testament texts.

The word *olam* carries as its primary and literal meaning, "eternity; unlimited duration."[2] This is most clear in texts that predicate it of God. Consider, for instance, Genesis 21:33 and Isaiah 40:28, which refer to Jehovah as "the everlasting God" (*el* or *elohim olam*). Psalm 90:2 furnishes an even more intensive use of *olam* for God's absolute eternity with the expression "from everlasting to everlasting (*meolam ad olam*) you are God." As there is no doubt about the endlessness of God's own being, even so there can be no doubt of *olam*'s meaning in these texts.

At the same time, *olam* can refer to limited duration in the sense of a long, ancient, or indefinite period.[3] For instance, the Bible uses *olam* in reference to the "everlasting hills" (*giboth olam*) in Genesis 49:26; in Psalm 78:69 to the earth itself; and in Deuteronomy 15:17 to a lifetime of service for a "perpetual" slave (*ebed olam*). These figurative or hyperbolic uses of *olam* do not take away from the fact that its basic meaning is that of unending duration, from which the "less proper" or figurative uses arise. As Stuart notes, such usages are a common feature of languages, including our own. For example, Stuart says that we might speak of experiencing "endless troubles" or a "perpetual scourge."[4] Such uses are, of course, hyperbole; it may *seem* to us that our troubles will never end or are without remission. That said, the figurative is grounded in the literal and makes no sense apart from it.

How, then, shall we understand the word *olam* in Daniel 12:2, the passage before us? What is determinative is that *olam* modifies both the word "life" (*khayim*) as well as the word "contempt" (*deraon*). Since it is clear that the life for the righteous is without end, as everyone would admit, it follows inexorably that the contempt that the wicked will experience must be endless as

---

2. Moses Stuart, *Exegetical Essays on Several Words Relating to Future Punishment* (Andover, MA: Perkins & Marvin, 1830), 47.
3. Stuart, *Exegetical Essays*, 50. See H. W. F. Gesenius, "עוֹלָם," *Gesenius' Hebrew-Chaldee Lexicon to the Old Testament* (Grand Rapids: Baker, 1979), 612–13.
4. Stuart, *Exegetical Essays*, 50.

well. Unless we are prepared to limit the duration of eternal life for believers, we have no justification for limiting the duration of hell. By the way, we shall encounter the same parallel in a New Testament example when we consider Jesus's words in Matthew 25:46, below.

Isaiah 66:24 (cf. Mark 9:47–48)

This verse reads:

> And they shall go out and look on the dead bodies of the men who have rebelled against me. For their worm shall not die, their fire shall not be quenched, and they shall be an abhorrence to all flesh.

Jesus clearly employs this verse from Isaiah as a metaphor for the sufferings of hell. In Mark 9:47–48 he states:

> And if your eye causes you to sin, tear it out. It is better for you to enter the kingdom of God with one eye than with two eyes to be thrown into hell, "where their worm does not die and the fire is not quenched."

It is significant that Jesus speaks of *undying* worms and *unquenchable* fire. If Jesus (and, for that matter, Isaiah) had in mind only a violent physical death, confined to the present life, such language would be inappropriate. Robert Reymond, citing Guthrie, observes of this verse:

> Because maggots, the larvae of flies, normally feed upon a corpse's flesh and are finally done with it (Job 21:26; 24:20; Isa. 14:11) whereas here the unrepentant sinner's "maggot" is said never to die and Gehenna's fire is said to be unquenchable, Guthrie appears to be correct when he states that Jesus' description of the unrepentant sinner's final state is that of "a state of continuous punishment."[5]

Our focus here is not on the exact meaning of the worm and fire imagery, i.e., whether one ought to take these figuratively or literally. We have already examined these issues, both generally in Question 30 (on the nature of hell) and even more specifically in Question 31 (whether the fires of hell are literal). However, on the issue of hell's duration these verses leave no doubt. As Shedd well observed, "Had Christ intended to teach that future punishment

---

5. Robert Reymond, "Dr. John Stott on Hell," *Presbyterion* 16 (Spring 1990): 47.

is remedial and temporary, he would have compared it to a dying worm, and not an undying worm; to a fire that is quenched, and not to an unquenchable fire."[6]

Matthew 25:41, 46

In my view, Matthew 25 is one of the three strongest chapters in the New Testament that establishes the endlessness of future retribution. (The other two passages occur in the book of Revelation; we shall consider these next.) The relevant verses read:

> Then he [the Son of Man] will say to those on his left, "Depart from me, you cursed, into the eternal fire (*to pyr to aiōnion*) prepared for the devil and his angels." (Matt. 25:41)

> And these will go away into eternal punishment (*kolasin aiōnion*), but the righteous into eternal life (*zōēn aiōnion*). (Matt. 25:46)

The Greek adjective translated "eternal" in these verses is *aiōnion*. This adjective carries the sense of "perpetual, never-ending, eternal, everlasting, without end."[7] However, just as we observed in the case of the Hebrew word *olam*, we note that certain contexts do not use the adjective *aiōnios* for eternity. In some passages, it refers to an "age" or period. Luke 1:70 (NASB), for example, says that God "spoke by the mouth of His holy prophets *from of old* (*ap aiōnos*)." Clearly, this cannot be a reference to eternity past. We find a parallel construction in Acts 3:21.[8] On the other hand, the Bible applies this adjective to God (e.g., the "eternal God"), as in 1 Timothy 1:17; Romans 16:26; Hebrews 9:14; and 13:8. In these latter passages, *aiōnios* means "eternal," as shown from their context and from the fact that God is the subject. Furthermore, Moses Stuart argues that *aiōnios* invariably refers to endless duration when the adjective is used to describe future time, such as is the case here.[9]

But what leaves no doubt about its meaning in the present verse is the context. As we noted in the case of Daniel 12:2, the fact that the duration of punishment for the wicked forms a parallel with the duration of life for the righteous is determinative. The adjective *aiōnios* describes both the length of punishment for the wicked and the length of eternal life for the righteous. One cannot limit the duration of punishment for the wicked without at the same time limiting the duration of eternal life for the redeemed. It would do

---

6. Shedd, *Doctrine of Endless Punishment*, 78.
7. Stuart, *Exegetical Essays*, 40.
8. See the discussion in Hermann Sasse, "αἰών, αἰῶνος," *TDNT* 1:199.
9. Stuart, *Exegetical Essays*, 46.

violence to the parallel to give it an unlimited meaning in the case of eternal life but a limited one when applied to eternal death.[10]

Revelation 14:9–11; 20:10

The relevant passages read:

> And another angel, a third, followed them, saying with a loud voice, "If anyone worships the beast and its image and receives a mark on his forehead or on his hand, he also will drink the wine of God's wrath, poured full strength into the cup of his anger, and he will be tormented with fire and sulfur in the presence of the holy angels and in the presence of the Lamb. And the smoke of their torment goes up forever and ever (*eis aiōnas aiōnōn*), and they have no rest, day or night, these worshipers of the beast and its image, and whoever receives the mark of its name." (Rev. 14:9–11)

> . . . and the devil who had deceived them was thrown into the lake of fire and sulfur where the beast and the false prophet were, and they will be tormented day and night forever and ever (*eis tous aiōnas tōn aiōnōn*). (Rev. 20:10)

In the most emphatic language possible, the above verses tell us that the torments of hell are without end. When we considered Matthew 25:46 above, we noted that, in some contexts, *aiōnos* could qualify nouns of limited duration. (Though, as we also observed, the context of Matthew 25 demands that we take *aiōnios* in its unlimited signification there.) But here, we find the emphatic forms *eis aiōnas aiōnōn* and *eis tous aiōnas tōn aiōnōn* ("unto the ages

---

10. Moses Stuart has articulated this principle as well as anyone possibly could, which applies not only here but with equal force to our earlier examination of Daniel 12:2:

"I take it to be a rule of construing all *antithetic* forms of expression, that where you can perceive the force of one side of the antithesis, you do of course come to a knowledge of the force of the other side. If *life eternal* is promised on one side, and *death eternal* is threatened on the other and opposite one, is it not to be supposed, that the word *eternal* which qualifies *death,* is a word of equal force and import with the word *eternal* which qualifies *life?* In no other case could a doubt be raised, with regard to such a principle. I venture to say that the exception here, (if such a one must be made), is without any parallel in the just principles of interpretation.

"If then the words *aiōn* and *aiōnios* are applied 60 times (which is the fact) in the New Testament, to designate the *continuance* of the future happiness of the righteous; and some 12 times to designate the *continuance* of the future misery of the wicked; by what principles of interpreting language does it become possible for us, to avoid the conclusion that *aiōn* and *aiōnios* have the same sense in both cases?" (*Exegetical Essays,* 56).

of the ages"). This construction only describes unending duration. As Sasse points out, the "twofold use of the term [*aiōnios*]" is designed "to emphasize the concept of eternity."[11] The fact that the forms used are plural in number further reinforces the idea of never-ending duration. Speaking of the Greek construction in this verse, the great biblical commentator Lenski observed:

> The strongest expression for our "forever" is *eis tous aiōnan tōn aiōnōn*, "for the eons of eons"; many aeons, each of vast duration, are multiplied by many more, which we imitate by "forever and ever." Human language is able to use only temporal terms to express what is altogether beyond time and timeless. The Greek takes its greatest terms for time, the eon, pluralizes this, and then multiplies it by its own plural, even using articles which make these eons the definite ones.[12]

We find this same emphatic construction in Revelation 1:6; 4:9; and 5:3, where it refers to the unending worship of God. Revelation 4:10 and 10:6 use it to describe God's own endless life. And Revelation 22:5 employs the construction to characterize the saints' everlasting reign.[13]

Note that the words "day and night" also point to the unending duration of the torment. This expression designates ceaseless activity. Revelation 4:8 and 7:15 use this same phrase to characterize the neverending worship of God. By juxtaposing the words "day and night" with "forever and ever" in 20:10, we have the most emphatic expression of unending, ceaseless activity possible in the Greek language.

Now, one might quibble, as Clark Pinnock does, that Revelation 20:10 is irrelevant to our discussion because it has only the Devil, the beast, and the false prophet in view, and these "cannot be equated with ordinary human beings, however we should understand their nature."[14] But one can scarcely take this objection seriously. First, the passage in Revelation 14 *does* mention ordinary human beings, as Pinnock himself admits.[15] Second, one need only read the verses immediately following, to the end of the chapter, in order to

11. Hermann Sasse, "αἰών, αἰώνος," *TDNT* 1:199.
12. R. C. H. Lenski, *The Interpretation of St. John's Revelation* (Columbus, OH: Wartburg, 1943), 48. I should note that I do not agree with Lenski that the eternal state for believers is "timeless" in the sense that God is timeless, i.e., existing outside of time—assuming that is what he meant to say. For us as creatures, we may more correctly describe our eternal life as "endless life."
13. See the discussion in Robert A. Morey, *Death and the Afterlife* (Minneapolis: Bethany, 1984), 138.
14. Clark Pinnock, "The Destruction of the Finally Impenitent," *CTR* 4, no. 2 (Spring 1990): 257.
15. Ibid.

see that anyone whose "name was not found written in the book of life . . . was thrown into the lake of fire" (v. 15).

REFLECTION QUESTIONS

1. What do the annihilationists and universalists teach about the eternality of hell? Explain how they differ from the traditional, biblical approach, as well as how they differ from one another.

2. Since the Hebrew word *olam* can mean either "eternity" or an indefinite period of limited duration, how can we know whether a passage such as Daniel 12:2 teaches a limited or an unlimited period of punishment for the wicked? Likewise, address this same issue for the Greek word *aiōnion,* used in Matthew 25:41, 46.

3. How would the metaphors of worms and fire, as used by Jesus, lead one to conclude that hell is of unlimited duration?

4. How does the original language of Revelation 14:9–11 and 20:10 strongly point to the eternality of hell?

5. Some have argued that one cannot cite Revelation 20 to argue for the eternal conscious punishment of human beings because this passage speaks only of the Devil, the beast, and the false prophet. Evaluate this argument.

What Do Universalists Teach about Hell?

Statement of the Position

Universalism is the teaching that everyone will finally be saved. Beyond this common theme, however, one finds significant diversity within the universalist camp.[1]

Many universalists claim Christian allegiance, affirming that it is only through Jesus Christ that God has secured salvation for all humankind. John A. T. Robinson, Nels F. S. Ferré, and more recently Robin Parry[2] are well-known proponents of this type of universalism, teaching that eventually everyone will come to receive Christ as savior. However, other universalists are "pluralists," such as John Hick. These argue that God has provided multiple paths to secure the salvation of all; Christianity is just one of many possible ways.[3]

Until recently, universalism had gained little audience among professing evangelicals. But in recent years a vague form of the teaching appears to have found a niche in the evangelical community through pop preacher Rob Bell, whose inexplicably popular—and often sarcastic and flippant—*New*

---

1. For a good, fairly recent article surveying contemporary universalist arguments and responses to them, see Gerald R. McDermott, "Will All Be Saved?," *Themelios* 38, no. 2 (2013): 232–43.
2. See, for example, Robin A. Perry, "A Universalist View," in *Four Views on Hell*, eds. Stanley N. Gundry and Preston Sprinkle (Grand Rapids: Zondervan, 2016).
3. The varieties of universalism in relationship to pluralism and to the Christian faith are a great deal more nuanced than space permits us to examine here. For more information, see Trevor Hart, "Universalism: Two Distinct Types," in *Universalism and the Doctrine of Hell*, ed. Nigel M. de S. Cameron (Grand Rapids: Baker, 1992), 1–34. Throughout this chapter, I shall focus mostly on the so-called Christian variety of universalism.

York Times bestseller *Love Wins* suggests a universalistic model without affirming it outright.[4]

Biblical Passages Offered in Support of Universalism

Many universalists attempt to offer direct biblical support for their position. We shall examine some of the more commonly presented passages.

Acts 3:21

In this verse, Peter states that Jesus presently remains in heaven "until the time for restoring (*apokatastaseōs*) all the things about which God spoke." According to the universalist, this shows that God will eventually restore everything and everyone to himself.

While the word *apokatastaseōs* can be translated "restitution" or "restoration," many commentators note that it "can also mean *establishment* of something formerly envisioned or agreed upon. . . . With such a meaning, the phrase could be rendered 'the establishment of all the things which the prophets predicted.'"[5] This sense would correspond nicely with the earlier statement in 1:6, which uses the same root word in the context of establishing the kingdom.[6] However, this reference to prophetic fulfillment in no way implies universal salvation.

Romans 5:12–21; 1 Corinthians 15:22

These passages contrast Adam with Christ. Just as "many" died through Adam's transgression, even so, the free gift of salvation also abounds to the "many" (Rom. 5:15). Verse 18 is especially pertinent: "Therefore, as [Adam's] one trespass led to condemnation for all men, so one act of righteousness [i.e., Christ's work of salvation] leads to justification and life for all men." Likewise, 1 Corinthians 15:22 states that "in Christ all shall be made alive." From these verses, the universalist concludes that God actually grants eternal life to all.

---

4. I use the words "vague" and "suggests" advisedly. Bell often couches his mocking ridicule of the biblical doctrine of eternal, conscious punishment in the form of loaded, straw-man questions, framed so that universalism would be the only attractive conclusion. In other places, he presents universalist arguments forcefully, but does so by putting the statements in the mouth of others, e.g., as reporting what "some Christians think." But in yet other instances, he provides himself with wiggle room by claiming to be agnostic about the final answer to the question. I note one such "escape clause" (Rob Bell, *Love Wins* [New York: HarperCollins, 2011], 115), where he entertains the possibility that some may perpetually choose to reject God, finally concluding that the truth of this scenario is unknowable. Such equivocations notwithstanding, not a few have come away with the impression that Bell is a universalist.

5. John B. Polhill, *Acts*, NAC (Nashville: Broadman, 1992), 135.

6. F. F. Bruce, *Commentary on the Book of Acts: The English Text with Introduction, Exposition, and Notes*, NICNT (Grand Rapids: Eerdmans, 1954), 85; Howard I. Marshall, *Acts*, TNTC 5 (Downers Grove, IL: InterVarsity, 2008), 94.

What these verses actually teach, however, is that all who are in Adam are condemned and die, whereas all who are in Christ are justified and receive salvation. All human beings are in Adam through natural birth, whereas only believers are in Christ through spiritual rebirth (John 3:3, 7; 1 Peter 1:23). The texts do not say that all are in Christ, but rather teach that all *who are in Christ* will receive salvation.[7] Note especially Romans 5:17, which speaks of the necessary condition of receiving the free gift of grace. Scripture everywhere gives faith as the sole condition for receiving salvation (Acts 16:31; Rom. 10:9–10; 1 Cor. 1:21; Eph. 2:8–10; 1 Tim. 4:10; Heb. 10:39).

As for 1 Corinthians 15:22, even if one were to insist that this passage applies to all people without exception, it still would not teach universalism. The wicked as well as the righteous will be raised from the dead and in that sense "made alive." But theirs is a resurrection of shame and judgment and not of salvation (Dan. 12:2).

Ephesians 1:10; Philippians 2:10–11; Colossians 1:19–20
In Ephesians 1:10 Paul says that in "the fullness of time" God is going to "unite all things" (*anakephalaiōsasthai*) in Christ. The same thought occurs in Philippians 2:10–11, in which a day will come when everyone is going to confess Jesus as Lord and Savior. Colossians 1:19–20 captures this same idea when it speaks of "reconcil[ing] to himself all things," effecting "peace by the blood of his cross." From these verses, some universalists conclude that everyone will someday confess Christ as Lord and be united to God.

Now, it is certainly true that every knee someday will bow to Christ and that eventually a day of universal peace will come. However, it does not follow from this that everyone will be saved. Commenting on Ephesians 1:10, Arnold discusses the word *anakephalaioō*, which some translations render as "to unite all things." He translates this word as "to bring everything under the headship of."[8] While all will eventually come under Christ's headship, this does not mean that all will submit willingly or in a saving way. Arnold observes:

> Behind [this word] lies the idea of a rebellion in the creation—of things on earth (humans and the institutions they control) and in heaven (the realm of angels and spirit beings) ... but there will come a time when all of creation will have to submit to his authority as sovereign Lord. ... Christ is the one who will serve as God's agent in bringing all the rebellious

---

7. See Roy E. Ciampa and Brian S. Rosner, *1 Corinthians*, PNTC (Grand Rapids: Eerdmans, 2010), 763–64; Gordon D. Fee, *1 Corinthians*, NICNT (Grand Rapids: Eerdmans, 1987), 749–50; Craig Blomberg, *1 Corinthians*, NIVAC (Grand Rapids: Zondervan, 1994), 304.
8. Clinton E. Arnold, *Ephesians*, ZECNT (Grand Rapids: Zondervan, 2010), 88.

creatures in all of creation under God's sovereignty. Paul expressed a similar idea to the Philippians when he declared that there will be a day when "at the name of Jesus every knee should bow, in heaven and on earth and under the earth, and every tongue confess that Jesus Christ is Lord, to the glory of God the Father" (Phil. 2:10–11).[9]

Bruce similarly understands the reconciliation mentioned in Colossians 1:20 in terms of "pacification." (Here Bruce is using the term "pacification" in the military sense of quelling or suppressing the hostile forces of opposition and imposing peace through force.) Bruce states, "The peace effected by the death of Christ may be freely accepted, or it may be imposed willy-nilly. This reconciliation of the universe includes what would otherwise be distinguished as pacification."[10] This applies not only to rebellious human beings but to the hostile spiritual forces of evil as well. A number of other scholars take the "pacification" understanding of the language used in these passages.[11]

1 Thessalonians 5:9
Unitarian Universalist authors Buehrens and Church observe that this was the famous eighteenth-century universalist John Murray's "favorite text: 'God has not destined us for wrath, but for salvation.'"[12] This passage is offered to demonstrate God's intention to save all—an intention that he realizes.
    In response, we observe that Paul is addressing *Christians*, not unbelievers. (Notice the reference to "brothers" in verse 1.) However, even if one were to take verse 9 without such a restriction, it still would not prove universalism. Strictly speaking, God does not "destine" or "send" anyone to hell; a person goes there by his or her own choice.[13]

1 Timothy 2:4–6
    This passage states that God desires the salvation of all (v. 4). Furthermore, in verse 6, Paul teaches that Christ gave his life as a ransom for all. Christ's

---

9. Ibid., 89.
10. F. F. Bruce, *The Epistles to the Colossians, to Philemon, and to the Ephesians*, NICNT (Grand Rapids: Eerdmans, 1984), 76.
11. Besides Arnold and Bruce, see also Larry Dixon, *The Other Side of the Good News* (Wheaton, IL: Victor Books, 1992), 59; Richard J. Melick Jr., *Philippians, Colossians, Philemon*, NAC 32 (Nashville: Broadman, 1991), 227; Douglas J. Moo, *The Letters to the Colossians and to Philemon*, PNTC (Grand Rapids: Eerdmans, 2008), 135–36; and Peter T. O'Brien, *Colossians, Philemon*, WBC 44 (Nashville: Thomas Nelson, 2000), 56.
12. John A. Buehrens and F. Forrester Church, *Our Chosen Faith: An Introduction to Unitarian Universalism* (Boston: Beacon, 1989), 32.
13. See especially Question 36 (though I touch on this issue in certain other questions as well).

work, the universalist concludes, therefore redeems all without exception and thus saves everyone by it.

This conclusion is unwarranted. When verse 4 speaks of God desiring "all" people to be saved, many commentators believe that Paul is speaking of all kinds or classes of people—i.e., people from every race, nation, and station in life, rather than "all men individually, one by one."[14] This would make sense especially in light of Paul's opponents, who argued that salvation was only available to certain groups, specifically to law-keeping Jews.[15] At the same time, it is also true that God does delight in the salvation of sinners without qualification (John 3:16), as a thing pleasing in itself.[16] That some fail to attain it through nothing other than their own willful obstinacy does not take away from the fact that God would delight in their salvation if they would but choose it (Luke 15:10; Ezek. 18:32; 33:11). On either understanding, this text does not support universalism.

As for Christ giving himself as "a ransom for all," if "all" refers merely to all kinds or classes of people, then this passage would in no way imply universalism. However, even if one took the "all" to refer to all without exception, it is certainly true that Christ's death is in and of itself a complete satisfaction of justice for sin, sufficient to redeem all humankind from all of their sins. However, as the Bible makes clear repeatedly, in order for this entirely sufficient redemption to discharge the debt of any particular sinner, the sinner must receive it by faith (Acts 13:39; Rom. 3:26, 30; 4:5; 5:1; 10:10; Gal. 2:16; 3:8, 11, 24).

1 Timothy 4:10

This verse states that the living God "is the Savior (*Sōtēr*) of all people, especially of those who believe." From this, the universalist concludes that God actually grants eternal salvation to all people, meaning that all will go to heaven.

That this verse cannot possibly teach universal salvation is obvious by the qualifier "especially of those who believe." If Christ were the savior both of believers and of unbelievers in the same way and without exception, then Paul ought simply to have said that Christ is the savior of all people and left it at that. Since, according to the universalist, unbelievers are just as eternally

---

14. William Hendriksen, *Exposition of the Pastoral Epistles*, NTC (Grand Rapids: Baker, 1957), 95. See his discussion on 93–95. Others holding this position include Calvin, *Commentary on 1 Timothy*; and George W. Knight III, *The Pastoral Epistles*, NIGTC (Grand Rapids: Eerdmans, 1992), 119.

15. Knight, *The Pastoral Epistles*, 119.

16. Francis Turretin, *Institutio Theologiae Elencticae* (Geneva, 1679–85), 4.17.33. See the discussion in W. G. T. Shedd, *Dogmatic Theology*, ed. Alan W. Gomes (Phillipsburg: P&R, 2003), 346–49.

saved as believers are, for Paul to say that believers are "especially saved" by Christ would make no sense whatever if universalism were true.

How, then, are we to understand the all-important qualifying phrase, "especially of those who believe"? There are at least two main ways of attacking this issue, neither of which is friendly to universalist conclusions.

The first consideration is the proper translation of the word rendered "especially" in some translations. The underlying Greek word is *malista*. Commentators have observed that in certain passages *malista* carries the sense of "namely," "to be precise," or "that is to say."[17] If such is the correct understanding of *malista* here, then it would make the most sense to take "all" in the sense of "all kinds" or "all classes," or "people from every walk of life," as discussed above.[18] Accordingly then, we would paraphrase the verse along the following lines: "[God] is the Savior of all kinds of people, namely of believers from every walk of life."

On the other hand, assuming "especially" really is the correct translation for *malista* here (which I suspect to be the case), then the issue becomes one of discerning the sense in which God is the savior of all people over and against the special sense in which he is the savior of believers in particular.

Some, such as Calvin, Grudem, Guthrie, Hendriksen, and A. T. Robertson, say that the word *sōtēr* (translated "savior") often carries the sense of one who delivers or preserves.[19] Hendriksen points out that *sōtēr* commonly described human and divine deliverers in the ancient world, such as emperors and pagan deities. Granting the common use of this word in Roman culture, it would not be surprising for Paul to reference the true Preserver and Deliverer of human beings, who "makes his sun rise on the evil and on the good, and sends rain on the just and on the unjust" (Matt. 5:45). Paul's reasoning, then, becomes an argument from the lesser to the greater. Calvin observes:

> The word *sōtēr* is here a general term, and denotes one who defends and preserves. [Paul] means that the kindness of God extends to all men. And if there is no man who does not feel the goodness of God towards him, and who is not a

---

17. See, e.g., Knight, *The Pastoral Epistles*, 203–4; William D. Mounce, *Pastoral Epistles*, WBC 46 (Nashville: Thomas Nelson, 2000), 256.
18. See Knight, *The Pastoral Epistles*, 203–4.
19. Calvin, *Commentary on 1 Timothy*, commenting on 4:10; Wayne Grudem, *Systematic Theology* (Grand Rapids: Zondervan, 1994), 662; Donald Guthrie, *The Pastoral Epistles*, TNTC (Nottingham, England: IVP Academic, 2009), 110; Hendriksen, *Exposition of the Pastoral Epistles*, 154–56; Archibald Thomas Robertson, *Word Pictures in the New Testament*, vol. 4, *The Epistles of Paul* (Nashville: Broadman Press, 1931), 580.

partaker of it, how much more shall it be experienced by the godly, who hope in him?[20]

It might also be that the word "savior" carries the same meaning in both instances, i.e., as the eternal savior from sin and judgment, but that in the case of unbelievers God is their savior only *potentially*, whereas for believers he is their savior *actually*.[21] This makes good sense to me, and I would explain it along the same lines as what I have stated in the discussion of 1 Timothy 2:6. That is to say, considered in and of himself, God is the Savior of all because he made a provision for salvation that will save all who confide in it. Yet, this provision actually saves only those who embrace it by faith. This would be analogous to speaking of a certain drug as the "cure for a particular disease"—granting, of course, that a drug will only cure in reality those who take it.

Theological Arguments Offered in Support of Universalism

A God of Love Would Not Send People to an Eternal Hell
The Bible everywhere declares that God is love (e.g., 1 John 4:8). One of the most common arguments in the universalist's arsenal is that "so horrible a view as eternal hell" is thoroughly incompatible with a God that is "boundless love."[22]

In response, the universalist correctly notes that God is love but then incorrectly concludes that a God of love could not and would not permit recalcitrant sinners to send themselves to eternal perdition. For a complete discussion of this, see Question 36, "How Can a God of Love Send People to an Eternal Hell?"

The Existence of Hell Would Destroy the Happiness of Heaven
According to universalists, if any of the human family were suffering eternally in hell this would destroy the happiness of those in heaven and even of God himself. Universalist author J. A. T. Robinson states, "In a universe of love there can be no heaven which tolerates a chamber of horrors, no hell for

---

20. Calvin, *Commentary on 1 Timothy*, 4:10.
21. Millard J. Erickson, *Christian Theology* (Grand Rapids: Baker, 1985), 829–30, 1021; Gordon D. Fee, *1 and 2 Timothy, Titus* NIBC 13 (Peabody, MA: Hendrickson, 1998), 106; Thomas D. Lea and Hayne P. Griffin Jr., *1, 2 Timothy, Titus* NAC 34 (Nashville: Broadman, 1992), 96. Robertson, who seemed to endorse the earlier view that we ought to understand *sōtēr* in the more generic sense of "deliverer" when applied to unbelievers, nevertheless also cites White approvingly in support of the present view (*Word Pictures in the New Testament*, 4:580).
22. Nels F. S. Ferré, *The Christian Understanding of God* (New York: Harper, 1951), 238.

any which does not at the same time make it hell for God."[23] Similarly, Ferré urges, "If eternal hell is real, love is eternally frustrated and heaven is a place of mourning and concern for the lost."[24]

I deal with this claim at some length in Question 37 and Question 38, "How Can We Be Happy in the Eternal State If There Are People Suffering in Hell, including Some of Our Loved Ones?"

The Existence of Hell Would Destroy God's Sovereignty and Omnipotence

As shown in some of the biblical passages cited above, God genuinely desires all to be saved. If in fact some are not saved, then, according to the universalist, it would follow that God cannot actualize his desire. This is unthinkable, however, granting that God is sovereign and omnipotent. J. A. T. Robinson states, "Judgment can never be God's last word, because if it were, it would be the word that would speak of his failure. . . . God would have failed and failed infinitely," and therefore "God would simply cease to be God."[25] Likewise, Ferré declares, "Christ is Love, and Love never fails. To say that Love fails is to insult God."[26] Ferré concludes, "The final victory of universal Love is universal salvation."[27]

In response, I note that God is indeed sovereign (Ps. 115:3; Isa. 45:7; 46:10; Dan. 4:34–35; Eph. 1:11) as well as omnipotent (Job 42:2; Isa. 44:24; Jer. 32:17; Matt. 19:26). But it will not do for us to draw conclusions about what must follow from God's sovereignty and omnipotence when such conclusions contradict Scripture's express teaching.

As the universalists themselves repeatedly acknowledge, we know from Scripture that God endowed human beings with moral freedom. His decision to do so is itself an exercise of his sovereignty. The freedom with which he created human beings enabled them to reject him out of their own self-caused volition. The choice to remain separate from God is chargeable to the creature and not to the creator. What *is* chargeable to the creator, so to speak, is his decision to create such beings in the first place, and then to allow them to choose contrary to him. Nevertheless, this is God's right to create human beings after such a fashion and it is not our place to limit his sovereignty in this matter. To deny God that freedom based on some preconceived assumption that flies in the face of Scripture's express testimony is in itself an affront to his sovereignty and omnipotence.[28]

---

23. John A. T. Robinson, *In the End, God . . . : A Study of the Christian Doctrine and the Last Things* (Eugene, OR: Cascade Books, 2011), 116.
24. Ferré, *The Christian Understanding of God*, 237.
25. Robinson, *In the End, God*, 101–2.
26. Nels F. S. Ferré, *Christ and the Christian* (London: Collins, 1958), 245.
27. Ibid., 248. See also Ferré, *The Christian Understanding of God*, 219.
28. While it is true that believers will not be able to sin in the eternal state, Adam, as originally created, was able to sin and able not to sin. Nevertheless, in the eternal state we will still be

REFLECTION QUESTIONS

1. According to this chapter, the universalists employ a faulty theological method. What method do they employ and what is wrong with it? Why is it important to use the correct procedure for answering this (and other) such questions?

2. Evaluate the biblical arguments that universalists offer in support of their position. Do you find any of them plausible? If so, which ones?

3. Reconcile the passages that declare God's universal desire for the salvation of all individuals with the fact that not all will be saved in the end. Does this mean that God's purposes are ultimately frustrated?

4. Explain the texts that appear to speak of Christ as the actual savior of all people without exception, such as 1 Timothy 2:4–6 and 1 Timothy 4:10. How can these passages be true if some people fail to attain salvation?

5. Evaluate the universalist argument drawn from the claim that a God of love would not send people to an eternal hell. (Refer to Question 36 if necessary.)

---

free, despite being unable to sin as Adam could. The key point here is that moral freedom consists in one's actions being *self-caused* and not forced. This is true whether we are considering Adam as originally created or us in the eternal state. For a more detailed treatment of free will and how that relates to the freedom of choice, see the discussion in Question 27.

What Do Annihilationists Teach about Hell?[1]

Basic Statement of the Annihilationist Position

Annihilationism is the teaching that God will "condemn [the wicked] to extinction, which is the second death."[2] Those who remain impenitent will simply pass out of existence; they will be no more.

Within this basic model, several variations emerge. Some hold that the wicked simply go out of existence at death. Others teach that God resurrects them, punishes them for a limited amount of time (depending on the severity of their crimes), and then annihilates them. Regardless of their differences, all annihilationists agree that God eventually will permanently remove the wicked from existence.

What Is the Main Attraction of Annihilationism?

I believe that annihilationism is attractive primarily for emotional reasons. For example, well-known evangelical author John R. W. Stott admits that his own meditations on the doctrine of hell have led him to say, "Well, emotionally, I find the concept intolerable and do not understand how people can live

---

1. Some of the material in this chapter has been adapted from Alan W. Gomes, "Part One: Evangelicals and the Annihilation of Hell," *Christian Research Journal*, Spring 1991, 15–19; and Alan W. Gomes, "Part Two: Evangelicals and the Annihilation of Hell," *Christian Research Journal*, Summer 1991, 9–13.

2. Clark Pinnock, "Fire, Then Nothing," *Christianity Today*, March 20, 1987, 40. John Stackhouse has more recently dubbed the position "terminal punishment" (see John G. Stackhouse, "Terminal Punishment," in *Four Views on Hell*, eds. Stanley N. Gundry and Preston Sprinkle [Grand Rapids: Zondervan, 2016], 61). Nomenclature aside, Stackhouse seems largely to recapitulate the arguments of earlier annihilationists, particularly Edward Fudge, and does not add anything especially new to the debate.

with it without either cauterizing their feelings or cracking under the strain."[3] Theologian Clark Pinnock's complaint is even more strident: "Everlasting torment is intolerable from a moral point of view because it makes God into a bloodthirsty monster who maintains an everlasting Auschwitz for victims whom he does not even allow to die."[4]

Note that universalists typically echo these same sentiments.[5] Annihilationists reject universalism, however, primarily because they cannot reconcile it with what they regard as the clear biblical teaching that not everyone is going to be saved.

Moral Arguments Offered by Annihilationists against the Doctrine of Eternal, Conscious Punishment

The annihilationists frequently complain that it would be immoral for God to inflict everlasting torture on his creatures. Endless torment would represent a punishment far in excess of the offense committed, which would make God unjust, vindictive, and bloodthirsty. This would be completely out of character with the God of love portrayed in the Gospels.[6]

Because others besides annihilationists—for example, universalists—level these same accusations against the classic position of eternal, conscious punishment, I have chosen to treat this class of objection under two separate questions. For an answer to these charges, see Question 35, "Does Eternal Punishment Really Fit the Crime?" and Question 36, "How Can a God of Love Send People to an Eternal Hell?"

Linguistic Arguments Offered to Support Annihilationism

The annihilationists believe that they can make a case for their theory based on the meaning of key biblical terms used to describe the ultimate fate of the wicked. We shall examine some of the biblical words that annihilationists rely upon most heavily.

Words Translated "Destroy," "Perish," and "Cut Off"

Annihilationists believe that words like "perish," "destroy," "cut off," and "consume" indicate total annihilation. Concerning these words, Fudge

3. David L. Edwards and John R. W. Stott, *Evangelical Essentials: A Liberal-Evangelical Dialogue* (Downers Grove, IL: InterVarsity, 1988), 314–15.

4. Clark Pinnock, "The Destruction of the Finally Impenitent," *CTR* 4, no. 2 (Spring 1990): 253.

5. See Question 33.

6. See, for example, Pinnock, "Fire, Then Nothing," 40; "The Destruction of the Finally Impenitent," 246–47, 253–55. See also Edwards and Stott, *Evangelical Essentials*, 318; Stephen Travis, *I Believe in the Second Coming of Jesus* (Grand Rapids: Eerdmans, 1982), 199.

declares himself "confident that the ordinary man in the street can tell us what those words usually mean to him,"[7] which is to say, total annihilation.

The most common term translated "destroy" in the Old Testament is the Hebrew word *abad*. It describes the fate of the wicked in passages such as Proverbs 11:10. However, should we understand this destruction to mean total annihilation?

Certain Old Testament passages make clear that *abad* need not mean annihilation.[8] The word has a range of meaning. For example, as Morey observes, Numbers 21:29 says that the people of Chemosh were "destroyed" (*abad*). But this is a reference to their being sold into slavery, not to their annihilation. First Samuel 9:3 and 20 uses it to speak of Saul's lost donkeys (*athonoth abadoth*). In this context, the word means "lost," not "annihilated." In Psalm 31:12, a vessel is "broken" (*abad*), not annihilated. Here, the meaning is that the vessel is rendered unfit for use, not that it has lapsed into nonexistence. It simply is not true that *abad*, "without exception,"[9] must mean annihilation.[10]

Some passages speak of evil doers as "cut off." Fudge and Pinnock both cite Psalm 37:22, 28, 34, and 38 as representative.[11] These verses, they believe, prove the entire annihilation of the wicked. The word used here is *carath*. However, note that this same word describes the Messiah (Dan. 9:26), who certainly was not annihilated. Even if one admits that the wicked are "annihilated" in the sense of being removed from earthly existence, this would not prove that they are removed from *any* existence.

Turning to the New Testament, the annihilationists claim that the Greek word *apollymi* conveys the sense of total annihilation. Stott cites Matthew 2:13, 12:14 and 27:4, which refer to Herod's desire to destroy the baby Jesus, and the later Jewish plot to have him executed. Stott then mentions Matthew 10:28 (NIV; cf. James 4:12): "Do not be afraid of those who kill the body but cannot kill the soul. Rather, be afraid of the One who can destroy [*apolesai*] both soul and body in hell."[12] He regards this "destruction" as referring to the soul's total annihilation in hell. Stott also offers the contrast between believers and unbelievers as manifest proof: "If believers are *hoi sozomenoi* (those who are being saved), then unbelievers are *hoi apollumenoi* (those who are

---

7. Edward W. Fudge, "'The Plain Meaning': A Review Essay," *Henceforth* 14 (1985): 23–24.
8. Morey has a good discussion of the examples that I am presenting here (Robert A. Morey, *Death and the Afterlife* [Minneapolis: Bethany, 1984], 109).
9. Edward W. Fudge, "The Final End of the Wicked," *JETS* 27 (September 1984): 326.
10. For the sake of brevity, I have considered only the one Hebrew word, *abad*. However, note that there are several other Hebrew words that translators often rendered as "destroy" or "ruin." For a discussion of these, see Morey, *Death and the Afterlife*, 108–11. For additional evidence that "destroy" does not mean "annihilate," see also Harry Buis, *The Doctrine of Eternal Punishment* (Philadelphia: P&R, 1957), 124–26.
11. Edward W. Fudge, *The Fire That Consumes* (Fallbrook, CA: Verdict, 1982), 92–93; Pinnock, "Destruction of the Finally Impenitent," 250–51.
12. Edwards and Stott, *Evangelical Essentials*, 315.

perishing). This phrase occurs in 1 Corinthians 1:18, 2 Corinthians 2:15; 4:3, and in 2 Thessalonians 2:10."[13] Stott believes that this language of destruction points to the total annihilation of the wicked.

However, careful scrutiny of passages using these words shows that they do not teach annihilation. Consider 1 Corinthians 1:18, one of the passages that Stott cites. This passage tells us that "the message of the cross is foolishness *to those who are perishing* [*tois apollymenois*]" (NIV, emphasis added). This participle is in the present tense, which, as Reymond rightly notes, "describes *existing* people who are *presently* perishing. The verb does not suggest that their *future* state will be non-existence."[14]

As Reymond points out, Luke 15:8–9 uses the word to describe the lost but *existing* coin. In Luke 15:4, 6 it describes the lost but *existing* sheep. Luke 15:17, 24 uses this term to describe the prodigal but *existing* son.[15] Murray Harris cites other passages, such as John 11:50, Acts 5:37, 1 Corinthians 10:9–10, and Jude 11, where the concept of destruction, *apōleia*, or perishing, *apolysthai*, need not imply annihilation.[16] Indeed, as Oepke remarks in the *Theological Dictionary of the New Testament*, "What is meant here [in passages speaking of divine judgment] is not a simple extinction of existence, but an everlasting state of torment and death."[17]

It is true that commentators and translators often render *apōleia* as "destruction" or "ruin." But "destruction" refers to the unsuitability of an object to fulfill its designated function. Roger Nicole gives a very lucid illustration that captures this. We speak of an automobile as wrecked, ruined, demolished, or "totalled," "not only when its constituent parts have been melted or scattered away, but also when they have been so damaged and twisted that the car has become completely unserviceable."[18]

Words Translated "Consume"

Pinnock states that the Bible repeatedly "uses the imagery of fire consuming (not torturing) what is thrown into it. The images of fire and destruction together strongly suggest annihilation rather than unending torture."[19]

13. Ibid.
14. Robert Reymond, "Dr. John Stott on Hell," *Presbyterion* 16 (Spring 1990): 53.
15. For a fine discussion of these terms, see Albrecht Oepke, "ἀπώλεια," *TDNT* 1:397; Reymond, "Dr. John Stott on Hell," 53.
16. Murray J. Harris, *Raised Immortal: Resurrection and Immortality in the New Testament* (Grand Rapids: Eerdmans, 1985), 184. See also Lenski's excellent treatment of this word, in which he notes, "The term never means annihilation, neither does any synonymous term nor any description of what it represents" (R. C. H. Lenski, *The Interpretation of St. Matthew's Gospel* [Columbus, OH: Wartburg, 1943], 297).
17. Oepke, "ἀπώλεια," *TDNT* 1:397.
18. Roger Nicole, "Universalism: Will Everyone Be Saved?," *Christianity Today*, March 20, 1987, 34.
19. Pinnock, "Destruction of the Finally Impenitent," 250.

Pinnock then cites Malachi 4:1 as a case in point. Likewise, Stott claims that the main function of fire is not to cause pain but to secure destruction, as in the case of an incinerator. The Bible speaks of a consuming fire and of burning up the chaff "with unquenchable fire" (Matt. 3:12; cf. Luke 3:17). Stott concludes, "The fire itself is termed 'eternal' and 'unquenchable' but it would be very odd if what is thrown into it proved indestructible. Our expectation would be the opposite: it would be consumed forever, not tormented forever. Hence it is the smoke (evidence that the fire has done its work) which 'rises forever and ever' (Rev. 14:11; cf. 19:3)."[20]

First, as Morey and others have shown conclusively, the Hebrew words translated "consume" are used in many contexts where the meaning cannot possibly be annihilation (e.g., Ps. 78:45; Lam. 3:4; Ezek. 13:13; etc.).[21] Therefore, we should not assume automatically that the mere presence of the word "consume" in and of itself proves annihilation. Context is determinative.

Second, let us grant that fire normally represents that which consumes or annihilates its fuel until nothing but ashes are left. Normal fire then goes out once it consumes the fuel. The fire of judgment, however, is no normal fire: The Bible describes it as an "eternal" fire (Jude 7) that "is not quenched" (Mark 9:48). The fact that the smoke is said to rise "forever and ever" is not evidence that "the fire has done its work," as Stott wrongly states, but rather that the fire is *doing* its work through a process of endless combustion. Stott replaces the unquenchable fire of Jesus with the quenchable fire of the annihilationists. The same argument holds for the undying worms (Mark 9:48). Worms can live as long as there is food for them to consume. Once the worms consume their food supply, they eventually die. In contrast, the Bible likens the torments of hell to undying, not dying worms. This is because their supply of food—the wicked— never ceases to exist.

Annihilationist Answers to Verses Used in Support of Eternal, Conscious Punishment

The annihilationists believe that they are able to answer the key verses advanced by the adherents of eternal, conscious punishment. Let us consider a couple of the main ones and see whether they succeed.

Matthew 25:46

Observe the words of John Stott:

At the end of the so-called parable of the sheep and goats, Jesus contrasted "eternal life" with "eternal punishment"

---

20. Edwards and Stott, *Evangelical Essentials*, 316.
21. Morey, *Death and the Afterlife*, 110–11.

(Matt. 25:46). Does that not indicate that in Hell people endure eternal conscious punishment? No, that is to read into the text what is not necessarily there. What Jesus said is that both the life and the punishment would be eternal, but he did not in that passage define the nature of either. Because he elsewhere spoke of eternal life as a conscious enjoyment of God (John 17:3), it does not follow that eternal punishment must be a conscious experience of pain at the hand of God.[22]

Stott is completely wrong in his assertion that the passage "does not define the nature of either [eternal life or eternal punishment]." The mere fact that it says that the wicked experience "punishment" (Greek *kolasin*) proves two inescapable facts by the nature of the case: the existence of the one punished and the conscious experience of the punishment. If either of these two is lacking, then punishment is not occurring—at least not in any meaningful sense of the term.

Someone cannot be punished eternally unless that someone is there to receive the punishment. As Gerstner points out, one can exist and not be punished, but one cannot be punished and not exist. Nonentities cannot receive punishment.[23]

Mere existence is not enough, however. One cannot "punish" a rock or a tree, even though these might exist. The annihilationists sometimes complain that we "smuggle" the word "conscious" into our descriptions of punishment.[24] But really, the adherent of the traditional view need not "smuggle" anything into the description. Punishment, per se, is conscious or it is not punishment. As Shedd has pointed out, a punishment that one does not feel is simply not a punishment. It is an odd use of language to speak of an insensate (i.e., unfeeling), inanimate object receiving punishment. To say, "I punished my car for not starting by slowly plucking out its spark plug wires, one by one" would evoke laughter, not serious consideration.

Revelation 20:10

This text reads, "and the devil who had deceived them was thrown into the lake of fire and sulfur where the beast and the false prophet were, and they will be tormented day and night forever and ever." What can annihilationists possibly say in the face of this text?

---

22. Edwards and Stott, *Evangelical Essentials*, 317.
23. John Gerstner, "The Bible and Hell: Part 1," *His*, January, 1968, 38.
24. Pinnock, "Destruction of the Finally Impenitent," 256.

Clark Pinnock on Revelation 20:10

Pinnock states, "[in Rev. 20:10] it is the Devil, the beast, and the false prophet who are the only ones present, and they cannot be equated with ordinary human beings, however we should understand their nature. John's point seems to be that everything which has rebelled against God will come to an absolute end."[25]

First of all, even if the point that the *annihilationists* wish to make is that "everything which has rebelled against God will come to an absolute end," *John's* point is that the Devil, beast, and false prophet will be tormented day and night, forever and ever. To read the text is to refute their interpretation.

Second, Pinnock's statement that the Devil, beast, and false prophet "cannot be equated with ordinary human beings, however we should understand their nature" proves nothing. Obviously, an angel's nature differs from a human being's nature. But the point of "equivalence" is not the nature of the beings (i.e., angels as disembodied spirits vs. human beings as persons with both a spirit and a body), but their ultimate *fate*. The fate of wicked humans is most assuredly "equated" with the fate of the Devil and his angels, as numerous passages make plain (e.g., Matt. 25:41; Rev. 14:11; 19:20; 20:15).

Besides, even in terms of nature, the Devil (and other angelic beings) can be equated with humans in this very relevant respect: both are personal, sensate (i.e., feeling) beings, who can experience conscious torment.[26] See, for example, Matthew 8:29, where the demons exclaim to Jesus, "Have you come here to torment us before the time?" This shows clearly that demons can be tormented.

If Pinnock allows that Revelation 20:10 proves that the Devil experiences unending torment, as the first part of his argument taken by itself seems to imply, he will have annihilated one of the main pillars of his position: that God could not punish with unending torment finite creatures, incapable of committing infinite sin.[27] Since none of the annihilationists is prepared to ascribe infinity (and, thereby, true deity) to Satan, they must abandon their so-called moral argument. On the other hand, if Pinnock denies even the Devil's endless torment, as the last part of his argument seems to say, then he runs completely afoul of the words of the text.

John Stott on Revelation 20:10

Let us see how John Stott handles this same passage. Stott declares, "The beast, the false prophet and the harlot however are not individual people but

---

25. Ibid., 257.
26. In saying that the Devil and demons can "feel" torment, I am not suggesting that they can feel pain in a physical sense. We have already examined this thoroughly in Question 31.
27. This is one of the moral arguments against the doctrine of eternal, conscious punishment that I shall address in Question 35.

symbols of the world in its varied hostility to God. In the nature of the case, they cannot experience pain. Nor can 'death and Hades,' which follow them into the lake of fire (20:13)."[28]

It is not at all clear that the beast, the false prophet, and the harlot mentioned in this text are "symbols of the world in its varied hostility to God" and not specific individuals. But let us grant Stott's premise. Surely Stott must admit that the world which he says they symbolize comprises *individual people* who are the ones exercising the hostility. At some level, then, these symbols must designate real people.[29] The same can be said for the expression "death and Hades." It is individuals, held in the power of death and occupying hades, whom God casts into the lake of fire. Verses 13–15 of the same chapter make this exceedingly clear.

Even if we were to suppose that the beast, the false prophet, and harlot are merely abstract symbols with absolutely no real reference to individual people (though just what they *would* symbolize in that case is anyone's guess), then what about the Devil? Is Stott prepared to say that the Devil is a mere symbol? Certainly, Stott believes in a personal devil! But the text says, "and the devil who had deceived them was thrown into the lake of fire and sulfur where the beast and the false prophet were, and they will be tormented day and night forever and ever."[30]

Edward Fudge on Revelation 20:10

Many within the annihilationist camp recognize Edward Fudge as the standard-bearer for the position. What does he say in response to this verse?

> This is the single most problematic text in the whole Bible for the extinction of all evil, even though it does not specify human beings. In view of the overwhelming mass of material otherwise found throughout Scripture, however, one ought to remember the general hermeneutical rule that calls for interpreting the uncommon in light of the common and the obscure in light of the more clearly revealed.[31]

---

28. Edwards and Stott, *Evangelical Essentials*, 318. It is possible that Stott essentially borrows this line of argument from Edward Fudge. I have examined Fudge's futile attempt to evade this passage below.
29. Beale, who takes the beast and the false prophet figuratively, nevertheless regards the figure as pointing to "unbelieving institutions composed of people" (G. K. Beale, *The Book of Revelation: A Commentary on the Greek Text*, NIGTC [Grand Rapids: Eerdmans, 1999], 1029).
30. See also ibid., 1030.
31. Fudge, "Final End of the Wicked," 332.

I can paraphrase the essence of Fudge's response as follows: "We know that annihilationism must be true. Therefore, this verse cannot possibly mean what it says." Since Fudge provides no alternative explanation for what the text does or possibly can mean, he offers no argument to refute.

REFLECTION QUESTIONS

1. Define "annihilationism." How does this teaching differ from universalism? From the traditional teaching of eternal conscious punishment?

2. What sorts of arguments do annihilationists and universalists have in common? What are the underlying flaws of the particular arguments they share?

3. Evaluate the strength of the linguistic arguments that the annihilationists offer for their position, such as those based on words like "destroy" and "consume."

4. What do you think are the strongest arguments both in favor of and against annihilationism?

5. Give your assessment of the annihilationists' attempts at explaining the key passages offered in defense of eternal conscious punishment, particularly Matthew 25 and Revelation 20.

Does Eternal Punishment Really Fit the Crime?[1]

A s we observed in Question 33 (concerning universalism) and Question 34 (dealing with annihilationism), those who object to the doctrine of eternal, conscious punishment reject the teaching as immoral. Noted annihilationist Clark Pinnock regards the doctrine of endless punishment as "morally flawed" and a "moral enormity."[2] If the "outrageous doctrine" of the so-called traditionalists were true, God would be a "cruel" and "vindictive" deity—in fact, he would be "more nearly like Satan than like God, at least by any ordinary moral standards." Indeed, the traditionalist's God is a "blood-thirsty monster who maintains an everlasting Auschwitz for victims whom he does not even allow to die."[3]

Opponents commonly argue that endless torment represents a punishment far in excess of the offense committed. Rob Bell queries, "Have billions of people been created only to spend eternity in conscious punishment and torment, suffering infinitely for the finite sins they committed in the few years they spent on earth?"[4] John Stott urges that if the traditional teaching were true, there would be "a serious disproportion between sins consciously committed in time and the torment consciously experienced throughout

---

1. Some of the material in this chapter has been adapted from Alan W. Gomes, "Part One: Evangelicals and the Annihilation of Hell," *Christian Research Journal*, Spring 1991, 15–19; and Alan W. Gomes, "Part Two: Evangelicals and the Annihilation of Hell," *Christian Research Journal*, Summer 1991, 9–13.
2. Clark Pinnock, "Fire, Then Nothing," *Christianity Today*, March 20, 1987, 440; Clark Pinnock, "The Destruction of the Finally Impenitent," *CTR* 4, no. 2 (Spring 1990): 246–47, 253.
3. Pinnock, "Destruction of the Finally Impenitent," 246–47, 253.
4. Rob Bell, *Love Wins* (New York: HarperCollins, 2011), 102; cf. 175.

eternity."[5] Likewise, Pinnock states, "it would amount to inflicting infinite suffering upon those who have committed finite sin. It would go far beyond an eye for an eye and a tooth for a tooth. There would be a serious disproportion between sins committed in time and the suffering experienced forever."[6] God's character totally opposes such vindictiveness, which is utterly unacceptable to "sensitive Christians."[7]

Do Sins Committed in Time Really Deserve Eternal Punishment?

The great nineteenth-century American theologian W. G. T. Shedd presented a solid answer to this faulty line of argument. I can do no better than to summarize and paraphrase it here.

The claim that "sins committed in time cannot be worthy of eternal suffering" is fallacious. It assumes, as Shedd points out, that a crime's heinousness relates directly to the time it takes to commit it. However, such a connection is nonexistent. Some crimes, such as murder, may take only a moment to commit, whereas it may take a thief several hours to load up a moving van with someone's possessions. Yet, murder is a far more serious crime than theft and merits a correspondingly more serious and enduring penalty.[8]

Second, we must take into account the nature of the object against which someone sins, as well as the nature of the sin itself, to determine the degree of heinousness. This, in turn, defines both the intensity as well as the duration of the punishment deserved. Shedd observes, "To torture a dumb beast is a crime; to torture a man is a greater crime. To steal from one's own mother is more heinous than to steal from a fellow citizen." The criminal act is the same in each case (i.e., stealing and torture), as is the person committing the act. But "the different worth and dignity of the objects upon whom his action terminates makes the difference in the gravity of the two offenses."[9] How much more serious, then, is even the slightest offense against an absolutely holy God, who deserves our complete and perpetual allegiance?[10] Indeed, sin against an absolutely holy God is absolutely serious. For this reason, the

---

5. David L. Edwards and John R. W. Stott, *Evangelical Essentials: A Liberal-Evangelical Dialogue* (Downers Grove, IL: InterVarsity, 1988), 318.

6. Pinnock, "Destruction of the Finally Impenitent," 255.

7. Pinnock, "Fire, Then Nothing," 40.

8. See W. G. T. Shedd, *The Doctrine of Endless Punishment* (1886; repr., Minneapolis: Klock & Klock, 1980), 152–53.

9. Ibid., 152.

10. St. Anselm argued cogently for the infinity of sin's guilt when committed against an infinitely holy God. See his epochal, eleventh-century work, *Cur Deus Homo?* ["Why the God-Man?"], especially Book 1, Chapters 20–24 (239–51) (St. Anselm, *Cur Deus Homo?*, in *St. Anselm: Basic Writings*, trans. S. N. Deane [La Salle, IL: Open Court Publishing, 1962]).

unredeemed suffer absolute, unending alienation from God; this alienation is the essence of hell.[11]

It is the annihilationist's theory that is morally flawed. Their God is not truly holy, for he does not demand that sin receive its due. David Wells correctly states that if God's life is perfectly holy and his character is pure, then sin, considered in itself, is infinitely unpardonable and "not merely momentarily mischievous."[12] Surely this was what Jesus had in mind when he said that even to call one's brother a fool will render a person "liable to the hell of fire" (Matt. 5:22). Now, the annihilationist holds that the fires of hell stand for total annihilation. But given the annihilationists' scruples about "the punishment fitting the crime," how could they justify even *annihilating* someone for all eternity for so seemingly slight an infraction as this? Clearly, Jesus has a different view of sin's seriousness than these "sensitive" annihilationists.[13]

Besides, even if one were to grant the annihilationsts' faulty premise underlying their argument, Robert Reymond observes that God could hardly annihilate the sinner for his or her sin, since annihilation is eternal in its effect.[14] At most, God could inflict a punishment of limited duration upon the sinner and then, having expunged the finite debt, forthwith admit him or her to glory. Thus, the annihilationist has actually argued for universalism, a position they reject as unbiblical. Again, the underlying foundation of their argument is faulty, as we have already shown, and therefore supports neither universalism nor annihilationism.

---

11. One might object that if all sin is worthy of absolute punishment, there could be no degrees of punishment in hell, in direct contradiction to certain biblical passages (e.g., Matt. 10:15; 11:21–24; 16:27; Luke 12:47–48; John 15:22; Heb. 10:29; Rev. 20:11–15; 22:12, etc.). From one standpoint, all sins do indeed receive the same penalty: complete alienation from God. Nevertheless, the way in which any particular individual experiences that alienation depends on the degree of that person's depravity. Realize, too, that the redeemed will all experience the presence of God in heaven, even though some will have a greater capacity for enjoying that presence than others. See Question 18, "Will There Be Degrees of Punishment Assigned to Unbelievers at the Final Judgment?"
12. David F. Wells, "Everlasting Punishment," *Christianity Today*, March 20, 1987, 42.
13. Concerning this verse, Shedd offers this insightful observation: "A human tribunal punishes mayhem, we will say, with a six-month imprisonment because it does not take into consideration either the malicious and wicked anger that prompted maiming or the dishonoring done to the Supreme Being by the transgression of his commandment. But Christ, in the final assize, punishes this offense endlessly, because his all-seeing view includes the sum total of guilt in the case, namely, the inward wrath, the outward act, and the relation of both to the infinite perfection and adorable majesty of God. The human tribunal does not punish the inward anger at all; the divine tribunal punishes it with hellfire: 'For whosoever shall say to his brother, You fool, is in danger of hellfire' (Matt. 5:22)" (W. G. T. Shedd, *Dogmatic Theology*, ed. Alan W. Gomes [Phillipsburg: P&R, 2003], 917).
14. Robert Reymond, "Dr. John Stott on Hell," *Presbyterion* 16 (Spring 1990): 57. Note that the annihilationists are at pains to stress annihilationism's "eternal effect" throughout their writings.

Hell's Eternality Is Required by the Ongoing Accumulation of Guilt[15]

Regardless of whether one conceives of hell's pains as operating "from the inside out" (as I have suggested in Question 31), or as an infliction imposed by God from without, or as a combination of these, the fact remains that hell's sufferings are punitive, which is to say that they are aimed at satisfying justice. Certainly most annihilationists grant this, as do a good many universalists. Their complaint, generally, is not that God would be wrong to punish sinners, but that eternal punishment is excessive—like giving a sentence of life in prison for a parking violation.

What such individuals fail to take into account is that the sinner's suffering in hell does not expiate his or her guilt but actually provides occasion for a further increase of it. Does anyone seriously think that the incorrigibly wicked love God and thank him for exercising his judgment against them? Revelation 16:9–11 is sufficient all by itself to dispatch any such notion. No, the denizens of hell hate God because he eternally frustrates their own quest for godhood and happiness without him. He alone is of supreme worth and not them. And this they find deplorable.

Now, this hatred of God is itself a grievous sin and aggravates their store of guilt. This guilt in turn requires further punishment, which effects in them an even greater hatred of God, which further multiples their guilt, ad infinitum.[16] When we stop to realize this, we see that—far from the punishment of hell giving justice more than its due—the sufferings of sinners in the lake of fire actually can only approximate a true satisfaction of justice, coming as close to satisfying an infinite debt as a finite creature can do. For believers, Christ paid fully the debt of sin owed to divine justice when he died on the cross. However, Christ, being both God and man, could offer a satisfaction of infinite worth, even though he suffered for a finite duration of time. This is why the God-man alone could pay for the sins of all humankind—indeed, for an infinite number of humans, if such were possible—without having to suffer for all eternity. But the closest that a sinner in hell can come to paying the debt owed to justice is to suffer without end.[17]

---

15. See Archibald Alexander, *Universalism: False and Unscriptural* (Philadelphia: Presbyterian Board of Publication, 1851), 65–68.
16. Not to trivialize it, but a fair analogy might be a credit card debt in which one makes only the minimum monthly payment. The principal of the debt is never reduced because of the interest that continues to accrue.
17. Shedd, though arguing a slightly different but closely related point, makes this observation: "The suffering of the criminal can never overtake the crime. And the only way in which justice can approximately obtain its dues is by a never-ceasing infliction. We say approximately, because, tested strictly, the endless suffering of a finite being is not strictly infinite suffering; while the guilt of sin against God is strictly infinite. There is no overpunishment in endless punishment" (*Dogmatic Theology*, 916).

The Sinner's Own Conscience Will Confirm the Rightness of Eternal Punishment

Those suffering in hell will recognize the rightness of their fate. This will furnish no comfort to them but only multiply their misery.

The Scriptures declare that no one will be able to gainsay the appropriateness of punishment for violating God's law, "so that every mouth may be stopped, and the whole world may be held accountable to God" (Rom. 3:19). The account of the rich man and Lazarus amply bears out this truth. The rich man asks for a measure of relief for his suffering. Abraham refuses (Luke 16:25–26), reminding him of how his earthly life led him to this fate:

> When Abraham reminds him of the principles of justice by which his destiny has been decided; when he tells him that having taken his choice of pleasure in the world which he has left, he cannot now have pleasure in the world to which he has come; the wretched man makes no reply. There is nothing to be said. He feels that the procedure is just. . . . Dives, the man in hell, is a witness to the justice of eternal punishment.[18]

REFLECTION QUESTIONS

1. Name certain positions and individuals who reject the doctrine of eternal punishment as excessive and therefore unjust. What sorts of statements do they make against it? What do you think of such statements?

2. Some have said that the doctrine of hell is immoral because sins committed in time cannot possibly deserve eternal punishment. What is the key fallacy underlying this argument?

3. How does the nature of the person against whom one sins relate to the punishment that is due for the offense? What are some examples that would clearly illustrate this?

4. If sinners in hell are paying for their sins, why would there not come a time when they have paid the debt in full and therefore be entitled to release?

5. Will sinners in hell acknowledge that God is right in punishing them in this way? What evidence is there for this?

---

18. W. G. T. Shedd, *Sermons to the Natural Man* (New York: Scribner's, 1871), 351–52.

How Can a God of Love Send People to an Eternal Hell?

In a universe of love there can be no heaven which tolerates a chamber of horrors, no hell for any which does not at the same time make it hell for God. He cannot endure that, for *that* would be the final mockery of his nature—and he will not.[1]

In Question 35 we have just considered whether God could be just if the doctrine of hell as eternal conscious punishment were true. We now turn to the often-asked question of whether God could be *loving* if the doctrine of hell were true. This is an issue that troubles a great many people, leading some to reject the doctrine of hell or even to dismiss the Christian faith altogether.

The Biblical Facts about God's Love and Hell
The biblical facts related to this question are straightforward enough.

First, the Bible plainly informs us that God is a God of love. So many verses teach this that it is neither practical nor necessary to cite them all. Besides, those who raise the question we are considering do not dispute that point. Nevertheless, should anyone ask for biblical proof, 1 John 4:8 is sufficient. Here John flatly states, "God is love." This verse expresses God's love in the strongest possible terms. This text does not tell us merely that God is

---

1. John A. T. Robinson, *In the End, God . . . : A Study of the Christian Doctrine and the Last Things*, ed. Robin Parry (Eugene, OR: Cascade Books, 2011), 116. We will find the answer to the issue of whether the existence of hell would make God himself miserable in Question 37 and Question 38. The point of the citation for this present chapter relates to the issue of whether hell is compatible with God's love.

loving or that he behaves in a loving way, true as that may be. Instead, the verse tells us that God *is* love. *God's very nature and character are love*, and it is from this that all of his loving actions flow. A more theological way of saying this is that love is one of God's attributes. (I shall say more about the divine attributes in a moment.)

At the same time, the doctrine of eternal, conscious punishment for those who finally reject Jesus Christ as their savior is also a settled truth of Scripture. I have already established this doctrine in several of the questions in Section B, "The Eternal State of Unbelievers (Hell)."

Therefore, the twin truths that God is love and that hell is real are the "brute facts" with which we must work. They are true whether a person likes them or can reconcile them in his or her mind. At the same time, there is more that we can say from the Bible and from reason to explain, or at least clarify, how these two facts are mutually consistent.

Dissecting the Objection

People who pose this question or dilemma usually frame it as follows: "How can a God of love send people to an eternal hell?" Since this is the most common form of the objection, I shall use it as the basis for our discussion. The two parts we must now consider are: (1) the "God of love" part; and (2) the "send people to hell" part.

The idea that God's attribute of love is inconsistent with hell is based on a faulty view of the divine attributes generally and of the divine attribute of love specifically. Then, the notion that God "sends people to hell" is potentially misleading.

I shall examine each of these aspects in turn.

God's Love and His Other Attributes

The Divine Attributes in General

Before considering God's attribute of love, it is important to understand how the divine attributes work generally in order to clear up some common misconceptions.

I must start by establishing that *God is equal to his attributes*. Another way of putting it is to say that all of God's attributes are essential to what and who he is. This means that if one were to remove any of God's attributes—such as holiness, wisdom, or love—the result would not be simply a watered-down version of God. Rather, one would not have God at all.

This is different from the way it works with creatures. For example, we can easily imagine a holy human being or a holy angel who ceases to be holy. In that case, we simply have an unholy version of the human or angel who used to be holy. Consider Lucifer, for example, whom God created holy but who stopped being so after he fell. Lucifer is still Lucifer—it is just that he is no longer a holy Lucifer but is now an unholy Lucifer. However, with God it is not like this. If one were to remove holiness from God, then one would not have an unholy God but one would not have God at all.

Now, if all of God's attributes are essential to what and who he is, then from this it follows that no attribute is superior or more central than another. All of his attributes are equally important, for they define his very being. If all of his attributes are essential to who and what he is, then you cannot have one attribute that is more essential. Remove any one of them and you no longer have God.

Sometimes people are tempted to focus on the divine attributes that they like best and shortchange or even deny the ones they do not like. This sometimes happens by making an attribute that they personally find attractive—typically, love—then call the shots, so to speak, by subordinating all the other attributes to it. Alternatively, they may simply deny entirely the ones they do not like. What we must do instead is to affirm all of God's attributes as all essential to who he is, and then seek to understand how they all work together in harmony.[2]

God's Holiness

The same Bible that tells us "God is love" also declares, "God is holy." Indeed, to emphasize this point the angelic hosts cry out, "Holy, holy, holy is the Lord of hosts" (Isa. 6:3; cf. Rev. 4:8). To say that God is holy means that he is separate from all sin, unrighteousness, and depravity. Stated positively, God is holy because he is upright in his being and therefore in all of his actions.

The Bible speaks of this uprightness as God's "righteousness" or "justice." The fundamental idea here is conformity to a standard. God's righteousness is not an external standard to which he conforms. Rather, the standard is God himself, which is who and what he is. "Unrighteousness," on the other hand, is any deviation that falls short of that standard on the part of any of his moral creatures. This becomes evident when one looks at certain biblical passages that juxtapose and contrast sin, lawlessness, and uncleanness on the one hand with righteousness on the other (e.g., Rom. 3:9–10; 5:7–8; 6:19). "Righteousness thus entails doing what is right or what conforms to God's laws." Righteousness is God's "moral and spiritual order" for all moral beings, both human and divine.[3] Truly God is righteous in all that he is and does (Dan. 9:14).

---

2. See the very fine statement of this truth in W. G. T. Shedd, "The Atonement, a Satisfaction for the Ethical Nature of Both God and Man," *Theological Essays* (New York: Scribner's, 1877), 273.

3. Robert Saucy and Alan Gomes, "Justification and the New Perspective," *Sundoulos*, Spring 2011, 15.

How is God's holiness/righteousness relevant to the doctrine of hell, the subject of our question? As we have observed, because God is righteous, he unalterably opposes any deviation from this righteousness, which is sin. God's *wrath* is the natural expression of his holiness when he is confronted with sin, as many biblical passages make plain (e.g., Rom. 1:18; 2:5, 8; Eph. 5:6; Col. 3:6). We see God's ultimate and final expression of his wrath by consigning the finally impenitent to the lake of fire at the end of the age (Rev. 14:10).

God's holiness, then, actually presents us with the other side of the dilemma we are considering. That is, if we find it difficult to reconcile how a God of love can punish creatures eternally in hell, we should find it equally difficult to understand how a God of holiness can admit sinful creatures to heaven.

The Harmony of God's Love and Justice

Happily, the Bible tells us that God's love and his justice operate in perfect harmony. We see this preeminently in the provision for dealing with the sin problem—a provision that God himself has provided in the atonement of Jesus Christ. "God shows his love for us in that while we were still sinners, Christ died for us" (Rom. 5:8).

God, out of his boundless love for us, sent his only son to save us (John 3:16). In saving us, he delivers us from the divine wrath that we would otherwise have had to bear ourselves (1 Thess. 1:10). Just how does Christ's death deliver us from God's wrath? Very simply, Jesus averts God's wrath by bearing that wrath in our place and as our substitute (Isa. 53:4–6, 10–11). This turning away of wrath is what the Bible means by the word "propitiation" (Greek *hilasmos*); a propitiation is that which turns away wrath. Jesus himself is the "propitiation for our sins" (1 John 2:2). This propitiation demonstrates God's great love for us because even when we had no love for God, God "loved us and sent his Son to be the propitiation for our sins" (1 John 4:10). But this same propitiation also demonstrates his justice, because God expressed the fullness of his wrath against sin by punishing Jesus Christ in our place. God set forth Christ "as a propitiation by his blood . . . to show his righteousness at the present time, so that he might be just and the justifier of the one who has faith in Jesus" (Rom. 3:25–26).

Consequently, a proper understanding of God's provision for salvation should forever put to rest the notion that God's love and wrath against sin are incompatible. In fact, the doctrine of hell demonstrates God's supreme love for us more than anything else does. Theologian Roger Nicole stated it well: "The doctrine of hell gives us an insight into the unfathomable goodness of God. He has done whatever was needed to snatch us away from this horrifying destiny, even to the point of absorbing hell itself in our place in order to redeem us."[4]

---

4. Roger Nicole, "Universalism: Will Everyone Be Saved?" *Christianity Today*, March 20, 1987, 39.

Does God "Send People to Hell"?

The notion that God sends people to hell is accurate in a certain sense. If by "send to hell" one means that God himself will cast unrepentant sinners into the lake of fire (Rev. 14:10; 20:15; cf. Matt. 25:41) then that is true enough. However, in another real and very important sense, God does not send anyone to hell; people send themselves there, by their own choice. Powell states:

> If the question be raised, How can a loving God send men to an everlasting Hell? It must be replied that God does not choose this destiny for men; they freely choose it for themselves. God simply concurs in their self-chosen way and reveals the full consequences of their evil choice.[5]

Let us ponder this important point in more detail, for it is critical in answering the question before us.

When God created humankind, he fashioned a creature of great worth and dignity. Unlike the other creatures recorded in the creation account of Genesis, he created men and women alone in his image. Among other things, this image entails a moral likeness to God, including the capacity for self-determination and meaningful ethical choices. One of those meaningful ethical choices—indeed, the most meaningful choice of all—is whether to love and serve God or to spurn his love. Those who reject God thereby *choose* hell, which is separation from God. What God is guilty of, so to speak, is respecting the free will of creatures that he created in his own image by allowing them to exercise their choice to reject him. God thus acknowledges the worth of human creatures by continuing to uphold their existence and by allowing them to choose their own path.[6]

And what path has the unrepentant sinner chosen? It is, in essence, to be "God," which is to be the center of his or her own autonomous universe, in which one's own desires reign supreme. The obstinate rebel will not bow the knee—or at least not willingly or with joy—because submitting to the will of another is abhorrent to such a one. Yet, these sinful creatures, being creatures, live in God's universe, governed by God's moral laws, with God as its Lord. God's moral laws work as invariably as his physical laws, and one either conforms to them or they dash him to pieces.

Now, one of those invariable moral truths is that the rational creature, whether human or angelic, can only find happiness in submission to God as the ground of all joy. Conversely, when one willingly separates from God and substitutes oneself as his or her own god, that individual cannot but be wretched. This is simply the way the moral universe works. Sinners may rail

---

5. Ralph E. Powell, "Hell," *BEB* 2:954–55.
6. See Question 27 for a more detailed and nuanced discussion of free will.

against this with all their being, but they may just as well rage against the law of gravity.

We already observed that we should not see the fire of hell as a material punishment applied from without, but rather as a dreadful picture of the inward, spiritual consumption of a tormented conscience working from within.[7] This is equally true of the other biblical metaphors, such as undying worms that gnaw but do not finally consume. This, however, is the fate that the finally unrepentant have freely chosen; this is what they have made of themselves. To use the scriptural turn of phrase, God "gave them up" to the sinful desires of their own hearts (Rom. 1:24). It is a well-known maxim that "God punishes sin with sin," and it is true enough here. God punishes the sinner by, in effect, allowing the sinner free rein to punish him or herself. This is true only to a relative degree in this present age, but in the age to come God will give them over to themselves without restraint.

We should also note that the lost in hell would never choose to leave their condition for heaven, granting that the essence of heaven is joyful submission to God. To those who set their affections totally upon themselves—who are "curved inward," as St. Augustine put it—heaven would be a kind of suffering even worse than hell itself. No doubt they would choose all the fringe benefits of a life with God, but only if they could have it without God himself. But this cannot be.

Conclusion

As we have seen, the question of how a God of love could send people to an eternal hell finds its simple and final answer in the cross of Christ. As the great nineteenth-century theologian W. G. T. Shedd put it so eloquently:

> The Christian Gospel—the universal offer of pardon through the self-sacrifice of one of the divine persons—should silence every objection to the doctrine of endless punishment. For as the case now stands, there is no necessity, so far as the action of God is concerned, that a single human being should ever be the subject of future punishment. The necessity of hell is founded in the action of the creature, not of the Creator. Had there been no sin, there would have been no hell; and sin is the product of man's free will. And after the entrance of sin and the provision of redemption from it, had there been universal repentance in this life, there would have been no hell for man in the next life. The only necessitating reason, therefore, for endless retribution that now exists is the sinner's impenitence. Should every human individual, before

---

7. See Question 31, "Are the Fires of Hell Literal?"

he dies, sorrow for sin and humbly confess it, hades and gehenna would disappear.[8]

REFLECTION QUESTIONS

1. Do you find some of God's attributes more attractive or personally appealing than others? Has anything in this chapter challenged your thinking on this?

2. What does the Bible mean when it says that God is holy? What are the implications of God's holiness in relation to hell?

3. How does Christ's atonement demonstrate the harmony of God's justice with his love?

4. Does God send people to hell? In what ways is this true or not true?

5. How does the truth of the atonement answer the question of whether a God of love can send people to hell?

---

8. W. G. T. Shedd, *Dogmatic Theology,* ed. Alan W. Gomes (Phillipsburg: P&R, 2003), 930.

How Can We Be Happy in the Eternal State If There Are People Suffering in Hell, including Some of Our Loved Ones? (Part 1)

> Heaven, to those who truly love all, can be heaven only when it has emptied hell. . . . If eternal hell is real, love is eternally frustrated and heaven is a place of mourning and concern for the lost.[1]

> In a universe of love there can be no heaven which tolerates a chamber of horrors, no hell for any which does not at the same time make it hell for God.[2]

The above quotes, written by the famous universalists Nels Ferré and John A. T. Robinson, express one of the key reasons they reject the doctrine of hell. They correctly believe that heaven will be a place of complete happiness, but incorrectly conclude that it could not be so if hell exists. Though these authors are wrong to reject the doctrine of hell, they nevertheless raise a serious concern that often weighs on the minds of many who do affirm hell as scriptural and therefore true. How can the eternal state (ES) be a place of complete bliss for us, not to mention for God, if people suffer in hell for all eternity? The question is especially acute for those of us (including me) who have loved ones who reject God's salvation in Christ. Consequently, this is an issue of deep emotional and practical concern.

---

1. Nels Ferré, *The Christian Understanding of God* (New York: Harper, 1951), 229, 237.
2. John A. T. Robinson, *In the End, God* (Eugene, OR: Cascade, 2011), 116.

Where Do We Begin?

In answering this question, I shall take two truths as starting points: (1) hell as eternal, conscious punishment is true; and (2) neither God nor we (believers) will have any sadness in the ES.

We have already demonstrated the reality of hell elsewhere in this book, and have also cited verses showing our supreme happiness in the ES. As for *God's* complete and total happiness, Romans 9:5 tells us that God "who is God over all" is also "blessed forever." Besides, if God were sad in the ES then we would have to be as well, given our complete and total love for him. Since we will not be sad, we can conclude that he will not be either.

Consequently, we can approach this question calmly and with the assurance that even though hell is a settled fact, it is equally a fact that neither God nor we will be distraught about it. Whether one accepts the solution to the problem that I shall offer, we can rest confidently in the final outcome. At the same time, I believe that the Bible does give us some information about why and how our complete happiness can coexist with hell's reality.

Establishing the Biblical Facts

Before we seek a solution to our conundrum, we must first lay out the relevant biblical data, or brute facts, with which we must work. After we have demonstrated those facts, we can then consider a model to harmonize them.

Here are the relevant biblical facts, which I shall demonstrate:

1. Our attitude toward sinners should be (and someday will be) the same as God's.

2. God loves sinners and desires to save them, not punish them.

3. God hates sinners and desires to punish them.

4. God's people love sinners and desire for God to save them, not punish them.

5. God's people hate sinners and desire for God to punish them.

It appears that some of the above biblical facts stand in direct conflict. Nevertheless, we know that they cannot be if they truly reflect the teaching of Scripture. In the next chapter, I shall offer a model for harmonizing these seemingly discrepant ideas. First, however, I must establish that the above five points are indeed what the Bible teaches.

Our Attitude toward Sin and Sinners Should Be the Same as God's

If our attitudes should and will be the same as God's on this question—and on any other moral question, for that matter—then we can look at verses that speak of God's attitude toward the finally unrepentant and use them to determine what our own ought to be and will be. Likewise, if we have verses that tell us how human beings in right relationship to God (e.g., Jesus; the saints in glory) feel about God's judgment of the wicked, then we may justifiably conclude that such feelings are consistent with God's own.

The Bible tells us that there is a general coincidence of our feelings with God's, i.e., when we are acting in right relationship to him. Consider Acts 13:22 (cf. 1 Sam. 13:14); Matthew 18:23–35; Ephesians 4:32 and 5:1. We could readily cite many verses beyond these.

I hasten to add that in our present sinful state we do not mirror perfectly God's feelings and attitudes; indeed, we frequently do not act and feel the way that God acts and feels. Nevertheless, the Bible commands us to be like God in all of our moral actions (Matt. 5:48), and does illustrate for us the proper human attitude, as we shall see below.

God Loves Sinners and Desires to Save Them, Not Punish Them
This second point is not especially controversial and one that I can establish easily from passages throughout the Bible.

Ezekiel 18:23; 33:11
In these verses, God himself declares emphatically, "I have no pleasure in the death of the wicked, but that the wicked turn from his way and live" (33:11). This pronouncement follows on the heels of prophecies of future judgment for Israel's disobedience, which God offers in order to induce sinners to repent to avoid their impending destruction.

The word translated "pleasure" used here "denotes the direction of one's heart or passion."[3] Here, God expresses his heart's passion for sinners to repent and escape judgment, which "is not a fixed, deterministic fate that operates regardless of human action."[4] Block summarizes the thrust of these statements well: "This oracle presents an important dimension of the divine character. God does not desire death, not even for the wicked. He appeals for all to repent and find life in his grace."[5]

Luke 15:4–10
In the parables of the lost sheep and the lost coin, we see that heaven rejoices when a sinner turns from his or her sin and is saved. Though verse 10 mentions specifically God's angels as rejoicing, Jesus also speaks of the joy in

---

3. David Talley, "חפץ," *New International Dictionary of Old Testament Theology and Exegesis*, 5 vols., ed. Willem A. Van Gemeren (Grand Rapids: Zondervan, 1997), 2:231–34.
4. Iain M. Duguid, *Ezekiel*, NIVAC (Grand Rapids: Zondervan, 1999), 383.
5. Daniel I. Block, *The Book of Ezekiel: Chapters 25–48*, NICOT 26 (Grand Rapids: Eerdmans, 1998), 253.

heaven generally (v. 7). This certainly would include God, who preeminently resides in heaven (Matt. 6:9).

Luke 15:11–32

In the parable of the prodigal son, we see the father's great longing for the son's repentance. The father in this parable, who represents God,[6] responds to the son's coming to his senses (v. 17) with great compassion (v. 20) and jubilant celebration (v. 23). Recapitulating the idea of the parables immediately preceding, the father summarizes the source of his inexpressible joy in verse 32: "It was fitting to celebrate and be glad, for this your brother was dead, and is alive; he was lost, and is found."

John 3:16; Romans 5:6, 8

These verses show that God desires to forgive sinners so much that he made a provision for their forgiveness. In a stupendous act of self-sacrifice, he took the initiative and sent his only dear and beloved son to provide a way of deliverance from their sins. And he did this while the world was yet hostile to him.

1 Timothy 2:4

This verse states that God "desires all people to be saved and to come to the knowledge of the truth." The verb translated "desires," which is rendered "wills" in some translations, is a form of *thelō*, which refers to the desires or inclinations of the heart. This shows that God truly desires the salvation of all.[7]

God Hates Sinners and Desires to Punish Them

Scripture attests to this point just as much as it does to the previous point, despite being less agreeable to some people.

Deuteronomy 28:63

Here the Lord warns his people about the consequences for disobedience when he brings them into the land:

> And as the LORD took delight (Hebrew *sus*) in doing you good and multiplying you, so the LORD will take delight (*sus*) in bringing ruin upon you and destroying you.

---

6. Commentators readily grant that the father in this parable depicts God, whether explicitly or by way of allegorical reference. For example, see Darrell L. Bock, *Luke*, NIVAC (Grand Rapids: Zondervan, 1996), 412. Other commentators on Luke making this same point are Stein, Nolland, Green, Garland, and Marshall.

7. "God's *thelein* is . . . resolute and complete willing. . . . 1 Tim. 2:4 [speaks] of God's gracious and majestic will to save all" (Gottlob Schrenk, "θέλω," *TDNT* 3:47).

The verb translated "take delight" is *sus*, which means, "to exult, rejoice."[8] This verb, appearing twice in this verse, expresses God's delight, both in doing good to his covenant people and in bringing ruin upon them should they disobey. As Grisanti observes, "In the midst of a litany of covenant curses, Moses affirms that Yahweh can take delight in prospering or devastating his vassal nation, depending on their response to the covenant stipulations (Deut 28:63)."[9]

Some, such as Wright, attempt to soften the force of this by claiming that verse 63 "must be taken as rhetorical, not literal,"[10] while others, such as Block, see the statement as "hyperbolic."[11] Yet, Block admits,

> Where previously Yahweh had delighted in causing Israel to flourish, now he will delight in their destruction. The notion is troubling to modern readers, but read within the ancient conceptual environment, it contrasts sharply with the notions of Israel's neighbors. Where others attribute such calamities to demonic forces and hostile deities, Yahwism refuses to take the easy way out. These statements reflect the other side of Yahweh's passion: When his people trample underfoot his grace, his passions will be ignited against them.[12]

Psalms 5:5–6; 7:11; 11:5, 7

These psalms, taken in their plain and natural sense, speak of God's feelings about the wicked. Concerning the arrogant, the bloodthirsty, the deceitful, and all who do wrong, the psalmist declares that God "hate[s]" and "abhors" them (5:5–6). He "feels indignation [with the wicked] every day" (7:11) and "his soul hates" them (11:5), in contrast to "the righteous," whose deeds "he loves" (11:7).

2 Thessalonians 1:6–8

Paul declares that it is "just" for God to exact vengeance on those who persecute God's saints. In so far as such infliction expresses God's righteousness, he does and must take delight in it, for God delights in his own righteousness (Jer. 9:24).

8. Heinz-Josef Fabry, "שׂושׂ/שׂישׂ" *TDOT* 14:50–58.
9. Michael A. Grisanti, "שׂושׂ," *New International Dictionary of Old Testament Theology and Exegesis*, 5 vols., ed. Willem A. Van Gemeren (Grand Rapids: Zondervan, 1997), 3:1223.
10. Christopher J. H. Wright, *Deuteronomy*, NIBC 4 (Peabody, MA: Hendrickson, 1996), 283.
11. Daniel I. Block, *Deuteronomy*, NIVAC (Grand Rapids: Zondervan, 2012), 651–52.
12. Ibid., 661.

But Does Not the Bible Teach That God "Hates the Sin but Loves the Sinner"?
In a word: No. From the above texts, we observe that God hates evil *doers* and not merely their evil *deeds*. He hates the "workers of iniquity" and not merely the iniquities that they work (Ps. 5:5, KJV).

One major problem with this statement is that it wrongly abstracts the sinner from his or her sin. Note that on the day of judgment, God will cast *sinners* into the gehenna of fire and not merely their *sins* in the abstract (whatever that would mean).

God's People Love Sinners and Desire for God to Save Them, Not Punish Them
While it is true that God's people are sometimes inconsistent in their desire to see God save the lost, we are talking here about the ideal, even if we do not always realize this in practice in our present sinful condition. Nevertheless, we do see this attitude perfectly represented in some of the biblical writers, who wrote under inspiration, and especially in the Lord Jesus Christ himself, who embodied the attitude of perfect humanity in all things.

Luke 6:28
Jesus instructs his followers to "bless those who curse you" and to "pray for those who abuse you." Jesus is admonishing his people to pray for their enemy's good, which preeminently must include their salvation and the repentance on which it depends.

Romans 9:1–3
Paul describes his "great sorrow and unceasing anguish" of heart over the hardhearted rejection of the gospel by his Jewish brethren. Paul then makes this stunning statement in verse 3: "For I could wish that I myself were accursed and cut off from Christ for the sake of my brothers, my kinsmen according to the flesh." Though such is not possible, of course, it nevertheless expresses the degree to which he agonizes over the terrible fate that awaits them if they do not turn from their sins.

Luke 19:41–44
In this passage, Jesus weeps over Jerusalem because they would not come to him as their only source of life and deliverance from their coming destruction. He laments in great sorrow: "Would that you, even you, had known on this day the things that make for peace! But now they are hidden from your eyes."

Acts 26:28–29
Paul, in his audience with King Agrippa, admits that he wishes that Agrippa, and indeed all men and women, would become Christians. Specifically, he preached repentance for the forgiveness of sins so that Agrippa might turn and be saved (vv. 18, 20).

God's People Hate Sinners and Desire for God to Punish Them
This point is perhaps the most controversial of the five. But again, the Scriptures surely teach this. Though we can find verses throughout the Bible to support this point, I shall draw particularly on the so-called imprecatory psalms and certain passages in Revelation.

In some of the imprecatory psalms, we find the psalmist calling down God's vengeance against his enemies, apparently with no admixture of pity or any desire on the psalmist's part for God to show them mercy. In the book of Revelation, we find texts where the saints in glory anxiously await and rejoice in God's coming vengeance—again, with no apparent concern for these individuals' repentance.

A False Solution
Some, and most famously C. S. Lewis in his *Reflections on the Psalms,* attempt to solve the problem by suggesting that the writers of such psalms express sentiments that are "devilish," "naïve," "childish," filled with "malice," "diabolical," "petty and vulgar," "contemptible," and "vindictive"—to cite but a few of Lewis's choice descriptions.[13] Lewis's proposed solution is to say that the psalmists were clearly speaking contrary to God's will. At best, they provide us with an example of what attitude we *ought not to have*—attitudes that God neither condones in others nor harbors himself toward the wicked.

Lewis's solution, which is not only wrong but also blasphemous, fails on several counts.

These psalms contain nothing to suggest that the psalmist has a malignant or unholy attitude, or is expressing sentiments that God finds displeasing in any way. Rather, we may often rule this out from the overall context, such as the flow of the argument in Psalm 73. An unbiased reading of this psalm shows that the psalmist's attitude is in no way contrary to God's will but that God's will actively informs the psalmist's passion for recompense. Contrast this with texts in which the biblical writer's sin *is* evident, such as we find with David and Bathsheba, and his detailed confession of it in Psalm 51. If the psalmist were uttering "diabolical" sentiments contrary to God's own, and especially imputing such diabolical sentiments to God himself, then God would be remiss in letting such utterances remain in Scripture without qualification.

Most decisively, the texts that show the saints in heaven crying out for vengeance absolutely refute this view. These martyrs are in a thoroughly sanctified state—in heaven, no less—and yet express precisely the same attitude that we find in these Old Testament psalms.

---

13. C. S. Lewis, *Reflections on the Psalms* (New York: Houghton Mifflin, 1958, 1986), 20–33.

Psalm 7:6, 9, 12, 17

In these verses, the psalmist David implores God to arise against his enemies in anger, and returns to God a song of praise in view of his coming righteous retribution.

Psalm 11:5–6

When we considered this psalm earlier, we saw that God hates the wicked. David aligns his own feelings toward the wicked with God's, asking God to rain fiery coals on their heads.

Psalm 31:6, 17

David declares that he "hate[s] those who pay regard to worthless idols." Notice that David does not merely declare his hatred of idols or idolatry, but his hatred of the idolaters themselves. He further implores God to put the wicked to shame and to send them to hell (i.e., sheol).[14]

Psalm 58

In yet another Davidic psalm, David implores God to "break the teeth" in the mouth of the wicked (v. 6) and to make them to be like a snail that dissolves into slime (v. 8). He exults that the righteous will rejoice when beholding God's vengeance against these enemies, and that the satisfaction the righteous will take in this punishment will be their reward.

Psalm 73

One should study carefully and in its entirety this very important imprecatory psalm, penned by Asaph. The evident good fortune of the wicked drives the psalmist nearly mad, almost like a beast. In this life, the ungodly appear to prosper at every turn even as they trample upon the righteous with seeming impunity. Yet, it is only in contemplating their coming destruction at God's hand that the psalmist finds solace.

Psalm 139:19–22

Here David declares his "complete hatred" for God's enemies, praying for their destruction. As the verses before and after his declaration make clear, there is nothing vile or "diabolical" in David's expressions of unmitigated hostility for those who "rise up" against his Lord. Indeed, in verses 23–24 he invites God to search the sincerity of his heart and reveal any untoward motives to him. There is no reason to conclude from the overall flow of this psalm that

---

14. As discussed in Question 8, sheol can refer either to the grave or to a place of disembodied punishment, i.e., hades. In either case, David is imploring God to punish the wicked. Besides, to wish even physical death upon the wicked is to thereby wish spiritual death upon them as well, granting that the wicked who die will experience punishment in hell.

any rebuke from God will be forthcoming, but that here is only perfect alignment with God's own heart (Ps. 5:5).

Jeremiah 12:1; 17:18; Lamentations 1:21–22

To cite but one Old Testament author outside of the psalms, consider Jeremiah. In these verses, he calls down God's judgments against his enemies, asking God to "bring upon them the day of disaster" and to "destroy them with double destruction" (Jer. 17:18). Though we could multiply Old Testament citations of this sort, this one is sufficient to make the point that the imprecatory psalms are no anomaly.

2 Thessalonians 1:6–10

We have already considered this verse in relation to how *God* feels about the wicked. In context, Paul is discussing how God considers it just to exact retribution on those who are afflicting his people. The divine vengeance that God will unleash at Christ's second coming is specifically in view, when he will send away to eternal destruction those who ultimately reject Christ.

What does this verse tell us about how *we* should/will feel about the eventual punishment of the wicked? Paul does not offer this information to add additional stress or sorrow to his readers, who were already suffering for their faith. Rather, he declares that this retribution will bring delight to God's people, "when he comes on that day to be glorified in his saints, and to be marveled at among all who have believed" (v. 10). Knowing that God's people rejoice in the exercise of God's righteousness (Ps. 35:27), Paul brings this to his readers' minds so that they might derive comfort from it in the midst of their persecution at the hands of the ungodly.

Revelation 6:9–11

In this dramatic scene, the dead saints who had been "slain" (*esphagmenōn*) for their testimony to Jesus cry out loudly for vengeance, imploring, "how long before you will judge and avenge our blood on those who dwell on the earth?" Here these saints seem to have no concern for their persecutors' repentance but only for their swift punishment.

Though some have wrongly argued that "the vindictiveness shown here is problematic," Osborne correctly correlates the attitude of these slain saints with the imprecatory prayers of David, concluding, "This cry does not constitute an ethical low in the book but rather . . . a high point for divine justice."[15] Besides, as we have already observed, it is difficult to see how the martyred saints, now free from the taint of indwelling sin that beset them through their earthly lives, could desire anything base or malignant.

---

15. Grant R. Osborne, *Revelation*, BECNT (Grand Rapids: Baker, 2002), 286.

Revelation 19:1–4

In these verses, the saints in glory cry "Hallelujah" as they express satisfaction at the smoke of those who murdered the saints arising "forever and ever." Again, we see no anguish on the part of these saints but only great joy, which transitions seamlessly to their eagerly anticipated marriage supper of the Lamb and the final and permanent reign of the Lord God Almighty (vv. 6–7).

Conclusion

We have seen that the Bible presents a variety of facts about how God and we should, do, and will feel about the wicked. Nevertheless, it may not be obvious how we are to harmonize what appear to be contradictory statements. On the one hand, both God and the saints long for the repentance of sinners and desire their salvation, not their destruction. However, other passages show that both God and the saints do desire to see the wicked punished. How can we harmonize these seemingly opposite ideas and attitudes? And, not to lose sight of our original purpose, how might these verses answer the question before us, which is how can both we and God be happy in the ES if people are suffering in hell for all eternity, particularly our loved ones?

REFLECTION QUESTIONS

1. How important to you personally is the answer to the issue treated in this question? Have you ever worried about whether you can be happy in heaven if some of your loved ones from this life will not be there?

2. React to the biblical passages that show both God and the saints actually desiring the punishment of sinners. Is this something you find difficult to accept?

3. What was your opinion of the statement, "God hates the sin but loves the sinner" before reading this chapter? After?

4. What do you think of C. S. Lewis's proposed solution to the imprecatory psalms?

5. Before reading the proposed solution in the next chapter, how might you harmonize the seeming discrepancies in the biblical data examined in this chapter?

How Can We Be Happy in the Eternal State If There Are People Suffering in Hell, including Some of Our Loved Ones? (Part 2)

In Part 1 of our discussion, I laid out the biblical facts relevant to answering this question, some of which seem to be in direct opposition. In this second part, I shall show how these facts are consistent, and then draw some practical applications.

To answer this question, I must draw upon important theological principles elicited from certain biblical doctrines. The doctrines from which I shall draw these applications are God's attributes of justice and mercy, and the biblical teaching of vicarious atonement.[1]

Justice, Both Human and Divine

We begin with the nature of justice, particularly in terms of how moral beings do (or at least should) *feel* about retributive justice.

We start with God. God is just,[2] and in consequence of this, he must punish sin.[3] Because God is just, when a moral creature violates his law God is displeased until he receives satisfaction for the offense. The biblical concept of *propitiation* expresses this. Mentioned in such verses as 1 John 2:2

---

1. While I shall use principles drawn from these doctrines to make my case, I shall not undertake any sort of detailed demonstration of the doctrines themselves. Those interested should consult the works of many fine evangelical systematic theologians, such as Berkhof, Culver, Grudem, Hodge, Horton, and Shedd.
2. Ezra 9:15; Psalms 7:11; 50:6; 71:19; 116:5; Isaiah 45:21; Revelation 16:7.
3. Exodus 34:6–7; Psalms 7:11–13; 129:4; Proverbs 21:12; Isaiah 11:4; Nahum 1:3; Romans 1:17–18; 2:5–10; 3:5–6, 25; 2 Thessalonians 1:6.

and Romans 3:25, a propitiation (Greek *hilasmos*) is that which appeases, and therefore turns away, anger. This is the consistent meaning of the word, whether in secular Greek (classical) literature or in the Bible.[4] Stated otherwise, God is unhappy until justice is satisfied, and justice is satisfied through punishment.

Note that this satisfaction is not merely transactional—as if balancing impersonal debits and credits on a financial spreadsheet—but relates to God's *feelings* as well. For instance, Ezekiel 5:13 declares that God is "comforted" (KJV; Hebrew *nakham*) when he punishes sin.[5]

Our own sense of justice mirrors God's, in that it elicits the same sense of satisfaction when punishment is meted out. Though some may suppress or attempt to deny this, it is universally true in all cultures throughout the ages. Shedd states, "There is that within us all, which answers, Yea, and Amen [at evil receiving its just recompense]. Such a balancing of the scales is assented to, and demanded by the moral convictions."[6]

Recall our earlier examination of the imprecatory psalms and texts such as Revelation 6:9–11. The desire for vengeance in these texts is not sinful but a normal, holy emotion. Indeed, for the martyrs in heaven, the fact that justice is still out of kilter, so to speak, delays or defers their complete happiness, which they will not experience until God sets everything right through punishing the wicked.

We can leverage our own moral intuitions to see that this is true. We find ourselves greatly vexed when evil people appear to get away with and even reap reward for their wickedness. For instance, we find it despicable that twisted, malevolent individuals profit by exploiting the poor and helpless, or gratify themselves by raping children. The thought of them doing so with impunity and never getting what they have coming to them would and should significantly augment our outrage.

It is for this reason that we see the saints taking delight in the display of God's attribute of justice, manifested in the punishment of sinners. We must keep in mind, however, that in our present state of sin our desire for vengeance is often warped and tinctured with malice, a lack of proportion, and other defects. In the biblical passages examined in Part 1, these saints manifest a pure, holy desire for retribution, unmixed with such sinful elements.

But Does Not Punishing Sin Actually Result in Unhappiness?

Some would urge that surely the opposite must be true, namely, that inflicting punishment on another, however deserving, ought to result,

---

4. See Leon Morris, *The Apostolic Preaching of the Cross* (Grand Rapids: Eerdmans, 1960).
5. The ASV and KJV render *nakham* as "comforted." The ESV and RSV translate it as "satisfy." The NASB has "appeased," while the NIV gives "avenged."
6. W. G. T. Shedd, *Sermons to the Natural Man* (New York: Scribner's, 1871), 351.

automatically and in and of itself, in unhappiness on the part of the one in-flicting it. At least, they say, this would be true for a compassionate and loving person. Moreover, would not such unhappiness equally apply to compassionate individuals who may be merely aware of this punishment, even if they themselves are not the ones inflicting it? Since the saints in heaven are the most compassionate and loving of all people, would they not especially be distraught as they contemplate the complete misery of those in hell—whether or not they themselves have any role in inflicting it?

The notion that inflicting punishment on the guilty would always, au-tomatically, and in and of itself, result in unhappiness does not commend itself to the moral intuitions of the vast majority of humankind throughout the ages. Nevertheless, I grant that this may be true for some. Just as sin can distort one's sense of justice, sin can also distort one's sense of mercy, making it all consuming and elevating it beyond any proper bounds. Such a distortion, coupled with the abuses that one often finds in carrying out justice in the human realm, may lead some to regard punishment as auto-matically repellent and to reject it entirely. However, to have a distorted or excessive sense of "mercy" is just as morally faulty as to have a warped or excessive sense of "justice." The fact that the saints in glory do indeed rejoice in God's vengeance against evil doers is adequate in itself to show us the proper attitude.

Therefore, *considering sinners only and purely in terms of their sin and what it deserves*, there is no cause for unhappiness on the part of the one who inflicts punishment on them, nor for those who contemplate such punish-ment. Rather, the knowledge that sinners receive their due causes satisfaction at seeing the scales of justice balanced and the violation of God's holy law avenged. We experience this even now, though in an imperfect and distorted way. In the eternal state (ES) we shall experience this even as God does and be fully at peace with it.

Mercy, Both Human and Divine

Surely, the account I have given above cannot be the whole story. As we saw in Part 1, Christians greatly desire the salvation of the unsaved and even weep for them until they repent. Why, then, would we not weep for all eter-nity over those who never, ever repent?

God's Attribute of Mercy

As before, we begin with the divine attributes, but this time with the at-tribute of mercy.

As we observed in Part 1, God desires to punish sinners. However, as we also saw, many passages show that God yearns to show mercy to sinners and to pardon them. Both of these are true, and we must avoid making the mistake of thinking that God can have only one emotion at a time toward the sinner. To do so "overlooks the complex nature, the infinite plenitude, of the Godhead."[7]

These two inclinations and desires in God—to punish sin as well as to pardon it—may appear to be at odds, such that in order for him to satisfy the one he could not satisfy the other. But this is not so. God is able to satisfy both through the atonement of Jesus Christ, which is a vicarious punishment for sin.

Christ's Atonement: A Manifestation of Justice and Mercy

Christ's death is a vicarious punishment for sin, which orthodox theologians also call a vicarious "satisfaction." It is a vicarious punishment because the offender's sin receives punishment, with a substitute receiving the punishment in the sinner's place (i.e., vicariously). It is also a satisfaction because this punishment exactly satisfies God's righteous requirements and demand for punishment. Therefore, in the case of a vicarious satisfaction, God mercifully spares the sinner by satisfying justice through punishing a substitute in the sinner's place. In this way God can show mercy to the sinner, but justice also receives its due.

Note that because Jesus is not only man but also God, the eternal Son of the Father and second person of the blessed Trinity, that it is God himself—in the person of the Son—who receives the stroke in the sinful creature's place. Here we do not have some disconnected, unrelated third party who bears the punishment, whose suffering is a matter of divine indifference. Far from it! Shedd states the matter beautifully:

> God is inherently inclined to forgive; and there is no proof of this so strong as the fact, that he does not shrink from this amazing *self*-sacrifice which forgiveness necessitates. The desire to save his transgressing and guilty creatures wells up and overflows from the depths of his own compassionate heart, and needs no soliciting or prompting from without. Side by side in the Godhead, then, there dwell the impulse to punish and the desire to pardon; but the desire to pardon is realized in act, by *carrying out* the impulse to punish, not indeed upon the person of the criminal, but upon that of his substitute. And the substitute is the Punisher Himself![8]

Now, from God's perspective, pardoning the sinner through a vicarious satisfaction is superior to punishing the sinner. In the former case, God is able to satisfy both his inclination to punish sin as well as his inclination to

---

7. W. G. T. Shedd, "The Atonement, a Satisfaction for the Ethical Nature of Both God and Man," *Theological Essays* (New York: Scribner's, 1877), 270.

8. Ibid., 272–73.

show mercy. When he punishes the actual sinner, however, he is only able to satisfy his attribute of justice. This explains why God urges sinners to repent: because his preference is for them to turn from their sins and live. Were he just as happy condemning them as saving them, their repentance would be a matter of indifference to him, which it is not.[9]

The Case of the Terminally Unrepentant

A critical matter remains yet unanswered. If God's desire to show mercy is frustrated by those who never repent, would not God eternally long for their salvation—a longing that in the case of those in hell is never satisfied? Even if we grant that God is able to satisfy his inclination to punish such sinners for their wickedness, would not God also be sad about being unable to show mercy to these same sinners, who are in hell for all eternity? Would this not mean that God is, at best, eternally conflicted? Would not his satisfaction at the punishment of their sin, on the one hand, be tainted, diminished, offset, or perhaps even overwhelmed by an unremitting eternal sorrow over his inability to show them mercy?

The answer to this has to do with a change that occurs in the sinners themselves, in which they cease to be objects of pity.

Considering those who find themselves eventually in hell, God, out of his yearning to pardon, furnished opportunity after opportunity for them to repent and turn from their sins. For many he did so clearly through the preaching of the gospel. For others he displayed his holiness through conscience and through the manifestation of his attributes in nature.[10] During their lifetimes, when he offered them opportunities that they rejected, God grieved over their rejection and longed for them to "turn . . . and live" (Ezek. 18:23).

Now, some resist God's overtures of mercy for part of their lives but at some point eventually do repent. In these cases, God no longer grieves but rejoices, because he can now exercise mercy toward them (Luke 15:7, 10). Others, however, reject and reject and reject until they have finally hardened themselves so much against all offers of clemency that they have made themselves unalterably fixed in their spurning of divine mercy. I refer to such individuals as terminally hardened, meaning that as a result of persistent and steadfast rejection of divine overtures of grace, such individuals

---

9. We must here observe briefly that divine forgiveness is not automatically or unconditionally bestowed upon the sinner. Forgiveness requires an act on the sinner's part, which is faith and the repentance which is part of faith. Notice that in Ezekiel 33:11, which we examined in Part 1, God does *not* say, "I have no pleasure in the death of the wicked and so therefore the wicked will live." Rather, he says, "I have no pleasure in the death of the wicked, *but that the wicked turn from his way and live*" (emphasis added). Therefore, when God desires the salvation of the wicked, he also desires their repentance and faith, through which he may suitably apply to them his provision of satisfaction.

10. See Question 16.

have placed themselves beyond any hope of repentance, and therefore of salvation.[11]

Once sinners have terminally hardened themselves against all offers to repent, God no longer yearns for their salvation but has given them up to their own desires, because of their persistent unwillingness to acknowledge him (Rom. 1:28). These have ceased to be objects of pity but have made themselves purely objects of wrath. Therefore, the fitting emotion toward such individuals is no longer sorrow for their lack of repentance but only pure indignation and wrath for their final, total, and irrevocable spurning of grace. This remaining emotion toward such individuals finds its expression in their punishment and their punishment alone.

Proverbs 1:24–33 bears careful scrutiny, as it well illustrates the case of sinners who have completely perverted their wills and rejected all of God's many overtures to effect repentance. Observe that God bears absolutely no pity toward these; they evoke only mocking and derision (v. 26). He no longer yearns for their salvation but only for their punishment, which is satisfied ultimately in hell.

When Does This Terminal Hardening Occur?

Those who continually spurn grace and die rejecting God's offer of pardon have fixed their moral character and inclinations to where they remain unalterably opposed to God for all eternity. Such individuals would never repent even in the afterlife, as we observed in a previous question.[12] For some, however, this hardening occurs even well before they die.

The fact that terminal hardening may occur before death helps us account for the imprecatory psalms and also for why the saints in glory implore God for vengeance rather than for him to show mercy on their persecutors still on earth. Such cases stand in stark contrast to Jesus's cry on the cross, "Father, forgive them, for they know not what they do" (Luke 23:34), or to Stephen's request that God not hold his death by stoning against his perpetrators (Acts

---

11. I have chosen to speak of these individuals as "terminally hardened" rather than as "reprobate" because the concept of reprobation is typically found in discussions of election to salvation, standing as its opposite. My treatment in this section is not allied to a particular view of the divine decrees, whether Arminian or Reformed. Though I do hold to a Reformed position on election, I am here looking at matters from the *human* side and am not staking out a position on how a prior divine decree, permissive or otherwise, may factor in to this. Whatever one's take on the question of election, all parties grant (or should grant) that human beings make responsible, self-caused choices that affect their own moral condition, sometimes to the degree mentioned here. Certainly, an Arminian would acknowledge this. But classic Reformed theologians affirm this as well. Shedd, an unquestionably Reformed writer, states, "On the side of reprobation, the efficient cause of perdition is the self-determination of the human will" (W. G. T. Shedd, *Dogmatic Theology,* ed. Alan W. Gomes [Phillipsburg: P&R, 2003], 342).
12. See Question 14.

7:60). In the former cases, it was clear to the psalmists and to these saints in glory that they were dealing with terminally hardened individuals. They would know this because God made it clear to them. For example, Psalm 7:12 suggests that the psalmist understands that the repentance of the individuals on whom he calls down judgment will not be forthcoming. It is for this reason that we do not find in such texts any sense of pity or a desire for their repentance but only a clamor for judgment.

But What about Our Loved Ones?

But is it not counterintuitive to think that we could ever feel this way about our finally unsaved loved ones—those nearest and dearest to us—who never, ever repent?

Realize that in the ES we shall see their sin of persistent rejection the way that God sees it: with full clarity and insight. Packer remarks, "The mistake here is to assume that in heaven our feelings about others will be as at present, and our joy in God's justice, as one of his moral perfections, will be no greater than it is now."[13] In the ES we will see the times that God extended his offer of pardon to them and their stubborn and persistent rejection of it. We will see their sin precisely as it is: as an egregious affront to an immaculately holy God. We will comprehend fully the gravity of rejecting God's supreme sacrifice of his only son, extended at great personal cost, and the perversity of will that such persistent rejection represents. Pache well summarizes, "Since, in heaven, we shall love God in a perfect, entire way, how can we still feel attached to those who, right to the end, sought to remain His enemies?"[14]

Practical Applications

Based on what we have seen, what specific guidelines ought to inform our attitudes toward sinners in this life and hell in the next?

Our Default Desire Should Be for the Repentance of Sinners

Our greatest, primary, and default desire ought to be for the good of all persons, in a way consistent with God's holiness. Practically speaking, this means that we should desire and pray for the repentance of all persons, so that they may find life in God through his provision of vicarious satisfaction.

Apart from receiving a special revelation from God, which would be highly unusual, we have no way of knowing who may have hardened him/herself beyond any hope of repentance. Although the Bible describes such individuals in passages like Hebrews 6:4–8, it is difficult for us to know to whom

---

13. J. I. Packer, "Is Hell out of Vogue in This Modern Era?," *United Evangelical Action,* September–October 1989, 11.
14. René Pache, *The Future Life* (Chicago: Moody, 1962), 317. See also Roger Nicole, "Universalism: Will Everyone Be Saved?" *Christianity Today,* March 20, 1987, 38.

such descriptions apply, since we cannot see the heart as God does. Therefore, our desire and prayer should be that the sinners we encounter will "turn . . . and live" (Ezek. 18:23). We continue to long for their repentance while hope remains, feel sadness so long as they have not yet repented, and continue to feel it until they do. We feel this sadness because we see how their sin hurts them and how it is an affront to God. We yearn that the sinner might embrace the depth of that blood-soaked divine love that bore the pains of hell in the sinner's place.

When someone does repent, we should rejoice along with the hosts of heaven that a sinner has found mercy (Luke 15:7, 10). Moreover, we also rejoice that the atonement of God's dear Son has met the demands of justice. Our longing for justice is pacified and our sense of outrage over whatever sins they have committed—however heinous—has been stilled because "Jesus paid it all."

We must at all costs avoid the malignant attitude of Jonah toward the Ninevites, who begrudged their repentance because he knew that God would pardon them if they turned from their sins (Jonah 4:1–3). May it never be so for us! We must always desire sinners' repentance, so that God will pardon them.

Our Desire for the Finally Impenitent Should Be for Their Punishment Only

Once individuals have hardened themselves beyond any possibility of salvation, we should (and eventually shall) then rejoice in their punishment, for in this God sets matters aright in his moral universe.

Again, rarely if ever would we know in this life whether a person will be or has already been given up by God (Rom. 1:28). We will, however, know this in the afterlife and see matters with perfect clarity and insight. Nevertheless, even in this life we should find the doctrine of hell comforting and not a cause of disquiet. The fact of eternal punishment means that the finally unrepentant will receive their due and that God will balance the scales of justice. Like the psalmist who saw the end of the incorrigibly wicked when he inquired of the Lord (Ps. 73:17), we too should be satisfied to know that God will make it right in the end.

REFLECTION QUESTIONS

1. Do you find the solution presented in this chapter convincing? Discuss the strengths and weaknesses of it.

2. Assuming that you are not convinced by the argument presented here, are you nevertheless satisfied that there will be no sadness in the ES, whether or not we can explain why that will be so?

3. Has your thinking changed or deepened in any way about God's attributes of justice and mercy because of what you have read in this chapter?

4. Think about your own sense of mercy and justice. Can you relate personally to any of the illustrations given in this chapter?

5. Is your "default desire" for the repentance of sinners? Ask God to give you an even deeper sense of compassion for the lost.

Did Jesus "Descend into Hell" Like the Apostles' Creed Says? (Part 1)

[I believe in] Jesus Christ, his only Son, our Lord;
Who was conceived by the Holy Ghost, born of the
    Virgin Mary;
Suffered under Pontius Pilate, was crucified,
    died, and was buried.
He descended into Hell (hades).
The third day he rose from the dead;
He ascended into heaven; and sits on the right hand of
    God the Father Almighty;
From there he shall come to judge the living and the dead.

So read the statements about the Lord Jesus Christ as contained in the "received form" of the Apostles' Creed, one of Christendom's earliest and most venerable declarations of faith. Accepted by Protestants, Catholics, and Eastern Orthodox believers alike, the creed sets forth basic and straightforward affirmations about Christ, largely paraphrasing the language of Scripture. At least that is so with one highly enigmatic exception: the statement that Christ "descended into Hell."[1] While the other particulars about Christ are direct, clear, and undisputed, what are we to make of this descent into hell (DH)?

Historically, there is nothing even close to agreement about the meaning of this clause, much less whether it is true. As the late seventeenth-century Dutch theologian Hermann Witsius once quipped, "There are almost as many dissertations concerning the *descensus* [descent] as there are flies in the height of summer."

---

1. Latin *descendit ad inferna* [or, *ad inferos*]; Greek *katabē eis ton Hadēn*.

It is not hard to see why. An exceedingly complex and bewildering array of theological, biblical, and historical issues come into play when trying to untangle the meaning and validity of this arcane expression. Moreover, some of the biblical passages involved in its explanation and defense are among the most interpretively difficult in all of Holy Scripture.

Because of the massive difficulty in untangling this issue, we shall consider it in two parts. In Part 1, I shall address the following aspects:

1. What is the Apostles' Creed?

2. When and how did the "descent into hell" language find its way into the creed?

3. What are some of the main interpretations for what the descent into hell means?

4. What are the main Bible verses offered in support of these various interpretations?

Then, in Part 2, I shall evaluate the truth and validity of the descent into hell, as discussed in Part 1.

What Is the Apostles' Creed?

Neither the Apostles nor a subcommittee of the Apostles penned the Apostles' Creed. However, I freely grant that the creed is "apostolic" in the sense that it presents a distillate or "*Reader's Digest* condensation" of apostolic—that is to say, biblical—teaching about the basic themes of the Christian religion.

As Philip Schaff recounts, the creed "cannot be traced to an individual author" but took its main shape in the first four centuries, arising in the Western portion of the church.[2] Some believe that its earliest known roots go back to the *Romanum* of around AD 150.[3] The *Romanum* was an early form of a baptismal creed, used in the instruction of new converts in the rudiments of faith, which they recited upon their full inclusion into the church at their baptism. Versions of this creed developed and received elaboration both in the Latin-speaking Western territories and in the Greek-speaking Eastern areas of the church, with minor wording adjustments taking place until around AD 750.

---

2. Philip Schaff, *Creeds of Christendom*, 3 vols. (Grand Rapids: Baker, 1985), 1:16.
3. Randal E. Otto, "*Descendit in Inferna*: A Reformed Review of a Creedal Conundrum," *WTJ* 52 (1990): 143; David P. Scaer, "He Did Descend to Hell: In Defense of the Apostles' Creed," *JETS* 35, no. 1 (March 1992): 94.

When and How Did the "Descent into Hell" Language Get into the Creed?

The earliest forms of the creed do not contain the "descent into hell" or "hades" language. It does not appear in the *Romanum*, mentioned above, nor is it present in the Nicene (AD 325) and Constantinopolitan (AD 381) versions of the creed. The language "made its sudden and almost noiseless appearance" in the creed connected with the Council of Sirmium in 359—a council not of orthodox but of Arian origin.[4]

Rufinus, a priest of Aquilea, wrote a commentary on the creed in AD 390 that sheds some interesting light on the mysterious origins of this expression. He states that the clause, found in the Aquelian version of the creed but not in the Roman or Eastern versions, was equivalent in meaning to saying "he was buried" (*sepultus est*). Pearson, commenting on this, observes that "in the Aquilean Creed, where this article was first expressed, there was no mention of Christ's burial," the DH language being substituted in its place.[5] Thus, "the intention of the Aquileian alteration of the creed was not to add a new doctrine, but to explain an old one," by expressing his burial using the language of a descent into hell, with "hell" being but a synonym for the grave.[6]

The later Athanasian Creed of the late fifth/early sixth century contains the DH, and like the Aquelian version leaves out the burial language.[7] The DH expression does not reappear in the creed until AD 650.[8]

The medieval and modern forms of the creed contain both "he was buried" and "he descended into hell."[9]

Main Interpretations of the Descent into Hell

There is a myriad of views on what the DH means. Cataloging the different positions is greatly complicated by the fact that elements of one opinion often combine with facets of others, making it difficult to categorize neatly the options. However, I shall look at a representative sample of some of the main representations of the DH, both ancient and modern.

---

4. D. A. Du Toit, "Descensus and Universalism: Some Historical Patterns of Interpretation," in *Universalism and the Doctrine of Hell*, ed. Nigel M. de S. Cameron (Grand Rapids: Baker, 1992), 75. The Arian party, which had been repudiated and declared heretical at Nicea in 325 AD, denied the deity of Christ.

5. John Pearson, *An Exposition of the Creed* (London, 1715), 226.

6. W. G. T. Shedd, *Dogmatic Theology*, ed. Alan W. Gomes (Phillipsburg: P&R, 2003), 838. See also Pearson: "It appeareth therefore that the first intention of putting these words in the Creed was only to express the burial of our Saviour, or the descent of his body into the grave" (*Exposition of the Creed*, 226–27).

7. Shedd, *Dogmatic Theology*, 839.

8. Wayne Grudem, "He Did Not Descend into Hell: A Plea for Following Scripture Instead of the Apostles' Creed," *JETS* 34, no. 1 (March 1991): 105.

9. Otto, "*Descendit in Inferna*," 144; Shedd, *Dogmatic Theology*, 839.

One finds two broad categories of interpretations: a figurative or meta-phorical "descent" and a literal, "local" descent, i.e., to the netherworld of spirits. Metaphorical views take the DH as a kind of figure of speech that stands for real experiences in the life of Jesus that relate to his death, burial, and resurrection. Unlike the local descent views, the metaphorical presentations do not affirm that Christ took an actual journey to a place called hell. The literal or local descent understandings, on the other hand, teach precisely that: Between his death and resurrection, Jesus traveled to hell (hades), understood as a realm of spirits—whether angelic or human, wicked or righteous. As we shall see, just what he may have done there, and to/with whom, varies considerably among the views.

Metaphorical Views

The Descent into Hell Means That Christ Was Truly Buried in the Grave
By saying that Christ descended to hell, adherents of this position mean simply that Christ literally died and went to the grave. By "grave" they may have the literal grave (e.g., tomb) in mind, or "grave" in the more general sense of "being dead"—or both.

As noted above, this may well have been the original understanding of the clause, if we are to believe Rufinus. This is also the view taken by the Westminster Assembly in Questions 46, 49, and 50 of the Westminster Larger Catechism.

The Descent into Hell Refers to the Suffering in Christ's Human Soul on the Cross
Calvin taught that we ought to understand the DH as Christ suffering the pains of hell while on the cross. Specifically, Christ experienced in his human soul the pains of a damned and abandoned man, separated from his Father, as he bore the judicial penalty for the sins of humankind.[10]

According to Mary Rakow, Calvin's reinterpretation of the DH in a "psychological, existential" sense was a "radically new" take on it. The later Heidelberg Catechism adopted Calvin's explanation of the DH in Question 44.

Local Descent Views

The Descent into Hell Was to Liberate Old Testament Believers from Hades
In the interval between Christ's burial in the tomb and his resurrection, proponents of this view say that Christ, in his disembodied, preresurrected state, took a journey to hades, understood as the realm of the dead. He did

---

10. See John Calvin, *Institutes of the Christian Religion* 2.16.10.

so in order to liberate the Old Testament believers who were awaiting deliverance and to transport them to heaven, which was now made possible by Christ's atoning work. Several early church writers suggest this idea, including Ignatius of Antioch and Tertullian.[11] The apocryphal, noncanonical Gospel of Nicodemus presents an elaborate picture of this deliverance, in which Christ crushes Satan and frees the Old Testament patriarchs from hades.[12]

Underlying this position is a two-compartment theory of hades. On this reckoning, before the work of Christ, hades was the abode of the wicked and the righteous alike; hades is here understood as the netherworld or region of the dead generally. The wicked resided in the lower chamber of hades in a state of suffering, while the righteous remained in an upper location, known variously as Abraham's bosom (*sinus Abrahae*); paradise; or, in Roman Catholic theology specifically, the *limbus patrum* or limbo of the fathers.[13] Though a place of comfort and free of suffering, it was still not heaven, and those abiding there did not enjoy God's direct presence.[14] Christ, whose soul descended to hades while his body was still in the tomb, extracted these captive saints and ushered them directly into heaven, thus emptying the *limbus patrum*. From that point forward, believers who died in the Lord went straight to heaven.

The Descent into Hell Is a Triumphal Proclamation to the Wicked in Hades
According to this position, Christ literally descended to hades, but primarily in order to proclaim his victory over hell's malevolent denizens. The message announced was not one of salvation or deliverance but of final condemnation. The audience in question may have been fallen angels, wicked humans, or both.

Some combine this view with the preceding, in which case the DH both liberates the righteous from hades and announces condemnation and defeat to the wicked there. In the depictions of Christ's "harrowing of hell," as found frequently in religious art and iconography throughout Christendom, "Christ is represented as breaking down the portals of death, crushing Satan, and taking Adam, Eve, and . . . the patriarchs by the hand."[15]

One exponent of this view was Martin Luther. His famous Easter sermon preached at Torgau in 1533 describes the DH "in vivid and colorful strokes."[16]

---

11. See discussion in W. Hall Harris III, "The Ascent and Descent of Christ in Ephesians 4:9–19, *BibSac* 151 (April–June 1994): 198–99.
12. Friedrich Loofs, "Descent to Hades (Christ's)," *Encyclopaedia of Religion and Ethics*, 12 vols., ed. James Hastings (New York: Charles Scribner's Sons, 1911), 4:660.
13. *Limbus* = "edge; border"; *patrum* = "of the fathers."
14. Thomas Aquinas, *Summa Theologiae* 3.52.5.
15. Karl Heinz Neufeld, "Descent into Hell," *ECT*, 1:435.
16. Du Toit, "Descensus and Universalism," 89. The date commonly assigned to this sermon is in dispute. See David V. N. Bagchi, "Luther versus Luther? The Problem of Christ's Descent into Hell in the Long Sixteenth Century," *Perichoresis* 6, no. 2 (2008): 190n42.

According to this sermon, Christ descended to hell, not in his soul alone but in both body and soul, triumphing over "the power of death and Satan," and delivering us "from eternal damnation, and even from the jaws of hell"[17]

The Descent into Hell Entailed a Gospel Proclamation of Salvation to the Unsaved in Hades

This position is in some ways the opposite of the one immediately preceding. Whereas in the triumphal proclamation view Christ descends to hades in order to deliver a message of condemnation and defeat for the wicked, in this version he proclaims a message of salvation for the wicked. In other words, God gives the wicked in hades a chance to believe. In some accounts, this might be a first chance to believe given to those who never heard the gospel during their lifetimes, whereas in other explanations Christ presents a second chance to those who died in a state of conscious rejection. Some versions of this include the idea that all will be saved through this postmortem opportunity.

Some of the early church fathers suggested teaching along these lines, including Irenaeus and Clement of Alexandria,[18] with Origen pressing the teaching specifically in support of universal salvation.[19] Among modern writers, Bloesch, Best, and Hanson have set forth this position of a postmortem chance to believe.[20] Historically, the church has overwhelmingly rejected the idea of after-death conversion as incompatible with the overall scriptural teaching on the fate of the wicked.[21]

Bible Passages Commonly Offered in Defense of the Descent into Hell

Acts 2:27, 31

> For you will not abandon my soul to Hades, or let your Holy One see corruption. . . . [David] foresaw and spoke about the resurrection of Christ, that he was not abandoned to Hades, nor did his flesh see corruption.

It is obvious why some would use this verse to support the DH. Adherents of metaphorical and local descent views alike draw upon it.

---

17. *Formula of Concord,* Epitome, 9.4.
18. R. J. Bauckham, "Descent into Hell," *NDT,* eds. Sinclair B. Ferguson and David F. Wright (Downers Grove, IL: InterVarsity, 1988), 194; Neufeld, "Descent into Hell," 434.
19. Du Toit, "Descensus and Universalism," 84.
20. Donald Bloesch, "Descent into Hell," *ED,* 339; John H. Elliott, *1 Peter,* AB (New Haven, CT: Yale University Press, 2000), 733; Karen H. Jobes, *1 Peter,* BECNT (Grand Rapids: Baker, 2005), 248.
21. I have dealt with the issue of postmortem conversions already in Question 14.

Those who equate the DH with Christ's burial in the grave take the words "my soul" in this passage as equivalent to "me," and the word "hades" as meaning "the grave"—both of which are within the range of meaning for these words.[22] Those who apply this to a literal, local descent typically take the text as meaning that Christ, between his burial and resurrection, went to hades as a disembodied soul.

Ephesians 4:8–10

> Wherefore he saith, When he ascended up on high, he led captivity captive, and gave gifts unto men. (Now that he ascended, what is it but that he also descended first into the lower parts of the earth? He that descended is the same also that ascended up far above all heavens, that he might fill all things.) (KJV)

Certain biblical commentators, ancient and modern, take the reference to Christ's descent "into the lower parts" or "lower regions" as having a descent into hades in view. Among modern scholars, Clinton Arnold is representative. He understands these "lower regions" as a reference to the underworld or hades, "where Christ proclaimed his victory over the hostile principalities and powers."[23] While some might see the descent as performed in order to liberate Old Testament believers, for example, held in the *limbus patrum* (see above), Arnold's position falls under the triumphal proclamation rubric.

1 Peter 3:18–20

> For Christ also suffered once for sins, the righteous for the unrighteous, that he might bring us to God, being put to death in the flesh but made alive in the spirit, in which he went and proclaimed to the spirits in prison, because they formerly did not obey, when God's patience waited in the days of Noah, while the ark was being prepared, in which a few, that is, eight persons, were brought safely through water.

Loofs identifies this highly enigmatic passage, together with 1 Peter 4:6 (below), as a one of the two classic texts offered in support of the DH.[24] However, historically the doctrine of the DH "developed independently of 1

---

22. See the discussions in Question 5 and in Question 8.
23. Clinton E. Arnold, *Ephesians*, ZECNT (Grand Rapids: Zondervan, 2010), 252, 254.
24. Loofs, "Descent into Hades," 659.

Peter in the New Testament,"[25] and adherents of the DH pressed this passage into service somewhat later.

All three of the local descent positions mentioned above draw upon this text. Clement of Alexandria, for instance, used it to establish that "all persons have the possibility of hearing the Gospel, of repenting, and of being saved."[26] Origen, mentioned earlier, used this text to prove universalism, the teaching that God would save all eventually.[27] Those who take the view that the DH is about a triumphal proclamation of condemnation to wicked humans and/or fallen angels, also point to it. For instance, Arnold sees "significant lines of correspondence" between 1 Peter 3:19 and Ephesians 4:8–10, which he takes as a reference to Christ "descending to the underworld and proclaiming a message of victory over the rebellious demonic powers."[28]

1 Peter 4:5–6

> . . . but they will give account to him who is ready to judge the living and the dead. For this is why the gospel was preached even to those who are dead, that though judged in the flesh the way people are, they might live in the spirit the way God does.

Some have used this text to teach that Christ offered a postmortem opportunity of salvation for unbelievers, either to those who never heard the gospel or to those who rejected it when alive. Others see a reference to Old Testament believers, who were waiting for Christ to preach the gospel to them.[29]

REFLECTION QUESTIONS

1. Had you heard about Christ's "descent into hell" as contained in the Apostles' Creed before reading this chapter? What did you think it meant?

2. Does the fact that the DH language was added relatively late to the creed raise any questions in your mind about whether it should be retained?

3. After looking at the survey of different views for the DH, do you find any of them plausible?

---

25. Elliott, *1 Peter*, 706.
26. Ibid., 707.
27. Ibid., 708.
28. Arnold, *Ephesians*, 254.
29. See the discussion of these different views in Jobes, *1 Peter*, 270; Simon E. Kistemaker, *Exposition of James, Epistles of John, Peter, and Jude*, NTC (Grand Rapids: Baker, 2002), 163–64.

4. Considering the biblical texts offered in support of the DH, how much support do you feel that they truly offer for a DH?

5. Based on what you have read thus far (i.e., in Part 1), do you believe that Christ "descended into hell," and if so, how would you understand that?

Did Jesus "Descend into Hell" Like the Apostles' Creed Says? (Part 2)

In Part 1, we looked at the history of the "descent into hell" (DH) language in the Apostles' Creed, the various ways in which theologians have understood it, and the main biblical passages offered in its support. In Part 2, we shall consider whether these passages actually teach a DH and whether we ought to retain the doctrine.

A Word about Creeds and Confessions of Faith

Christians have produced many valuable statements of faith over the centuries that serve to express the church's understanding of what the Bible teaches on a variety of important topics. These statements distill the essence of biblical teaching on crucial issues and serve several very useful functions in the life of the church. These include instructing new believers in the rudiments of the faith and clarifying a church's stand on controversial issues, particularly in the face of heresies and other fundamental errors.

At the same time, the authority of a creed—any creed—is relative, not absolute. A creed is only as good as the scriptural basis on which it rests. As a concise summary of biblical teaching, a creed has great value. However, when it departs from the Bible we must depart from it, however ancient or widely held.

The Descent into Hell Is Not Original to the Creed

Even apart from the question of how much authority a document such as Apostles' Creed ought to have, one could argue that that the DH is a late intrusion that does not belong in it in the first place. Shedd observed,

> If, then, the text of the Apostles' Creed shall be subjected, like that of the New Testament, to a revision in accordance with

the text of the first four centuries, the Descensus ad inferos [descent into hell] must be rejected as an interpolation.[1]

The alien character of this late addition sticks out like the proverbial sore thumb when compared to the rest of the creed. The original clauses of the creed present subject matter that is straightforward and clearly stated, touching on core, universally agreed-upon doctrines of the faith that remain beyond dispute. Not so for the DH. There is no explicit Bible verse stating that Jesus descended into hell, and we find myriad interpretations among Christians about how to understand this clause.[2] Even if one were to adopt the view that the DH means nothing more than Christ's burial—which all admit is an undisputed fact—then all the statement would do is to transform or restate the already existing and very clear statement that "he was buried" into an obscure one.

Some "Theologically Correct" Explanations May Not Really Explain the Descent into Hell

Some of the explanations for how to understand the DH are theologically correct in themselves. Nevertheless, that does not mean that these statements necessarily explain the DH language of the creed.

Consider Calvin's interpretation of the DH: that the DH is a metaphor for Christ's sufferings on the cross. Calvin offers a profound and thoroughly scriptural discussion of Christ's spiritual agony and sense of abandonment by God.[3] However true and precious as these truths may be, do they accurately explain the meaning of the phrase "he descended into hell" as contained in the creed?

Among other problems, the DH language of the creed comes *after* the burial, whereas in Calvin's view this descent into hell took place while on the cross, before his death and entombment.

The Biblical Texts Used in Defense of the Descent into Hell May Be Explained Differently

The obscurity of the DH language is matched only by the extreme difficulty one encounters when attempting to explain some of the main biblical texts offered in its defense. Some of these texts, such as the passage about the "spirits in prison" in 1 Peter 3 and the "descended into the lower regions" in Ephesians 4, are anything but clear and stand as among the most interpretively difficult passages in the entire Bible. Indeed, concerning 1 Peter 3:19–22, Martin Luther, one of the greatest biblical commentators of all times,

---

1. W. G. T. Shedd, *Doctrine of Endless Punishment* (1886; repr., Minneapolis: Klock & Klock, 1980), 70–71.
2. See Wayne Grudem, "He Did Not Descend into Hell: A Plea for Following Scripture Instead of the Apostles' Creed," *JETS* 34, no. 1 (March 1991): 113.
3. See Calvin, *Institutes* 2.16.10.

admitted in one of his sermons on 1 Peter: "This is a strange text and certainly a more obscure passage than any other passage in the New Testament. I still do not know for sure what the apostle means." At minimum, this should give us pause before erecting a doctrine on such an edifice—particularly one that is enshrined in a creed that purports to express the basic, foundational truths of the catholic (i.e., universal) faith of all Christians everywhere.

To illustrate the point, let us consider briefly some of the alternative interpretations that commentators have offered for the key texts we examined in Part 1—interpretations often unsupportive of the DH position. Even if we are not able to decide which view is correct on these exceedingly challenging passages, most if not all of these interpretations are entirely plausible, which in itself should at least temper our enthusiasm for using them to prove a DH.

Acts 2:27–31

It seems best to take this passage in Acts 2 as referring to Christ's burial, not to a local descent to the underworld. This is clear from the context, in which Peter draws a comparison between the corruption of David's *body* over against the incorruption of Christ's *body.*

Why, then, does Peter speak of Christ's *soul* not being abandoned to *hades?* Why did he not say instead, "You will not abandon my *body* to the *grave?*" As noted in Question 8, the biblical writers sometimes use "hades," which is equivalent to the Hebrew word "sheol," to designate the grave. Furthermore, the word "soul" in this text does not refer to Christ's immaterial nature—as if his "soul" took a journey to hell after it separated from his body. Rather, the word "soul" can stand for the entire person, as equivalent to the pronoun "me." This is a common use of the word "soul," as discussed earlier.[4] Here the following rendering of verse 27 is to be preferred: "You will not abandon *me* to the *grave,* nor will you let your Holy One see decay."

Now, one might counter that if Peter were talking about Christ's burial then this would actually serve as a proof of the DH, provided one takes the DH as a metaphor for Christ's burial, as some do. But if the DH means nothing more than his burial, then it presents us with a needless repetition, granting that the final version of the creed contains both the expression "he was buried" and the words "he descended into hell." We would therefore lose nothing by removing the DH language and gain much clarity by doing so.

Ephesians 4:8–10

I begin by observing that "there is no obvious reference to hades or hell here in Ephesians."[5] Different Bible translations render variously, however, what the text does say. The KJV reads, "he also descended first into the lower

---

4. See Question 5.
5. Peter T. O'Brien, *Ephesians*, PNTC (Grand Rapids: Eerdmans, 1999), 294.

parts of the earth," and the NASB follows this rendering as well. However, other modern versions translate it so as to equate the lower regions with the earth. For instance, the ESV reads, "he also descended into the lower regions, the earth," while the NET Bible has "the lower regions, namely, the earth." The NIV takes this approach as well: "he also descended to the lower, earthly regions." Grammatically speaking, these latter translations take the phrase "of the earth" as carrying the meaning, "the lower regions, which are the earth."[6]

Many commentators believe that the translation that equates "the lower parts" with "the earth" supports the notion that the descent in question is not a descent from earth into hades but rather the descent from heaven to earth that took place at the incarnation. Some commentators further broaden this to include not only the incarnation proper but also Christ's death and burial.[7]

It is also significant that the idea of a DH may be incompatible with certain other themes in Ephesians generally. As Snodgrass insightfully observes, "In Ephesians the conflict with the powers takes place in the heavenly realms, and Christ's victory is by exaltation, not descent (see 1:20–23; 6:10)."[8] Furthermore, considering Scripture outside of Paul's writings, the ascent/descent language in John clearly has the incarnation in view, in which Christ moves from heaven to earth and not from earth to hades (e.g., John 3:13; 6:62; 16:28).[9]

1 Peter 3:18–22

As noted earlier, this is one of the most difficult texts to understand in the entire New Testament. For this reason alone, one should be cautious in building a doctrine upon it.

First, observe that nowhere does this passage mention the words "descent" or "hell."[10] Peter does say, however, that Christ preached to imprisoned spirits that were disobedient in the days of Noah. Be that as it may, many commentators understand this in ways incompatible with a DH.

---

6. Specifically, they take the Greek *tēs gēs* as an epexegetical genitive or genitive of apposition. Hoehner observes that this grammatical construction is common in Ephesians (see Harold W. Hoehner, *Ephesians: An Exegetical Commentary* [Grand Rapids: Baker, 2002], 531, 535).
7. Grudem, "He Did Not Descend into Hell," 108; O'Brien, *Ephesians*, 295–96; Hoehner, *Ephesians*, 536; Klyne Snodgrass, *Ephesians*, NIVAC (Grand Rapids: Zondervan, 1996), 202. Older commentators adopting this view include Shedd and Calvin. So Bales: "Since the Reformation, and particularly in the last 150 years or so, the view that the descent in Eph. 4:9 refers to Christ's incarnation (understood variously as his earthly ministry and/ or his redemptive death and/or his burial in the ground) has gained a strong following" (William Bales, "The Descent of Christ in Ephesians 4:9," *CBQ* 72 [2010]: 84–85).
8. Snodgrass, *Ephesians*, 201–2. Hoehner makes this same point (*Ephesians*, 535).
9. Hoehner, *Ephesians*, 535.
10. John H. Elliott, *1 Peter*, AB (New Haven, CT: Yale University Press, 2000), 638.

The "Libidinous Angels" View

One view that has gained much currency among commentators, but which frankly seems strange (to me at least), is what I have dubbed the "libidinous angels" view. According to this, the "spirits in prison" refer to fallen angels who, in the days before the great flood, came down to earth and had sexual relations with earthly women. Adherents of this view equate these wicked angels with the "sons of God" in Genesis 6:2, and the Nephilim or giants of verse 4 were the mutant love children, as it were, of this illicit union. Because of this foul transgression, God consigned these angels to a kind of spiritual "prison" in an inferior level of heaven, as punishment and in order to prevent them from further mischief.

Advocates ground this position in the purported parallels between the language of 1 Peter and a tradition recounted in lurid detail in the noncanonical book of 1 Enoch. Space does not permit an examination of 1 Enoch, but interpreters who adopt the libidinous angels view believe the similarities in wording and overall story line between 1 Enoch and 1 Peter are too close to be coincidental.[11]

If one were to grant this line of interpretation, there are aspects that would pose significant barriers for those who would use this text to establish the DH. The most obvious one is that the preaching directed at these fallen angels (thought to be a message of condemnation) did not take place in hell but in one of the lower levels of heaven—presumably the second heaven—in which these angels find themselves imprisoned. Furthermore, not only would this preaching have taken place in the heavenlies and not in hell, but it also would have occurred as part of Christ's *ascension*, while en route to the highest level of heaven. Thus, on this reckoning, what we would have is an *ascent* into *heaven* and not a descent into hell, and one occurring after his resurrection, not before.[12]

Christ Preaching through Noah

Another major interpretation of this passage is the idea that Christ preached to humans (not angels), who were alive in Noah's own day, immediately before the flood. According to this position, Christ preached through

---

11. One finds both nonevangelical and conservative evangelical commentators who adopt this theory. A detailed account of the view in 1 Enoch, and its parallels with 1 Peter, may be found in Elliott, 697–705. Schreiner, a recent evangelical commentator, regards the evidence for this theory to be "impressive" (Thomas Schreiner, *1, 2 Peter, Jude*, NAC 37 [Nashville: B&H, 2003], 188).

12. On these two points, see Elliott, *1 Peter*, 654, 658–59, 690, 702–3, 706; and Schreiner, *1, 2 Peter, Jude*, 188–89. Kistemaker, though rejecting the libidinous angels view, nevertheless sees Peter as referring to a preaching of condemnation against imprisoned demonic spirits in the heavenlies, not in hades (see Simon J. Kistemaker, *Exposition of James, Epistles of John, Peter, and Jude*, NTC [Grand Rapids: Baker, 2002], 142, 145).

Noah to his contemporaries in the power of the Holy Spirit. In other words, Noah was God's human instrument through whom Christ preached "in the Spirit." Many in church history have advocated this view, including contemporary writers such as Grudem, Feinberg, and Erickson.[13]

Such a position, if true, would lend no support to a DH. In this view, the preaching took place in Noah's own day, not during the interval between Christ's death and resurrection. In addition, the spirits in prison refer to the spirits of disembodied *humans* who *currently* reside in prison, presumably in hades, but who were very much alive on earth when Christ addressed them through Noah.

1 Peter 4:6

Most modern commentators do not connect 1 Peter 4:6 with 1 Peter 3:18 but see them as addressing different issues.[14] When the text says, "the gospel was preached even to those who are dead," the consensus is that Peter is talking about Christians who had died at the time of his writing but who were alive when they heard and believed the gospel.[15] This understanding best fits the context of Peter's argument, which Schreiner explains as follows:

> Pagans probably dismissed the Christian faith by pointing out that believers died in the same way as unbelievers. Peter explained that the gospel was proclaimed to believers while they were still alive so that they would live in the spirit in God's presence, even though they experienced the temporal judgment of physical death.[16]

This interpretation is almost certainly correct. That being the case, this verse lends zero support to the idea that Christ descended into hell, whether to preach the gospel or for any other reason.

Other Theological and Logical Problems with the Descent into Hell

Even beyond its thin and dubious biblical support, the DH presents a variety of theological and logical difficulties. I shall mention only a few of these very briefly.

---

13. For advocates of this position, see Millard Erickson, "Did Jesus Really Descend to Hell?," *Christianity Today*, February 7, 2000, 74; John Feinberg, "1 Peter 3:18–20, Ancient Mythology, and the Intermediate State," *WTJ* 49 (1986): 303–36; and Wayne Grudem, *The First Epistle of Peter: An Introduction and Commentary*, TNTC (Grand Rapids: Eerdmans, 1996).
14. Karen H. Jobes, *1 Peter*, BECNT (Grand Rapids: Baker, 2005), 272; Scot McKnight, *1 Peter*, NIVAC (Grand Rapids: Zondervan, 1996), 227.
15. Elliott, *1 Peter*, 734; Grudem, "He Did Not Descend," 111; Jobes, *1 Peter*, 272; J. Ramsey Michaels, *1 Peter*, WBC 49 (Waco, TX: Word, 1988), 237; Schreiner, *1, 2 Peter, Jude*, 198–99, 208.
16. Schreiner, *1, 2 Peter, Jude*, 198–99.

A Number of Verses and Biblical Themes Run Counter to the Descent into Hell
There is every indication that Jesus, when he died, went immediately to the presence of his heavenly Father and no indication whatever that he took a detour via hell. Jesus declared to the thief on the cross, *"today you will be with me in paradise"* (Luke 23:43, emphasis added). Furthermore, as Jesus was about to die he cried out with a loud voice, exclaiming "Father, into your hands I commit my spirit!" (Luke 23:46). The most straightforward way of understanding this is that Christ went directly into God's presence immediately upon his death, as do all the righteous.[17] Note that we find this same language on Stephen's lips in Acts 7:59, immediately before passing directly into the divine presence.

An Erroneous Two-Compartment View of Hades Underlies Some Versions of the Descent into Hell
As observed in Part 1, some versions of the DH maintain that the godly of the Old Testament era were held in an upper compartment of hades or sheol known variously as Abraham's bosom, paradise, the *limbus patrum*, etc. Here they were said to be free from suffering but, nevertheless, separate from God's direct presence as they awaited Christ to liberate them and carry them heavenward. Calvin was quite correct when he labeled this view a "fable."[18] We have already seen that sheol, when it does not refer simply to the grave, is always and only a place of punishment for the wicked.[19] We have also seen that Old Testament believers, upon their deaths, went directly into God's blessed presence,[20] based on the work that Christ would do on their behalf in the fullness of time.

Space does not permit me to illustrate the manifold problems with the two-compartment theory. It is sufficient to note, as Shedd has pointed out, that the righteous in the Old Testament era went *up* to be with God at their deaths, not downward to a compartment of hades (Eccl. 3:21, cf. 12:7).

The Omission of the Descent into Hell from the Gospel Accounts Strongly Suggests That It Never Occurred
Shedd and others have observed that if Christ had actually made a local descent into hell between his death and resurrection, this "would have been one of the great cardinal facts connected with the incarnation." Granting that the gospel writers include details of far less moment than this, it is inconceivable

---

17. See Grudem, "He Did Not Descend," 112–13. See also the earlier discussion on the intermediate state for believers in Question 6 and Question 7.
18. See Calvin, *Institutes* 2.16.9.
19. Question 8.
20. Question 6.

that they would not include something of this magnitude. Shedd states the problem very well:

> St. Matthew speaks of the descent of Christ into Egypt, but not of his descent into Hades. Such an act of the Redeemer as going down into an infernal world of spirits would certainly have been mentioned by one of the inspired biographers of Christ. The total silence of the four gospels is fatal to the tenet.[21]

Additionally, Shedd points out that in Paul's recitation of the essential elements of the gospel in 1 Corinthians 15:3–4, he makes no mention whatever of a DH, even though this would be exactly the place for him to do so had it taken place.

The Descent into Hell Has Been Used to Justify Theologically Heterodox Ideas
Historically, the DH has been pressed into service to promote a variety of theological mischief. As we observed in Part 1, those who have advocated the possibility of postmortem conversions as well as universalism often invoke the DH in their argumentation.[22]

This fact would not be sufficient in it itself to reject a DH. After all, even true doctrines can be misused, warped, and abused. However, given its many other biblical and theological problems, I simply add this to the list of reasons to get rid of the DH.

Conclusion

It is best to reject the DH clause in the Apostles' Creed. It is difficult to secure any agreement about what this language even means, and many of the explanations of it entail unbiblical teaching. Even when one strains to offer an interpretation of it that fully comports with the Bible, it is not worth the verbal gymnastics required to contort the phrase "he descended into hell" to fit such teaching. Besides, the DH was not originally a part of the Apostles' Creed in the first place.

As a practical matter, I concur with Otto's conclusion:

> While the intention behind the original insertion of the article is dubious at best . . . the church has generally continued to hold to the article, this despite the fact that no consensus has been or apparently can be reached on its meaning. To

---

21. W. G. T. Shedd, *Dogmatic Theology*, ed. Alan W. Gomes (Phillipsburg: P&R, 2003), 841.
22. For the problems with the idea of postmortem conversions, see Question 14 and for a refutation of universalism, see Question 33.

include such a mysterious article in the creed, which is supposed to be a summary of the basic and vital tenets of the faith, seems very unwise.[23]

REFLECTION QUESTIONS

1. How much authority do you believe that confessions of faith ought to have in the life of the church? In your own life?

2. Concerning the biblical passages that some have offered in defense of the DH, do you see any of the non-DH interpretations presented here as plausible or even probable?

3. Do you believe that if a DH really had taken place that the writers of Scripture, including the gospel authors, should have given it prominent mention?

4. Having read Parts 1 and 2 of this issue, what do you believe are the strongest arguments in favor of a DH? Against it?

5. What is your overall conclusion about whether to retain or remove the DH language from the creed?

23. Randall E. Otto, "*Descendit in Inferna:* A Reformed Review of a Creedal Conundrum," *WTJ* 52 (1990): 150.

Scripture and Ancient Sources Index

40 QUESTIONS SERIES

40 QUESTIONS SERIES